The Lillooet Language

First Nations Languages

The First Nations languages of the world, many of which are renowned for the complexity and richness of their linguistic structure, embody the cumulative cultural knowledge of aboriginal peoples. This vital linguistic heritage is currently under severe threat of extinction. This new series is dedicated to the linguistic study of these languages.

Patricia A. Shaw, a member of the Department of Linguistics at the University of British Columbia and coordinator of the First Nations Languages Program, is general editor of the series.

M. Dale Kinkade, professor in the Department of Linguistics at the University of British Columbia, is co-editor.

The Lillooet Language: Phonology, Morphology, Syntax is the first book in the series.

UBC Press gratefully acknowledges the support of the UBC Killam General Fund in the establishment of this series.

Jan van Eijk

The Lillooet Language:
Phonology, Morphology, Syntax

UBCPress / Vancouver

Printed in Canada on acid-free paper ∞

ISBN 0-7748-0625-7

Canadian Cataloguing in Publication Data
Eijk, Jan van, 1950-
   The Lillooet language

   (First Nations languages, ISSN 1206-9531)
   Includes bibliographical references.
   ISBN 0-7748-0625-7

   1. Lillooet language - Grammar. I. Title. II. Series.
PM1646.L7E44 1997   497'.9   C97-910493-9

This book has been published with the help of a grant from the Canadian Federation for the Humanities, using funds provided by the Social Sciences and Humanities Research Council of Canada.

UBC Press gratefully acknowledges the ongoing support to its publishing program from the Canada Council for the Arts, the British Columbia Arts Council, and the Department of Canadian Heritage of the Government of Canada.

Set in Stone by Francis J. Chow
Copy-edited by Francis J. Chow
Printed and bound in Canada by Friesens

UBC Press
University of British Columbia
6344 Memorial Road
Vancouver, BC V6T 1Z2
(604) 822-5959
Fax: 1-800-668-0821
E-mail: orders@ubcpress.ubc.ca
http://www.ubcpress.ubc.ca

Dedicated to the memory of
Sam Mitchell
Martina LaRochelle
and
Bill Edwards
My first Lillooet teachers

Contents

Figures and Maps / xv

Preface and Acknowledgments / xvii

Introduction / xxi

Symbols and Abbreviations / xxix

Part 1: Phonology
1 Phonemes: General Information and Phonetic Data / 3
  1.1   Retracted versus non-retracted phonemes / 3
  1.2   Dental, velar, and uvular glides / 4
  1.3   Laryngeal, velar, and uvular resonants / 4
  1.4   Dentals, laterals, and palatals / 4
  1.5   Stress / 5
  1.6   Questions of word phonology / 5
  1.7   Distribution of phonemes / 6
      1.7.1   Distribution of y y′ and z z′ / 7
  1.8   Neutralizations / 7
      1.8.1   The position −z/z′ / 8
      1.8.2   Neutralization between retracted and non-retracted phonemes / 8
      1.8.3   Unrounded versus rounded consonants / 10
  1.9   Phonetic data: details and special questions / 10
      1.9.1   Obstruents / 10
      1.9.2   Resonants / 11
      1.9.3   Vowels / 11
      1.9.4   Vowel-resonant sequences: special cases / 12
2 Movement of the Stress / 14
  2.1   Roots and suffixes / 14

2.2   Combinations with enclitics / 16
2.3   Combinations with prefixes / 17
3 Distribution of Schwa / 18
3.1   Cases #REC and #RC / 18
3.2   Elision of schwa / 19
3.3   Schwa and obstruents / 20
    3.3.1   Sequences #KEKC and CKEK# / 20
    3.3.2   Unstressed sequences #KECV∴ and ∴VCEK# / 21
    3.3.3   Schwa and #K K#: concluding remarks / 22
    3.3.4   Schwa and word-medial clusters / 22
3.4   Schwa and resonants / 23
3.5   The status of ʔ / 24
4 Internal Sandhi / 26
4.1   Vowel-consonant alternations and h-epenthesis / 26
4.2   Reduction of full root vowels / 27
4.3   Elision of stem-final -as / 28
4.4   Morphophonemic changes of consonants / 28
5 Retracted Phonemes / 29
5.1   Retracted roots / 29
5.2   Retraction of suffixes / 29
5.3   Retraction of the nominalizer s- / 30
5.4   Background of retraction / 30
6 Structure of Roots / 32
6.1   Roots: basic characteristics and main types / 32
6.2   Roots CVC / 33
    6.2.1   Roots CVC: examples / 34
6.3   Roots CVCC / 34
6.4   Roots CCVC / 35
6.5   Roots CV́CVC / 35
6.6   Roots CVCV́C / 35
6.7   Residual types / 35
7 Special Questions / 36
7.1   Aphaeresis and syncope / 36
7.2   Slow song speech / 36
7.3   Rhetorical lengthening / 36
7.4   Nursery talk / 36
7.5   Treatment of borrowings / 37

Part 2: Morphology
8 Introduction to Morphology / 41
8.1   Variable words / 41
    8.1.1   Stem formation: transposition and (in)transitivization / 43

8.1.2　Personal affixation: predicates and complements / 44
8.1.3　Factualization / 45
8.2　Invariable words / 46
8.3　Clitics / 46
9　The Nominalizer s- / 48
10　Stem-Forming Prefixes / 50
10.1　Productive stem-forming prefixes / 50
10.1.1　The prefix ʔəs- 'to have, to own' / 50
10.1.2　The stative prefix s- / 50
10.1.3　The resultative combination ka-...ˌa / 51
10.1.4　The prefix kəns- 'to try, to want to' / 51
10.1.5　The prefix n- / 51
10.1.6　The prefix nəkʷ- 'co-, fellow' / 52
10.1.7　Combinations of prefixes / 52
10.2　Unproductive prefixes / 53
11　Compounding / 54
12　Reduplication / 55
12.1　Survey of basic types / 55
12.2　Initial reduplication / 57
12.3　Final reduplication / 58
12.4　Consonant reduplication / 60
12.5　Total reduplication: types (4a) to (4c) / 61
12.5.1　Total reduplication (4a) to (4c): predictability of subtypes / 64
12.5.2　Total reduplication (4a) to (4c): residual types and special cases / 65
12.6　Total reduplication: type (4d) / 66
13　Interior Glottalization / 67
13.1　Cases $C_1VʔC_2$ / 67
13.1.1　Vowel-change / 68
13.1.2　Cases Cíʔiˁ, Cíʔiˁʷ / 68
13.1.3　Interior glottalization and consonant reduplication / 69
13.2　Cases CʔVC / 70
14　Aspectual Suffixes / 71
14.1　The suffix -p / 71
14.2　The suffix -əm / 72
14.3　The suffix -t / 72
14.4　The combination n-...-təm / 73
14.5　Conditioned suffixes / 73
15　Lexical Suffixes / 74
15.1　Lexical suffixes: combinations / 74
15.1.1　Combinations of lexical suffixes with each other / 74
15.1.2　Lexical suffixes and the prefix n- / 75

15.2   Primary lexical suffixes / 76
15.3   Connectives / 98
15.4   Residual suffixes / 98
16 Abstract Suffixes / 102
17 Reflexive and Reciprocal Suffixes / 105
17.1   Reflexive suffixes / 105
17.2   Reciprocal suffixes / 106
18 Intransitivizers and Transitivizers / 107
18.1   Plain stems / 108
18.1.1   Intransitivizers / 108
18.1.2   Transitivizers (Ia), (Ib), (IIa), and (IIb) / 109
18.1.3   Functions of transitivizers (Ia), (Ib), (IIa), and (IIb) / 110
18.1.4   Transitivizers (IIc) to (IIe) / 113
18.1.5   Distribution of intransitivizers and transitivizers / 117
18.1.6   Distribution of (in)transitivizers: special cases / 118
18.2   Somatic suffixes and (in)transitivizers / 118
18.3   Non-somatic suffixes and (in)transitivizers / 120
18.4   Nominal stems and (in)transitivizers / 122
18.5   Abstract suffixes and (in)transitivizers / 123
18.6   The reflexive suffix -cut / 123
18.7   Reflexive and reciprocal suffixes: detransitivization and
retransitivization / 125
18.8   Stative and resultative forms / 125
18.9   Summary of (in)transitivizers / 126
19 Numerals and Numerical Substitutes / 129
19.1   Cardinals and numerical substitutes / 129
19.1.1   Formation / 130
19.1.2   Prefixation, reduplication, and alternative forms / 130
19.1.3   Complex numerals and reduplication / 131
19.2   Suffixation / 131
19.3   Special questions / 131
19.4   Ordinals, numerical adverbs, and numerical-distributive adverbs / 132
19.4.1   Ordinals / 132
19.4.2   Numerical adverbs / 132
19.4.3   Numerical-distributive adverbs / 133
20 Verbal Substitutes / 134
20.1.   Interrogative verbs / 134
20.2   Relator-verbs / 135
21 Summary of Stem Formation / 134
21.1   Formal operations / 137
21.2   Aspect / 139

21.3   Control / 140
21.4   Transposition / 140
22 Personal Affixation / 142
  22.1   Survey of affixes / 143
  22.2   The possessive paradigm / 145
  22.3   Simple intransitive and transitive paradigms / 146
    22.3.1   The simple intransitive declarative paradigm / 146
    22.3.2   The simple transitive declarative paradigm / 147
    22.3.3   Special cases with transitivizers of type I / 149
    22.3.4   The simple passive paradigm / 150
    22.3.5   The simple imperative (intransitive and transitive)
             paradigm / 151
  22.4.   Complex forms / 152
    22.4.1.   Complex declarative intransitive forms / 152
    22.4.2   Complex declarative transitive forms / 154
    22.4.3   The complex passive paradigm / 155
    22.4.4   Complex imperative forms / 156
  22.5   Special questions / 156
    22.5.1   Imperatives 1P / 157
    22.5.2   Imperative stems / 157
    22.5.3   Expression of 1P transitive subject / 157
    22.5.4   -ɬk suffixes after obstruents / 157
    22.5.5   Reflexive and reciprocal forms / 158
  22.6   Object- and subject-centred forms / 158
  22.7   Indirect object-centred forms (nominalized transitives) / 159
  22.8   Summary of complements, nominal forms, and factual forms / 160
23 Invariable Words: General Remarks / 161
24 Personal Pronouns and Related Substitutes / 162
  24.1   Personal pronouns / 162
    24.1.1   Use of personal pronouns / 163
    24.1.2   Personal pronouns and predicates with a possessive marker / 164
  24.2   Interrogative and indefinite pronouns / 165
  24.3   Evasive pronouns / 165
  24.4   Possessive substitutes / 167
  24.5   The anticipatory pronoun niɬ / 167
  24.6   Remaining non-local substitutes / 167
25 Demonstrative Pronouns / 168
  25.1   Demonstrative pronouns: basic information / 168
    25.1.1   Semantics and examples / 169
  25.2   Suffixation with -wna/-na / 170
  25.3   Special forms after prepositions / 170

26 Demonstrative Adverbs / 171
   26.1   Local deictics / 171
       26.1.1 Semantics and use / 172
       26.1.2 Affixation / 173
       26.1.3 Special questions / 174
       26.1.4 Interrogative and indefinite local deictics / 175
       26.1.5 Morphosyntactic comments on local deictics / 175
       26.1.6 Local non-deictics / 176
   26.2   Temporal deictics / 176
       26.2.1 Temporal non-deictics / 176
27 Proper Nouns / 178
   27.1   Make-up of proper nouns / 178
   27.2   Use of proper nouns / 179
   27.3   Generic pet-names / 179
28 Full-Word Conjunctions and Adverbs (Particles) / 180
   28.1   Conjunctions / 180
       28.1.1 The conjunction X̓uʔ 'but' / 180
       28.1.2 The conjunction k̓á‿maɬ 'but' / 181
       28.1.3 The conjunction X̓u 'until' / 181
       28.1.4 The conjunction mútaʔ 'and' / 182
       28.1.5 The conjunction wi 'and' / 182
   28.2   Adverbs / 182
       28.2.1 The adverb mútaʔ 'again' / 182
       28.2.2 The adverb sénaʔ 'unfulfilled' / 182
       28.2.3 The adverb núkʷun' 'again' / 183
       28.2.4 The adverb nukʷɬ '(not) a bit' / 183
       28.2.5 The adverb X̓it 'also, too' / 183
       28.2.6 The adverb kaʔɬ 'for a while, once more, again' / 184
       28.2.7 The adverb zam' 'after all, as things are now, as things turned
            out to be' / 184
       28.2.8 The adverb ʔayɬ 'next, this time, and then' / 185
29 Sentence-Equivalents / 186
   29.1   List of sentence-equivalents / 186
   29.2   Variable words as sentence-equivalents / 188
30 Greetings, Exclamations, and Interjections / 189
   30.1   Greetings and related expressions / 189
   30.2   Exclamations and interjections / 191
31 Articles / 192
   31.1   Formal aspects / 192
   31.2   Semantics of the articles: general information / 193
   31.3   The category 'known': 'present' versus 'absent' / 193
       31.3.1   The category 'known': use of ki‿ / 194

31.4 The category 'unknown' / 195
31.5 The articles kʷ‿ and wi‿ / 196
31.6 Special questions / 197
    31.6.1 Merging of *‿a‿a into ‿a / 197
    31.6.2 Complex complements / 197
32 Enclitics / 199
32.1 Individual enclitics / 199
    32.1.1 The enclitic ‿maɬ 'adhortative' / 199
    32.1.2 The enclitic ‿tuʔ 'definite past' / 200
    32.1.3 The enclitic ‿an' 'evidential' / 200
    32.1.4 The enclitic ‿ƛ'uʔ 'well, but, so' / 200
    32.1.5 The enclitic ‿ƛ'ɬ 'demarcation of time' / 201
    32.1.6 The enclitic ‿ka 'obligation, expectancy' / 201
    32.1.7 The enclitic ‿kəɬ 'remote future, possibility' / 201
    32.1.8 The enclitic ‿k'a 'possibility, surmise' / 202
    32.1.9 The enclitic ‿kʷuʔ 'quotative' / 202
    32.1.10 The enclitic ‿xʷiɬ 'after all, it turned out to be' / 202
    32.1.11 The enclitic ‿qaʔ 'presupposed knowledge' / 203
    32.1.12 The enclitic ‿ha 'interrogative' / 204
    32.1.13 The enclitic ‿həm' 'antithesis' / 204
    32.1.14 The enclitic ‿wiʔ 'emphasis' / 205
    32.1.15 The enclitic ‿wən 'emphasis' / 206
    32.1.16 Position of enclitics / 206
32.2 The enclitic ‿a 'reinforcement' / 206
32.3 Combinations of enclitics / 207
    32.3.1 Combinations with ‿an' / 207
    32.3.2 Combinations with ‿a / 208
    32.3.3 Combinations with ‿xʷiɬ / 208
    32.3.4 Combinations with ‿qaʔ / 208
    32.3.5 Combinations with ‿ha / 208
    32.3.6 Combinations with ‿kʷuʔ / 209
    32.3.7 Combinations with ‿ka / 209
    32.3.8 Combinations with ‿k'a / 209
    32.3.9 Combinations with ‿maɬ / 210
    32.3.10 Combinations with ‿wiʔ / 210
    32.3.11 Combinations with ‿həm' / 210
    32.3.12 Combinations with ‿kəɬ / 210
    32.3.13 Combinations with ‿tuʔ and ‿ƛ'uʔ / 211
32.4 Combinations of enclitics: special cases / 211
    32.4.1 Double occurrences of ‿a / 211
    32.4.2 Combinations of enclitics with demonstrative pronouns / 212
32.5 Enclitics after indicative and subjunctive forms / 213

        32.5.1   Neutralization of subjunctive and indicative paradigms / 215
33 Proclitic Conjunctions / 217
    33.1   The conjunction ʔə̓ɬ 'before' / 217
    33.2   The conjunction kʷu̓ 'attribute-connector' / 217
34 Prepositions / 219
    34.1   Primary prepositions / 219
    34.2   Secondary prepositions / 221

Part 3: Syntax
35 Introduction to Syntax / 225
36 Mono-Clausal Sentences / 226
    36.1   Word order: general information / 226
        36.1.1   Word order: subject and object complements / 226
        36.1.2   Word order: adverbial elements / 230
        36.1.3   Word order: auxiliaries / 230
    36.2   Auxiliaries: types and use / 230
37 Multi-Clausal Sentences / 233
    37.1   kʷ-constructions / 233
    37.2   s-constructions / 234
    37.3   t-constructions / 234
    37.4   Subjunctive (c) constructions / 234
        37.4.1   ɬ-constructions / 234
        37.4.2   ʔi-constructions / 235
38 Syntax: Special Questions / 237
    38.1   The use of the passive / 237
    38.2   The structure of complex complements / 238
    38.3   Possessive complements / 239
    38.4   Single expression of the plural / 240
    38.5   Focusing elements / 241

Appendixes
39 A Lillooet Text / 245
    39.1   Text: 'Máhyeqs and the Mouse' / 245
    39.2   Comments / 247
40 Comparison of Lillooet Orthographies / 251

Notes / 253

Bibliography / 269

Index / 273

Figures and Maps

Figures
1 Chart of phonemes / 2
2 Combinatory possibilities of retracted and non-retracted phonemes / 9
3 Vowel-consonant combinations in roots CVC / 33
4 Chart of morphological operations / 40
5 Verbal and nominal categories / 44
6 Functions of transitivizers (Ia), (Ib), (IIa), and (IIb) / 113
7 Classification of transitivizers / 116
8 Classification of verbal paradigms / 143
9 Possessive affixes / 144
10 Object suffixes / 144
11 Subject suffixes / 145
12 Complex declarative intransitive forms / 152
13 Complex declarative transitive forms / 154
14 Complex passive forms / 155
15 Complements, nominal forms, and factual forms / 160
16 Personal pronouns / 162
17 Demonstrative pronouns / 168
18 Demonstrative adverbs / 171
19 Articles / 192
20 Order of enclitics / 207
21 Primary prepositions / 219

Maps
1 The Salish language area / xxii
2 The Lillooet language area / xxvi

Preface and Acknowledgments

This book presents a grammatical analysis of Lillooet, an Interior Salish language spoken in British Columbia, Canada. It was originally prepared as a doctoral dissertation for the University of Amsterdam. The dissertation was successfully defended in 1985 and distributed in a limited edition by the University of Amsterdam print shop. Material for the dissertation was collected in the summers of 1972, 1973, and 1974 in the town of Lillooet, and during various periods from 1975 through 1984 in Mount Currie and Lillooet. Subsequent field work was done for brief periods in 1988 and 1992, yielding some new insights that are incorporated into this edition.

Of the many people who helped me prepare this book, I wish to thank first of all my Lillooet-speaking consultants. I am especially grateful to the late Mr. Sam Mitchell of Fountain; the late Mrs. Martina LaRochelle of Lillooet; the late Mr. Bill Edwards of Pavilion; and Mrs. Marie Leo, the late Mrs. Rosie Joseph, Mrs. Margaret Lester, the late Mrs. Adelina Williams, the late Mr. Charles Mack Seymour, Mr. Joe Joseph, Mr. Alec Peters, and Mr. Ernie Pascal, all of Mount Currie. A special word of thanks is due to Ms. Lorna Williams and Ms. Marie Abraham, both of Mount Currie, who belong to a younger generation of Lillooet speakers and with whom I had many fruitful discussions on the linguistic analysis of Lillooet when the three of us were employed by the Mount Currie Cultural/Educational Centre between 1975 and 1984.

Of the linguists who have helped me, I am most deeply indebted to my dissertation supervisors, the late Dr. Simon C. Dik of the University of Amsterdam and Dr. M. Dale Kinkade of the University of British Columbia. I also owe a debt of gratitude to Dr. Aert H. Kuipers (formerly of the University of Leyden, the Netherlands, now retired), who guided the initial stages of my work on Lillooet. Others who deserve my gratitude are Dr. Henk F. Nater and Dr. John C. Rath, with whom I have had many vigorous (and invigorating) discussions on Salish and general linguistics that greatly enhanced my insight into linguistic matters; Mr. Randy Bouchard, who provided logistical and linguistic assistance during my first summer of field work; and Dr. Thomas M. Hess of the University of Victoria, British Columbia, Dr. Laurence C. Thompson (formerly of the University of Hawaii, now retired), M. Terry Thompson, Dr. Steven M. Egesdal, and the many other Salishists who gave insightful comments on earlier copies of my work, from which I greatly benefited. I also wish to thank Mr. Jan A. Timmers, who carefully read an earlier version of the completed dissertation and ferreted out a large number of typographical and other errors, and Dr. Willem F. Adelaar of the University of Leyden, who, as a member of my doctoral committee, identified a number of incorrect cross-references that had resulted from the final revision of the dissertation and also made very valuable suggestions for a deeper analysis of some of the issues raised in the earlier versions of this book. Dr. Nancy J. Turner of the University of Victoria deserves credit for involving me in the many Lillooet ethnobotanical research projects that she undertook while I was working on the language, which enabled me to collect a large number of botanical terms that I would otherwise have missed.

My research after 1985 has benefited greatly from input by Drs. Kinkade, Hess, and Egesdal, and (besides many others) Dr. Barry F. Carlson and Dr. Thomas Hukari, both of the University of Victoria, Dr. Anthony Mattina of the University of Montana, and Dr. Brent Galloway of the Saskatchewan Indian Federated College.

I gratefully acknowledge the support of the Netherlands Organization for the Advancement of Pure Research (ZWO), which provided me with the funds to carry out my first three summers of field work, through Research Grant 39-10. I also owe a debt of gratitude to the following persons and institutions for hiring me to work in Mount Currie in 1975-84: Mrs. Georgina Nelson and the Ts'zil Board of Education (Mount Currie), Dr. June Wyatt and Simon Fraser University (Burnaby), and Mr. Robert Irvine of Capilano College (North Vancouver). A special word of thanks is due to the Amsterdam University Society (AUV) and the Leyden University Foundation (LUF) for jointly sponsoring my airplane flight to the Netherlands in 1985, thereby enabling me to defend my dissertation. And a big thank-you is definitely in order for my sister Herma, who together with her (and my) friends Folkert Leemans, Fop Bos, and Els Bos-Hoffenaar organized the festivities after my dissertation defence.

From 1985 to 1989 my research on Salish was made possible by the Social Sciences and Humanities Research Council of Canada (SSHRCC), through Research Grant 410-85-0062 and Postdoctoral Fellowships 456-87-0358 and 457-88-0086. I also gratefully acknowledge the hospitality of the Department of Linguistics at the University of Victoria, where from 1985 to 1989

I enjoyed the status of Visiting Scholar, under the aegis of the former and current Department Heads, Dr. Henry J. Warkentyne and Dr. Joseph F. Kess.

Preparation of this book would not have been possible without the assistance and advice of Dr. Patricia A. Shaw of the Department of Linguistics at the University of British Columbia, and of the staff at UBC Press, in particular Ms. Laura Macleod, Ms. Camilla Jenkins, and Ms. Holly Keller-Brohman. I am also very grateful to Mr. Colin Carter of the Department of Computer Science at the University of Regina, who devised the Lillooet font that is used in this book and who has assisted me throughout with his seemingly limitless supply of patience and computer knowledge. Mr. Francis J. Chow deserves my gratitude for the meticulous way in which he has edited and typeset my manuscript.

It is with profound gratitude that I pay homage to my father and mother, Arie van Eijk (who passed away in 1988) and Annigje van Eijk-Van der Wilt, whose unstinting moral and financial support and keen interest in my work helped me through many a dark moment during the preparation of my dissertation. I am also deeply grateful to my mother-in-law, Angeline van Leeuwen-De Jong, whose delightful personality has been a constant source of joy and whose largesse made it possible for my wife and children to fly to the Netherlands in 1985 and share in one of the most important moments of my scholarly career. With deep respect I salute my late father-in-law, Henri Albert van Leeuwen, who passed away in 1980. I will be amply rewarded if my book reflects at least some of the commitment to quality and the virtues of good, hard work that these four people have consistently shown.

Last, but certainly not least, I wish to thank my wife, Sonja, for her patience and understanding during the long time it took me to prepare this book, and for her moral support at the many difficult moments when the grammatical complexities of Lillooet threatened to overwhelm me. Our two sons, Jesse and Mark, deserve my gratitude for the joy they have brought to my life and for showing me that there is life (a lot of it, in fact) outside linguistics.

Introduction

General

Lillooet is a Native American language spoken in British Columbia, Canada, in an area 160 to 300 kilometres northeast of Vancouver. It comprises two dialects, one spoken in and around Mount Currie (approximately 160 kilometres from Vancouver), the other spoken in and around Fountain (approximately 300 kilometres from Vancouver) (see Map 2, on p. xxvi, for the location of the various Lillooet-speaking communities). These dialects are completely mutually intelligible, the main differences being lexical. (For example, the terms for 'to work,' 'to eat,' and 'woman,' and for several types of salmon, are different in both dialects.) There is also a small phonological difference (see Section 1.8.1 of this book) and a syntactic difference (see Section 22.4.1).

Lillooet belongs to the Interior division of the Salish (or Salishan) language family. (The terms 'Salish' and 'Salishan' are used interchangeably.) With the other Interior Salish languages it shares (a) the occurrence of retracted (velarized) phonemes (see Section 1.1) and (b) the occurrence of uvular resonants (see Section 1.2). With its linguistic neighbours Shuswap and Thompson, and with northern Okanagan, Lillooet also shares (c) the occurrence of velar resonants (see Section 1.2); and with Shuswap, Thompson, and Coeur d'Alene it shares (d) the collapse of the Proto-Salish phonemes *ƛ' and *t' into one phoneme (ƛ' in Lillooet and Thompson, t' in Shuswap and Coeur d'Alene). Salish languages outside the Interior division do not have velar or uvular resonants or retracted phonemes. These languages (together with the Interior languages Okanagan, Columbian, and Kalispel) have retained ƛ' and t' as separate phonemes. For further information on Salish, see Thompson 1979b. For the Salish language area, see Map 1. A list of the Salish languages is provided under 'Salish languages' below.

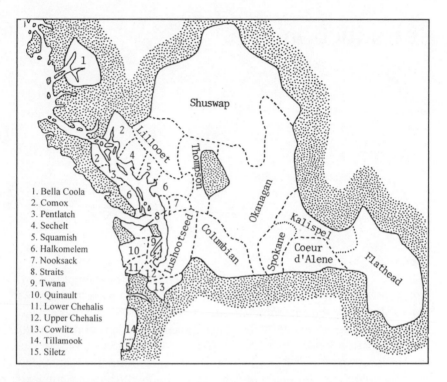

1. Bella Coola
2. Comox
3. Pentlatch
4. Sechelt
5. Squamish
6. Halkomelem
7. Nooksack
8. Straits
9. Twana
10. Quinault
11. Lower Chehalis
12. Upper Chehalis
13. Cowlitz
14. Tillamook
15. Siletz

Map 1 The Salish language area.

The theoretical framework of this book is that of classical structuralism, as developed in Europe by the School of Prague and in North America by Bloomfield. The morpheme is central to the description of the language, and the transcription is based on the principle of maximal morphological clarity, occasionally violating the bi-uniqueness requirement (see, for example, my treatment of phonetically labialized consonants in Section 1.8.3). The description follows the classical division into phonology, morphology, and syntax. Other descriptive models (even within structuralism) are by all means possible: one possibility would have been to integrate morphology and syntax into one morpho-syntax, a choice made feasible by the fact that Lillooet expresses a number of notions through affixes, whereas, for example, Indo-European languages generally use full words. (For example, pronominal objects and subjects in Lillooet are expressed through suffixes, of the type 'help-you-I' for 'I help you'; see Sections 8.1 and 22.) However, I deal separately with the structuring of words through various morphological operations under morphology and with the arrangement of such words under syntax.

Little has been published on the Lillooet language. Hill-Tout published a brief grammatical sketch of the language in his ethnographic report on the Lillooet (Hill-Tout 1905:156-176, 206-218). Although this sketch is inadequate by modern standards, Hill-Tout must be saluted for his pioneering efforts. Moreover, a number of his observations were very useful to me during the initial stages of my work on the language. (In particular, I was able to record a number of words that I found in his lists; because they were already fading from the memory of my consultants, these words would otherwise have passed into oblivion.)

A number of linguistics students also did field work on Lillooet in more recent periods, but their field notes and reports are difficult to obtain (if they are available at all). Mr. Randy Bouchard and Ms. Dorothy Kennedy have collected an immense amount of taped materials (mainly traditional legends told by a large number of elders, many of whom have unfortunately passed away), and they have taken down a large body of ethnographic information. Most of this material, however, has yet to be published. Current research on the language is being carried out by various young scholars from the University of British Columbia and Simon Fraser University.

Besides this book, my contributions to Lillooet linguistics consist of a number of papers submitted to various conferences on Salish and Neighbouring Languages (held annually at different locations) and of my publications since 1985 (see the bibliography). Also, as part of my work for the Mount Currie Community School (1975-84) and for the Lillooet Tribal Council (1992), I cooperated with native speakers of the language in the publication of materials in and about Lillooet, in a practical orthography that avoids the usual Amerindianist symbols but is entirely based on the standard Latin alphabet (and uses, for example, *lh* instead of ɬ, or *c* instead of x). For a bibliography of these materials, see Lillooet Tribal Council and Joseph et al. 1979, van Eijk 1981, van Eijk and Williams 1981, and Williams 1979 in the bibliography of this book. A conversion table showing both the Amerindianist symbols used in this book and the practical orthography used in the pedagogical materials is given in Section 40).

Salish languages
The geographical position of the Salish language area can be seen in Map 1. The Salish languages fall into four divisions, which are further divided into branches, individual languages, and major and minor dialects. In the following list, languages are indicated by Arabic numbers (1, 2, 3) and major dialects by lowercase letters (a, b, c). Minor dialects are given in parentheses after the languages or after the major dialects. Alternative names are

separated by the symbol =. An asterisk (*) indicates extinct languages and dialects.

I Bella Coola Division
   1) Bella Coola = Nuxalk
II Coast Division
  A) Central Branch
    1) Comox (Mainland Comox = Sliammon = Lhaamen; Island Comox)
    2) *Pentlatch
    3) Sechelt = Sechelt
    4) Squamish
    5) Halkomelem
      a) Upriver Halkomelem (Tait, Chilliwack, Chehalis, etc.)
      b) Downriver Halkomelem (Katzie, Musquiam, *Kwantlen, etc.)
      c) Island Halkomelem (Nanaimo, Chemainus, Cowichan)
    6) Nooksack
    7) Straits: falls into two closely related languages (regarded as dialects by some Salishists):
      7.1) Clallam
      7.2) Northern Straits = Lkungen (Saanich, Sooke, Lummi, Songish = Songees, Samish, Semiahmoo)
    8) Lushootseed = Puget Salish
      a) Northern Lushootseed (Upper Skagit, Lower Skagit, Snohomish)
      b) Southern Lushootseed (Skykomish, Snoqualmie, Duwamish, Suquamish, Muckleshoot, Puyallup, Nisqually, Sahewamish)
    9) Twana = Skokomish
  B) Oregon Branch
    1) *Tillamook
    2) *Siletz: very little is known about Siletz, and its relation to Tillamook is not entirely clear
III Tsamosan Division
  A) Inland Branch
    1) Upper Chehalis
    2) Cowlitz
  B) Maritime Branch
    1) Lower Chehalis
    2) Quinault
IV Interior Division
  A) Northern Branch
    1) Lillooet (Upper Lillooet = Fountain, Lower Lillooet = Mount Currie)
    2) Thompson

3) Shuswap
   a) Eastern Shuswap (Enderby, Athalmer = Kinbasket)
   b) Western Shuswap (Canim Lake, Deadman's Creek)
B) Southern Branch
   1) Okanagan
      a) Northern Okanagan (Head of the Lakes, etc.)
      b) Southern Okanagan (Colville, Methow, etc.)
   2) Columbian (Wenatchi = Peskwaus, Moses Columbian, Chelan, Entiat)
   3) Kalispel
      a) Spokane
      b) Kalispel
      c) Flathead
   4) Coeur d'Alene

For some languages and dialects, names other than the ones above are (or were) in use, but most of those names are either antiquated, used inconsistently, or used very rarely. In some cases, the name of a dialect is also the name of a community where that dialect is spoken. The same dialect may then also be spoken at other places. For example, the Fountain dialect of Lillooet is also spoken in Pavilion, Lillooet, and other places. Of course, there are minor differences between communities within each dialect area, and there are personal and family idiolects. For example, the dialect of Skookumchuck, which lies within the southern (Mount Currie) dialect area, is said to be somewhat different from the speech of Mount Currie, but I have not had any opportunity to study this issue in detail.

The Lillooet people
The Lillooet people have inhabited their homeland since time immemorial, and their traditional culture is based on an intimate economic and spiritual relationship with their habitat. Economically, the Lillooet relied and still rely on their environment for food, clothing, utensils, building materials, and religious objects and ceremonies.

One of the main sources of food was and is salmon, which are caught during their annual return from the ocean to their native streams and lakes. All five species of Pacific salmon (chinook or spring, pink or humpback, coho or silver, sockeye or red, and chum or dog) occur in the Lillooet homeland, although they are not evenly distributed. Deer are hunted for their meat and their hides. When tanned, the hides are used for making traditional dresses and moccasins. Berries, of which a large number of varieties are available, are a prized foodstuff. Huckleberries and saskatoon berries are particularly popular. Soapberries are used for making a

Map 2 The Lillooet language area.

KoolAid-like beverage (one part soapberry juice in a number of parts of water) and for the ever-popular 'Indian ice cream': soapberry juice whipped into a foam and served as a dessert.

The western redcedar is extremely important in the traditional culture. The roots are used for making various types of baskets (basket cradles, berry baskets, shopping and storage baskets, etc.). These baskets are still widely used by the Lillooet themselves, but a large number are sold as souvenirs. The wood of the cedar provides excellent building material for both houses and dug-out canoes.

A tree of similar importance is the Douglas-fir. Its wood is used for lumber and as material for a wide variety of utensils, such as the handle and hoop of traditional dipnets, while the boughs, which are endowed with a special spiritual power, function predominantly in traditional religious activities. For example, persons undergoing religious training would wipe themselves dry with Douglas-fir boughs after a bath.

The traditional religion centres on the maintenance of a good relationship with Nature. Game animals and other sources of food and nonalimentary materials were treated with great respect. For example, a special ceremony surrounded the catching and preparing of the first salmon of the season. Guardian spirits could be obtained through vision quests. Pubescent individuals, especially pubescent women, had to undergo elaborate rites in order to prepare them for the social and religious duties of adulthood.

The usual winter dwelling was the semi-subterranean house, described in Teit 1906:212-213. In summer, temporary shelters, such as lean-to's, were used.

The Lillooet language not only served to facilitate social interaction but was (and is) also the repository of a tremendously rich oral history: countless myths and legends, jokes, and other types of stories were handed down from one generation to the next. A favourite character in the myths and legends is Coyote, a trickster who on the one hand provides invaluable services to mankind – such as freeing salmon from a trap set by a witch, so the salmon can now serve as food for the people – while on the other hand committing numerous acts of utter foolishness or depravity. (A traditional Coyote legend, with the original Lillooet text and a translation and analysis in Dutch, is given in van Eijk 1989.)

Other characters are Beaver, Frog, and Owl, the latter being a bogeyman who figures in scary stories told to children in order to keep them in line). A good collection of both myths and legends (sptak^{w}ɬ) and of more contemporary stories (sq^{w}áq^{w}əl'), as recorded from Lillooet elders, is given in Bouchard and Kennedy 1977, in the form of English translations of the Lillooet language originals. Further examples of Lillooet stories (partially overlapping with Bouchard and Kennedy) are given in Teit 1912 and Elliott 1931. Van Eijk and Williams 1981 offer a bilingual Lillooet-English collection of sptak^{w}ɬ and sq^{w}áq^{w}əl', with word lists and a grammatical sketch of the language, in the practical orthography that is currently used by the Mount Currie Community School and the Lillooet Tribal Council.

The foregoing overview gives, of course, only a very superficial description of the traditional Lillooet culture. For fuller accounts, see Hill-Tout 1905(1978) and Teit 1906(1975). Excellent descriptions of food plants and plants in Native technology (also with reference to the Lillooet) can be found in Turner 1978 and 1979. Many aspects of the Lillooet culture are also represented in the collections of stories mentioned above.

The arrival of the white man on the scene in the nineteenth century had a profound impact on the old culture. Forced acculturation led to the disappearance of a large number of ancient customs, and it forced the Lillooet language into disuse among younger generations, so that today only a few people under the age of fifty are fluent in the language. In recent years, the Lillooet have taken a renewed pride in their rich heritage; a number of customs are regaining their former use, while interest in and use of the old language is also increasing. It is the author's hope that this book will contribute to the increased use of the Lillooet language.

For a discussion of the white man's impact on British Columbia's Native cultures and languages, see Duff 1964. For a discussion of the suppression of Native languages, see Levine and Cooper 1976.

The name 'Lillooet'

The name 'Lillooet' is derived from líl'wat, the name of an old settlement partially coinciding with the present-day boundaries of Mount Currie. In its anglicized version, it became the name of the town of Lillooet (which partially overlaps with an old settlement called saλ' in the Lillooet language) and the name of the Lillooet people. Traditionally, the Lillooet refer to themselves by the name of each settlement in the Lillooet language and culture area, combined with the suffix -məx/-əmx 'person' (as in líl'wat-əmx 'person from líl'wat [Mount Currie]'). The name líl'wat is unanalyzable: the explanation 'wild onion' given by Boas in Teit 1906:292 is spurious and almost certainly results from a confusion of líl'wat with the word qʷlə́lwaʔ 'little onion' (diminutive of qʷláwaʔ 'onion'). Although the Lillooet in pre-contact times did not seem to have had a common term for themselves, the term sλ'áλ'y'əmx (or sλ'áλ'imx), which originally seemed to cover only the bands from Seton up to the Lillooet-Fountain area, is now also used fairly regularly for the entire nation. The terms Upper and Lower Lillooet, which are also used in the literature, basically coincide with the Fountain and Mount Currie dialect areas, respectively, with the boundary (such as it is) falling around D'Arcy.

Symbols and Abbreviations

C	consonant
V	vowel
Ç	retracted consonant (see Section 1.1)
C̱̃	non-retracted correlate of Ç (see Section 1.1)
Ṿ	retracted vowel (see Section 1.1)
Ṽ	non-retracted correlate of Ṿ (see Section 1.1)
Q	uvular
T	consonant other than Ç C̃ or Q (see Section 1.8.2)
K	obstruent
R	resonant
Cʷ	labialized consonant
A	full vowel (a ạ i ị u ụ)
E	weak vowel (ə ə̣)
√	root
Ø	zero-morpheme
#	word boundary
[..]	phonetic transcription
..[..]..	merger (see Section 4.4)
(..)	optional element (see Section 7.1)
*	reconstructed, rejected or excluded form
◊	marks divergences between type I and type II paradigms (see Section 22.3.2)
>	develops into
<	is developed from
-	indicates morpheme boundaries within words
‿	connects clitics to each other and to full words
UC	unique constituent
IC	immediate constituent
P	plural

S	singular
1, 2, 3	1st, 2nd, 3rd person
subj.	subject
obj.	object
tr.	transitive
intr.	intransitive
poss.	possessive
art.	article
reinf.	reinforcing enclitic
adh.	adhortative
ant.	anticipatory pronoun
fact.	factualizer
nom.	nominalizer
quot.	quotative
res.	resultative
smb.	somebody
smt.	something
id.	idem
BE	Bill Edwards
CM	Charlie Mack
LW	Lorna Williams
ML	Marie Leo
MLaR	Martina LaRochelle
RJ	Rosie Joseph
SM	Sam Mitchell
F	Fountain dialect
M	Mount Currie dialect
CdA	Coeur d'Alene
Kal.	Kalispel
Sh.	Shuswap

Part 1:
Phonology

Figure 1

Chart of phonemes

Consonants (C)

		Labial	Dental-Lateral		Dental-Palatal		Velar		Uvular		Laryngeal	
			Dent.	Lat.	Dent.	Pal.	Unr.	R.	Unr.	R.	Unr.	R.
Obstruents (K)	Plos. plain	p	t			c c̣*	k	kʷ	q	qʷ		
	Plos. glott.	p'		ƛ'	c'		k'	k'ʷ	q'	q'ʷ		
	Fric.			ɬ		s ṣ*	x	xʷ	x̣	x̣ʷ		
Resonants (R)	Nas. plain	m	n									
	Nas. glott.	m'	n'									
	Liqu. plain			l ḷ*								
	Liqu. glott.			l' ḷ'*								
	Glides plain				z	y	y	yʷ	ʕ	ʕʷ	h	w
	Glides glott.				z'	y'	y'		ʕ'	ʕ'ʷ	ʔ	w'

Vowels (V)

	Front		Back	
High	i i̦*		u u̦*	
Mid	e ȩ*			
Low	a a̦*			

* = retracted phonemes (see Section 1.1). For borrowed phonemes, see Section 7.5. For stress (´), see Section 1.5.

1
Phonetic Phonemes: General Information and Data

Lillooet has 52 segmental phonemes: 44 consonants (symbolized C) and 8 vowels (V). Consonants fall into 22 obstruents (K) and 22 resonants (R). There is one suprasegmental phoneme, a dynamic stress ('). Here we discuss retracted phonemes (Section 1.1), classification of phonemes (Sections 1.2 to 1.4), stress (Section 1.5), questions of word phonology (Section 1.6), distribution of phonemes (Section 1.7), and neutralization (Section 1.8). Phonetic data are given in Sections 1.1 to 1.4 and in 1.8 and 1.9.

1.1. Retracted versus non-retracted phonemes

As Figure 1 shows, the phonemes ǀ ǀ' c̣ ṣ (symbolized Ç) and a̱ i̱ u̱ ə̱ (V̱) are the retracted counterparts of ǀ ǀ' c s (symbolized C̃) and a i u ə (Ṽ). Retraction is basically velarization with concomitant tensing, phonetically symbolized on consonant symbols as [~] written through (not above) these symbols. Plain (non-retracted) ǀ ǀ' are [l l'] (resembling English 'clear l' of 'lip'), while retracted ǀ ǀ' are [ɫ ɫ'] (resembling English 'dark l' of 'pill'); c s are [č š] (resembling English 'ch' and 'sh' of 'chip' and 'ship'), while c̣ ṣ are [c s] (ṣ resembles Arabic ṣād; the retraction of the tongue-root in c̣ ṣ leaves only the tongue-tip to articulate the closure, in contrast to c s, where the whole tongue-blade is left free to make the closure); and a i u ə are broadly [ɛ e o ə], while a̱ i̱ u̱ ə̱ are [a ɛ/ė ɔ ʌ] ([ė] resembles the vowel of German 'mehr,' while [e] resembles the vowel of German 'Mehl'; note that a and i̱ overlap phonetically in [ɛ]; for further details on vowels, see Sections 1.8.1 to 1.8.2 and Section 1.9.3). In most roots where retraction occurs, it is characteristic of all phonemes that are susceptible to it (see also Section 1.8.2). Moreover, Ç V̱ replace C̃ Ṽ in certain suffixes when these follow retracted roots; for example, qəl 'bad' > qəl-wíl'x 'to get spoiled' (versus ʔáma 'good' > ʔama-wíl'x 'to get better, to get back to life'; -wíl'x inchoative suffix. For details on retracted phonemes, see Section 5.

1.2. Dental, velar, and uvular glides

The dental, velar, and uvular glides (z z′ ɣ ɣ′ ʕ ʕ′ ʕʷ ʕ′ʷ) are classed as resonants, rather than as voiced fricatives, because (1) they oppose plain versus glottalized members (like m m′ n n′ l l′ ! !′ y y′ w w′, but unlike the fricatives); and (2) like the other resonants, they do not occur in the positions C—C and C—# (see Section 1.7).

Phonetically, z z′ are lax fricatives, varying from a purely dental articulation (with the tongue-tip more forward than in English 'z′) to an interdental pronunciation (where z z′ sound somewhat like lax variants of English voiced 'th′). The former pronunciation is generally more common in the Fountain dialect (F), whereas the latter is more common in the Mount Currie dialect (M). In phonetic transcriptions, we use [z z′] for both F and M variants; after vowels, z′ in M allows the variant [l′] beside [z′], e.g., x̌əz′p [x̌əz′p x̌əl′p] 'ember(s)';[1] z z′ vary freely with y y′ in certain positions (see Section 1.7.1). The resonants ɣ ɣ′ ʕ ʕ′ ʕʷ ʕ′ʷ are lax velar and pharyngeal glides pronounced with a wide aperture (the articulation of ʕ is further back than that of the uvular obstruents).[2] For velar and uvular resonants, see also Section 1.3.

1.3. Laryngeal, velar, and uvular resonants

The phonemes h ʔ are classed as resonants because they do not occur in the positions C—C and C—# (see Section 1.7). Within the group of resonants, h ʔ stand apart by being voiceless,[3] and by the frequent occurrence of ʔ in word-initial position (other cases of glottalized resonants are rare here; see Section 1.7). The resonants w w′ are phonetically bilabial non-laryngeal [w w′]; however, by classing w w′ as the rounded counterparts of h ʔ, we can interpret ʕ ʕ′ ʕʷ ʕ′ʷ as the uvularized counterparts of h ʔ w w′, respectively; ɣ ɣ′ then follow the pattern as the velarized counterparts of y y′.[4]

1.4. Dentals, laterals, and palatals

Lillooet has six phonemes (t n n′ c′ z z′) that are phonetically dental (i.e., the tongue-tip takes a slightly more forward position than in the English alveolars; for z z′ see also Section 1.2). We class t n n′ with the laterals and c′ z z′ with the palatals, because n n′ belong to one 'close contact' pronunciation type with t and the laterals, whereas z z′ belong to another 'close contact' pronunciation type with c′ and the palatals. By 'close contact' we mean certain combinations CəR CəR where əR əR is phonetically syllabic [R̩] and the preceding C is released through (that is, in 'close contact' with) əR əR. We have the following cases:

(1) When əm əm′ follow a labial consonant (p p′ m m′), or when ən ən′ follow a dental-lateral consonant (t ƛ′ ɬ n n′ l l′ ! !′), əm əm′ ən ən′ are [m̩ m̩′

ŋ ŋ'], and the preceding consonant has a velic release through əm əm' ən ən'. Examples: ƛ'épƛ'pəm [ƛ'épƛ'pm̩] 'dark,' kʷáməm [kʷɛ́mm̩] 'to get smt.,' sm'ə́m'łac [šm'm̩'łɛč] 'girl' F, xʷík'tən [xʷék'tn̩] 'knife,' kʷánəns [kʷɛ́nn̩š] 'to catch smt.,' ʔítən [ʔétn̩] 'to eat' F, xʷíl'ən [xʷél'n̩] 'to look for smt., tr.,' ƛ'éna? [ƛ'ŋ̩ɛ?] 'ear.' Where əm əm' follow a non-labial consonant, or where ən ən' follow a non–dental-lateral consonant, they are [əm əm' ən ən'], e.g., xʷíl'əm [xʷél'əm] 'to look for smt., intr.,' xʷík'əm [xʷék'əm] 'to butcher fish,' sápən [šɛ́pən] 'daughter-in-law.'

The vowel ə prevents close contact between a preceding consonant and a following nasal: pəmp [pʌmp] 'fast,' łə́nkaya [łʌ́nkɛyɛ] 'cast-iron pot,' łə̧np [łʌnp] 'sound of things shaking, rattling.'

(2) When əl əl' ə̧l ə̧l' follow a lateral consonant, they are [l̩ l̩' ł̩ ł̩'] and the preceding lateral is released through [l̩ l̩' ł̩ ł̩']: łíləl [łéll̩] 'to sprinkle,' łəl'kám' [łł̩'kém'] 'to weed,' ƛ'əlc [ƛ'lč̩] 'high-elevation cranberry,' qʷəl'qʷal'ə́l't [qʷəl'qʷɛl'l̩'t] 'to talk, to have a conversation,' sálə̧l [sáłł̩] 'to drip in a string (like syrup),' sƛ'áƛ'ə̧l's [šƛ'áƛ'ł̩'š] 'to carry smt. in one's mouth (like a dog carrying a bone),' ƛ'ə̧lp [ƛ'ł̩p] 'vibrating sound (like a string being plucked).' After non-lateral consonants (and also after the dentals t n n'), əl əl' ə̧l ə̧l' are [əl əl' ʌł ʌł'], e.g., kí?kəl' [ké?kəl'] 'unwilling to do smt.,' pálpə̧lt [pátpʌłt] 'stubborn,' pəl'p [pəl'p] 'lost,' qə̧l [qʌł] 'bad.' The sequences *ə̧l *ə̧l' *ə̧l *ə̧l' are excluded (see Section 1.8.2).

(3) When əz əz' follow a dental-palatal obstruent or z z', they are [z̧ z̧'] (elsewhere they are [əz əz']). The obstruents c s are phonetically [c s] (non-velarized) before əz əz': ʔúcəz [ʔócz̧] 'good, straight(forward), okay,' ʔúcəz'qam' [ʔócz̧'qɛm'] 'to steer a canoe,' ti‿staˤ'ésəzh‿a [..sz̧hɛ] 'the squirrel,' x̌zézəm' [x̌z̧ə̧m'] 'a little bit bigger.'[5] As shown in Section 1.8.1, the sequences *əz *əz' do not occur.[6]

1.5. Stress

In polysyllabic Lillooet words, one vowel has a dynamic stress (written '). Stress is phonemic, as shown by such pairs as máqa? 'snow' versus maqá? 'poison onion' F, and ƛ'ámin 'fur' F versus ƛ'amín 'axe' F. Stress is mobile: it can move to a later vowel as suffixes and/or enclitics are added, e.g., ʔúxʷalmixʷ 'Indian, person' > ʔuxʷalmíxʷ-kan 'I (-kan) am an Indian, a person,' ʔuxʷalmíxʷ‿ti? 'that (‿ti?) is an Indian, a person.' For details on the movement of the stress, see Section 2.

1.6. Questions of word phonology

Lillooet words fall into two main classes: full words and clitics (the latter are divided into proclitics and enclitics). A full word may consist of a root, or of a root marked by various forms of reduplication, or pre- or suffixation, or by interior glottalization ($C_1VC_2 > C_1V?C_2$), or by any combination of these operations. Compounding also exists, but is rare and unproductive. For further details on word classes and morphological operations, see Section 8.1.

The favourite root-shape of full words is C_1VC_2, while $C_1VC_2C_3$ is also relatively common. For details on root-shapes, see Section 6. Morphological operations may lead to epenthesis or elision of ə ə̣ (see Section 3), or to vowel-consonant alternations, merging of consonants, or other changes (see Section 4). For retraction in suffixes after retracted roots, see Section 1.1. For the distribution of stress in roots and in combinations of roots with suffixes and/or enclitics, see Section 1.5. Restrictions on the (co)occurrence of phonemes are discussed in Sections 1.7 and 1.8. Glottalized resonants may be characteristic of morphemes as such (e.g., sil 'cloth' versus psil' 'daylight'), but plain resonants may also become glottalized as a result of a morphological operation. For instance, with 'consonant reduplication' ($C_p\acute{V}C_q > C_p\acute{V}C_pC_q$), we have pun 'to find' > púpən' 'to find smt. by accident' (*púpn' excluded; see Section 1.7). Certain suffixes, e.g., -q^w 'head, animal,' glottalize a postvocalic resonant in the preceding morpheme, e.g., x̌zum 'big' > x̌zum'-q^w 'big animal.' Resonant glottalizations that result from morphological operations will be discussed under these operations (see Sections 12 [introductory remarks], 12.4, and 15.2 [fifth paragraph]).

1.7. Distribution of phonemes

Vowels do not occur word-initially, and not adjacent to another vowel.[7] Word-finally, vowels are rare: ạ i̩ u̩ ə ə̣ do not occur here at all (except for borrowings), i u in only a few words, and a in a larger number of words. The distribution of a ạ i i̩ u u̩ (collectively symbolized A) is different from that of ə ə̣ (both called 'schwa' and symbolized E) in two respects: (1) ə ə̣ are elided more easily from a number of positions as a result of suffixation; (2) on the other hand, ə ə̣ are used to break up certain consonant clusters where these would arise from a morphological operation. As the last statement implies, consonants may occur in clusters, but of limited length; longer clusters are broken up by epenthetic E. In particular *CRC and *CR# are excluded, and where a morphological operation would give rise to these sequences we have CREC CERC CEREC and CER# instead (see pun > púpən' in Section 1.6). Where R is h or ʔ we have special variants (see Sections 3.5 and 4.1). With obstruents, the sequences #KKC and CKK# are generally (but not always) avoided, and we have #KEKC and CKEK# instead. For further details on consonant clusters and the distribution of schwa, see Section 3.

Glottalized resonants other than ʔ do not occur word-initially except in certain reduplicative formations. Retracted phonemes, velar and uvular resonants, and h are of comparatively rare occurrence.[8] Velar and uvular resonants and h do not occur in suffixes.[9] For the special status of y and y′, see Section 1.7.1. For neutralizations of phonemic oppositions, see Section 1.8.

1.7.1. Distribution of y y′ and z z′

Comparison with other Salish languages shows that Proto-Salish *y *y′ generally developed into z z′ in Lillooet.[10] However, we do have y y′ in the following cases:

(1) Free variation of z z′ with y y′ before a suffix or enclitic beginning in a coronal (i.e., a dental or lateral consonant or a palatal obstruent), e.g., huz′ 'to be about to do smt.' > húz′-ɬkan/húy′-ɬkan 'I (-ɬkan) am about to do smt.,' húz′‿ti?/húy′‿ti? 'that one (‿ti?) is about to do smt.'; ƛ′laz′ 'canoe' > ƛ′laz′-s/ƛ′lay′-s 'his (-s) canoe.' Here also belongs qʷ́əz-ən/qʷ́əy-ən 'to use smt., tr. (-ən)' (*qʷ́əz-n/qʷ́əy-n [with *Cn#] excluded; see Section 1.7). In F y y′ are the normal variants, whereas in M z z′ are the normal variants (in texts I write variants as they occur).

(2) y y′ (to the exclusion of z z′) before a coronal consonant within morphemes and also in fixed combinations (i.e., those where the morpheme ending in y y′ never occurs without a following morpheme beginning with a coronal). Examples are: sqayt 'top, summit,' ?ayɬ 'to have just done smt.,' -ay′ɬ 'child,' sáy′-səz′ 'to play' (reduplicative form without simplex), q′áy-ləx 'to jump, run away' (q′ay- UC; -ləx 'body, self'), cáy-ləx 'to crawl' (cay- UC; -ləx 'body, self'), may-t 'to fix, to be in session (ab. Indian doctor)' (may- 'to fix'; -t formative), máy-s-ən 'to fix smt., tr. (-ən)' (-s 'shape').

(3) Occasional variation of z with y in cases other than (1): we have on the one hand idiolectal variants such as zətp/yətp 'jelly-like,' and on the other hand cases where initial z is replaced by y in nursery talk, e.g., yaxt 'long,' yáxən 'to carry on one's back' instead of regular zaxt, s-záxən (for dropping of s- in the latter form, see also Section 7.1).[11]

(4) y y′ in borrowings and in irregular retentions of Proto-Salish *y *y′, as in yúnhana 'Carrier Indian,' xʷuy 'come on!' məxáy′a 'birchbark basket' F.[12]

The resonants y y′ do not vary with z z′: ?ayɬ, yúnhana, məxáy′a are never *?azɬ, *zúnhana, *məxáz′a.

1.8. Neutralizations

In this subsection we discuss three types of neutralizations: between Ṽ ~ V̬ in the position —z/z′ (Section 1.8.1), between non-retracted and retracted phonemes (Section 1.8.2), and between rounded and unrounded consonants (Section 1.8.3). For the neutralization of y y′ ~ z z′ before certain consonants, see Section 1.7.1(2). For the neutralization between certain vowel-resonant sequences and vowels, and between y′ ~ ? and w′ ~ ?, see Section 1.9.4.

1.8.1. The position −z/z′

In the positions −z and −z′, the opposition a ~ ạ is neutralized in M, and only the retracted vowel is pronounced here. However, my transcription reflects F, which has both a and ạ here, e.g., qʷəz-qʷáz 'blue' versus xʷʔạz 'no(t)'; xníz′-az′ 'gooseberry bush' versus pṣúṣ-ạz′ 'wild cherry bush.' In order to obtain the M form, one has to read a as ạ here. Where z z′ become y y′ (see Section 1.7.1[1]), ạz ạz′ are often pronounced ay ay′: xʷʔạz 'no(t)' > xʷʔáy‿X̣′uʔ (besides xʷʔáy‿X̣′uʔ) 'not yet, not at all' (‿X̣′uʔ 'well, but, so'), xʷʔay-s 'to refuse' (-s causativizer). The oppositions u ~ ụ, i ~ ị, and ə ~ ə̣ are neutralized in the position −z/z′ in both F and M: of i ~ ị and ə ~ ə̣, only i and ə are found here. As for u ~ ụ, in M only ụ is pronounced, in F only u (we write u throughout, e.g., kʷúz-xal 'to spread out berries to dry': [kʷoz..] in F, [kʷɔz..] in M). In M, we have retracted variants of a u also where these vowels are separated from z z′ by ʔ (or ʔ and an epenthetic ə before z z′), e.g., qáʔəz′ 'tired': [qέʔəz′] in F, [qáʔəz′] in M.

1.8.2. Neutralization between retracted and non-retracted phonemes

Writing Q for any uvular, Ç for any retracted consonant, Č for any non-retracted correlate of Ç, and T for any other consonant, we have the combinatory possibilities of these consonants with V (retracted vowels) and Ṽ (non-retracted vowels) shown in Figure 2.

As Figure 2 shows, we have the following restrictions:

(1) Before uvulars, the opposition Ṽ ~ V is neutralized, and we write Ṽ here. The phonetic variants of Ṽ before Q are similar to those of V elsewhere (e.g., the vowel of zuqʷ [zɔqʷ] 'dead' is phonetically like that of ṣtụt [stɔt] 'cricket' F, but different from the 'normal' variant of u, as in put [pot] 'just right'; for phonetics of vowels, see also Section 1.1). The normal variants of Ṽ [ε e o ə] appear when Ṽ, as a result of consonant reduplication (CₚV́C_q > CₚV́CₚC_q), is not immediately followed by Q any more, e.g., súqʷ′əm [šɔ́qʷ′əm] 'to skin an animal' > súsqʷ′əm′ [šúšqʷ′əm′] 'to skin small animals.' With the opposite phonetic change, we have, e.g., qʷúsəm [qʷóšəm] 'to shoot' > qʷúqʷsəm′ [qʷɔ́qʷšəm′] 'to shoot/hunt small animals.' The vowels in the preceding examples behave phonemically exactly like vowels that are not followed by Q, e.g., pun [pon] 'to find' > púpən′ [pópən′] 'to find smt. by accident.' The opposition Ṽ ~ V is also neutralized before ʔQ and only Ṽ is written here; a i u ə have the same phonetics before ʔQ as before Q, e.g., ɬaʔ [ɬέʔ] 'to get close' > ɬaʔqs [ɬaʔqš] 'to go ashore'; ʔúqʷaʔ [ʔɔ́qʷέʔ] 'to drink' > ʔúʔqʷaʔ [ʔɔ́ʔqʷέʔ] 'to drink a little bit.'[13]

(The sequence *ə̣ʔQ does not occur, and aʔQ arises where we would expect ə̣ʔQ; see Section 3.5 for aʔ replacing *ə̣ʔ. For restrictions on ə̣ʔ and ə̣ʔ within roots, see Section 6.2. For the general restraint on *ə̣ʔC, see Section 1.9.4.)

Figure 2

Combinatory possibilities of retracted and non-retracted phonemes

	−T		−Q		−Ç		−C̃	
	V̄	V	V̄	V	V̄	V	V̄	V
T—	TaT	TạT	TaQ	—	—	TạÇ	TaC̃	—
	TiT	TịT	TiQ	—	—	TịÇ	TiC̃	—
	TuT	TụT	TuQ	—	—	TụÇ	TuC̃	—
	TəT	Tə̣T	TəQ	—	—	Tə̣Ç	TəC̃	—
Q—	QaT	—	QaQ	—	—	QạÇ	QaC̃	—
	QiT	—	QiQ	—	—	—	QiC̃	—
	QuT	—	QuQ	—	—	QụÇ	QuC̃	—
	QəT	Qə̣T	QəQ	—	—	Qə̣Ç	QəC̃	—
Ç—	—	ÇaT	—	—	—	ÇaÇ	—	—
	ÇiT	ÇịT	—	—	—	ÇiÇ	—	—
	—	ÇuT	—	—	—	ÇuÇ	—	—
	—	ÇəT	—	—	—	ÇəÇ	—	—
C̃—	C̃aT	—	C̃aQ	—	—	—	C̃aC̃	—
	C̃iT	—	C̃iQ	—	—	—	C̃iC̃	—
	C̃uT	—	C̃uQ	—	—	—	C̃uC̃	—
	C̃əT	—	C̃əQ	—	—	—	C̃əC̃	—

(2) V does not occur adjacent to C̃, nor does V̄ occur adjacent to Ç (except for ÇiT, e.g., kʷli? 'green, yellow'; other cases of Ç not adjacent to V are rare but do occur, e.g., ṣṭuṭ 'cricket' F, çə́m'çm'əqʷ 'to get mired,' with the second ç not adjacent to V).[14] V Ç remain as such also when they become separated from each other by T, e.g., √X̣'al 'to bite' > s-X̣'áX̣'əḷ'-s 'to carry in one's mouth' (s- stative prefix, -s transitivizer). V in the position T—T retains its retraction also in reduplicated forms, e.g., √ɬuṭ 'to squash a bug' > ɬú́ɬt-ən' 'to squash it well.'

(3) There is no *ÇVQ or *QVT (except for QəT, in qəmḷá? 'young, newly hatched fish,' recorded from CM only). Moreover, *QiÇ does not occur, while other cases of QVÇ, such as qəḷ 'bad,' are rare. Neither do we have *CVQ (see [1] above). Hence, uvulars and retracted phonemes tend to exclude each other.[15]

1.8.3. Unrounded versus rounded consonants

Before and after u ụ all velars and uvulars are phonetically rounded.[16] In these positions we write rounded or unrounded consonants depending on what is morphophonemically indicated. We have three sets of cases here:

(1) Inherently rounded consonants that remain rounded when, as a result of a morphological operation, they do not border on u ụ any more, e.g., páqʷuʔ 'to be afraid' > páqʷʔ-an 'to scare smb., tr.'; cukʷ 'finished' > cəkʷ-cúkʷ 'to be all finished' (here kʷ in the first syllable proves that kʷ in the second syllable is inherently rounded).

(2) Secondarily rounded consonants that are unrounded when they are separated from u ụ, e.g., cʼaʔx-ús [..xʷóš] 'ashamed' (-us 'face') versus cʼaʔx id.

(3) Cases where it cannot be determined whether a consonant is inherently or secondarily rounded, due to a lack of relevant derivations, e.g., xʷúxʷən' 'to heave a deep sigh.'

We write Cʷ in cases (1) and (3), and C in case (2).[17]

1.9. Phonetic data: details and special questions

Basic phonetic information is given in Sections 1.1 to 1.4 and Section 1.8. In what follows, we discuss details and special questions concerning obstruents (Section 1.9.1), resonants (Section 1.9.2), vowels (Section 1.9.3), and certain vowel-resonant sequences (Section 1.9.4).

1.9.1. Obstruents

Plain (non-glottalized) plosives are sometimes slightly aspirated. Glottalized plosives are pressure stops (ejectives), as described by Heffner (1960:136-137) and O'Connor (1973:41). In glottalized plosives, the oral and glottal release are simultaneous, Kʼ being opposed to Kʔ Kʼʔ ʔK and ʔKʼ (e.g., sqʼan 'thornberry,' qʔam 'to nurse, breastfeed,' qʼʔáłʼmən 'hungry' M, łaʔqs 'to go ashore,' naʔqʼ 'rotten').[18] Glottalized qʼ qʼʷ are affricates [qʼˣ qʼˣʷ], but plain q qʷ are not: [q qʷ] (henceforth we will write [qʼ qʼʷ] for [qʼˣ qʼˣʷ]). The articulation point of the uvulars is quite close to that of the velars; the fricatives x̌ x̌ʷ have a rather sharp friction (and a rather high degree of stridency) that sets them apart from the velars x xʷ (in the same way, qʼ qʼʷ are distinguished mainly by their fricative off-glide from q qʷ). Velars are almost, but not completely, assimilated with uvulars when they adjoin these.

The affricate c [č] is opposed to both ts [tš] and cs [čš], e.g., panʼc 'to have a meal with smb., intr.,' pʼanʼts 'to return smt./smb.,' panʼcs 'to share a meal with smb., tr.' The palatals c [č] and s [š] have a more dental-alveolar pronunciation before t: [ć ś] ([ć] resembles Serbo-Croatian ć; with [ś] we have, for example, cilkst [čelkśt] 'five'). Before cʼ (ə)z (ə)zʼ, c s are [c s] (non-velarized), e.g., ʔúczan [ʔóczɛn] 'to straighten, fix smt.,' sʔúcəz 'good, okay' (for the pronunciation of əz əz′ after c s, see Section 1.4[3]). Sequences of two identical obstruents are pronounced long (symbolized [:]), e.g., ƛ′ákkan [ƛ′ɛ́k:ɛn] 'I go.' The sequence tc (as in npətcán′ 'to cover a door opening with a piece of cloth') is [tč], but also allows a pronunciation [č:], phonetically indistinguishable from cc [č:].[19]

1.9.2. Resonants

The nasals n n′ sometimes have a velar pronunciation [ŋ ŋ′] before velar obstruents (but not before other velars). Glottalization of resonants consists of a tightening of the vocal cords rather than a complete closure (the latter is the case in glottalized obstruents and in the resonant ʔ). As a result, glottalized resonants are (1) pronounced with 'creaky voice' but not as ejectives, and (2) phonetically closer to non-glottalized resonants than glottalized obstruents are to non-glottalized obstruents.[20]

In glottalized resonants other than ʔ, the glottal stricture is strongest near the onset of the resonant before a stressed vowel but near the outset in other positions. However, there is a difference between R′ on the one hand and Rʔ ʔR and ʔR′ on the other: e.g., ti‿sqláw′‿a 'the beaver, the money,' ti‿qʷláwʔ‿a 'the onion,' wáʔwit 'they are,' and ʔáʔwʹət 'a little bit later'; the one example with R′ʔ, sqlawʹʔúl 'a real beaver' (i.e., not money), is not accepted by all consultants.[21] Sequences of two identical resonants are pronounced long, occasionally with a hiatus.

1.9.3. Vowels

As we saw in Sections 1.1 and 1.8.2(1), the main variants of a i u are [ɛ e o] when not in the position —(ʔ)Q,[22] but [a ɛ/ė ɔ] when in the position —(ʔ)Q. The phonetic values [e o] of i u tend to be rather high, approaching [i u], and this higher quality is clearly noticeable in the neighbourhood of dental and non-velarized laterals and palatals. Examples are psil′ [pšel′ pšil′] 'daylight,' lúləm′ [lóləm′ lúləm′] 'jealous in matters of love (suspecting one's partner of infidelity).' Outside this subsection we write [e] for [e i] and [o] for [o u]. As mentioned in Section 1.1, the vowels a̦ i̦ u̦ are [a ɛ/ė ɔ].

Aside from those sequences əR that are in close contact with a preceding consonant (see Section 1.4), and the sequences əR that are discussed in Section 1.9.4, the vowel ə has the following variants: [ʊ] (resembling English 'u' of 'pull') between rounded velars and after w w′: kʷə́kʷa? [kʷúkʷɛ?] 'grandmother'; [ɪ] (resembling English 'i' of 'pit') between dentals and/or non-velarized laterals or palatals: ɬəsp [ɬɪšp] 'rash (on skin)'; and [ə] between labials and/or unrounded velars: pə́pla? [pə́plɛ?] 'one animal,' kə́xkəx [kə́xkəx] 'elder sister.' Between non-uvulars of different places of articulation, ə is influenced by both (as in səxp 'numb,' where ə is less palatal than in ɬəsp 'rash'). In the rare cases where ə occurs next to h or ?, it has the value [ə] but with some influence from the other consonant (as in hə́ləz 'humpback salmon' M, with a value between [ə] and [ɪ]. Before un-rounded uvulars, ə is [ʌ], before rounded uvulars it is [ɔ̌]: pəq [pʌq] 'white,' stəx̌ʷ [štɔ̌x̌ʷ] 'true, very.' After uvulars, ə has almost the same variants as before uvulars (however, in, for example, sx̌əp 'piled up evenly' the vowel is open [ə], but not as open or back as [ʌ]).

The vowel ə̣ is [ʌ], but adjacent to rounded consonants it also allows a variant [ɔ̌]: sɬə̣k [štʌk] 'lazy, motionless,' xʷə̣lp [xʷʌɬp xʷɔ̌ɬp] 'breeze.' For cases ə̣R with close contact, see Section 1.4(2).

The variants of ə ə̣ are somewhat shorter than those of the full vowels (A). This shorter length is indicated only, by [ˇ], in the case of [ɔ̌]. There is no phonetic difference between cases of ə ə̣ that represent root vowels and cases of ə ə̣ that result from epenthesis.

1.9.4. Vowel-resonant sequences: special cases

Sequences ə̣R (where R is a glide other than z z' or h ʔ) have the following pronunciations before C or #:

phonemic:	əɣ	əɣ́	ə ˁ	ə ˁ′	əˁʷ	əˁ′ʷ	əy	əy′	əw	əw′
phonetic 1:	[ə̂ɣ	ə̂ɣ́	â ˁ	â ˁ′	ɔ̂ˁʷ	ɔ̂ˁ′ʷ	ey	ey′	uw	uw′]
phonetic 2:	[ə̂(:)	ə̂(:)ʔ	â(:)	â(:)ʔ	ɔ̂(:)	ɔ̂(:)ʔ	e	e?	o	o?]

The symbol [ˆ] indicates velarization (in [ə̂]) or pharyngealization (in [â] and [ɔ̂]). Phonetic variants 1 are generally heard in slower types of speech, variants 2 in more rapid types of speech. Examples of variants 2 of əy through əˁ′ʷ include: məyp [mə̂(:)p] 'numb (to feel "pins and needles"),' nləɣ́c [n̩lə̂(:)ʔč] 'corked,'[23] pəˁp [pâ(:)p] 'dull, faded (of colour),' ˁə́ˁcəp [ˁâ′(:)ʔcəp] 'caught in a trap,' x̌'ə́ˁʷx̌'ˁʷəm [x̌'ɔ̂′(:)x̌'ˁʷəm] 'hard,' pəˁ′ʷqʷ [pɔ̂(:)ʔqʷ] 'to bump one's head.'

Before # and non-uvular consonants, the sequences əy əy′ are opposed to i in slower speech and when under the stress: sx̌ʷis [šx̌ʷeš] 'to smile' versus x̌ʷəys [x̌ʷeyš] 'to love, to like smt./smb.' (in more rapid speech both forms tend to merge into [(š)x̌ʷeš]).[24] Outside the stress, əy əy′ are virtually indistinguishable from i iʔ and we base our transcription on morphopho-nemic indications, e.g., cəycáyləx [čeč..] 'to crawl all over' (reduplication of cáyləx 'to crawl') versus pipáncək [pep..] 'summer' (no simplex); qaʔəý-ɬkán [qɛʔe?ɬkɛ́n] 'I (-ɬkan) am tired (qáʔəz′)' (with regular change z′ > y′; see Section 1.7.1) versus ɣiʔpúpzaʔ [ɣe?p..] 'potatoes start to shoot out' (ɣiʔp 'to grow,' -upzaʔ 'shoot of plant'). In the position —Q, the sequences əy əy′ are both phonetically and phonemically opposed to i iʔ: sqəyqə́qy′əxʷ [šqeq..] 'boys' (reduplication of sqə́qy′əxʷ 'boy') versus x̌'iq [x̌'ɛq, x̌'éq] 'to arrive here'; syʔə́yʼqcaʔ [šyʼéyʼqčɛʔ, šyʼéʔqčɛʔ] 'girl' M (reduplication of syáqcaʔ 'woman' M) versus kiʔx̌ [kɛʔx̌ kėʔx̌] 'cranky (like baby).'

The sequences əw əwʼ are [ʊw ʊwʼ], in direct opposition to u uʔ [o oʔ], when they occur under the stress, e.g., ləws [lʊwš] 'broken, shattered (like glass)' versus slúsəs [šlóšəš] 'flume'; təwʼp [tʊwʼp] 'to foam' versus pʼuʔƛ̓ [pʼoʔƛ̓] 'smoke coming up.'[25] Unstressed əw əwʼ also allow [o oʔ] besides [ʊw ʊwʼ], e.g. ləwsán [lʊwšén, lošén] 'to shatter smt., tr.,' stəwʼpálqʷ [štʊwʼpélqʷ, štoʔpélqʷ] 'cottonwood cambium layer.'

The sequences əh or əʔ do not occur before C or # (only unstressed before vowels).

The sequences aˤ aˤʼ uˤʷ uˤʼʷ iy iyʼ uw uwʼ have the following variants before C and #:

phonemic:	aˤ	aˤʼ	uˤʷ	uˤʼʷ	iy	iyʼ	uw	uwʼ
phonetic 1:	[â:ˤ	â:ˤʼ	ô:ˤʷ	ô:ˤʼʷ	ey	eyʼ	ow	owʼ]
phonetic 2:	[â:	â:ʔ	ô:	ô:ʔ	e:	eʔ	o:	oʔ]

Note that aˤ aˤʼ uˤʷ uˤʼʷ are distinguished from əˤ əˤʼ əˤʷ əˤʼʷ by relative length, and that iy overlaps phonetically with əy in [ey], that iyʼ overlaps with əyʼ and iʔ in [eʔ] (and with əyʼ also in [eyʼ]), and that uwʼ overlaps with əwʼ and uʔ in [oʔ]. Examples of variants 2 of aˤ, etc., include: ɬəˤɬáˤt [ɬâ(:)ɬâ':t] 'fast' F, spʼaˤʼ [špʼâ:ʔ] 'burnt-out area,' scuˤʷ [sčô:] 'stripe,' ncuˤʼʷk [n̦čô:ʔk] 'to have a stripe on one's back,' skíyʔamx [škéːʔɛmx] 'porcupine' F, takəm‿ʔíyʼ‿ƛ̓uʔ [tɛkəmʔéʔƛ̓oʔ] 'all (tákəm) those (‿ʔiʔ)' (‿ƛ̓uʔ 'well, just, so,' ‿ʔiyʼ < ‿ʔizʼ before ‿ƛ̓uʔ, cf. Section 1.7.1[1]; for the stress-shift from tákəm to the enclitic ‿ʔiyʼ, see Section 2.2[2]), səwsúwt [šuwšóːt] 'wet vegetation (from dew or rain),' and cwʼúwʼsaʔ [čwʼóʔšɛʔ] 'to play soccer' – reduplication of *cwʼ-úsa 'to kick (cwʼ-) a ball (-usaʔ)'; cf. pʼuʔƛ̓ [pʼoʔƛ̓] above, which consists of √pʼuƛ̓ 'to smoke' plus interior glottalization.

Before V, the sequences əR AR are [əR AR], e.g., láˤʷən [lô̜ˤʷən] 'to hide smt.,' ka-léw‿a [kɛlúwɛ] 'to land with a thud,' snúwa [šnówɛ] 'you (S).'[26]

The rare sequence əy is phonetically identical to i̦ [ɛ/ė]. We write əy where this is morphophonemically indicated: pəypə́pyʼət [pɛp.., pėp..] 'to quarrel' M (reduplication of pa̦yt 'to fight' M). We have no sequences of ə followed by other glides (for neutralization of ə ~ ə̦ before z zʼ and before uvular glides, see Sections 1.8.1 and 1.8.2).

2
Movement of the Stress

For the main facts about stress in Lillooet, see Section 1.5. Here we discuss the rules for the distribution of the stress in roots and suffixes (Section 2.1), in combinations with enclitics (Section 2.2), and in combinations with prefixes (Section 2.3).

2.1. Roots and suffixes

In both roots and root-suffix combinations, assignment of the stress follows two basic tendencies: (1) in words with at least one vowel A (a ạ i į or u ụ), the stress falls on the first A, whether or not that A is preceded by E (ə or ə̣); in words with only vowels E, the stress falls on the first E; (2) from the base established by the first tendency, the stress moves two vowels at a time, as long as it does not fall on the last vowel. These tendencies are discussed in rules (1) and (2) below. Additional rules, and exceptions, are discussed in rules (3) to (10).

(1) Assignment of the stress to the first A is attested by, e.g., k'áx-an' 'to dry it, tr.,' k'áx-xal 'to dry things, intr.,' cúɬ-un' 'to point at it, tr.,' cúɬ-xal 'to point at things, intr.,' ník'-in' 'to cut it, tr.,' ník'-xal 'to cut things, intr.,' sútik 'winter,' zúmak 'spring salmon,' zánuc 'driftwood,' ʔínwat 'to say what?,' kíl̲-us-əm 'to feel very bad (pained, embarrassed, etc.) about smt.,' sáƛ'-məx 'person from sáƛ',' ɬáp-ən 'to forget smt., tr.,' məc-xál 'to write, intr.,' qəl̲-wíl'x 'to get spoiled,' ləʕʷ-átkʷaʔ 'to hide water or liquor,' məc-ən-ɬkán 'I write it down.' Examples of words with vowels E only are léʕʷ-ən 'to hide it, tr.,' ʕʷél-ən 'to light it, tr.,' méc-ən 'to write it down, tr.' (cf. məc-xál, məc-ən-ɬkán above), xéɬ-xəɬ 'lively, brisk,' ʕʷél-ʕʷəl-əp 'forest fire.' Most cases of Aʔ act like E with regard to the stress, e.g., q'aʔ 'to eat' M > q'aʔ-ɬkán 'I eat'; cáʔxʷ 'glad' > caʔxʷ-kán 'I am glad.'

(2) Movement of the stress by two syllables is attested by, e.g., ʔúxʷalmixʷ 'Indian, person' > ʔuxʷalmíxʷ-kan 'I (-kan) am an Indian, a person,' ʔuxʷalmíxʷ-am 'to do smt. the Indian way' (-am intransitivizer); sútik

'winter' > sutik-áka? 'north wind (-aka?)'; cúɬ-un' 'to point at it, tr.' > cuɬ-un'-túmuɬ 'point at us (-tumuɬ)!' cuɬ-un'-tumuɬ-káɬap 'you folks (-kaɬ'ap) point(ed) at us'; ɬáp-ən 'to forget it, tr.' > ɬap-ən-ɬkáɬap 'you folks forget (forgot) it'; ləʕʷən-túmuɬ 'hide us!' > ləʕʷən-tumuɬ-káɬap 'you folks hid(e) us.'[1] Where E or A? are even-numbered from the counting base and should therefore attract the stress, E and A? are in fact ignored unless they are followed by another syllable with E: záxal'qʷəm' 'tall' > záxal'qʷəm'-ɬkan 'I am tall,' zaxal'qʷəm'-ɬkáɬap 'you folks are tall' (instead of the expected *zaxal'qʷə́m'-ɬkan, *zaxal'qʷə́m'-ɬkaɬap): cf. ɬap-ən > ɬap-ən-ɬkáɬap above, where E is not in a position to receive the stress (because it is odd-numbered from the counting base), so E counts for the assignment of the stress. An example with A? is luc' 'tight' > luc'-aká?-əm 'to hold on tightly, intr.' (-əm intransitivizer) versus lúc'-aka?-min 'to hold on tightly (-min), tr.' (-aka? 'hand').[2]

(3) All roots, including the ones with E or A?, use the root vowel as counting base when embedded in ka-..‿a 'suddenly, by accident, out-of-control' (Section 10.1.3), e.g., ka-qʼʷə́ɬ-kan‿a 'I got scorched (qʼʷəɬ-) by accident' versus qʼʷəɬp-kán id. (-p inchoative suffix [see Section 14.1]; the form with ka-..‿a suggests a lesser degree of control than the form with -p). When a root embedded in ka-..‿a is followed by more extensions, the stress moves from the root according to rule (2): ka-qʼʷəɬ-kan‿á‿kɬ 'I might get scorched' (‿kɬ 'remote future'; for stress on ‿á see Section 2.2[2]). Reduplicated stems with E, which regularly stress the first vowel, shift the stress to the second vowel when the word is embedded in ka-..‿a. Thus we have mə́təmtəp 'to get paralyzed' (via *mə́tmətp; see Section 3 for details on the dropping and insertion of ə) versus ka-mətmə́t‿a 'to get paralyzed suddenly.'

(4) Certain consonant clusters count as vowels with regard to the distribution of the stress. These clusters comprise either root-final clusters, e.g., ʕʷuy'ɬ 'to sleep' > ʕʷuy'ɬ-íc'a? 'pajamas, nightie' (-ic'a? 'clothing'); final clusters on so-called lexical suffixes (discussed in Section 8.1), e.g., x̌ʷ?úcin 'four' > x̌ʷ?ucin-álqʷ 'four sticks (-alqʷ)'; or word-final clusters resulting from a lexical suffix of the shape C(C) added to a root, e.g., ?úxʷalmixʷ 'Indian' > ?uxʷalmíxʷ-c 'to speak (-c) Indian.'

Consonant clusters involving non-lexical suffixes do not count as vowels. Cases that obtain here are: -s (1) transitivizer, (2) 3S poss.; -tumx 1S obj. (after the transitivizer -s); -c 1S obj. (after transitivizers other than -s; for -s, -c, and -tumx, see also Section 3.3.2), e.g., pún-c-kaɬ'ap 'you folks (-kaɬ'ap) found (pun) me (-c)' (cf. this form with p'an'ɬ-káɬap 'you folks return,' where n'ɬ counts as an extra vowel).[3]

(5) Some suffixes have two forms depending on whether or not they are stressed, e.g., -ílx/-ləx 'body,' -úlm'əxʷ/-lum'əxʷ 'earth, land, soil.' The first member of each pair is the basic form: when the stress, according to the

rules discussed so far, should fall on the suffix, the suffix keeps this form, as in √ʕəl 'strong' > ʕəl-ílx 'to exert oneself'; when the suffix cannot attract the stress, we have the second form, as in √taɬ 'upright' > táɬ-ləx 'to stand up (from sitting position).' In the same way we have zaʔx̌ʷ 'to thaw' > zaʔx̌ʷ-úlm'əxʷ 'ground is thawing' versus pus 'wet' > pús-lum'əxʷ 'wet ground.'

(6) There are a number of so-called 'strong' suffixes that attract the stress regardless of the above rules, e.g., -ʔúl 'real, original, par excellence,' -úɬ 'always,' -sút 'out of control,' -cút reflexive. Examples are: ʔúxʷalmixʷ 'Indian' > ʔuxʷalmixʷ-ʔúl 'a real Indian'; lúləm' 'jealous in matters of love' > lulm'-úɬ 'always jealous' (for the dropping of ə, see Section 3.2); q'íɬil 'to run' > q'iɬil-sút 'to run around, looking for help'; ɬúqʷ-xit 'to serve food to smb.' > ɬuqʷ-xi-cút 'to serve oneself' (with regular dropping of t; see Section 4.4). Of two consecutive strong suffixes, the second one attracts the stress in the only example recorded of such a combination: lulm'-uɬ-sút 'always jealous without reason.' Given enough extensions, the stress moves from the strong suffix according to rule (1): ɬuqʷ-xi-cút > ɬuqʷ-xi-cut-kaɬ'áp‿ha 'did you folks serve yourselves?' (‿ha question marker; see also Section 2.3[2]).

(7) Many roots CAR' are erratic with regard to the stress, e.g., √kʷʷul' 'to make' > kʷʷul'-ún' 'to make, create smt. (-un'), tr.' versus kʷʷúl'-xal 'to make (-xal), intr.,' kʷʷúl'-xit 'to make smt. for smb.' (-xit 'indirect object' transitivizer; see Section 18.1.4); √c'aw' 'to wash' > c'aw'-án 'to wash smt. (-an), tr.,' c'áw'-xal 'to wash (-xal), intr.' For the special status of roots CAʔ, see rule (2).

(8) The passive-former -əm acts as a suffix with a full vowel (A), so it does attract the stress after roots with E (in contrast to other suffixes with E; see [2]), e.g., téq-ən 'to touch (təq-) smt. (-ən), tr.' > təq-n-ém 'it is touched' (for -ən > -n see Section 3.2).

(9) The suffix -tam (which precedes -al'ap and -ɬkal'ap in forms where these suffixes refer to 2P object; see Sections 22.3.2 and 22.3.4) behaves like E, so it may not attract the stress, e.g., cuɬ-un'-tam-ɬkál'ap 'you folks are pointed at, we point at you folks,' cuɬ-un'-tam-ál'ap-as 'he (-as) points at you folks' (instead of the expected *cuɬ-un'-tám-ɬkal'ap, *cuɬ-un'-tam-al'áp-as): compare these cases with pun-tam-ɬkál'ap 'you folks are found, we find you folks' and pun-tam-ál'ap-as 'he finds you folks,' where the stress is regular because -tam is odd-numbered from the counting base.

(10) Cases (1) through (9) cover the vast majority of root-suffix combinations, but there remain some residual irregularities, e.g., ʔúmik 'to go upstream on water' > ʔumík-əm 'to go upstream by land or on water' (also n-ʔumík-əm; n- locative prefix, -əm intransitivizer), with an irregular stress-shift of one vowel.

2.2. Combinations with enclitics

With regard to the stress, all enclitics behave as though their vowels were

E or A?. This means that enclitics have a 'weak' stress status and tend to remain unstressed or to attract the stress only in special circumstances. We have the following two basic rules for the distribution of the stress in combinations of full words with enclitics:

(1) After words with E or A?, single enclitics do not attract the stress, and the stress falls on the (first) E or A? in the word that precedes the enclitics, e.g., X̌'éx‿ha 'is it tasty (X̌'əx)?' (‿ha question particle, showing the same reluctance to attract the stress as -ən in méc-ən, Section 2.1[1]). Note also léˤʷ-ən‿maɬ 'hide it!' (‿maɬ adhortative enclitic) versus ləˤʷ-ən-ɬkán 'I hid it'; qə́l‿ti? 'that (‿ti?) is bad (qəl)' versus qəl-ɬkán 'I am bad.'

(2) The addition of an enclitic may move the stress by two syllables at a time from the counting base, and the stress may also fall on an enclitic as long as it is not the last one in a string. Examples are: ?úxʷalmíxʷ 'Indian' > ?uxʷalmíxʷ‿ti? 'that is an Indian'; ?ə́lsəm-ɬkan 'I am sick (?ə́lsəm)' > ?álsəm-ɬkán‿kɬ 'I might (‿kɬ) get sick.' See also ɬuqʷ-xi-cut-kal'áp‿ha (Section 2.1[6]), with a stress-shift caused by ‿ha. Examples of enclitics attracting the stress are ka-xím'‿a 'he went out of sight' > ka-xím'‿a‿kʷú?‿tu? 'allegedly (‿kʷu?), he went out of sight, and did not return' (‿tu? 'definite past'), qʷacác 'he left' > qʷacac‿kʷu?‿k'á‿tu? 'he left allegedly, it seems (‿k'a)'; ka-qʷˤə́ɬ-kan‿a 'I got scorched' > ka-qʷˤəɬ-kan‿á‿kɬ 'I might get scorched'; húy'-ɬkan 'I will (huẑ) do it' > huy'-ɬkan‿hə́m'‿X̌'u? ka-máys-c‿a 'I will be able (ka-..‿a) to fix it (mays-c) after all (‿həm'‿X̌'u?).'

Note that a case like the last one, where an enclitic (with a weak vowel) attracts the stress away from the strong vowel u in the root parallels those where a vowel A? attracts the stress away from a 'strong' vowel (i.e., A), as long as A? is itself followed by a weak vowel (see luc'-aká?-əm in Section 2.1[2]).[4] The enclitic ‿kəɬ 'remote future, possibility' has this shape when stressed, but ‿kɬ when unstressed, e.g., qlil-min'-cih-as‿kə́ɬ‿tu? 'he (-as) might (‿kəɬ‿tu?) get mad (qlil) at (-min') you (-cih)' (‿kəɬ in combination with ‿tu? indicates a rather remote possibility) versus ?ə́lsəm-ɬkán‿kɬ 'I might get sick.'[5]

Note that a case like the last one, where an enclitic (with a weak vowel) attracts the stress away from the strong vowel u in the root parallels those where a vowel A? attracts the stress away from a 'strong' vowel (i.e., A), as long as A? is itself followed by a weak vowel (see luc'-aká?-əm in Section 2.1[2]).[4] The enclitic ‿kəɬ 'remote future, possibility' has this shape when stressed, but ‿kɬ when unstressed, e.g., qlil-min'-cih-as‿kə́ɬ‿tu? 'he (-as) might (‿kəɬ‿tu?) get mad (qlil) at (-min') you (-cih)' (‿kəɬ in combination with ‿tu? indicates a rather remote possibility) versus ?ə́lsəm-ɬkán‿kɬ 'I might get sick.'[5]

2.3. Combinations with prefixes

Most prefixes are never stressed; the few that are are limited in use. The following cases obtain here:

(1) lá- 'in,' ?á- 'towards,' ɬlá- 'from,' kná- 'around.' These prefixes are used in certain demonstrative adverbs, e.g., ɬlá-kʷu? 'from there (invisible spot).' Given enough extensions, the stress may move from these prefixes, e.g., ɬlá-kʷu? > ɬla-kʷ?-amx‿há‿?iz' 'are those (‿?iz') people (-amx) from there?' (see Section 3.5 for the dropping of u from ɬlákʷu?).

(2) The formative ?í-, used only in ?í-q'ʷˤəl-q'ʷˤəl 'June' (q'ʷˤəl 'ripe'), and recorded only from SM, and in n-?í-p'əlk'əqʷ 'lying head to tail (e.g., fish in a barrel)' (p'əlk'əqʷ 'to turn around').

3
Distribution of Schwa

The distribution of schwa (ə ə̣, collectively symbolized E) is one of the most difficult problems of Lillooet phonology. In the first place, ə ə̣ occur as stressed root vowels, in direct opposition to each other, e.g., pə́t-ən 'to cover (pət-), tr. (-ən)' versus ka-pə̣́t̲a 'to get squished (pə̣́t-)' (ka-..̲a 'suddenly, by accident'); ka-ɬə́k̲a 'to deflate, go down (like dough), to set-tle' versus ka-ɬə̣́k̲a 'to get very tired, to conk out.' Outside the stress, schwa may be elided or retained, or arise through epenthesis (epenthetic schwa is ə̣ before Ç, and ə elsewhere, i.e., there is no opposition between epenthetic ə̣ and epenthetic ə). Exceptions to the rules for retention, elision, and epenthesis lead to unpredictable (i.e., phonemic) cases of presence versus absence of schwa, e.g., ɬəsp-áka? 'rash (ɬəsp) on one's hand (-aka?)' versus k̲snan 'to send smb. on an errand'; sə́x-sə̣x 'silly, rather crazy' versus ?alk̲st 'to work' (see also Section 3.3.1 for these cases). Finally, in some cases the presence versus absence of schwa, or its exact position, is a matter of idiolect, e.g., pún̲ɬəp/pun̲ɬp 'juniper,' k'ín̲k'nət/k'ín̲k'ənt 'dangerous.' (In texts and sentences I write idiolectal variants as recorded, in the dictionary I give all forms, and in quotations out of context I give the form that seems to have the widest distribution.)[1]

Here we discuss elision of schwa in Section 3.2, and the occurrence of schwa adjacent to obstruents in Section 3.3. We discuss the occurrence of schwa adjacent to resonants in Section 3.4 (except for cases #REC and #RC, which are discussed in Section 3.1; this arrangement is chosen because it requires the least number of references ahead). In Section 3.5 we deal with cases A?/?A parallelling ER/RE.

3.1. Cases #REC and #RC
Word-initially, we have both #REC and #RC. The shape #REC is character-istic of roots, whereas the shape #RC is found exclusively with the prefixes l- 'in, on, at' and n- (1) 1S poss., (2) 'referent of root is situated in a larger setting.'

Examples of #REC are: nəqʷ 'warm (weather),' ʕʷəlín 'stomach,' ləhác' 'otter,' zəwátən 'to know,' məzác 'body.'

Phonetically, ɬ-, n- are [ḷ ṇ], but they also allow a pronunciation [ʔ| ṇ]:[2] ɬ-cʔa [ḷčʔɛ ʔ|čʔɛ] 'here,' n-citxʷ [ṇčetxʷ ʔṇčetxʷ] 'my house.'[3] When ɬ- or n- are preceded by a proclitic or a prefix ending in a vowel, ɬ- n- lose their own syllabicity and are pronounced [..Vl ..Vn] (with [V] belonging to the proclitic or prefix), e.g., ti͜ n-cítxʷ͜ a [ten..] 'my house' (ti͜ ..͜ a composite article). When preceded by a proclitic or a prefix ending in a consonant, ɬ- n- are [əR] or [Ṛ] (depending on the preceding consonant, cf. Section 1.4); we write əl ən in these cases, e.g., nəɬ͜ ən-ɬkʷʼáɬus͜ a [nəɬṇɬ..] 'my (absent) baskets' (nəɬ͜ ..͜ a composite article indicating absence).

3.2. Elision of schwa

When roots KEC are followed by a suffix beginning in a vowel, E is dropped, unless in the resulting form E is stressed, or the stress falls on the second vowel of the suffix (for stress, see Section 2). Thus we have √təq 'to touch' > tq-álk'-əm 'to drive, steer' (-alk' 'string,' -əm intransitivizer) versus téq-ən 'to touch, tr. (-ən)' (stress on the root), s-təq-əl'wás 'to have one's hands on one's hips' (s- stative prefix, -əl'wás 'in the middle'; stress on second vowel of suffix). Further examples of KEC > KC are: pəq 'white' > pq-us 'bald eagle' (-us 'face'), x̌ʷəm 'fast' > x̌ʷm-ákaʔ 'to do smt. fast' (-akaʔ 'hand'), √təɬ 'to string across' > tɬ-áyən 'to have one's net (-ayən) set out,' qəl̩ 'bad' > ql-ál'qʷəm 'ugly' (-al'qʷəm 'outward appearance'), √pəm 'fast' > pm-il̩x 'to hurry' (-ilx 'body').[4]

A root vowel that is dropped or retained in the first suffixation is also dropped or retained when the stress shifts in subsequent extensions; hence from tq-álk'-əm we have tq-alk'-əm-ɬkál'ap 'you folks (-ɬkal'ap) drive' versus téq-ən > təq-ən-ɬkál'ap 'you folks touch it.'

Roots REC do not drop schwa, e.g., nəqʷ 'warm (atmosphere)' > nəqʷ-álc 'warm in the house (-alc),' √ʕəl 'strong' > ʕəl-ílx 'to exert oneself' (-ilx 'body, oneself'). The retention of E here is in accordance with the rule that we do not have #RC within roots (see Section 3.1).

Unstressed sequences ..CEC drop E before a suffix (and also before an enclitic) beginning in a vowel, regardless of whether the stress remains before ..CEC or falls on the suffix or enclitic, e.g., cícəl 'new' > ti͜ cícl͜ a 'the new one' (ti͜ ..͜ a composite article), cicl-úsaʔ 'fresh fruit (-usaʔ)'; n-kéxkəx 'my older sister' > ti͜ n-kéxkx͜ a id., qáxʷəxʷ 'to break (down)' > qaxʷx̌ʷ-áwɬ 'car (-awɬ) breaks down'; ʔúm'ən 'to give smt. to smb.' > ʔúm'n-as 'he (-as) gives it to him,' ʔum'n-ítas 'they (-ítas) give it to him.'[5] Unstressed cases ..CEC also drop E when the stress falls on the second vowel of the suffix: tíʔtəx̌ʷ 'right (at it)' > tiʔtx̌ʷ-əl'wás 'midnight.' For sequences ..CREC before a vowel, see also Section 3.4.

When forms KV́CER are subjected to 'total' reduplication (i.e., reduplication of KV́C as unstressed KEC after KV́C), the result is usually KV́CKCER, as in téq-ən 'to touch, tr.' > téq-tq-ən 'to touch all over.' Such forms are probably derived via *KV́CKECER, with unstressed KEC reduplicating stressed KV́C (cf. səx-səx 'silly, rather crazy,' reduplication of √səx), and reduction of unstressed KEC to KC before ER (parallelling, say, the reduction of unstressed kəx to kx in ti̲n-kə́xkx̲a; see above).

3.3. Schwa and obstruents

In what follows, we discuss the general avoidance of sequences #KKC CKK# in favour of #KEKC CKEK# (Section 3.3.1) and the occurrence of unstressed #KECV.. ..VCEK# (Section 3.3.2); make concluding remarks on E adjacent to #K K# (Section 3.3.3); and discuss E and word-medial obstruent-clusters (Section 3.3.4).

3.3.1. Sequences #KEKC and CKEK#

Lillooet generally does not tolerate clusters #KKC: roots KEK drop E when unstressed before a vowel (as in pəq > pq-us [Section 3.2]), but they retain E when unstressed before C, e.g., pəq-mínst 'almost (-minst) white.' In the same way, sequences KEKC retain E in unstressed derivations, e.g., ɬəsp 'rash (on skin)' > ɬəsp-áka? 'rash on hand (-aka?)'; téq-ən 'to touch smt.' > təq-n-ás 'he (-as) touches it' (with regular reduction of -ən > -n; see Section 3.1).

#KEKC is also shown by forms with so-called 'total' reduplication, like cəqʷ-cíqʷ 'red' (from √ciqʷ id.), and by isolated cases such as pət-x̌íləm 'to make it worse' (pət- UC, x̌íləm 'to do smt. in a certain way'), c'əqʷ?íqʷ 'salmon stretcher' (unanalyzable; see also last paragraph of this section). We do have #KKC in a number of cases that involve s. These fall into: (a) #KsC, e.g., psx̌íx̌nəm 'Chilcotin Indian' (probably a borrowing from Shuswap), ksn-án 'to send smb. on an errand, tr. (-an)' (from √kəsən 'message, errand,' with irregular dropping of the first ə; cf. the regular treatment of ə in ɬəsp-áka? above);[6] and (b) #sKC: these cases involve the prefix s- (1) nominalizer/factualizer, (2) stative. An example with s- nominalizer is kʷzúsəm 'to work' > s-kʷzúsəm 'work, job' (cf. sək'ʷn-ás 'he [-as] breaks it [sə́k'ʷən]': the absence of ə in s-kʷzúsəm indicates a morpheme boundary; cf. also #RC versus #REC in Section 3.1).

Word-finally, we usually have CKEK# rather than CKK#, e.g., pún-ɬəp 'juniper' (pun- UC, -ɬəp 'tree, plant'; cf. stressed -áɬp in qʷn-aɬp 'Indian hellebore'), mám'təq 'to go for a walk' (reduplication of matq 'to be on foot'), n-qám't-ək 'to get hit (qam't) on the back (n-..-k)' (cf. n-qʷal'-k 'ache [qʷal'] in the back'), séx-səx 'silly, rather crazy' (reduplication of √səx id.). Here also belong isolated cases such as pipáncək 'summer' (unanalyzable). For sequences CKEK# resulting from *CEKEK#, see Section 3.3.2.

We do have a number of cases CKK#. These mostly concern suffixes with s, e.g., -s (1) transitivizer, (2) 3S poss.; -qs 'nose, point, direction,' -kst 'hand, arm,' -mənst 'unmarried,' -minst 'almost.' Examples are: p'an't 'to return (oneself)' > p'an't-s 'to return smt., smb., tr.'; citxʷ 'house' > citxʷ-s 'his house'; cixʷ 'to arrive over there' > cixʷ-qs 'end of smt. reaches over there'; √ʔal UC > ʔal-kst 'to work'; s-qayxʷ 'man' > qayxʷ-mánst 'unmarried man' (dropping of s- is regular); pəq 'white' > pəq-mínst 'almost white.' In kʷə́mp-əqs 'blunt (kʷəmp) point,' a final sequence of four consonants is avoided, but ə does not appear adjacent to s. We also have CKK# in pəckɬ 'leaf' (versus q'ə́ɬq'əɬ 'muskrat' M).

In some words the occurrence of schwa depends on idiolect: SM, for instance, does not pronounce ə in, among others, c'əqʷʔíqʷ, púnɬəp, pipáncək.

3.3.2. Unstressed sequences #KECV∴ and ∴VCEK#

As we saw in Section 3.2, roots KEC do not drop E when they are followed by a suffix that attracts the stress on its second vowel (in other words, when #KEC is followed by V∴, the result is #KECV∴, rather than #KCV∴ - see s-təq-əl'wás [Section 3.2]; the stative prefix s- that is added to #təq- does not disturb the pattern). Here also belong cases with the compound-former -aɬ (Section 11), e.g., qəl-aɬ-tmíxʷ 'storm' (qəl 'bad,' tmixʷ 'land, weather'), pəl'-aɬ-cítxʷ 'stranger, newcomer' (√pəl' 'to lose,' citxʷ 'house').

Word-finally, we tend to have ∴VCEK# rather than ∴VCK#. Suffixes that have the shape -K after V́C have the shape -EK after unstressed VC, as shown by kʷʷin 'how much, many?' > n-kʷʷin'-qʷ 'how many balls?' (n-..-qʷ 'ball, round object' glottalizes preceding resonant), but ʔá?ən'was 'two animals' > n-ʔá?ən'was-əqʷ 'two eggs'; x̌ʷʔú?cin' 'four animals' > n-x̌ʷʔú?cin'-əqʷ 'four eggs.' Where a suffix -K follows unstressed ∴CEC, the suffix is regularly extended to -EK, while ∴CEC drops E (in accordance with Section 3.2), e.g., qáxʷəx 'to break' > *n-qáxʷəxʷ-k > *n-qáxʷəxʷ-ək > n-qáxʷxʷ-ək 'to break one's back (n-..-k).' Further examples are: cécəw' 'design' > n-cécw'-ək 'design on back, fawn'; sá̰ləl 'to drip in a string (like syrup)' > n-sá̰l'l'-əc 'to drool, slobber' (n-..-c 'on the mouth,' with regular glottalization of preceding resonants). Here also belongs kə́n'ən' 'to get bumped' > n-kə́n'n'-əqs 'to bump one's nose' (for -qs > -əqs see also kʷə́mp-əqs [Section 3.3.1]).

Words of the type $K_1VK_2K_3$ usually yield $K_1\acute{V}K_2K_1K_2\partial K_3$ in total reduplications, e.g., ɬəsp 'rash (on skin)' > ɬə́sɬsəp 'rash all over'; sx̌ətq 'hole' > sx̌ə́tx̌təq 'holes'; sək'ʷp 'broken' > sə́k'ʷsk'ʷəp 'all broken up'; *caqt > cáqcqət 'tame'; and also pəckɬ ($K_1VK_2K_3K_4$) > pécpcəkɬ 'foliage.' The derivational history of ɬə́sɬsəp, etc. seems to be ɬəsp > *ɬə́sɬəsp (reduplication) > *ɬə́sɬəsəp (alleviation of final cluster) > ɬəsɬsəp (elision of ə before ..səp;

cf. *n-qáx^{w}əx^w-ək > n-qáx^{w}x^w-ək above). In fact, one occasionally hears K$_1$V́K$_2$K$_1$EK$_2$K$_3$ (ɬəsɬəsp, pəcpəckɬ, etc.) in careful speech. The word x^{w}ə́sx^{w}əst 'strong, overbearing (of behaviour or smell)' was never recorded *x^{w}ə́sx^{w}sət (x^{w}ə́sx^{w}əst has no simplex).

The following suffixes -K are never extended to -EK: -s (1) transitivizer, (2) 3S poss.; -c 1S obj. (after transitivizers other than -s). Examples are: x^{w}ítən-s 'to whistle (x^{w}ítən) at (-s),' sápən-s 'his (-s) daughter-in-law (sápən),' núk^{w}ʔan-c 'help (núk^{w}ʔan) me (-c).'

Suffixes -VRK are -V́RK under the stress, but outside the stress they divide into two types: one group drops the V and has an unstressed variant -REC, viz., -ilx/-ləx (Section 2.1[5]), while another group retains the V, but inserts E before K#: compare s-q^{w}m-álq^w 'pile (s-q^{w}m-) of logs (-alq^w)' versus pál?-aləq^w 'one (pál?-) log, one stick' and nəq^w-álc 'warm (nəq^w) in the house' versus pál?-aləc 'one house, the next house,' and note x^{w}ʔít-aləx^w 'having a big family,' with x^{w}ʔit 'much, many' and the UC -aləx^w. The ə in unstressed -lum'əx^w 'earth, land, soil' (besides stressed -úlm'əx^w, Section 2.1[5]) is certainly due to the same process.[7] However, the suffix -tumx 1S obj. (after the transitivizer -s) is always pronounced -tumx, never *-tuməx, both under and outside the stress, e.g., x^{w}ítən-s-tumx 'whistle at me!' The suffix -tumx (together with -s and -c) also has a peculiar status with regard to the stress (see Section 2.1[4]).

3.3.3. Schwa and #K K#: concluding remarks

From Sections 3.3.1 and 3.3.2, it follows that Lillooet tends to break up #KC and CK# when these sequences do not border on a stressed vowel, and to have #KEC CEK# instead. On the other hand, adjacent to a stressed vowel, Lillooet generally does not tolerate #KEC CEK# but has #KC CK# instead. Hence we have roots #KCV́.. ..V́CK# (e.g., ptak 'to pass by,' pl'uk^w 'to smoke,' səps 'door' M, mulx 'stick') but not #KECV́.. ..V́CEK#.[8] Moreover, roots KEC drop E before suffixes -V́.. (e.g., pəq > pq-us [Section 3.2]). We do have ..V́KEK# in the case of so-called 'final' reduplication (Section 12.3), e.g., √qax^w 'to break' > qáx^w-əx^w id.[9]

3.3.4. Schwa and word-medial clusters

Word-medially, clusters KKC CKK and CKKC are allowed, although in some idiolects these clusters are broken up by schwa, as in, for example, cáqcqət/cáqəcqət 'tame,' sx̌ə́tx̌təq/sx̌ə́təx̌təq 'holes,' sk^{w}ístq^{w}ʔam/ sk^{w}ístəq^{w}ʔam 'waterfall,' wáwəlckza?/wáwəlcəkza? 'poplar.' We never have schwa here when one of the K's is s as (part of) a suffix, e.g., X̌'íq-s-twitas 'they (-twitas) brought him' (X̌'íq 'to arrive,' -s transitivizer), ʔál-kst-kaɬ 'we (-kaɬ) worked (ʔal-kst)' (note the sequence of five consonants in the latter example).

3.4. Schwa and resonants

As mentioned in Section 1.7, the sequences *CRC and *CR# are excluded. Where a morphological operation would give rise to *CRC *CR#, we have CREC CERC CEREC and CER# instead. The following are examples of these formations.

CREC: With consonant reduplication (Section 1.6) we have, for example, ʔaw't 'to be late, behind' > ʔáʔw'ət 'to be a little bit later'; ʕʷəlp 'to burn' > ʕʷə́ʕʷľəp 'to burn a little bit'; saw't 'slave' > sə́sw'ət 'little slave' (with a change á > ə́); sqayxʷ 'man' > sqə́qy'əxʷ 'boy.' With total reduplication we have, next to RVC > RV́C-REC (as in √ləx̌ 'clear' > lə́x̌-ləx̌ 'intelligent, learned'), cases with longer words, e.g., sqayxʷ 'man' > sqáyqyəxʷ 'men'; q'əm'p 'ten' > n-q'ə́m'q'm'əp 'ten people'; cilkst 'five' > n-cílcləkst 'five people.' Without simplex we have, for example, k'ink'nət 'dangerous,' qʷámqʷmət 'funny.'

CERC: With consonant reduplication we have ʔán'was 'two' > ʔáʔən'was 'two animals'; q'əm'pálmən 'nine' > q'əm'pápəl'mən 'nine animals'; ʔálsəm 'sick' M > ʔáʔəl's_əm 'a little bit sick.'

We often have CREC and CERC as idiolectal variants, e.g., k'ink'nət/k'ink'ənt 'dangerous,' n-q'ə́m'q'm'əp/n-q'ə́m'q'əm'p 'ten people,' λ'áq'məkst/λ'áq'əmkst 'six,' wáwləckzaʔ/wáwəlckzaʔ 'poplar' (for wáwəlckzaʔ see also Section 3.3.4), mámlət/máməlt 'whitefish.' The forms with CERC are generally characteristic for SM's speech, while the forms with CREC are used more by other speakers.

Cases with CREK# (ʔáʔw'ət, sqáyqyəxʷ, etc.), rather than CERK#, possibly result from analogy to CKEK# (e.g., mám'təq [Section 3.3.1] or ɬəsɬsəp [Section 3.3.2]).[10]

Where unstressed sequences CREC are followed by a suffix or an enclitic beginning with a vowel, CREC may not simply drop E (as in Section 3.2), since this would lead to excluded *CRC. Hence CREC is retained, or we have CERC or CREC/CERC in free variation. Examples are: CREC – ʕə́lʕəl 'strong' > ti_ʕə́lʕəl_a 'the strong one,' ʕəlʕəl-ús 'strong-headed' (-us 'face, head'); CERC – sqáyqyəxʷ 'men' > ʔi_sqáyqəyxʷ_a 'the men'; CREC/CERC – nλ'ákmən 'trail, path' > ti_nλ'ákmən_a/ti_nλ'ákəmn_a 'the trail.' Note also cases like sxʷápməx 'Shuswap' > sxʷápəmx-əc 'to speak (-c) Shuswap,' where -c is extended to -əc (cf. Section 3.3.2), and ..pməx changes to ..pəmx. In the same way, we have s-nə́m'-nəm' 'blind' > nə́m'-ənm'-əp 'going blind' (-p inchoative aspectual marker; dropping of stative prefix s- is regular).[11]

The suffix -məx 'people, person' has this shape after V́C, but -əmx after ..C(V)C, e.g., sáx̌'-məx 'person from sax̌' (Lillooet),' sxʷáp-məx 'Shuswap' (√xʷap UC), s?íxʷɬ-əmx 'person from a different (s?íxʷɬ) place,' líl'wat-əmx 'person from líl'wat (Mount Currie),' sλ'íx̌'q't-əmx 'person from sλ'íx̌'q'ət (a place close to Lillooet)' (note also q'ət > q't in the last example).[12]

CEREC: In total reduplications of RVRK we have CEREC (or, to be precise, REREK) in the unstressed portion of the word: ʕʷəlp 'to burn' > ʕʷə́lʕʷələp 'to burn all over (like a forest fire)'; zaw't 'fed up' > záw'zəw'ət 'to be a bother, a nuisance.'[13]

CER#: With consonant reduplication we have, for example, pun 'to find' > púpən' 'to find smt. by accident'; sqʷal' 'to report' > sqʷə́qʷəl' '(to tell a) story.'

3.5. The status of ʔ

The resonant ʔ alternates with aʔ/ʔa under the same conditions under which other R's alternate with ER/RE, e.g., spzuʔ '(wild) animal (esp. black bear or grizzly)' > spzúzaʔ 'bird' (parallelling pun > púpən' [Section 3.4]); p'aʔxʷ 'more' > p'ə́p'ʔaxʷ 'a little bit more' (parallelling saw't > sə́sw'ət [Section 3.4]); káʔəw' 'to go far away, to move way out' > kə́kʔaw' 'a little bit further away'; caʔxʷ 'glad' > cáʔcʔaxʷ id.[14]

In a few words we have sequences Aʔ/ʔA (other than aʔ/ʔa) alternating with ʔ, e.g., qʷuʔ 'water' > qʷə́qʷuʔ 'small body of water, puddle'; pú'y'axʷ 'mouse' > pə́pu'y'axʷ 'little mouse' (also recorded as pə́pʔuy'axʷ); qʷuʔɬ 'blister' > qʷúʔqʷʔuɬ 'lots of blisters'; c'iʔ 'deer' > c'ə́c'iʔ 'fawn.'[15]

Roots KAʔ drop or retain A under the same conditions under which roots KEC drop or retain E (see Section 3.2), e.g., √p'iʔ 'to squeeze out' > p'ʔ-álmixʷ 'to milk' (-almixʷ 'breast, udder') versus p'íʔ-ən 'to squeeze smt. out, tr. (-ən)' (KAʔ stressed), s-p'iʔ-əl'wás 'squeezed in the middle' (stress on second vowel of suffix). Further examples of Aʔ > ʔ: q'aʔ 'to eat' M > q'ʔ-ál'mən 'hungry';[16] √ɬaʔ 'close' > ɬʔ-ilx 'to get close' (-ilx 'body'), ɬʔ-ús-ən 'to lean smt. against smt.' (-us 'face,' -ən transitivizer).

RAʔ becomes Rəʔ in waʔ 'to be (busy with)' > wəʔ-án 'to have, hold, keep' (-an transitivizer), but hiʔ 'powerful spirit, supernatural being' retains i in unstressed derivations: hiʔ-úlm'əxʷ 'land (-ulm'əxʷ) inhabited by hiʔ,' hiʔ-átqʷaʔ 'water (-atqʷaʔ) inhabited by hiʔ.' We have no other cases of RAʔ before -V́.

Unstressed sequences ..CAʔ are generally reduced to ..Cʔ before a suffix or enclitic starting in a vowel, e.g., skʷúzaʔ 'child, offspring' > ti‿n-skʷúzʔ‿a 'my (n-) child,' skʷuzʔ-úɬ 'stepchild' (-úɬ 'step-relative'); kʷúsaʔ 'to urinate (men or animals)' > kʷus̩ʔ-ál'mən 'to want (-al'mən) to urinate'; sqáx̌aʔ 'dog' > ti‿sqáx̌ʔ‿a 'the dog,' sqáx̌ʔ-i 'their (-i) dog.' However, cases ..ʔAʔ do not drop A, e.g., s'áʔaʔ 'crow' M > ti‿s'áʔaʔ‿a 'the crow'; sʕíʔiʔ 'magpie' > ʕiʔiʔ-íc'aʔ 'blanket (-ic'aʔ) made out of magpie skins'; p'íʔiʔ 'to get squeezed' > p'iʔiʔ-áɬməx 'belly (-aɬməx) gets squeezed (by tight pants, belt).'

A final ..CRAʔ is changed to ..CERʔ before V (cf. CREC > CERC-V [Section 3.4]): skíxzaʔ 'mother' > ti‿n-skíxəzʔ‿a 'my (n-) mother,' skíxəzʔ-i 'their (-i) mother';[17] ʔíʔwaʔ 'to go along' > ʔiʔəw'ʔ-ál'mən 'to want to come along.' We do not have *CRAʔ-V (which would parallel CREC-V).

In unstressed ..CAʔ, not only is A before a suffix -əC(C) dropped but the ə of the suffix also changes to a: √núkʼʷaʔ 'help, friend' > núkʼʷʔ-am 'to help, be of help' (-əm intransitivizer), núkʼʷʔ-an 'to help, tr. (-ən)'; ɬákʷuʔ 'from there' > ɬákʷʔ-amx 'person from there' (-məx 'person' changes to -əmx after unstressed ..uʔ – see Section 3.4; hence we have *ɬákʷuʔ-məx > *ɬákʷuʔ-əmx > *ɬákʷʔ-əmx > ɬákʷʔ-amx); sámaʔ 'white person' > sámʔ-ac 'to speak (-c) English' (-c changes to -əc after unstressed ..aʔ); √cʼíkʷʔ 'left (side)' > n-cʼíkʷʔ-aq 'left leg (n-..-q)'; páqʷuʔ 'afraid' > n-páqʷʔ-aq 'afraid from behind (n-..-q)' (a man's name); kə́laʔ 'first' > n-kə́lʔ-aqs-tən 'leader' (n-..-qs 'nose, direction,' -tən 'instrument').

With ..CRAʔ plus -əC(C) we get CəRʔ-aC(C), e.g., pə́plaʔ 'one animal' > n-pə́pəlʔ-aqʷ 'one egg' (n-..-qʷ 'round object').

For the alternation of h with a/ha, see Section 4.1.

4
Internal Sandhi

Here we discuss vowel-consonant alternations and h-epenthesis (Section 4.1), reduction of full root vowels (Section 4.2), elision of stem-final -as (Section 4.3), and morphophonemic changes of consonants (Section 4.4). Morphophonemic changes other than internal sandhi are: retraction of suffixes (Sections 1.1 and 5.2), resonant-glottalization (Section 1.6), movement of the stress (Section 2), and elision and epenthesis of schwa (Section 3).

4.1. Vowel-consonant alternations and h-epenthesis

A morpheme-final a, when followed by a suffix or an enclitic beginning in a vowel, changes to h or (under the stress) áh. Vowels other than a are always expanded with h regardless of the stress. Examples are: ʔáma 'good' > ʔámh-us 'pretty face (-us),' ti‿ʔámh‿a 'the good one'; sləmála 'bottle' M > ti‿sləmálh‿a 'the bottle,' sləmálh-i 'their (-i) bottle'; ɬə́nkaya 'cast-iron pot' > ti‿ɬə́nkayáh‿a 'the cast-iron pot,'[1] ɬənkayáh-i 'their cast-iron pot'; lcʔa 'here' > lcʔáh-as 'let it be (-as) here'; ltʔu 'there' > ltʔúh-as 'let it be there'; kʷasú 'pig' > ti‿kʷasúh‿a 'the pig,' kʷasúh-i 'their pig,' kʷuṣú 'pig' > ti‿kʷuṣúh‿a 'the pig,' kʷuṣúh-i 'their pig,' kʷuṣuh-áɬcʔa? 'pork' (-aɬcʔa? 'inside of body, meat'); tmíxʷ-i 'their land (tmixʷ)' > ti‿tmíxʷ-ih‿a id.; cítxʷ-i 'their house (citxʷ)' > ti‿citxʷ-íh‿a id.; -ci 2S obj. > pún-cih-as 'he (-as) found (pun) you,' nuk'ʷʔan-cíh-as 'he helped (núk'ʷʔan) you.' These changes may take place more than once in a complex: ti‿sləmalh-íh‿a 'their bottle,' ti‿ɬə́nkayáh-ih‿a 'their cast-iron pot.'

An exception is -su 2S poss. > -sw before a vowel, e.g., cítxʷ-su 'your house' > ti‿cítxʷ-sw‿a id.; cúwaʔ-su 'yours' (cúwaʔ 'own') > cuwaʔ-sw-ás‿ka‿ti? 'I wish (‿ka) that that (‿ti?) were yours' (-as 3S subjunctive). Note that -su cannot be interpreted as -səw (Section 1.9.4).

Before a suffix -əC(C), unstressed a regularly changes to h, while -əC(C) becomes -aC(C), e.g., nkʷúkʷca 'downstream area' > nkʷúkʷch-amx 'people from downstream' (-məx 'people, person' changing to -əmx after unstressed

..a, i.e., unstressed ..a is interpreted as though it were ..əh; cf. also sʔíxʷɬ-əmx, etc. in Section 3.4 for the behaviour of -əmx); hálʼa 'to be visible' > n-hálʼh-ac 'to groan' (n-..-c 'in the mouth,' with -c > -əc after ..a); nkʷúkʷca 'downstream area' > nkʷúkʷch-aqs (a geographical name; n-..-qs 'nose, direction').

Stressed Á changes to Áh before -məx 'people,' but not before other suffixes starting in C: ɬəlcʔá 'from here' > ɬəlcʔáh-məx 'people from here,' but lcʔa 'here' > lcʔá-wna 'right (-wna) here'; ɬəltʔú 'from there' > ɬəltʔúh-məx 'people from there,' but ltʔu 'there' > ltʔú-na 'right (-na) there.' In one case we have i > ih before an enclitic starting in C: cuwʔ-íh‿ka‿tiʔ 'that (‿tiʔ) should (‿ka) be theirs' (cúwaʔ 'one's own,' -i 'their'). Other vowels are not expanded before enclitics C..: cuwaʔ-sú‿ka‿tiʔ 'that should be yours,' ʔáma‿ka 'it would be good.'

Note that the alternations between h, a, and ha (e.g., ti‿ʔámh‿a versus ʔáma, or nkʷúkʷca versus nkʷúkʷchaqs) parallel the alternations between ʔ, aʔ, and ʔa (e.g., ti‿sqáx̌ʔ‿a 'the dog' versus sqáx̌aʔ 'dog,' or kélaʔ 'first' versus nkélʔaqstən 'leader'; see also Section 3.5 for alternations of ʔ, aʔ, and ʔa).[2]

4.2. Reduction of full root vowels

Root vowels A (other than in root-final Aʔ; see Section 3.5) are usually retained as such in unstressed derivations, e.g., √qʷalʼ 'to speak' > qʷalʼ-út 'to deliver a speech, to speak' (-út formative); √cʼawʼ 'to wash' > cʼawʼ-ús-əm 'to wash one's face (-us)' (-əm intransitivizer); lucʼ 'tight' > lucʼ-akʼáʔ-əm 'to hold on tight to smt., intr. (-əm)' (-akaʔ 'hand'). However, in a number of words A is often reduced to E, and we have pairs such as lam 'rum, liquor' > s-lam-ála/s-ləm-ála 'bottle' M (s- nominalizer, -ala 'container'); xʷíkʼəm 'to butcher fish' > xʷikʼm-áɬxʷ/xʷəkʼm-áɬxʷ 'shed for butchering fish (-aɬxʷ 'place where an action is carried out'); s-ɣap 'tree' > s-ɣap-ʔúl/s-ɣəp-ʔúl 'Douglas-fir' (-ʔúl 'real, original, par excellence'); xʷimán 'to keep store' > xʷiman-áɬxʷ/xʷəman-áɬxʷ 'store' (with a variation A ~ E in a portion of the word that is never stressed).

The pronunciations with E are the more usual ones in such cases, while the ones with A are used only in rather deliberate speech. There seems to be no predictability in formal terms as to which stems often reduce A to E and which do not. (In the dictionary I list both pronunciations, in texts the one that was recorded there, and in isolated examples usually the one with E.) Note that all of the above cases are opposed to those where we have E both in the stressed root and in the unstressed derivation, e.g., nəqʷ 'warm (atmosphere)' > nəqʷ-álc 'warm in the house'; ɬəsp 'rash (on skin)' > ɬəsp-ákaʔ rash on hand.' The root √cʼikʷaʔ 'left' has i in the only derivation where it is stressed, n-cʼíkʷʔ-aq 'left leg (n-..-q).' In all other derivations it is unstressed, and I recorded only ə for the first vowel, e.g., n-cʼəkʷʔ-ákaʔ 'left

hand.' Other roots CAC drop A entirely before certain suffixes -V́..: k̓ax
'dry' > n-k̓x-ín'was 'island' (n-..-in'was 'middle'); √kʷuz 'to get spilled' > kʷz-
ilx 'people milling about, commotion' (-ilx 'body').

Roots ʔAC(..) present a special problem: roots ʔAC retain their vowel in
unstressed derivations, e.g., √ʔac '(curved) area' > n-ʔac-áw'sxən 'knee'; √ʔal
'(curved) area' > n-ʔal-áka? 'shoulder.' However, some longer roots ʔAC..
allow a pronunciation without ʔA, e.g., ʔúqʷa? 'to drink' > qʷʔ-ál'mən
'thirsty' (-al'mən 'to want') beside ʔuqʷʔ-ál'mən.[3] With some roots ʔAC.. the
pronunciation without ʔA is the regular one, e.g., ʔac̓x̌ 'to be seen' > n-c̓x̌-
ús-xal 'to stare' (n-..-us 'with/in the face,' -xal intransitivizer).[4]

4.3. Elision of stem-final -as
The word kaɬás 'three' drops as before suffixes with full vowels (A), and
shifts the stress to these suffixes: kaɬ-qín 'three-year-old buck' (-qin 'head,'
here referring to antler), kaɬ-álqʷ 'three sticks, logs, trees (-alqʷ),' kaɬ-úlwiɬ
'three bottles, canoes (-ulwiɬ),' kaɬ-ásq'ət 'three days (-ásq'ət), Wednesday.'[5]
Any stem-final as is dropped before -aszanuxʷ 'year': ʔán'was 'two' > ʔan'w-
aszánuxʷ 'two years old'; kaɬás > kaɬ-aszánuxʷ 'three years old.' Note that
in the last three examples (kaɬ-ásq'ət, ʔan'w-aszánuxʷ, kaɬ-aszánuxʷ) we
have cases of haplology.

Unstressed stem-final as is not dropped before suffixes other than
-aszanuxʷ: ʔán'was 'two' > ʔan'was-álqʷ 'two logs, sticks, trees,' ʔan'was-
úlwiɬ 'two bottles, canoes,' ʔan'was-ásq'ət 'two days, Tuesday.'

4.4. Morphophonemic changes of consonants
Morphophonemic changes of consonants are usually characteristic of
certain morphemes only, and not of others (i.e., they do not depend on
overall phonotactic rules). For example, the transitivizer -xit merges final t
with the initial t c of following suffixes, e.g., cúɬ-xit 'to point smt. out (cuɬ-)
to smb.' > cuɬ-xi[t]-túmuɬ 'point it out to us (-tumuɬ)!' cúɬ-xi[t]-c 'point it
out to me (-c)!' However, in other cases t is retained before t c, e.g., ꞓʷuy't 'to
sleep' > n-ꞓʷúy't-tən 'bed' (n-..-tən 'setting'); √pət 'cover' > n-pət-c-án' 'to
cover an opening, to put a curtain before an opening' (n- 'in, at,' -c 'mouth,
opening'). In Part 2 (Morphology), I discuss these changes under the pertinent morphemes.

The only rule for consonants that is applied throughout is that two
glottal stops may not follow each other immediately. Where such a sequence should occur, the ʔ's merge (as in s?alélna? 'youngest in family' >
s?aləlna[?]-?úl' 'the very (-?ul') youngest in the family'), or the rule that
should bring the two ʔ's together is not applied (see the retention of A in
..?Aʔ, e.g., s?áʔa? > ti‿s?áʔa?‿a, in Section 3.5).

5
Retracted Phonemes

Basic information on retracted phonemes is given in Section 1.1. Restrictions on the co-occurrence of retracted and non-retracted phonemes are discussed in Section 1.8.2. Here we deal with the structure of retracted roots (Section 5.1), retraction of suffixes (Section 5.2), retraction of the nominalizing prefix s- (Section 5.3), and the background of retraction (Section 5.4).

5.1. Retracted roots
Retracted phonemes are relatively rare (see Section 1.7). Within roots we have the following cases:

(1) Roots where retraction affects all phonemes that take part in the retraction correlation, e.g., qә̣ḷ 'bad,' √sạ̣ḷ 'to drip in a string (like syrup),' √ḷә̣ş 'to cave in.'

(2) Roots where retraction is only partially applied. Here belong a fairly large number of cases Çi.., e.g., √c̓ḷip' 'to pinch,' √k̓ḷip' 'curly,' wә̣lík̓ 'sound made by frogs,' mә̣lín-ɬәp 'balsam fir.'

(3) Roots with a retracted vowel and with neutral consonants (T), i.e., consonants that do not take part in the retraction correlation, e.g., √ɬu̞t 'to squash smt. soft (esp. a bug),' √pә̣m 'fast.'

(4) One root that consists of neutral consonants (T) but acts as a root with retraction: c̓n̓-ál̓us әm 'to take aim' (see also Section 5.2).

All these types are referred to as 'retracted roots.'

5.2. Retraction of suffixes
As a rule, retracted roots require retracted phonemes in lexical suffixes and in certain transitivizing and intransitivizing suffixes (see Section 8.1 for suffix types): qә̣ḷ 'bad' > qә̣ḷ-wíl̓x 'to get spoiled' (-wíl̓x inchoative suffix; cf. ʔáma 'good' > ʔama-wíl̓x 'to get better, to come back to life'); √ƛ̓ʼaḷ 'to bite' > ƛ̓ʼáḷ-an 'to bite, tr. (-an)'; √ɬu̞t 'to squash smt. soft (esp. a bug)' > √ɬu̞t-u̞n̓ 'to

squash it, tr. (-un').' Due to analogy with non-retracted cases, suffix retraction is not always implemented, or we have alternative forms, e.g., pəmp 'fast' > pəmp-ṣút/pəmp-sút 'to run on without being able to stop' (-sút 'out of control'). In any case, of two suffix-vowels only the first one can be retracted, e.g., kʷúṣaʔ 'to urinate (men or animals)' > kʷuṣʔ-áɬʼnup 'to wet one's bed (-aɬʼnup)'; √kʼəl̓ 'to make a mark by scratching' > kʼl̓-úl̓mʼəxʷ 'boundary' (-ulmʼəxʷ 'earth, land, soil'); qəl̓ 'bad' > n-ql̓-áɬcʼaʔ 'cranky' (n-..-aɬcʼaʔ 'inside of body'). Moreover, the vowel i is never retracted before a neutral consonant (T) in a suffix, e.g., kʷl̓-iʔ 'green, yellow' (kʷl̓- id., -iʔ formative), kʷl̓-it 'brass' (kʷl̓- 'yellow,' -it formative), kʼl̓-ícʼaʔ 'buckskin/leather (kʼl̓-) coat (-icʼaʔ)': cf. these cases with qəl̓-wil̓ʼx above and with case 5.1(2).

Besides combinations of retracted roots with plain suffixes, we have cases with a retracted suffix after a plain root, e.g., xʷicʼam-áya 'see-saw' (√xʷicʼ 'board jumps up,' -am formative, -aya 'body'), mək'il̓-úlya 'sticky oil' (s-mík'il '[fish]oil,' -ulyaʔ UC – see also Section 15.4[27]; the final l of the root is retracted as a result of following -ulyaʔ).[1]

Where we have incomplete retraction in a root-suffix complex, we occasionally have irregular sequences of C̦ and V̦. Besides il̦ in mək'il̦-úlyaʔ above, we have, for example, c'n'-ál̦us-əm 'to take aim' (c'n'- UC, -al̦us 'eye,' -əm intransitivizer) with a sequence l̦u. There are a fairly large number of cases of unstressed C̦əT, as in ʔál̦səm 'sick' M (ʔál̦ṣ- UC, -əm aspectual suffix; see Section 14.2), and in some cases with reduplication, e.g., pm-il̦x 'to hurry' > pm-ím̦l̦'əx id.; s-pəl̦xʷ 'to stick out' > s-pəp̦l̦'əxʷ 'to stick out a little bit.'

5.3. Retraction of the nominalizer s-

The nominalizing prefix s- has this shape before non-retracted roots, e.g., s-qayxʷ 'man.' Before retracted roots it is generally also s-, although in some cases I recorded the variant ṣ- in addition to s-, e.g., s-pl̦ant/ṣ-pl̦ant 'skunk.' Where s- functions as a factualizer (Section 8.1.3), it is never retracted; neither is the stative prefix s- (Section 10.1.2) ever retracted (we have stative s- in, for example, s-ɬək 'lazy, motionless, plopped down,' never *ṣ-ɬək).

5.4. Background of retraction

Retracted phonemes occur in all Interior Salish (IS) languages, although not every IS language has the full set that Lillooet has. The origin of the retracted phonemes has been the subject of debate for some time (see Kuipers 1981 for a brief summary of the various opinions).[2] It is not clear why retraction affects certain roots and not others. A semantic factor may be at play here: Kuipers (1981:332) notes that 'one still finds cases where a vowel alternation plain-retracted has a symbolic value, for example, Li ɬək "get deflated, go down (of dough)" vs. ɬəḳ "get pooped, conk out."'

Many Lillooet words with retraction do indeed have a connotative value, either a negative one (negation, decay, unpleasantness) or a positive one (jocoseness, affection). There is a negative connotation in, for example, xʷʔaẓ 'not, no,' qəḷ 'bad,' ʔál̥ṣəm 'sick' M, l̥ə̣sp 'to cave in,' ɬə̣c̣ 'to cave in,' √pə̣t 'to get squished' (cf.? √pət 'to get covered up'), √ɬu̥t 'to get squashed (smt. soft, esp. a bug),' ɬə̣mk 'broken, not usable any more,' mác̣'u̥ɬ 'pus,' √c̣'u̥l̥ 'sour, bitter (of berries),' c̣'ạʔp 'sour (of smt. fermented),' pṣu̥ṣ 'wild ("bitter") cherry,' s-plạnt 'skunk' (cf. also ɬək and ɬəḳ in the above quote from Kuipers 1981). A somewhat jocose connotation is probably present in the proper names ṣu̥ṣpạʔ (cf. súspaʔ 'tail') and ṣə̣xám (cf. sxam 'foolish, irresponsible'), and in pə̣píḷạʔ 'to swing (as in the children's game)' and xʷic'am-áya (Section 5.2).

To be sure, not all words with retracted phonemes have a connotative value (at least not one that I can sense), e.g., ɬə́nkaya 'cast-iron pot,' pə̣mp 'fast,' ṣtu̥t 'cricket.' Also difficult to interpret is the pair ƛ'ḷ-ịlx 'to stand still in the air (e.g., a fishhawk)' versus ƛ'l-ilx 'to keep still (anybody, in general)' (both words from √ƛ'əl 'to stop,' -ilx 'body'). We also have ə̣ in a number of words referring to 'vibration/noise': c'ə̣np 'ringing sound,' tə̣sp 'to trill, vibrate (e.g., a table when hit with a fist)'; ƛ'ə̣lp (1) 'lots of noise (e.g., at a party),' (2) 'vibrating sound (more or less like tə̣sp)'; ɬə̣np 'to vibrate, make a vibrating sound' ('heavier' than tə̣sp, e.g., when a logging truck passes).

6

Structure of Roots

In this section we deal with the main aspects of Lillooet root structure. Only the roots of full words (not clitics) are considered. An exhaustive treatment of this topic remains a task for the future. Here we discuss the basic characteristics and main types of roots (Section 6.1) and separate root types (Sections 6.2 to 6.7).

6.1. Roots: basic characteristics and main types

The main root types, with approximate percentages computed on the basis of the lexicon, are: CVC, 65%; CVCC, 18%; CCVC, 5%; CV́CVC, 3%; CVCV́C, 2%; residual types, 7%. Many roots occur as such as free forms, e.g., cukʷ 'finished,' mulx 'stick,' pl'ukʷ 'smoke,' ƛ'ámin 'fur, wool' F, qan'ím 'to hear,' kʷtamc 'husband.' However, a number of roots occur exclusively with an affix, or reduplicated, or with interior glottalization, e.g., √ʕəl 'strong' > ʕəl-ílx 'to exert oneself' (-ilx 'body'), ʕə́l-ʕəl 'strong'; √x̌iq 'duck' > s-x̌iq 'duck,' x̌íq-am 'to hunt (-am) ducks'; √lakʷ 'loose, untied' > laʔkʷ 'to become loose, untied,' ləkʷ-lákʷ 'loose, untied.' A number of roots may be historically complex, containing an affix that is no longer recognized, e.g., pipáncək 'summer,' which goes back to the root *pan 'time, period' (Kuipers 1982:73). Within Lillooet, however, there is not enough indication to split up pipáncək into smaller units, hence we treat it as a single root of a residual type.

As we saw in Sections 3.1 and 3.4, #REC is not opposed to #RC within roots, and CER# is not opposed to *CR#. We interpret unstressed cases of #REC and CER# as CC (e.g., sápən 'daughter-in-law' is treated as CVCC, and məzác 'body' as CCVC). However, stressed cases of #REC and CER# (e.g., nəqʷ 'warm [atmosphere],' x̌ʷəm 'fast, quick') are classed under CVC. In the same way, stressed cases of CERC, e.g., x̌əlq' 'to roll,' are classed under CVCC; we have no cases of stressed CREC within roots.[1] Word-final a aʔ, although they alternate with h ʔ (see Sections 4.1 and 3.5), are treated as V Vʔ, both under and outside the stress (hence wa? 'to be' is CVC, and sáma? 'white man' is CV́CVC).

The following root types are discussed below: CVC (Section 6.2), CVCC (Section 6.3), CCVC (Section 6.4), CV́CVC (Section 6.5), CVCV́C (Section 6.6), and residual types (Section 6.7). Only CVC and CVCC are discussed in some detail; only examples are given of the other types.

The same consonant rarely appears more than once in the same root. Hence, roots CVC, CVCC, etc. are almost all C_1VC_2, $C_1VC_2C_3$, etc. (C_1 different from C_2, C_3; where the same consonant appears twice in a root, it has the same number, e.g., xax 'steam' is C_1VC_1; see also Sections 6.2.1 and 6.3).

6.2. Roots CVC

The root type CVC can be subdivided along the main division between the vowels (A versus E) and the main division between the consonants (K versus R). Within R we also distinguish between ? versus other cases of R (see comments [1] to [3] below for the special status of roots with ?). There are no cases of CE?, so we have the types shown in Figure 3.

Figure 3

Vowel-consonant combinations in roots CVC

	—K	—R	—?	—K	—R
K—	KAK	KAR	KA?	KEK	KER
R—	RAK	RAR	RA?	REK	RER
?—	?AK	?AR	—	—	—
	A			E	

Comments

(1) Cases CA? and CEC go together because they easily shift the stress to a suffix (see Section 2.1[2]). Of these roots, the types KA? and KEK KER drop their vowels when unstressed before V (see Sections 3.2 and 3.5).

(2) Cases ?AC stand apart from other cases of RVC because of the frequent occurrence of ? as C_1 while other cases of glottalized R' as C_1 are very rare (see Section 1.7).

(3) As Figure 3 shows, there are no cases of *?A? or *?EK *?ER.[2] As for *?A?, the root-shape C_1VC_1 is rare anyhow (see last paragraph of Section 6.1). As for *?EK *?ER, it is possible that a number of cases ?əC go back to *?əC, in the same way that C?əC appears where one would expect C?əC (see Section 3.5).

(4) As we saw in Section 1.7, velar and uvular resonants and h are relatively rare. In roots CVC we find h in, for example, hiʔ 'powerful spirit, supernatural being,' huzʼ 'to be about to do smt.,' √huqʷ 'frost,' √nah 'to name,' √zah 'right side,' √zuh 'safe,' √kʼih 'to pick up and put somewhere.' Velar and uvular resonants are found in, for example, √ɣap 'tree,' √ʕəl 'strong,' √ʕʷəl 'to burn,' √cəʕ 'to tear, rip,' √ʕəc 'to tie.'

6.2.1. Roots CVC: examples

Of each subtype of CVC three examples are quoted in the following list. Where possible, free forms are given; otherwise a form with the nominalizer s- or with the transitivizer -Vn (-Vnʼ) is given.

KAK   ƛʼak 'to go along,' cixʷ 'to get there,' put 'enough, just right'

KAR   x̌an 'to get hurt,' kʷʼin 'how much, how many?' qʷul 'full'

KAʔ   qʼaʔ 'to eat' M, cʼiʔ 'deer, meat,' qʷuʔ 'water'

ʔAK   s-ʔaxʷ 'slide (rocks or snow),' ʔiqʼ-in 'to scrape smt.' ʔus 'to be thrown out'

ʔAR   ʔáw-an 'to choose,' ʔim-in 'to rake smt.,' ʔúm-ən 'to give smt. to smb.'

RAK   lak 'to be around, to exist,' níkʼ-in 'to cut smt.,' luc 'tight.'

RAR   láw-anʼ 'to hang smt. up,' niw 'spouse' (term of address between spouses), múl-un 'to dip smt. in'

RAʔ   waʔ 'to be busy with, involved in,' máʔ-ən 'to blame smb.,' hiʔ 'powerful spirit, supernatural being'

KEK   ƛʼəx 'sweet, tasty,' cʼək 'finished, all gone,' pəq 'white'

KER   x̌ʷəm 'fast, quick,' qəl̓ 'bad,' sə́mʼ-ən 'to cut a hide'

REK   ləq 'even, okay,' mə́s-ən 'to put things close together,' ʕə́c-ən 'to tie smt.'

RER   lə́ʕʷ-ən 'to hide smt.,' ʕʷə́l-ən 'to light smt.,' lə́mʼ-ən 'to break smt. dry (dried salmon or bread, etc.)'

There are a few cases of C_1VC_1: xax 'steam,' kʷukʷ 'to be saved, helped out,' √mam 'spouse, one of a couple' (e.g., mam-áwʼs 'couple,' -awʼs 'together'), √waw 'to shout' (wáw-əlckzaʔ 'poplar,' -əlckzaʔ 'leaf').

A number of roots CVC show a mutual formal semantic resemblance, e.g., ɣə́p-ən 'to stand smt. up' ~ s-ɣap 'tree' ~ ɣíp-in 'to raise smb., to make smt. grow,' √kʷəm 'dull, blunt' M ~ √makʷ id. F (the latter two roots occur reduplicated: kʷə́m-kʷəm = məkʷ-mákʷ 'dull, blunt'). In the first example we have apophony (ə ~ a ~ i), in the second example apophony and metathesis.

6.3. Roots CVCC

Here belong, for example, çəmʼqʷ 'to get stuck in the mud,' s-qʼəmʼs 'mushroom,' s-manʼx 'tobacco,' sápən 'daughter-in-law,' ʔítən 'to eat' F, x̌əlq' 'to roll (down),' ƛ'əl'qʷ 'broken (rope),' mulx 'stick,' s-k'ʷalx̌ 'bald eagle,' ƛ'əlc 'cranberry.' A comparatively large number of CVCC roots have the shape CVIC or CVI'C (see the last five examples above). A few roots have the shape C₁VC₂C₁: səps 'door' M, kál'k-ən 'to delouse,' s-kəz'k 'prickly pear, cactus,' s-qəl'q 'rose,' qəl'q-ús 'necklace' (-us 'face').

6.4. Roots CCVC

A few examples will suffice here: ptak 'to pass by,' psil' 'daylight,' pl'ukʷ 'smoke,' xman' 'enemy,' qmut 'hat,' qyax̌ 'drunk,' wənáxʷ 'true,' ʕʷəlín 'stomach,' məzác 'body.'

6.5. Roots CV́CVC

Examples are: máwal' 'alive,' sútik 'winter,' zúmik 'spring salmon,' ʔácaqʷ 'baked,' ʔílaxʷ 'to soak smt. in order to get matter out of it (soak salt out of fish, dirt out of clothes, etc.),' míx̌at 'bear,' máqaʔ 'snow,' ƛ'ámin 'fur, wool' F, sámaʔ 'white man.'

6.6. Roots CVCV́C

Examples are: maqá ʔ 'poison onion' F, ƛ'amín 'axe' F, kataś 'three,' cal'át 'lake,' qan'ím 'to hear,' qʷal'ít 'pitch (in tree).'

6.7. Residual types

Only a few examples of residual types are given: ptakʷt 'to tell a legend,' kʷtamc 'husband' (CCVCC), tútkis 'stone hammer, hand maul' (CV́CCVC), x̌ʷʔúcin 'four' (CCV́CVC), etc.

7

Special Questions

Here we discuss five marginal aspects of Lillooet phonology: aphaeresis and syncope (Section 7.1), slow song speech (Section 7.2), rhetorical lengthening (Section 7.3), nursery talk (Section 7.4), and treatment of borrowings (Section 7.5).

7.1. Aphaeresis and syncope

A number of words starting in unstressed C(E)C.. are often pronounced without initial C or CE, as in the following cases (with the optional C or CE written in parentheses): (p)lan 'already, bygone, past,' (zə)wátən 'to know,' (cə)spíc'a? 'sweater,' (w'əw'p)lílc'a? 'caterpillar,' (p)mi̠lx 'to hurry.' The nominalizer s- is particularly often dropped, e.g., (s-)qáx̌a? 'dog.' For aphaeresis of forms with unstressed ?AC.., see Section 4.2. Words starting in ƛ'l or ɬl often drop l, e.g., ƛ'(l)az' 'canoe,' ɬ(l)ák̓ʷu? 'from there.'[1]

7.2. Slow song speech

In slow songs (especially in hymns) the vowels ə and ə̣ are often pronounced i and i̠ respectively, e.g., ptínusəm 'to think, worry' > ptínusim, qə̣l 'bad' > qi̠l. In texts I indicate these pronunciations by the notations ə̇ ə̣̇, e.g., ptínusə̇m, qə̣̇l.

7.3. Rhetorical lengthening

In running texts and in conversations, speakers may stress a particular word by pronouncing it with a considerably lengthened vowel. We write V··· in such cases: ƛ'a···k 'and he we··nt (he just kept on going)' (ƛ'ak 'to go').

7.4. Nursery talk

In nursery talk we find the following two phenomena:
(1) z > y (see Section 1.7.1[3] for details).
(2) Use of a special vocabulary, e.g., mi? 'sit down!' (cf. míca?q id.), múya?

'belly-button' (cf. méx̌ʷya? id.), yúya? 'boy's penis,' cíci? id. (cf. spəl'q 'penis'), túta? 'sleep!' (cf. Squamish ?ítut 'go to sleep'), ta? 'no! don't!' (cf. Shuswap tá?a [tá?a] 'no').[2]

7.5. Treatment of borrowings

Borrowings from other languages (mainly other Salish languages, English, and French, the latter usually through Chinook Jargon) are treated in two different ways in Lillooet:

(1) Some borrowings have their phonemes replaced with the nearest Lillooet equivalent, e.g., pankʷúpa 'Vancouver,' kʷuṣú 'pig' (Chinook Jargon *cosho* from French *cochon*; note that the presence of ṳ precludes the presence of s [š], the closest equivalent to French and Chinook [š]; cf. also Section 1.8.2).[3] In derivations, such forms show the same morphophonemic changes as words of a purely Lillooet origin, e.g., pankʷúph-amx 'people from Vancouver,' kʷuṣuh-áɬc'a? 'pork' (cf. Section 4.1).

(2) Other borrowings retain the original phonemes. I write such words in the font used for the English text in this book, but their Lillooet accretions are in the Lillooet font, as in milk-ám 'to milk' (-am 'to obtain'), ti‿radioh‿a 'the radio.' However, in two cases that have become part of the traditional Lillooet vocabulary, I reflect the non-Lillooet phonemes by special symbols in the Lillooet orthography: au in taun 'to go to town, to go shopping' and t' in t'áqa? 'salal berry' (borrowed from a Coast Salish language, probably Halkomelem or Squamish), t'áq?-az' 'salal berry bush,' s-t'əmáɬt 'cattle' (a borrowing from Shuswap, and recorded only in F). Where we have Lillooet words quoted in an English sentence, the Lillooet words are written in the orthography employed in this book, except in the case of Lillooet proper nouns, which in an English context are retranscribed in the Lillooet practical orthography explained in Section 40. Thus, for example, we will have máhyəqs (a woman's name) in a Lillooet text, but Máhyeqs in the English translation of that text.

Part 2:
Morphology

Figure 4

Chart of morphological operations

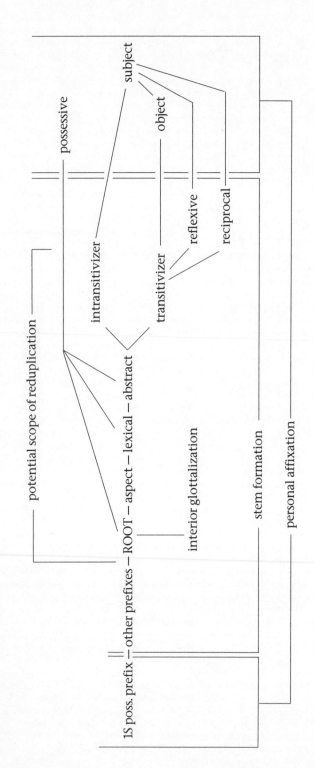

8
Introduction to Morphology

As we saw in Section 1.6, Lillooet words fall into full words and clitics. Here we discuss first full words: variable words (Section 8.1) and invariable words (Section 8.2). Variable words may be marked by the operations mentioned in Section 1.6, i.e., affixation, reduplication, and interior glottalization ($C_1VC_2 > C_1V?C_2$). With a few exceptions, invariable words may not be marked by these operations. Clitics are discussed in Section 8.3.

8.1. Variable words
The productive operations to which a variable word may be subjected are shown in Figure 4 (the unproductive operation of compounding is not considered here). Morphological operations can be divided into three types: (1) personal affixation, comprising possessive affixes (all suffixes, except for n- 1S possessive prefix) and object and subject suffixes; (2) stem formation, comprising non-personal prefixes (these have various functions), aspectual suffixes, lexical suffixes, abstract suffixes, intransitivizing and transitivizing suffixes, reflexive and reciprocal suffixes, reduplication, and interior glottalization;[1] and (3) factualization, which combines stem formation and personal affixation (see Section 8.1.3).

A full (variable) word may contain personal affixes or it may be a stem, i.e., a word without personal affixes. Stems may consist of a bare root or of a root marked by stem-forming operations (see also Section 6.1). Intransitivizers and transitivizers fall into various formal types that have specific functions besides their (in)transitivizing role. Some transitivizers may combine with each other into a new transitivizer. One type of transitivizer may follow intransitivizers, and some transitivizers may follow reflexive and reciprocal suffixes (these possibilities are not reflected in Figure 4). For the co-occurrence of transitivizers and object, reflexive, or reciprocal suffixes, see Section 8.1.1.

Personal affixes distinguish three persons in singular and plural. Some subject suffixes are complex, containing voice and mood markers. (Reflexive and reciprocal suffixes do not distinguish person or number. This, together with the fact that they may be followed by transitivizers, calls for classing them within stem formation rather than within personal affixation.) Possessive suffixes do not co-occur with subject suffixes other than 3S (see Section 24.1.2). Moreover, possessive affixes combine only with nominal, not verbal, stems (see Section 8.1.1).

Abstract suffixes refer to abstract concepts, e.g., -aĺmən 'wanting to,' -uz' 'playfully.' Some abstract and lexical suffixes may follow (in)transitivizers (not reflected in Figure 4, but see the introductory remarks to Sections 15 and 16). Lexical suffixes refer to concrete objects or concepts, e.g., -alqʷ 'stick, log, tree' or -aĺqʷəm' 'outward appearance.' Aspectual suffixes express notions such as 'changed state,' 'ongoing state,' etc.

Reduplication falls into four main types and various subtypes, each with special functions (expressing diminutiveness, collectivity, or aspectual notions). Reduplication may involve roots or aspectual, lexical, abstract, or (in)transitivizing suffixes (see Figure 4), but not prefixes. For interior glottalization (which has an aspectual function), see Section 13. For root structures see Section 6.

Prefixation is very limited compared with suffixation: there are 8 productive prefixes and about 200 productive suffixes. Special mention must be made of the nominalizing prefix s- (see also Sections 8.1.1 and 8.1.3).

The most important stem-forming operations are those that deal with (1) transposition (converting nominal stems into verbal ones and vice versa), (2) intransitivization and transitivization, and (3) aspect and control (the latter indicating the degree to which a state or action is controlled by the person involved in it). Aspect finds expression through formations such as √puɬ 'to boil, get boiled' > púɬ-əɬ 'boiling' (with final reduplication, expressing an ongoing process), s-puɬ 'boiled' (s- stative prefix, not to be confused with the nominalizer s-, above). Control involves mainly the use of certain transitivizers. Section 8.1.1 deals with the main points of transposition and (in)transitivization, and the attendant problem of word classes. For aspect and control, see also Sections 21.2 and 21.3.

Lillooet makes no tense distinctions. In what follows, we translate predicates in the present or past tense indiscriminately, unless the sentence in which such a form is used necessitates the choice of a certain tense.

Section 8.1.2 discusses the most important role of personal affixation: the addition of subject suffixes to stems, which then form full predications.

Morphological operations are discussed as follows: the nominalizer s- (Section 9), prefixes other than s- (Section 10), compounding (Section 11), reduplication (Section 12), interior glottalization (Section 13), aspectual suffixes (Section 14), lexical suffixes (Section 15), abstract suffixes (Section 16), reflexive and reciprocal suffixes (Section 17), intransitivizers and transitivizers (Section 18), numerals and numerical substitutes (Section 19), nominal and verbal substitutes (Section 20), summing up of stem formation (Section 21), and personal affixation (Section 22).

8.1.1. Stem formation: transposition and (in)transitivization

Stems fall into the following, partially overlapping, groups: (1) intransitive and transitive stems, (2) nominal and verbal stems. Transitive stems are those that end in a transitivizer, e.g., -ən in ʔác'x̌-ən 'to see smt./smb.,' or -anʼ in k'áx-anʼ 'to dry smt.' Transitive stems must take an object, reflexive, or reciprocal suffix, although the object suffix for 3S is zero. On the other hand, object, reflexive, and reciprocal suffixes may only be affixed to transitive stems; reflexive and reciprocal suffixes may be (but do not have to be) followed by a transitivizer, which then must be followed by an object suffix.

Stems that do not end in a transitivizer are intransitive and may not be followed by object, reflexive, or reciprocal suffixes. Intransitive stems may be divided into three formal groups:

(1) Verbalized stems (i.e., those with an overt intransitivizer), e.g., ʔác'x̌-əm 'to see, have vision,' ʔíƛ'-əm 'to sing,' k'áx-xal 'to dry things' (-əm, -xal intransitivizers).

(2) Nominalized stems (i.e., those with the nominalizing prefix s-), e.g., s-qayxʷ 'man,' s-ɣap 'tree,' s-qʷəm 'mountain.' Here also belong nominalized stems based on verbalized stems, e.g., s-ʔíƛ'-əm 'song.'

(3) Unmarked stems (i.e., those without intransitivizer or -əm). These comprise on the one hand nouns, e.g., qʷuʔ 'water,' tmixʷ 'land,' and on the other hand verbal stems, corresponding to the English categories intransitive verb, adjective, and numeral, e.g., ƛ'ak 'to go,' ʔac'x̌ '(to be) seen,' k'ax '(to be) dry,' qʷul '(to be) full,' pálaʔ '(to be) one.'

Hence we have on the one hand transitive stems (all verbal and all overtly marked) and on the other hand intransitive stems, which may be verbal or nominal, and unmarked or overtly marked (Figure 5).

The difference between nouns and intransitive and transitive verbs is that nouns may take possessive affixes whereas verbs may not. Hence, from tmixʷ 'land' and s-ʔíƛ'-əm 'song,' we may form n-tmixʷ 'my (n-) land' and n-s-ʔíƛ'-əm 'my song,' whereas we may not combine ʔíƛ'-əm or other verbs with possessive affixes.

In the above examples, I give only cases of (in)transitivizers or s- on bare roots. Other forms of affixation, reduplication, or interior glottalization generally do not affect the nominal or verbal status of a stem, although certain operations may be limited to one type of stem (e.g., interior glottalization and the addition of aspectual suffixes are limited to verbal stems). Some lexical suffixes and one form of reduplication may have a

Figure 5

Verbal and nominal categories

	Marked			Unmarked			
Transitive	ʔác'x̌-ən 'to see it'	k'áx-an' 'to dry it'		—			Verb
Intransitive	ʔác'x̌-əm 'to see'	k'áx-xal 'to dry'	ʔíx̌'-əm 'to sing'	ʔac'x̌ 'seen'	k'ax 'dry'	pála? 'one'	
	s-qayx^w 'man'	s-ɣap 'tree'	s-ʔíx̌'-əm 'song'	q^wu? 'water'	tmix^w 'land'		Noun

transpositional effect, but these cases are unproductive or otherwise problematic, and they have been left out of the above discussion. We will deal
with them in the sections on lexical suffixation (Section 15) and reduplication (Section 12).

The formal difference between nouns and intransitive verbs is weak,
since both are represented in the group of unmarked stems. Moreover,
nouns and intransitive verbs use the same types of subject suffixes (see
Section 8.1.2). Nouns, intransitive verbs, and transitive verbs may be used
in both predicates and complements (see Section 8.1.2).

8.1.2. Personal affixation: predicates and complements

By combining a stem with a subject suffix we obtain a sentence-word (or
predication). We have the same subject suffixes for nouns and intransitive
verbs:

(a) sqáyx^w-kan 'I (-kan) am a man (sqayx^w)'
(b) nk'yáp-kan 'I am a coyote (nk'yap)'
(c) X̌'ák-kan 'I go (X̌'ak)'
(d) q^wənq^wánt-kan 'I am poor (q^wənq^wánt)'
(e) sqayx^w 'he is a man' (no overt marker for 3S subj.)
(f) nk'yap 'he is a coyote'
(g) X̌'ak 'he goes'
(h) q^wənq^wánt 'he is poor'
(Lillooet makes no gender distinctions. We translate the third person as
'he' unless 'she' or 'it' is necessitated.)

In the transitive paradigm the object suffixes precede the subject suffixes. Also, the 3S transitive subject suffix is -as (hence not unmarked as in
the intransitive paradigm):

(i) núk'^w?-an-c-as 'he (-as) helped (√nuk'^w?) me (-c)' (-an transitivizer)

(j) núkʷ́ʔ-an-as 'he helped him' (no overt marker for 3S obj.)

A predicate with a third person subject or object may be combined with an article and used as an object or subject complement to another predicate. With the composite article ti‿..‿a (ti‿ 'present, known, singular,' ‿a reinforcing enclitic required by certain articles; see Section 31), we have, for example:

(k) ƛ'ak   ti‿nk'yáp‿a
     go   art.‿coyote‿reinf.
     'the coyote goes'

(l) nk'yap   ti‿ƛ'ák‿a
     coyote   art.‿go‿reinf.
     'it is a coyote who goes'

(m) núkʷ́ʔ-an-c-as   ti‿sqáyxʷ‿a
     help-tr.-1S obj.-3S subj.   art.‿man‿reinf.
     'the man helped me'

(n) sqayxʷ   ti‿nukʷ́ʔ-an-c-ás‿a
     man   art.‿help-tr.-1S obj.-3S subj.‿reinf.
     'it is a man who helped me'

Note that the predicate in Lillooet precedes the complement. The fact that in (n) we have a complement with an overtly marked subject suffix (-as), based on the predicate in (m), shows us that ti‿nk'yáp‿a and ti‿ƛ'ák‿a in (k) and (l) are not merely based on the stems nk'yap and ƛ'ak but rather that these complements are based on full predicates (nk'yap 'he is a coyote' and ƛ'ak 'he goes').[2]

It is clear that on the syntactic level there is no difference between nouns and verbs, since both nouns and verbs can take the predicate or the complement position.[3] Hence, 'noun' and 'verb' are strictly morphological terms with no syntactic relevance.[4]

Subject suffixes distinguish between a subjunctive and an indicative paradigm, which, however, coincide in a number of forms (all the above forms are either indicative or neutral). For tables of Lillooet subject and object suffixes, and basic paradigms, see Sections 22.1 to 22.3. For details on predicates and complements, see Section 22.6.

8.1.3. Factualization

Factualization is the addition of the nominalizer s- together with the addition of either a subject suffix to a transitive stem or a possessive affix (functioning as a subject suffix) to an intransitive stem. Factualized forms (factuals) are not used by themselves but rather function as dependent (subordinate) clauses, which have to be preceded by a higher predicate, e.g., with kánəm 'why':

(a) kánəm   s-ƛ'ak-s
   why   nom.-go-3S poss.
   'why did he go?'
(b) kánəm   s-núk'ʷʔ-an-c-as
   why   nom.-help-tr.-1S obj.-3S subj.
   'why did he help me?'

Factual forms do not distinguish between indicative and subjunctive. For details on factualization, see Section 22.

8.2. Invariable words

Invariable words generally do not allow the operations that may be applied to variable words. However, some invariable words have limited affixing or reduplicating possibilities. For example, from the adverb xʷʔaz 'not, no' we may form xʷʔá̰ʔz'-aɬ 'good for nothing, unwilling to do anything' with either reduplication of ʔ or interior glottalization and with the suffix -aɬ (see Section 13.1.3).

Invariable words comprise most pronominals: personal pronouns (Section 24), demonstrative pronouns (Section 25), and demonstrative adverbs (Section 26). Other invariables are proper nouns (Section 27), particles (adverbs and conjunctions [Section 28]), so-called sentence-equivalents (Section 29), and greetings, exclamations, and interjections (Section 30). The invariables are also briefly discussed in Section 23.

8.3. Clitics

Clitics comprise proclitics and enclitics. Clitics are invariable, although personal proclitics contain some morphological rudiments (see Section 22.4.1). Proclitics serve many different functions (see below), whereas enclitics are adverbial (reinforcing, interrogative, quotative, etc.) markers.

The difference between clitics and affixes is that clitics are mobile whereas affixes are not. For an example of proclitics versus prefixes, compare ti‿ and n- in:

(a) ti‿n-citxʷ‿a   >   ti‿x̌zúm‿a   n-citxʷ
   art.‿my-house‿reinf.   art.‿big‿reinf.   my-house
   'my house'   'my big house'

where the proclitic article ti‿ is separated from citxʷ but the prefix n- is not.

Enclitics fall into two groups: (1) the reinforcing element ‿a, which is required after words that are preceded by ti‿ or by other articles, as in example (a) above; and (2) elements that follow the first word in a sentence, such as the question-marker ‿ha in:

(b) nukʷˀ?-an-cíh-as‿ha   >   wá?‿ha   nukʷˀ?-an-cíh-as
    help-tr.-you-he‿question   be‿question   help-tr.-you-he
    'did he help you?'   'is he helping you?'

where the transitivizer, the 2S object suffix -cih, and the 3S subject suffix -as stay after nukʷˀ?-, but the interrogative enclitic ‿ha moves to the first word. For further differences between suffixes and enclitics, see Section 2.2.

Proclitics are divided into articles (Section 31), proclitic conjunctions (Section 33), prepositions (Section 34), and personal proclitics (Section 22.4.1). Enclitics are discussed in Section 32.

9

The Nominalizer s-

The nominalizer s- occurs in many lexicalized combinations with marked and unmarked intransitive stems. There are four types of nominalized stems:

1   s- on marked stems

X̌'íq-xal 'to bring'	s-X̌'íq-xal 'smt. brought'
k'ʷzús-əm 'to work' M	s-k'ʷzús-əm 'work, job' M
ptínus-əm 'to think'	s-ptínus-əm 'thought, mind'
ʔíX̌'-əm 'to sing'	s-ʔíX̌'-əm 'song'

2   s- on unmarked stems

ʔúqʷaʔ 'to drink'	s-ʔúqʷaʔ 'drink, beverage'
q'aʔ 'to eat' M	s-q'aʔ 'food' M
ʔíłən 'to eat' F	s-ʔíłən 'food' F
qʷal'út 'to speak, deliver a speech'	s-qʷal'út 'speech, serious talk'

3   s- on unmarked stems that do not occur in free use but occur in combination with an intransitivizer

mán'x-əm 'to smoke'	s-man'x 'tobacco'
q'ʷláw'-əm 'to pick berries'	s-q'ʷlaw' 'picked berries'
p'áms-əm 'to make a fire'	s-p'ams 'fire, firewood'
núk'ʷʔ-am 'to (be of) help'	s-núk'ʷaʔ 'friend, relative'

4   s- on unmarked stems that occur neither in free use nor in combination with an intransitivizer

s-qayxʷ 'man'
s-k'əm'c 'door' F
s-qáx̌aʔ 'dog'

Various derivations prove that in (4) we do have a prefix rather than a root sC.., e.g., s-qáy-qyəxʷ 'men' ('total' reduplication always involves the first two consonants of the root), qayxʷ-án-cut 'to act like a man, to do it the man's way' (-an transitivizer, -cut reflexive suffix). Quite often, s- is dropped in careless speech, e.g., qáx̌a? 'dog' (see also Section 7.1). A number of words starting in sC probably contain the nominalizer s- in petrified form, but no arguments for prefix status of s could be obtained here, e.g., skím'wət 'tiger lily.' (Still, considering the productive status of s-, I consider these cases to contain s- as well.)

As we saw in Section 8.1.1, nouns may take possessive affixes, unlike verbs, which may not. Hence, the difference between the nominalized forms in (1) to (3) and their non-nominalized counterparts is that the nominalized forms may take possessive affixes.[1] There are also nominalized transitive forms, which are discussed in Section 22.7. As we saw in Section 8.1.3, s- is also used productively in factualized forms.

10
Stem-Forming Prefixes

As we saw in Section 8.1, prefixation in Lillooet comprises the possessive prefix n- and stem-forming prefixes. The latter fall into (1) the nominalizer s-, discussed in Section 9, (2) six other productive prefixes, (3) nine unproductive prefixes, and (4) prepositional prefixes, used exclusively with certain deictic roots and discussed in Section 26. Here we discuss the six other productive stem-forming prefixes (Section 10.1) and the nine unproductive stem-forming prefixes (Section 10.2).

10.1. Productive stem-forming prefixes

Of the productive stem-forming prefixes, that described in Section 10.1.1 is verbalizing in that it transforms nominal stems into verbal ones. The prefixes covered in Sections 10.1.2 to 10.1.6 are neutral in that they do not change the verbal or nominal status of the stem to which they are attached.

The prefixes covered in Sections 10.1.2 to 10.1.4 are attached only to verbal stems. (Of these prefixes, those in Sections 10.1.2 and 10.1.3 are aspectual, and their place within the Lillooet aspectual system is discussed in Section 21.1. When combined with transitive stems, they influence the choice of transitivizer; see Section 18.8.) The prefixes in Sections 10.1.5 and 10.1.6 may be combined with verbal and nominal stems. In Section 10.1.7 we discuss combinations of productive prefixes.

10.1.1. The prefix ?əs- 'to have, to own'

The prefix ?əs- expresses 'to have, to own,' e.g., citxʷ 'house' > ?əs-cítxʷ 'to have a house.' The final s of this prefix merges with the nominalizer s-, e.g., s-qáx̌a? 'dog' > ?əs-qáx̌a? 'to have a dog,' s-kʼʷzúsəm 'job, work' > ?əs-kʼʷzúsəm 'to have a job.'

10.1.2. The stative prefix s-

The addition of the stative prefix s- to a stem indicates a state resulting from an action. Intransitive stems with stative s- are best translated by a present (active) or past (passive) participle, e.g., s-kic 'lying (position)' (√kic 'to lay down, put down'), s-míca?q 'sitting' (míca?q 'to sit down or up'), s-ɬəc 'piled up' (√ɬəc 'to pile up'), s-məc 'written' (√məc 'to write'). Intransitive stems combined with s- usually do not have other affixes, although I recorded a few cases with lexical suffixes, e.g., s-táɬ-ləx 'standing' (táɬ-ləx 'to stand up,' -ləx 'body'), or intransitivizers, e.g., s-wákʷ-xal 'carrying under one's clothes, being pregnant' (√wakʷ 'to put under one's clothes,' -xal intransitivizer). With a transitive stem we have s-?ac'x̌-s 'to be watching over' (?ac'x̌ 'to be seen,' -s transitivizer). See also Section 10.1.5(3).[1]

10.1.3. The resultative combination ka-..ꞈa

The prefix ka-, which always co-occurs with the reinforcing enclitic ꞈa, expresses 'suddenly, after much trying, by accident.' With intransitive stems we have, for example, nq'san'k 'to laugh' > ka-nq'sán'k ꞈa 'to burst out laughing'; ʕʷuy't 'to sleep' > ka-ʕʷúy't ꞈa 'to fall asleep.' With transitive stems we have, for example, ka-?ac'x̌-s-kán ꞈa 'I (-kan) caught sight (?ac'x̌-s) of it,' ka-ʕʷə́l-s-kan ꞈa 'I managed to get it lit (ʕʷəl-s).' For these forms, see also Section 18.8.

The combination ka-..ꞈa also expresses 'to manage to, to be able to,' as in ?ác'x̌-əm 'to see, have vision, intr.' > ka-?ác'x̌-m ꞈa 'to be able to see, to manage to see.' The underlying notion of ka-..ꞈa is that of a lack of control: something just happens suddenly or by accident without a person controlling the event, or a person finally manages to achieve something. The combination ka-..ꞈa has the following effects on stems with E:

(1) Stems with E behave like stems with A with regard to the stress; see Section 2.1(3).

(2) Stems CECC, when embedded in ka-..ꞈa, are changed to CCEC: x̌əlq' 'to roll down' > ka-x̌ləq' ꞈa 'it rolled down (suddenly)'; ɬəmk 'broken, not usable any more' > ka-ɬmə́k ꞈa 'to break (like an old rope when pulled), to come loose (rotting hide of a dead animal)'; s-x̌ətq 'hole' > ka-x̌tə́q ꞈa 'hole is created suddenly.'

(3) Stems of the type $C_1ÉC_2$-$C_1(E)C_2$ are C_1EC_2-$C_1ÉC_2$ when embedded in ka-..ꞈa: mə́t-əmt-əp 'paralyzed' (from *mə́t-mət-p; see Section 3.4 for the behaviour of ə) > ka-mət-mə́t ꞈa 'to get paralyzed.'

10.1.4. The prefix kəns- 'to try, to want to'

The prefix kəns- expresses 'to try, to want to,' e.g., kʷzúsəm 'to work' > kəns-kʷzúsəm 'to try (want) to work'; qʷúsxit 'to shoot' > kəns-qʷúsxit 'to try (want) to shoot.'

10.1.5. The prefix n-

Lillooet has a prefix n-, which is used in four cases:

(1) Locative n-: The addition of n- to a stem indicates that the referent of the stem is on or inside something else (n-X 'X is inside or on something else'), e.g., c'ip' 'cold (object)' > n-ċip' 'cold (liquid)' (a liquid must of necessity be contained in something else, such as a cup, bowl, etc.); qəmp 'hot' > n-qəmp 'hot (liquid)'; c'áw'xal 'to wash' > n-c'áw'xal 'to wash dishes (i.e., in a sink or dishpan)'; k'ax 'dry' > n-k'ax 'container is dry inside'; wəq'ʷ 'to be carried away by water, to drown' > n-wəq'ʷ 'to float on top of the water (like ice-flows)'; káwləx 'to move away' > n-káwləx 'to move away on water'; q'áyləx 'to jump, run away' > n-q'áyləx 'to swim'; k'ímaɬc 'frozen, ice' > n-k'ímaɬc 'ice on top of water.' Locative n- is also required by certain lexical suffixes; see Section 15.1.2(2).

(2) n- and reduplication: n- is used in combination with certain forms of reduplication to refer to the category 'persons' in numerals and numerical substitutes, e.g., cilkst 'five' > n-cílcləkst 'five persons.' For details, see Section 19.

(3) n- and s-: There are a few cases of n-s- that refer to a certain attitude (s- is taken to be the stative prefix [Section 10.1.2]), e.g., n-s-x̌ák-x̌k-ət 'bossy' (√x̌ək 'to correct smb.'; for -t see Section 14.3), n-s-liɬ'q 'generous' (liɬ'q 'easy'). Without simplex we have n-s-p'x̌iɬ' 'stingy,' n-s-káza? 'stuck-up, conceited.'

(4) n- and -təm: The combination n-..-təm is used as an aspectual marker. For examples, see Section 14.4.

I do not know whether n- in these cases goes back to one prefix that has semantically diversified, or whether we have a set of semantically different but homophonic prefixes.

In a number of cases we have nC.. without parallelling forms C... Because nC in these cases has the phonetic characteristics of n-C [ṇC ?ṇC] (see Section 3.1), I postulate n-C.. here, e.g., n-ka? [ṇkɛ?] 'where?' (no simplex *ka?).

10.1.6. The prefix nək'ʷ- 'co-, fellow'
The prefix nək'ʷ- expresses 'co-, fellow,' e.g., ?úx''almix'' 'Indian' > nək'ʷ-?úx''almix'' 'fellow Indian'; sáma? 'white man' > nək'ʷ-sáma? 'fellow white man'; k'ʷzúsəm 'to work' > nək'ʷ-k'ʷzúsəm 'to work with, to be smb.'s colleague.' This prefix is probably an atrophied form of √núk'ʷa? 'friend, to help.' If this is the case, forms with nək'ʷ- can be considered compounds (cf. also Section 11).[2]

10.1.7. Combinations of prefixes
Productive stem-forming prefixes may occur in combinations, but not all conceivable combinations were in fact recorded. Moreover, certain prefixes (e.g., those in Sections 10.1.2 and 10.1.3) are in complementary distribution. Where prefixes co-occur, there may be mergers, as in the following cases:

(1) ?əs- merges s with the nominalizer s- (Section 10.1.1).

(2) ?əs-, the factualizer s-, and stative s- merge with n- (Section 10.1.5)

into n-, where n- would follow ʔəs-, etc. immediately: n-qláw'-tən 'wallet' (√qlaw' 'money,' n-..-tən 'setting, container'), also 'to have a wallet' (instead of *ʔəs-ən-qláw'-tən); n-q'áyləx 'to swim' > nít̲X̲'u? n-q'áyləx-s 'and then (nít̲X̲'u?) he (-s) swam' (instead of *s-ən-q'áyləx-s with the factualizer s-; cf. nít̲X̲'u? s-cut-s 'and then he said [cut]');[3] n-kákəl'-s 'to follow (n-kákəl'-), tr. (-s)' (with stative prefix s- merged with n-). The nominalizer s- does not combine with n- either, e.g., s-k'əm'c 'door' F versus n-k'əm'c 'edge of water (lake, river).'

The resultative prefix ka- precedes n-, and ka- itself may be preceded by the factualizer s-, as in the following example, with n-q's-an'k 'to laugh' (-an'k 'belly') and n- 1S poss.:

xʷʔaz̲   kʷ̲ən-s-ka-n-q's-án'k̲a
not   that̲my-fact.-suddenly-laugh̲reinf.
(not that there was the fact of my suddenly laughing)
'I did not burst out laughing'

The prefix n- 1S poss. merges with stem-forming n- (Section 10.1.5), e.g., n-qláw'-tən (1) 'wallet,' (2) 'my wallet.'

10.2. Unproductive prefixes

None of the unproductive prefixes has a clear meaning except (2) below. The following is a list of all recorded cases with the prefix in question:

(1) pət-: pət-x̌íləm 'to make smt. worse' (x̌íləm 'to do smt. in a certain way')

(2) piʔɬ-: 'without': piʔɬ-qmút 'without a hat (qmut)' (name of a mountain)

(3) t-: t-xʷúxʷəl-k'ʷ-əm 'to roll a cigarette' (√xʷul 'to roll,' -k'ʷ 'around,' -əm intransitivizer). t- also occurs in the combination s-t- (s- nominalizer) in a number of names of animals: s-t-páʕ-əltxʷ 'grey horse' (√paʕ 'grey'), s-t-p'úm-əltxʷ 'buckskin-coloured horse' (√p'um 'to smoke skins'), s-t-q'ʷúɬ-əltxʷ 'brown horse' (√q'ʷuɬ 'scorched'), s-t-əqʷy-áltxʷ 'dappled grey horse' (√qʷy- UC, -əltxʷ/-altxʷ 'outside, skin'),[4] s-t-q'ʷáq'ʷipa? 'doe' (also c'-q'ʷáq'ʷipa? - see [5] below - √q'ʷáq'ʷipa? UC).

(4) c-: c-əkʷlí? 'sorrel horse' (kʷli? 'green, yellow').

(5) c'-: c'-q'ʷáq'ʷipa? 'doe' (see also [3] above), s-c'-q'ʷúl-aka? 'thumb,' s-c'-q'ʷúl-axən 'big toe' (√q'ʷul limited to these words, cf.? q'ʷul 'full,' -aka? 'hand,' -axən 'foot').

(6) sa-: sa-káw-amx 'Prairie Indian, Cree' (√kaw 'far away,' -amx irregular variant of -məx 'people'). sa- may be related to the nominalizer s-.

(7) na-: na-páw-alckza? 'rattlesnake plantain, "snake-weed"' (√paw 'to swell,' -alckza? 'leaf'), na-kéw 'clearing in forest' (√kəw 'to clear land'). na- may be related to the prefix n- (Section 10.1.5).

(8) ʔí-: ʔí-q'ʷəl-q'ʷəl 'June' (q'ʷəl 'ripe, done'), n-ʔí-p'əlk'-əqʷ 'lying head-to-tail (e.g., fish in a barrel)' (p'əlk'əqʷ 'to turn around').

11
Compounding

Besides affixation, reduplication, and interior glottalization, Lillooet employs compounding: the joining of two full words, or roots of words, through intermediate -aɬ-. The stress falls on the second root. Lillooet compounds are subordinating: the second root refers to the object characterized by the first (like English 'killjoy,' rather than English 'governor-general'). As mentioned in Section 8.1, compounding is unproductive.

All recorded cases of compounding are given here. They are as follows: qəl̓-aɬ-tmíxʷ 'storm' (qəl̓ 'bad,' tmixʷ 'land'),[1] ləp'-aɬ-k'ʷúnaʔ 'cured (by burying) salmon eggs' (√ləp' 'to bury,' k'ʷúnaʔ 'salmon eggs'), pəl'-aɬ-cítxʷ 'stranger' (√pəl' 'to lose,' citxʷ 'house'), p'əc-aɬ-léqəm 'first snow of winter (which knocks down the grass)' (√p'ac 'to knock down grass,' √léqəm 'grass, hay'), wəq'ʷ-aɬ-yáʔqʷ 'heavy rain in autumn (washes out dead fish)' (wəq'ʷ 'to get carried away by water,' yaʔqʷ 'fish is dead after spawning'), ɬəq'-aɬ-səm?ám 'one who elopes with smb. else's wife' (√ɬiq' 'to steal,' səm?ám 'wife'; also pronounced ɬəq'-a-səm?ám, with ɬ dropped), zəw-aɬ-tmixʷ 'one who knows (zəw-) the land (tmixʷ).' The following may also belong here: c'əq'aɬtúmx 'wild burdock' (cf. c'əq'p-án 'to stick smt. onto smt.,' -tumx 1S obj.; the meaning of this word would then be 'sticks-on-me,' with a unique use of a suffix as the second member in the compound).

A special case is presented by the phrases kʷuˌxáʔˌa kʷúkʷpəy' 'God, Lord' (xaʔ 'high,' kʷúkʷpəy' 'chief'), kʷuˌxáʔˌa tmixʷ 'Heaven' (tmixʷ 'land'), kʷuˌƛ'ápˌa ʕʷəlp 'Hell' (ƛ'əp 'deep,' ʕʷəlp 'to burn'); kʷuˌ...ˌa article 'evidential' (see Section 31). These phrases are often shortened into compound glosses: xaʔ-a-kʷúkʷpəy', xaʔ-a-tmixʷ, ƛ'əp-a-ʕʷélp.

There are no cases of root-root compounds (without -aɬ- or -a-), unless one wishes to consider cases with nəkʷ- (Section 10.1.6), -sup' (Section 15.2[26]), or -sqáx̌aʔ (Section 15.2[31]) compounds.

12
Reduplication

Reduplication plays an important part in Lillooet stem formation. There are four basic types, each falling into a number of subtypes and leaving a number of residual types. A fifth type is formed by combinations of the four basic types. Reduplication serves a number of functions (expressing diminutiveness, collectivity, and aspectual notions, or functioning merely as a lexicalizing device).

Section 12.1 provides a list of the basic types together with their subtypes. These types are discussed in detail in Sections 12.2 to 12.6, together with the residual types. In some cases reduplication is accompanied by resonant-glottalization. Resonant-glottalization is fairly unpredictable; here we give cases without further comments, except in the case of consonant reduplication (Section 12.4).

Reduplication may also lead to schwa epenthesis (see Sections 3.3 and 3.4) or to alternations of ʔ with Aʔ/ʔA (see Section 3.5). Of the four types of reduplication, two (initial and total reduplication) may operate only on roots. However, the other two (consonant reduplication and final reduplication) select as their locus the stressed vowel, and as such may operate on roots or suffixes and, in the case of consonant reduplication, even across morpheme boundaries (see Section 12.4 for details). Reduplication does not involve prefixes, except for one case (see the end of Section 12.5).

Following Uhlenbeck 1992 and Jensen 1990, we treat reduplication as an operation different from affixation. Also, Lillooet reduplication is partial rather than complete, in that only a part of the targeted string is copied. However, in so-called 'total' reduplication, which copies the first CVC of the root, the effect may be that of complete reduplication where the targeted string consists of a root CVC.[1]

12.1. Survey of basic types
In the formulae that symbolize the various types, I write 1, 2, p, q, etc. for

C₁, C₂, Cₚ, C_q, etc., and I do not write unstressed schwa. Where A is used twice in such a formula, it represents identical full vowels.

1 Initial reduplication
   (a) 11√2, 11(A)2√3: kə-káw' 'far' (√kaw 'far, away'), kə-kl'áxʷ 'muskrats' (kl'axʷ 'muskrat'), qʷə-qʷal'út 'to talk (qʷal'út) loudly, to bawl out.'
   (b) 1Á-1A2: xʷí-xʷitən' 'to keep whistling' (xʷítən 'to whistle'), s-tá-taɬləx 'to keep standing up (e.g., a bear on its hind legs)' (s-táɬləx 'standing up').
   (c) 1√12: This type is treated as a special case of consonant reduplication; see (3b).
2 Final reduplication
   (a) p√qq: ɬíl-əl 'to sprinkle, be sprinkling' (√ɬil 'to sprinkle'), púɬ-əɬ 'to boil, be boiling' (√puɬ 'to get boiled'), p'líx̌ʷ-əx̌ʷ 'boiling over, flowing over' (√p'lix̌ʷ 'to boil over, flow over'), pálla? 'to get together (people, two streams, etc.)' (pála? 'one').
   (b) p√qV√q√q: təl-al-íl 'to keep sprinkling' (cf. ɬíl-əl above), λ̓'əɬ-əɬ-əɬ 'to keep shivering' (√λ̓'əɬ 'to shiver'), p'líx̌ʷ-ix̌ʷ-íx̌ 'to keep boiling over' (cf. p'líx̌ʷ-əx̌ʷ above).
3 Consonant reduplication
   (a) p√pq: x̌ʷ?ú?cin' 'four (x̌ʷúcin) animals,' x̌ʷm-íml'əx 'to hurry up' (x̌ʷəm 'fast, quick,' -ilx 'body'), s-pzúza? 'bird' (s-pzu? '[wild] animal'). Many cases also change Á to É, e.g., kaɬás 'three' > kaɬéɬs 'three animals'; s-qlaw' 'beaver' > s-qléləw' 'little beaver'; x̌zum 'big' > x̌zézəm' 'a little bit bigger.'
   (b) 1√12 (see also [1c]): pápla? 'one (pála?) person,' púpən' 'to find (pun) smt. unexpectedly,' s-qʷéqʷəm' 'little mountain, hill' (s-qʷəm 'mountain'). With change Á > É we have pépla? 'one (pála?) animal,' céc̓l'əkst 'five (cilkst) animals.' In fact, (3b) is a subset of (3a) in that in (3b) p = 1.
4 Total reduplication
   (a) 12-1√2: s-yəp-yáp 'trees' (s-yap 'tree'), s-nək'ʷ-núk'ʷa? 'friends, relatives' (s-núk'ʷa? 'friend, relative'), qʷən-qʷánt 'poor, destitute' (√qʷan 'to want, desire'), cəqʷ-cíqʷ 'red' (√ciqʷ id.).
   (b) 1√2-12: s-qʷém-qʷəm 'mountain range' (s-qʷəm 'mountain'), s-qáy-qyəxʷ 'men' (s-qayxʷ 'man'), ɬə́s-ɬs-əp 'rash (on skin) all over' (ɬəs-p 'rash'), cí?-c?iʕ'ʷ 'to bleed (cí?iʕ'ʷ) all over,' s-púl'-pəl' 'stash of nuts made by squirrel' (no simplex),² kéx-kəx 'older sister' (no simplex, but cf. s-kíx-za? 'mother'), cá?-c?axʷ 'glad' (ca?xʷ id.), léx̌-ləx̌ 'smart, well educated' (√ləx̌ 'clear').
   (c) 12-1(A)2.:: s-k'əl-k'líp'qʷ 'curly hair' (s-k'lip'qʷ id.), p'ən'-p'an'án 'to fold smt. up' (p'an'án 'to fold, bend smt.'), məc-məcxál 'to write (məcxál) a lot.'

(d) 1V2-1V2-1V́2: ɬəp-ɬəp-ɬə́p 'to keep blinking' (√ɬəp 'to blink'), ka-mul-mul-múl̲a 'to get further into the water' (√mul 'to put smt. into the water'), pəx̌-pəx̌-páx̌ 'to keep peeling' (√pax̌ 'to peel'), kʷət-kʷət-kʷə́t-ax̌ʷac 'heart is really pounding' (kʷət-p-áx̌ʷac id., -ax̌ʷac 'chest').

5 Combinations of reduplication types

(a) Combination of (4a) and (3b): λ̓'əq-λ̓'íq 'light (of colour)' > λ̓'əq-λ̓'ə́λ̓'q 'weasel in white phase'; cəqʷ-cíqʷ 'red' (√ciqʷ id.) > cəqʷ-cə́cqʷ 'little red ones'; s-qəl-qál'xʷ 'rooster' > s-qəl-qə́ql'əxʷ 'little rooster'; s-qə́qx̌aʔ 'pup' (s-qáx̌aʔ 'dog') > s-qəx̌-qə́qx̌aʔ 'pups'; s-qə́qy'əxʷ 'boy' (s-qayxʷ 'man') > s-qəy-qə́qy'əxʷ 'boys'; s-qə́qw'əc 'little potato' (s-qawc 'potato') > s-qəw-qə́qw'əc 'little potatoes.'

(b) Combination of (4b) and (3b): lə́x̌-ləx̌ 'smart, well educated' (√ləx̌ 'clear') > l'ə́l'x̌-ləx̌ 'a little bit smart'; ʕə́l-ʕəl 'strong' > ʕə́ʕəl'-ʕ'əl 'a little bit strong.'

(c) Combination of (4c) and (3a): ɬəp-ɬəpn-ún'ɬ 'forgetful' (ɬápən 'to forget,' -úɬ 'always'), qʷəl'-qʷal'ə́l't 'to have a conversation' (qʷal'út 'to speak, hold a speech').

(d) Combination of (4a) and (2a): púɬ-əɬ 'to boil' > pəɬ-púɬ-əɬ 'rapids'; cíq-əq 'to get stabbed' > cəq-cíq-əq 'to get stabbed all over.'

(e) Remaining cases, e.g., s-pzúzaʔ 'bird' (s-pzuʔ '[wild] animal') > s-pə-pzúzaʔ 'birds' – (3a) plus (1a); qíqəl' 'weak' (no simplex) > qíqqəl' 'getting weak' – (3a) plus (2a); ɬá-ɬaxʷ 'patch-blanket' (√ɬaxʷ 'patch') > ɬə́ɬ-ɬaxʷ 'little patch-blanket' – (1b) plus (3a).

Except for types (1a) and (1b), all reduplication types are productive. The following will now be discussed: initial reduplication (Section 12.2), final reduplication (Section 12.3), consonant reduplication (Section 12.4), total reduplication (4a) to (4c) (Section 12.5), and total reduplication (4d) (Section 12.6). Combination types are discussed throughout Sections 12.2 to 12.5.

12.2. Initial reduplication

Type (1a) is a repetition of the first consonant of the root. It expresses plurality or collectivity in kə-kl'áxʷ 'muskrats,' and in kʷə-kʷíkʷs 'little (kʷikʷs) things,' s-k'ə-k'xʷús 'hail, tears, beads' (s-k'xʷus 'hailstone, tear, bead'), s-qʷə-qʷyíc 'hares, rabbits' (s-qʷyic 'hare, rabbit'), x̌ə-x̌zúm- 'big (x̌zum) things' (not recorded by itself but in, for example, n-x̌ə-x̌zúm-anaʔ 'big ears (n-...-anaʔ),' qʷə-qʷlítaʑ 'jackpines' (qʷlítaʑ 'jackpine'), s-qʷə-qʷl'íp 'lots of black tree moss' (s-qʷl'íp 'black tree moss'). As mentioned above, this type of reduplication is unproductive, and many speakers use only the non-reduplicated forms (e.g., s-qʷyic, n-x̌zúm-anaʔ, qʷlítaʑ', s-qʷl'ip), employing the plural articles (see Section 31) to express the plurals of these words. (On the other hand, some cases with initial reduplication, e.g., kə-kĺáxʷ, s-qʷə-qʷyíc, are occasionally used without reference to the plural.) However, in s-pə-pzúzaʔ 'birds' (s-pzúzaʔ 'bird'), the initial reduplication is actively used for expressing the plural. A special case is cə-cítxʷ 'houses, village' (citxʷ 'house'), which refers explicitly to a collective of houses (versus ʔi‿cítxʷ‿a 'houses,' with the plural article ʔi‿..‿a, which refers to a number of individual houses that do not form a collective).[3]

In the numerals 'three' and 'four,' type (1a) in combination with the prefix n- (Section 10.1.5) refers to the category 'persons' rather than 'animals' or 'objects': n-kə-kaɬás 'three (kaɬás) persons,' n-x̌ʷə-x̌ʷʔúcin 'four (x̌ʷʔúcin) persons.'

The rest of the type (1a) cases have no clear function, e.g., kə-káw 'far' (√kaw 'far, away'), qʷə-qʷaĺút 'to talk loudly, to bawl people out' (qʷaĺút 'to speak, deliver a speech'), x̌ə-x̌lún 'to be short of smt.' (x̌lun id.), x̌ʼə-x̌ʼák-a 'to go right through' (x̌ʼak 'to go'; for -a see Section 12.5.2).

We also have 11V́.. in a number of cases without simplex, e.g., qʼʷəqʼʷúʔɬ 'bone,' pəpíɬaʔ 'to swing (children's game).' These cases might represent fixed reduplications or they might be borrowings.[4]

There are two residual types of (1a): (1) 1a1V́.., e.g., pa-páw 'swimming bladder' (√paw 'to swell'); and (2) 1i1V́.., which seem to express repetitiveness: pi-pálaʔ 'one (pálaʔ) at a time,' ʔi-ʔánʼwas 'two (ʔánʼwas) at a time' (the other numerals do not allow this reduplication), pʼiy-a-pʼánʼt-a 'to go back and forth' (also pʼənʼ-a-pʼánʼt-a – cf. Section 12.5.2; pʼanʼt 'to return'; the sequence iya in pʼiy-a-pʼánʼt-a presents a unique case of internal sandhi).

Type (1b) is a repetition of the first consonant and vowel of roots CA.., with the first A in the reduplicated form receiving the stress. It expresses 'continuation' in s-tá-taɬləx, xʷí-xʷitən (Section 12.1), s-ʔí-ʔix̌ʼ 'to sing little songs' (ʔíx̌ʼ-əm 'to sing'), and qʼá-qʼawam 'to howl' (cf. s-qʼáwam 'wolf'). The function of this type is less clear in s-nʼá-nʼatxʷ 'morning' (natxʷ 'tomorrow,' s- nominalizer), pá-pakʷ 'sliced salmon or meat, strips of salmon' (pákʷ-an 'to slice smt.'), ɬá-ɬaxʷ 'patch-blanket' (s-ɬaxʷ 'patch'), pʼú-pʼuqʷ '"grey" huckleberry' (pʼəqʷ-pʼúqʷ 'grey').[5]

12.3. Final reduplication

Type (2a) is a repetition of the consonant after the stressed vowel of the word, regardless of whether or not that consonant is the final one in the word. Type (2a) generally expresses an ongoing process, usually one that is bound to lead to an expected result. (For example, something that is pút-əɬ 'boiling' will become s-puɬ 'boiled' [s- stative prefix (Section 10.1.2)]; pállaʔ 'to get together' will lead to pálaʔ 'one.') Besides the examples in

Section 12.1 we have, for example, x̌ʷús-əs 'to foam' (cf. s-x̌ʷús-um 'soap-berry'), qáxʷ-əxʷ 'to break' (s-qaxʷ 'broken'; s- stative prefix), ʕʷə́lʼ-əlʼ 'to bubble' (√ʕʷəlʼ 'bubble'), cə́kʷ-əkʷ 'to get pulled' (cə́kʷ-ən 'to pull, tr. [-ən]ʼ), kʼáʔ-aʔ 'laid up' (s-kʼaʔ 'to have come to a [permanent] stop, e.g., a rock ly-ing somewhere [also used for a lazy person]ʼ; s- stative prefix), kʼə́ppəx̌ 'to knock constantly (like a hailstorm hitting a roof)' (kʼəpx̌-xál 'to knock, intr. [-xal]ʼ), X̌ʼqʷ-áwʼwʼəs 'to get together' (s-X̌ʼqʷ-awʼs 'together,' with -awʼs 'group, collective' – Section 15.2[117]; and √X̌ʼəqʷ UC), ʔállas 'to get worse' (ʔálas 'really, very much [either good or bad]ʼ; note the semantic narrow-ing in ʔállas).[6]

The function of final reduplication is sometimes difficult to detect, e.g., in ʔáwʼwʼət 'too late (e.g., for an appointment), to miss the train or bus' (ʔawʼt 'to be late, to come behind in a race'): from a Lillooet point of view, ʔáwʼwʼət refers to the ongoing process (one is ʔawʼt until one catches up with the person with whom one had the appointment, or until one catches the next bus or train), whereas ʔawʼt refers to the irreversible state (if one is ʔawʼt, one cannot catch up any more with the winner of the race). ʔáwʼwʼət ~ ʔawʼt in a sense parallels pálla? ~ pála? (see above). Final reduplication also conveys the notion that the participant in the action designated by the form with final reduplication is not entirely in control of that action, as indicated by the choice of the transitivizer s- after such forms (see Section 18.1.3). For the place of final reduplication in the Lillooet aspectual system, see also Section 21.2.

In some cases we have resonant-glottalization, as in qʷúlʼ-əlʼ 'to get full (qʷul), e.g., a rain-cloud,' but in pə́lləp 'to get sold' M (pəlʼp 'lost') we have a rare case of deglottalization.

Type (2b) expresses in general a continuation or intensification of a state or action. Besides the cases in Section 12.1, we have, for example, x̌ʷəm 'fast, quick' > x̌ʷəm-am-ə́m 'to hurry up'; ʕʷə́lʼ-əlʼ 'to bubble' > ʕʷəlʼ-alʼ-ə́lʼ 'bubbles come up when smb. dives into the water'; zuqʷ 'dead' > zuqʷ-əqʷ-úqʷ 'to struggle through (e.g., travelling through heavy snow until exhaustion).' The stressed vowel in cases of type (2b) has the same quality as the root vowel; the quality of the unstressed vowel varies with each case. An entirely isolated case within type (2b) is xʷələp-ap-ə́p 'to whirl around' (xʷəl-p 'to spin around'), with the irregular reduplication of the third consonant of the stem.

Unique is the reduplication type exhibited by X̌ʼal-ál 'tired' (cf. X̌ʼál-əl 'stopped, not able to keep going,' with type [2a]). Note also kalál 'soon' (cf.? kálən 'to follow, pursue, tr.') and qʷacác 'to leave, set out' (cf.? qʷə́c-ən 'to shake, tr.,' qʷə́c-əc 'to have [finally] started on smt., to be busy with smt.').[7]

For a comparative historical treatment of final reduplication in Salish, including Lillooet, see van Eijk 1990b.[8]

12.4. Consonant reduplication

Consonant reduplication repeats the consonant before the stressed vowel once more after this vowel, regardless of whether or not this vowel is in the root (see also the discussion below). Stressed Á also changes to É in most cases of consonant reduplication. (On formal grounds, it is unpredictable which cases change Á to É or which retain Á; cf. pápla? versus pə́pla? [Section 12.1].)

In most cases, consonant reduplication expresses diminutiveness. Thus, besides s-pzúza?, s-qlə́ləw', s-qʷə́qʷəm', s-qə́qx̌a?, s-qə́qy'əxʷ, s-qə́qw'əc, and the combination types x̌'əq-x̌'ə́x̌'q, s-qəl-qə́ql'əxʷ (all from Section 12.1), we have səmyə́ɣəw' 'little lynx' (səmyáw' 'lynx'), nax̌ʷə́x̌ʷt 'worm' (nax̌ʷít 'snake'), s-y'ə́y'qca? 'girl' M (s-yáqca? 'woman' M), s-m'əm'ɬac 'girl' F (s-múɬac 'woman' F), ʔíʔmac 'little grandchild' (ʔímac 'grandchild'), twiw't 'boy, young man' (twit 'good hunter'), m'ə́m's-məs 'calf' (mús-məs 'cow').

With words denoting a quality, consonant reduplication expresses a weakening of that quality ('a little bit X'), or a weak comparative ('a little bit Xer'): ʔáʔəl'səm 'a little bit sick' M (ʔál̩səm 'sick' M), ʔáʔma 'pretty, cute, funny' (ʔáma 'good'), n-x̌'pə́pəm' 'a little bit deeper' (n-x̌'pam' 'deep'), x̌zə́zəm' 'a little bit bigger' (x̌zum 'big'), p'ə́p'ʔaxʷ 'a little bit more' (p'a?xʷ 'more'), ʔáʔw'ət 'a little bit later' (ʔaw't 'late, behind'). A diminutive function also underlies mám'təq 'to go for a walk,' from matq 'to be on foot.' With numerals, consonant reduplication makes reference to the category 'animals' (see x̌ʷʔúʔcin', cə́cl'əkst, pə́pla? in Section 12.1) or 'persons' (pápla? [Section 12.1]; cúɬaka? 'seven' > n-cúcɬaka? 'seven persons,' with n-, Section 10.1.5[2]). For details on numerals, see Section 19.

In a number of cases, forms with consonant reduplication have completely lexicalized (although originally they are probably diminutivizing), e.g., púpən' 'to find by accident' (pun 'to find'), lúləm' 'jealous in matters of love' (lúm-ən 'to accuse, suspect smb., tr.'), cícəl 'new' (cf.? cil-kst 'five,' with -kst 'hand'), qíqəl' 'weak' (no simplex, but cf.? qlil 'angry'), scwaw'xʷ 'creek' (no simplex, but cf. Shuswap cwex 'creek'), n-sísx̌-l'əx 'to move from one conveyance to another' (n-síx̌-ləx id.).

Consonant reduplication may occur within roots (as in all of the above examples), or it may operate across morpheme boundaries. In the latter case, the final consonant of the morpheme preceding a suffix is repeated in that suffix, e.g., x̌ʷm-íml'əx 'to hurry up' (< *x̌ʷm-ilx; x̌ʷəm 'fast, quick,' -ilx 'body'), pal?-á?qa? 'one-year-old buck' (pála? 'one,' -aqa? 'barrel, cylindrical object'), w'əw'p-l-íl̩c'a? 'caterpillar' (√wəp 'hair,' here also with consonant reduplication, -l- connective, -ic'a? 'skin'), ɬəp-ɬəp-n-ún'ɬ 'forgetful' (ɬáp-ən 'to forget, tr.,' -úɬ 'always'). In one case, consonant reduplication takes place within a suffix: x̌əcp-qíqən'-kst 'hundred' F (*x̌əcp element used in numerical units, -qin'-kst 'finger[tip]'). In sum, consonant reduplication always involves the consonant preceding the stressed vowel, regardless of whether or not that vowel is in the root.⁹

The tendencies for resonant-glottalization accompanying consonant reduplication are as follows:

(1) Cases CV́(..)R yield CV́C(..)R'; see, for example, s-qə́qy'əxʷ, lúləm', x̌ʷʔú?cin' above.

(2) Cases RV́K yield R'V́R'K or RV́R'K; see, for example, s-m'ə́m'łac, mám'təq above.

(3) Resonants followed by (A)? are not glottalized (e.g., pála? 'one' > pápla? 'one person'), but resonants following ? may be glottalized, e.g., s-kə́kəl?-am'x 'elder relative, "any person older than you"' (*s-kə́l?-amx; kə́la? 'first,' -amx < -məx 'person'; see also Sections 3.4 and 3.5 for morphophonemics). In some cases, resonant-glottalization does not take place, even if there is no (A)? following, e.g., cícəl 'new.'

Some forms show double consonant reduplication, e.g., twə́ww'ət '(little) boy' (twiw't 'boy, young man,' twit 'good hunter'), scwə́ww'əxʷ 'little creek' (scwaw'xʷ 'creek,' cf. Shuswap cwex id.), qə́qqəl' 'rather weak' (qíqəl 'weak,' no simplex). All recorded cases here show Á > É. Note also w'əw'p-l-ílc'a? 'caterpillar' (analyzed above), with consonant reduplication of the root and subsequent suffixation, stress-shift, and reduplication of the suffix -l-.

Consonant reduplication leaves the following residual types:

(1) pV́q > (a)pV́pqa(?): kʷ'win 'how much, how many?' > kʷ'ík'ʷna? 'a few, a little bit'; q'əltwáxʷ '(to wage) war' > q'əltawáw'xʷa '(to have a) race,' X̌'xʷun 'to beat smb. in a contest, tr.' > X̌'əxʷ-X̌'axʷúxʷna? 'to try to beat each other (in a game)'; səm?am-úz' 'mistress, "blanket-wife"' > səm?am-úmza? id., X̌'əqʷəntwal'-úz' 'to wrestle, to play-fight' > X̌'əqʷəntwal-úlza? id. (recorded with deglottalized l), ləˤʷilx-úxza? 'to play hide-and-seek' (ləˤʷ-ílx 'to hide [ləˤʷ-] oneself,' -ilx 'body,' -uz' 'play-').¹⁰ Note the deglottalization of z' in the last three words.

(2) 1É2 > 1í12: sə́q-ən 'to quarter, split smt., tr.' > sísq-ən' 'to split wood'; √X̌'əp 'clothing' > X̌'íX̌'p-tən 'skirt' M.

(3) pÁq > pÁpAq: x̌əcp-qíqin'-kst 'hundred' M (*x̌əcp numerical unit, -qin'-kst 'finger[tip]').

12.5. Total reduplication: types (4a) to (4c)

Total reduplication of types (4a) to (4c) involves a repetition of the first two consonants of the root. In most cases it expresses collectivity/plurality, as in s-yəp-yáp, s-nək'ʷ-núk'ʷa?, s-qʷə́m-qʷəm, s-qáy-qyəxʷ, łə́s-łsəp, cí?-c?iˤʷ, s-k'əl-k'líp'q'ʷ, p'ən'-p'an'án, məc-məcxál, and in the combination types s-qəx̌-qə́qx̌a?, s-qəw-qə́qw'əc, s-qəy-qə́qy'əxʷ, pəł-pú́łəł, cəq-cíqəq (all in Section 12.1), and in, for example, təp-túp-un' 'to beat smb. up' (túp-un' 'to punch smb., tr.'), s-x̌ə́t-x̌təq 'holes' (s-x̌ətq 'hole'), ˤʷə́l-ˤʷəl-əp 'to burn all over (as in a forest-fire)' (ˤʷəl-p 'to burn'), sə́kʲʷ-skʲʷ-əp 'all broken up' (səkʲʷ-p 'broken up'), kə́ɬ-kɬ-ən 'to take completely apart' (kə́ɬ-ən 'to take apart, to take off, tr.'), qʷən-qʷnúx̌ʷ 'many people sick' F (qʷnux̌ʷ 'sick' F).

The idea of collectivity is clearly present in, for example, s-qʷə́m-qʷəm 'mountain range' (rather than a set of individually recognizable mountains). In the same way, certain words allow total reduplication only when one aspect of their meaning is taken under consideration, e.g., pə́c-pcəkɬ 'foliage' (pəckɬ 'leaf'), which is not used for a group of individually recognizable leaves (the latter concept can be expressed only by pəckɬ in combination with one of the plural articles).[11]

Likewise, certain words allow total reduplication of a form with consonant reduplication, but not of the same form without consonant reduplication. Besides s-qəx̌-qə́qx̌aʔ 'pups' (s-qə́qx̌aʔ 'pup' < s-qáx̌aʔ 'dog'), we do not have *s-qəx̌-qáx̌aʔ or *s-qáx̌-qx̌aʔ for 'dogs,' and besides s-qəw-qə́qw'əc 'little potatoes' (s-qə́qw'əc 'little potato' < s-qawc 'potato'), we do not have *s-qəw-qáwc or *s-qáw-qwəc for 'potatoes': collectivity can be represented by a litter or a handful, but not by a number of rather large individual objects.

Many terms for persons show obligatory total reduplication when they are used in the plural (i.e., when they are combined with one of the plural articles; see Section 31). Besides s-nəkʲʷ-núkʲʷaʔ 'friends, relatives,' s-qáy-qyəxʷ 'men,' s-qəy-qə́qy'əxʷ 'boys,' we have, for example, s-məɬ-múɬac 'women' F (s-múɬac 'woman' F), s-yəq-yáqcaʔ 'women' M (s-yáqcaʔ 'woman' M), səw-sáw't 'slaves' (saw't 'slave'; note deglottalization of w' in the first syllable of the reduplicated form), s-kʲʷəm-kʲʷúkʲʷm'it 'children' (s-kʲʷúkʲʷm'it 'child'), ʔəm-ʔíʔmac 'grandchildren' (ʔíʔmac '[little] grandchild'), təw-twíw't 'young men' (twiw't 'young man'). A number of terms for persons do not allow total reduplication, or they allow total reduplication in certain idiolects but not in others, e.g., s-taʔ 'aunt,' c'ə́c'p'aʔ 'grandfather' M, s-pápzaʔ 'grandfather' F.[12] The word kʷə́kʷaʔ 'grandmother' does not allow total reduplication, but in F there is the form kʷáʔ-kʷaʔ 'grandmothers,' based on the root √kʷaʔ (not used by itself) that underlies kʷə́kʷaʔ.

A special case is presented by ʔúxʷalmixʷ 'Indian' and sámaʔ 'white man,' which yield the reduplicative forms ʔəxʷ-ʔúxʷalmixʷ 'to act like an Indian, to do smt. the Indian way' and səm-sámaʔ 'to act like a white man, to do smt. the white man's way.' The total reduplications of these forms are not used for pluralization purposes (hence 'the Indians' is ʔi‿ʔuxʷalmíxʷ‿a, with the plural article ʔi‿..‿a, never *ʔi‿ʔəxʷ-ʔuxʷalmíxʷ‿a). Also, the reduplication in the above cases transposes ʔúxʷalmixʷ and sámaʔ from nominal to verbal stems. For a survey of the various morphological means by which Lillooet expresses the concepts 'to act like' or 'to pretend to be,' see van Eijk 1988.

Like ʔúxʷalmixʷ and sámaʔ, certain terms referring to localities allow total reduplication not for pluralization purposes but in order to express 'to go along the X.' These total reduplications also transform nominal stems into verbal ones. Examples are: n-k'əm'c 'shore, beach' > n-k'əm'-k'm'əc 'to walk along the shore, beach'; k'mus 'edge (of cliff)' > k'əm-k'mús 'to walk along the edge'; n-káh-ạw's 'railroad track' > n-káh-kh-ạw's 'to walk along the railroad track.' These cases, and ʔəxʷ-ʔúxʷalmixʷ, səm-sámaʔ are the only ones where reduplication has a transpositional function.

Total reduplication in combination with the prefix n- (Section 10.1.5[2]) is used in some numerals and other words to refer to 'persons' (rather than 'animals' or 'objects'), e.g., cilkst 'five' > n-cíl-cləkst 'five persons.' For details, see Section 19.

Total reduplication is lexicalized in a number of words, e.g., s-qəl-qál'xʷ 'rooster,' kə́x-kəx 'older sister,' káw-kəw 'sagebrush,' sáy'-səz' 'to play,' kən-knáp 'thunder,' wəl-wəlqʷúsəm 'lightning' (all without simplex, but for kə́x-kəx cf. s-kíx-zaʔ 'mother'), ɬət-ɬút 'squishy, soft' (ɬút-ụn 'to squash smt., especially a bug'), ʕə́l-ʕəl 'strong' (cf. ʕəl-ílx 'to exert oneself,' -ilx 'body'). A fairly large number of adjective-like words have both total reduplication and the suffix -t or -əm (see Section 14.2-3), e.g., pạ́l-pəl-t/pạ́l-pl-ət 'stubborn,' k'ín-k'ən-t/k'ín-k'n-ət 'dangerous,' qʷám-qʷm-ət 'funny,' kíx-kx-ət 'lively,' qʷən-qʷán-t 'poor' (√qʷan 'to want'), xə́ɬ-xɬ-əm 'lively, brisk' (√xəɬ 'active'), kə́xʷ-kxʷ-əm 'dark blue (like bruise)' (kəxʷ-p 'to get bruised'), pə́ʕ-pʕ-əm 'grey(ish)' (pəʕ-p 'faded').

All colour terms, except pəq 'white' and kʷḷi? 'green, yellow,' are either of the shape 1V́2-12-əm (see kə́xʷ-kxʷ-əm, pə́ʕ-pʕ-əm above) or of the shape 12-1V́2, e.g., cəqʷ-cíqʷ 'red,' qʷəz-qʷáz 'blue,' qʷ'əx̌-qʷ'íx̌ 'black.'

Forms such as s-qəx̌-qə́qx̌aʔ, s-qəw-qə́qw'əc (see above), or s-qəy-qə́qy'əxʷ 'boys' (< s-qə́qy'əxʷ 'boy' < s-qayxʷ 'man') show that here also total reduplication involves the first two consonants of the root, not the first two consonants of the stem with consonant reduplication (for example, -qəy- in s-qəy-qə́qy'əxʷ repeats q..y of s-qayxʷ, not q..q of s-qə́qy'əxʷ). For this aspect of total reduplication, see also the conclusion to Section 13.1 and the reference there.

Lexicalized forms that combine total and consonant reduplication are ɬəp-ɬəpn-ún'ɬ, qʷəl'-qʷal'-ə́l't (Section 12.1[5c]), and, for example, pəqʷ-pəqʷʔ-úʔɬ 'afraid of everything' (páqʷuʔ 'afraid,' -úɬ 'always'), c'aʔ-c'aʔx-úxɬ 'bashful' (c'aʔx 'shy,' -úɬ 'always'), kʷəm-kʷə́kʷəm 'weasel in brown phase' (no simplex).

Remarkable are the cases cəqʷ-cécqʷ 'little red ones' (cəqʷ-cíqʷ 'red'),[13] qʷəz-qʷə́qʷəz' 'little blue ones' (qʷəz-qʷáz 'blue'), qʷ'əx̌-qʷ'ə́qʷ'x̌ 'little black ones' (q'ʷəx̌-q'ʷíx̌ 'black'): here the application of consonant reduplication to a form with total reduplication expresses plurality as well as diminutiveness. This contrasts with the regular cases, where consonant reduplication applied to total reduplication expresses diminutiveness (e.g., s-qəl-qál'xʷ 'rooster' > s-qəl-qə́ql'əxʷ 'little rooster'), or where plurality plus diminutiveness is expressed by total reduplication of a form with consonant reduplication (e.g., s-qə́qx̌aʔ 'pup' > s-qəx̌-qə́qx̌aʔ 'pups').

As a rule, reduplication does not involve prefixes. However, in s-qʷal' 'to report' (s- stative prefix [Section 10.1.2]; here with partial loss of its original meaning) > səqʷ-sqʷál 'spreading news around, squealing, gossiping,' we have a unique case of a prefix being involved in reduplication (note the regular case s-qʷəl'-qʷal'-úɫ 'tattletale,' with s- not reduplicated).

12.5.1. Total reduplication (4a) to (4c): predictability of subtypes

The structure of a stem often indicates which type of total reduplication such a stem selects:

(1) Stems 1(A)2.'. always select type (4c), e.g., məcxál 'to write' > məc-məcxál 'to write a lot.' These stems are also the only ones that select type (4c).

(2) Stems 1É2(..) almost always select type (4b), e.g., kə́x-kəx 'older sister'; s-qʷəm 'mountain' > s-qʷə́m-qʷəm 'mountain range'; ɫəsp 'rash' > ɫə́s-ɫsəp 'rash all over.' The only exceptions recorded here are kʷət-kʷə́t 'hollow spot on top of breastbone' (cf. kʷət-p-áx̌ʷac 'to pant') and c'əz'-c'éz'x̌ʷəm 'sleet' F (no simplex).

(3) Stems 1V́ʔ(A)C always select type (4b), e.g., caʔxʷ 'happy' > cá?-c?axʷ id.; cíʔiʕ'ʷ 'to bleed' > cíʔ-c?iʕ'ʷ 'to bleed all over.' Basically, these are cases with interior glottalization, for which see also Section 13.1.

(4) Stems 1A2 and 1Á2.. usually select type (4a), e.g., s-ɣap 'tree' > s-ɣəp-ɣáp 'trees'; s-núk'ʷaʔ 'friend, relative' > s-nək'ʷ-núk'ʷaʔ 'friends, relatives.' However, numerals 1Á2.. that combine the prefix n- with total reduplication in order to refer to 'persons' always select type (4b), e.g., cilkst 'five' > n-cíl-cləkst 'five people' (see also Section 19 and n-cúkʷ-cəkʷ below). Moreover, cases with total reduplication and the suffix -t (e.g., k'ín-k'ən-t/k'ín-k'n-ət 'dangerous') are usually of type (4b):[14] it is not possible to establish whether such forms result from 1A2-12 plus -t or from total reduplication of 1A2-t, because in most of these cases the total reduplication and the affixation of -t operate in tandem. Finally, there are also isolated cases of 1A2(..) that select type (4b), e.g., s-púl'-pəl' 'stash of nuts made by squirrel,' s-qáy-qyəxʷ 'men.'

(5) Stems 1V́12(..), i.e., stems 1V́2(..) with consonant reduplication, select type (4a), even where their underlying stems, i.e., 1V́2(..), select type (4b). Hence we have s-qayxʷ 'man' > s-qáy-qyəxʷ 'men'; s-qə́qy'əxʷ 'boy' >

s-qəy-qə́qyʼəxʷ 'boys'; s-X̣ʼəqʷ 'to have a spot (on one's skin)' > s-X̣ʼə́qʷ-
X̣ʼəqʷ 'spotted, variegated' versus s-X̣ʼəqʷ-X̣ʼə́X̣ʼqʷ 'to have little spots'; kə́la?
'first' > s-kə́l-kla? 'ancestors' versus s-kəl-kə́kla? 'elders.'[15] Stems 1V22, i.e.,
stems with final reduplication, also select type (4a) only, e.g., pú꜔-ə꜔ > pə꜔-
pú꜔-ə꜔ (Section 12.1[5d]).

The following cases show types (4a) and (4b), both selected by the same
root: c'ə꜖ʼ-c'ú꜖ʼ 'sour, bitter (about berries)' versus c'ú꜖ʼ-c'ə꜖ʼ 'Oregon grape'
(known for its tart taste); cukʷ 'to quit, be finished' > cəkʷ-cúkʷ 'all finished'
versus n-cúkʷ-cəkʷ 'several people are finished.' Next to k'əx-k'áx 'dry' (k'ax
id.) one also uses k'áx-k'əx id., which seems to be slightly less correct than
k'əx-k'áx or k'ax. Note also cəq-cáq 'tame' (cf. cáq-an 'to tame, tr.') versus
cáq-cq-ət 'Spruce grouse, Franklin's grouse, "foolhen"' (which is known for
the fact that it is easily caught); c'əx-c'áx 'ashamed of what one did' (√c'ax
'shy, ashamed') versus c'áx-c'x-ət '(a) shameful (thing)'; nəqʷ-núqʷ 'warm
(of atmosphere)' (√nuqʷ id.) versus nú?-ən?uqʷ 'to get warmed up (person)'
(nu?qʷ 'to get warm [atmosphere, weather]'). For the latter case, and total
reduplication of cases with interior glottalization in general, see also Section 13.1.

The various reduplication types and the stems that usually select them
are given in the following table:[16]

	1(A)2.	1É2(..)	1V́?(A)C	1Á2(..)	1V́12(..)
(a)	–	rarely	–	mostly	always
(b)	–	mostly	always	some cases	–
(c)	always	–	–	–	–

12.5.2. Total reduplication (4a) to (4c): residual types and special cases

Total reduplication types (4a) and (4b) leave the following special cases
and residual types:

(1) 1(V)2-a-1V́2-a, 1(V)2-a-1V́12-a: expresses repetitiveness or persistence,
e.g., X̣ʼək-a-X̣ʼák-a 'to go all the way through without stopping; long un-
derwear in one piece, snowsuit' (X̣ʼak 'to go along'),[17] ləq'-a-láq'-a (1) 'to turn
pages fast,' (2) type of design on basket (the design is alternately woven
over and under the roots from which the basket is made; cf. láq'-an' 'to flip
smt. over, e.g., a page; to take a cover off'), ʕim-a-ʕím-a 'to get rumpled up,
to be made smaller by getting rumpled up' (ʕím-ləx 'to make oneself
smaller, e.g., a snake coiling itself up,' -ləx 'body'), zəx̌-a-zə́z'x̌-a 'to play
checkers, to move a little bit at a time' (zə́x̌-ən 'to move smt.'). Without
simplex we have, for example, X̣ʼəq'-a-X̣ʼə́q'-a 'grasshopper when flying'
(refers to the clicking sound it makes), cək-a̡-cə̡k-a 'blue jay' (refers to the
sound it makes when it is forecasting bad weather or bringing bad news).

(2) 1Á2-1A2: tín-tin 'bell' (borrowed from Chinook Jargon), mús-mus 'cow'

(borrowed from Chinook Jargon), c'íxʷ-c'ixʷ 'fishhawk, osprey' (no simplex). These cases were also recorded tín-tən, mús-məs, c'íxʷ-c'əxʷ. Further examples of 1Á2-1A2 are the onomatopoetic formations lík-lik (unidentified little swamp bird), ʕít-ʕit 'snipe,' mík-mik (unidentified little black bird with yellow beak, smaller than blackbird), káy-kay (also q'áy-q'ay) 'blue jay when forecasting good weather, when bringing good news.'

12.6. Total reduplication: type (4d)

This type, which consists of the double repetition of 1V2, is used to indicate a continuous action, often combined with the idea of increased intensity. Besides the examples in Section 12.1(4d) we have, for example, ʔuy-ʔuy-ʔúy 'to keep sobbing' (no simplex), ʕʷəl-ʕʷəl-ʕʷə́l-ən 'to walk all over' (metaphorical use of ʕʷə́l-ən 'to burn, to set fire to,' as in [from a song] ʕʷəl-ʕʷəl-ʕʷə́l-ən-ɬkan ti‿tmixʷ‿a 'I walk all over the land [tmixʷ]'). The following is from a story I collected: ʔáta? x̌aw'-x̌aw'-x̌áw'n'‿a ɬ‿ƛ̓'ák-as 'he (-as) went (ƛ̓ak) that way (ʔáta?), all along the low (x̌áw'ən') part' (for ‿a see Section 26.1.3).

13
Interior Glottalization

A number of Lillooet roots C_1VC_2 can appear in the shape $C_1V?C_2$. We call this operation 'interior glottalization.' This term generally refers to an incipient change or a change in progress (the term 'inchoative' or 'ingressive' may be applied here). This operation (which can be described as a form of infixation) is applied almost exclusively to roots C_1AC_2, and it seems to have the same function as the suffix -p, which operates mainly on C_1EC_2 (see Section 14.1). Roots CVR usually have R glottalized when interior glottalization is applied. As a rule, roots CAC that are subjected to interior glottalization yield the stress to a suffix under the same conditions as those under which roots with E yield the stress (see Section 2.1[1]), e.g., √c'ax 'shy, ashamed, embarrassed' > c'áx-an' 'to poke fun at, tr. (-an')' versus c'a?x-ús 'ashamed, shy' (c'a?x id., -us 'face'); √huqʷ 'frost' > s-húqʷ-lum'əxʷ 'frozen ground (-lum'əxʷ)' (s- nominalizer) versus hu?qʷ-úlm'əxʷ 'ground is getting frozen' (for -lum'əxʷ/-úlm'əxʷ see also Section 2.1[5]).

Interior glottalization is discussed in Section 13.1. There is also a second, totally unproductive type of interior glottalization, i.e., C?VC, which has no clear function and is discussed in Section 13.2.

13.1. Cases $C_1V?C_2$
Examples of $C_1V?C_2$ are: ma?kʷ 'to get dull' (about blade) F (məkʷ-mákʷ 'dull [blade]' F), n-ti?qʷ 'water gets muddy, dirty' (n-təqʷ-tíqʷ 'water is muddy, dirty'), nu?s 'to get damp' (nəs-nús 'damp'), la?kʷ 'to get loose, untied' (ləkʷ-lákʷ 'loose, untied'), n-li?x̌ 'water gets clear' (n-ləx̌-líx̌ 'water is clear'), çú?əl̓ 'to get stretched' F (çúl̩-ləx 'to stretch oneself reaching for smt.' F), ca?k 'to cool off' (cək-cák 'cool'), c'a?ɬ 'to get chilled' (c'əɬ-c'áɬ 'chilled'), n-su?ƛ̓ 'to get drained out' (n-súƛ̓-un' 'to drain water out, tr.'), ki?l̩-ús 'to get embarrassed, hurt' (kíl̩-us-əm 'to be embarrassed, hurt'), ká?əw̓ 'to go out further' (káw-ləx 'to move away'), ɣi?p 'to grow (up)' (ɣíp-in' 'to raise smt./smb.'), qʷá?əz̓ 'to get blue' (qʷəz-qʷáz 'blue'), q'ʷú?c 'to get

fat' (qʷʼuqʼʷc 'fat'), zaʔx̌ʷ 'to melt' (zəx̌ʷ-záx̌ʷ 'melted'). See also cʼaʔx, huʔqʷ-ulmʼəxʷ above (in the introductory remarks).

In a number of cases we have $C_1VʔC_2$ with no counterparts in Lillooet but in other Salish languages, e.g., pʼiʔs 'shrivelled up, wrinkled' (Sh. pʼəses 'become wrinkled'; cf.? Lillooet pʼəs 'vagina'), naʔqʼ 'to rot, rotten' (CdA naqʼ 'organic substance is rotten,' Kal. naqʼ 'rotten, putrid,' Sh. nʔeqʼ 'rotten'). Finally, there are cases $C_1VʔC_2$ for which I did not find a counterpart without ʔ in Lillooet or in other Salish languages, e.g., cʼiʔqʼ 'to get dirty,' kʼʷiʔxʷ 'pitched, containing pitch (wood),' paʔq 'red-hot' (cf.? pəq 'white'), x̌aʔs 'tired, aching (from exercise).'[1]

Although the ʔ resulting from interior glottalization is not part of the original root, it consists of total reduplication as though it were a root consonant, e.g., nuʔqʷ 'to get warm (atmosphere, weather)' (nəqʷ-núqʷ 'warm') > nú?-ənʔuqʷ (via *núʔ-nuʔqʷ) 'to get warmed up (about a person)'; miʔX̌ 'dirty' (no simplex) > míʔ-əmʔiX̌' id., x̌aʔs 'tired, aching (from exercise)' > x̌áʔ-x̌ʔas 'aching all over.' Compare these cases with, for example, s-qə́qx̌aʔ 'pup' (s-qáx̌aʔ 'dog') > s-qəx̌-qə́qx̌aʔ 'pups,' where the second q of s-qə́qx̌aʔ, which results from reduplication, is not counted for further reduplication. As explained in van Eijk 1993b (following Broselow 1983), the different treatments of the inserted elements results from the fact that the ʔ targets the root and is therefore part of the morphological IC structure of the word and accessible to total reduplication (which targets only material that falls within the morphological confines of the root), whereas the inserted consonant that results from consonant reduplication targets the stressed vowel and is therefore part of the prosodic structure of the word and not accessible to total reduplication.

13.1.1. Vowel-change

In a few words, forms $C_1AʔC_2$ are parallelled by forms C_1EC_2: s-piʔkʷ 'crumb, anything broken off' (pə́kʷ-ən 'to spill [pəkʷ-], tr. [-ən]'); kʼaʔX̌' 'to get dirty' (s-kʼə́X̌'-kʼəX̌' 'dirty'); máʔ-əmʔat 'paralyzed' (reduplication of *maʔt) versus mə́t-əmt-əp 'paralyzed' (reduplication of *mət-p).

13.1.2. Cases Cíʔiˤ', Cíʔiˤʷ

In roots CiQ where Q is a uvular resonant, interior glottalization yields the form CíʔiQ. Phonetically, the first i in these forms is like the second i [ė] (cf. n. 13 of Section 1). Examples are: łíʔiˤ' 'to get scattered' (łiˤ'-ín 'to scatter them, tr.'), líʔiˤʷ 'to fall apart' (líˤʷ-in 'to dismantle smt., tr.'), síʔiˤʷ 'loose' (síˤʷ-in 'to loosen it, tr.'), kʼíʔiˤʷ 'in pain, run down, suffering from tuberculosis' (s-kʼiˤʷ 'delicate, frail'), cíʔiˤʷ 'to bleed' (cf. Sh. cʔiˤʷ 'to bleed'). These cases also allow total reduplication, which involves Ciʔ: líʔ-əlʔiˤʷ 'falling apart,' cíʔ-cʔiˤʷ 'bleeding all over.' The first i in such forms with total reduplication varies from [ė] to a pronunciation that resembles the central phonetic value of i, a closer [e].

13.1.3. Interior glottalization and consonant reduplication

Some words show a combination of consonant reduplication and interior glottalization: $C_1A?C_1C_2$. (In terms of rule ordering, consonant reduplication precedes interior glottalization: $C_1AC_2 > C_1AC_1C_2 > C_1A?C_1C_2$.[2]) This operation seems to express 'happens to be, improvised, any old way.' Roots C_1EC_2 change E to i as a result of the consonant reduplication (cf. Section 12.4, residual type [2]). Examples are: xí?x̌əw' 'raw, uncooked' (about smt. that really should be cooked; cf. s-x̌iw' 'raw [in general]'), zá?zəq' 'tea-biscuits, smt. baked with baking powder' (cf. s-zaq' 'bread'), k̓í?k̓əxʷ 'dug, tunnelled' (e.g., about a hole made by a muskrat in a riverbank; cf. also k̓í?k̓əxʷ cípwən 'hole in the ground for storing vegetables [instead of a proper larder]': cípwən 'root-house, larder'; cf. also s-k̓əxʷ 'hole'), ʕí?ʕ'əc 'tied any old way' (ʕéc-ən 'to tie it, tr.'). Without simplex we have kí?kəl' 'unwilling to do smt.,' n-zí?zəʕ 'every' (cf.? CdA yaR 'assemble, be many, crowd').[3]

A number of words have the shape $C_1Á?C_1C_2$-at (with the aspectual suffix -at; see Section 14.5[1], which is limited to these cases).[4] This formation indicates that a process has gone to its very end: k̓á?k̓'x-at 'dried out' (k̓'ax 'dry'), q'ʷí?q'ʷl'-at 'overripe, overcooked' (q'ʷəl 'ripe, cooked,' note ə ~ i). Here also belongs zú?z'əqʷ-at 'dead (zuqʷ) for sure.'

A special set of cases is formed by ?ú?c-at 'good for nothing, not capable of doing anything' and xʷ?á?z'-at id. (?uc 'to be not so-and-so,'[5] xʷ?az 'no[t]'). In these cases the consonant preceding V́ (i.e., the consonant involved in the reduplication and/or interior glottalization) is ?; I do not know whether here we have both reduplication and interior glottalization with the ?'s resulting from each operation merging, or the application of only one operation. However, the first solution seems more likely in that it would conform to the general pattern of formations with -at. (For merging of glottal stops, see also Section 4.4.) Remarkably, we have a root CCVC (not CVC) in xʷ?á?z'-at. For ?ú?c-at see also ?uc-át-p in Section 14.1.

A number of cases $C_1Á?C_1C_2$-at were also recorded with -?úl 'really, par excellence' (Section 16): k̓a?k̓'x-at-?úl 'completely dried out,' q'ʷí?q'ʷl'-at-?úl 'completely overripe, overcooked.'

There are also a few cases of the type $C_1A?C_1C_2$-at-ím'. The suffix -ím' is limited to these cases and its function is unclear. Cases at hand are: xʷu?xʷk̓'ʷ-at-ím' 'to drag smt. on the ground' (√xʷuk̓'ʷ 'to drag'), ƛ̓i?ƛ̓'qʷ-at-ím' 'to sew by hand' (cf. ƛ̓əqʷ-úm 'to sew'; the deletion of ? from ƛ̓əqʷ?- is unexplained). Note also za?-əz?ac-at-ím' 'to wash by hand,' which has a combination of interior glottalization, total reduplication, and -aɬ-ím' (√zac 'to rub things between one's hands').

13.2. Cases CʔVC

In two cases we have $C_1VC_2 > C_1ʔVC_2$: s-kʷ'ʔap 'straight (like a candle)' F (kʷ'əp-kʷ'áp id.), x̌ʷ'ʔuḷ (name of a mountain, cf. unretracted √x̌ʷul 'ridge'). In one case we have $C_1VC_1 > C_1ʔVC_1$: wəʔáw 'to shout' (cf. wáw-əlckzaʔ 'poplar,' -əlckzaʔ 'leaf'). Note also s-əmʔám 'wife' versus mam-áw's 'couple' (-aw's 'together'). Without any parallelling form we have, for example, cʔas 'to come,' xʷ'ʔaz 'no(t),' xʷ'ʔuxʷ 'to give off smell.'

14
Aspectual Suffixes

Lillooet has seven aspectual suffixes, which are discussed in Sections 14.1 to 14.5. These suffixes generally express notions such as 'incipient state' or 'ongoing state,' although in a number of cases, especially where no simplex without the suffix can be found, they seem to have lost part of their function and the forms in question are completely lexicalized.

14.1. The suffix -p
The suffix -p expresses an incipient change or a change in progress, e.g., nəqʷ-p 'warming up (weather)' (nəqʷ 'warm [weather, atmosphere]'), nə́m'-ənm'-əp 'to go blind' (s-nə́m'-nəm' 'blind,' s- stative prefix [Section 10.1.2]), kʷəm-p 'to get dull (blade)' M (kʷə́m-kʷəm 'dull [blade]' M). The function of -p is thus the same as that of interior glottalization (Section 13); formally -p is in complementary distribution with interior glottalization in that -p operates only on roots CEC whereas interior glottalization operates on roots CAC (see Section 13.1).

There are a few root-doublets CEC ~ CAC, with CEC selecting -p and CAC selecting interior glottalization: besides nəqʷ-p (above), we have nuʔqʷ id., and besides kʷəm-p (above) we have maʔkʷ id. F (see also Section 13.1 for nuʔqʷ, maʔkʷ). Besides mə́t-əmt-əp 'paralyzed,' we have má́ʔ-əmʔat id. (both forms with total reduplication), while pəˤ-p 'pale, faded' (cf. pə́ˤ-pˤəm 'grey[ish], light of colour') is parallelled by páʔəˤ 'pale, fading, faded' (cf. pəˤ-páˤ 'grey[ish]'). Note also ləq'-p 'flipped over (like a blanket)' versus láq'-əq' 'to get opened (blanket), to get flipped over' (the difference between ləq'-p and láq'-əq' is difficult to establish); for láq'-əq', cf. láq'-an' 'to open smt., to take the cover off, tr.'), and cəx̌ʷ-p-áɬiw's 'to sweat' (-aɬiw's '[outside] of body') versus cíx̌ʷ-əx̌ʷ 'stream comes down.'[1]

Completely unusual is ʔúʔcaɬ 'good for nothing, can't do anything' versus ʔucáɬ-p 'no longer good (e.g., a fish that is no longer fit to eat, or a person who has been drunk for a few days).' In the latter case -p is added not just to a root CVC but to an extended stem (ʔuc 'to be not so-and-so'; for -aɬ see Section 14.5). For ʔúʔcaɬ see also Section 13.1.3.

The inchoative function of -p is not always explicit (at least not from a non-Lillooet point of view), e.g., ʕʷəl-p 'to burn' (ʕʷə́l-ən 'to light smt., tr.'), qəm-p 'hot' (qə́m-ən 'to heat smt., tr.'). Here we have more a physical state that is maintained over a certain period of time.

14.2. The suffix -əm

The suffix -əm has a rather elusive function. It probably refers to something like 'continued state.' In most occurrences it combines with total reduplications of roots CEC, e.g., xə́ɬ-xɬ-əm 'lively, brisk' (√xəɬ 'active'), cə́ɬ-cɬ-əm 'light, bright' (cəɬ-p 'daylight breaking'), pə́ʕ-pʕ-əm 'grey(ish)' (pəʕ-p 'faded'), qə̣l-q̣l-əm 'noisy' (cf.? qə̣l 'bad'), qʷə́t-qʷt-əm 'dark of complexion' (tə́qʷ-tqʷ-əm id., cf. √tiqʷ 'dark, muddy'), kə́x-kxʷ-əm 'dark blue' (kəxʷ-p 'to get bruised'), kə́w-kw-əm 'cleared (land), having no underbrush' (kəw-xál 'to clear land'), ƛ'ə́k'-ƛ'k'-əm 'silent' (ka-ƛ'ə́k'‿a 'to fall silent'), kʷə́z-kʷz-əm 'smooth' (kʷə́z-ən 'to shine smt. up, to polish smt., tr.') c'ə́x̌-c'x̌-əm 'clean' (c'ə́x̌-ən 'to clean smt., tr.'). For function and patterning of -əm, see also -t (Section 14.3).

There are a few cases of -əm after non-reduplicated roots: s-nə́qʷ-əm 'sun' (nəqʷ 'warm [weather],' s- nominalizer), s-cáqʷ-əm 'red saskatoon berry' (√caqʷ 'reddish,' s- nominalizer), ƛ'áq'-əm-kst/ƛ'áq'-m-əkst 'six' (ƛ'aq' 'to cross over,' -kst 'hand'). Note that in the last two cases, -əm appears after roots CAC rather than CEC.

The suffix -əm is probably etymologically related to the intransitivizer -əm (see Section 18). In a number of cases, -əm appears in fixed combinations, e.g., ʔáḷṣ-əm 'sick' M (no simplex *ʔaḷṣ).

14.3. The suffix -t

The function of -t is as difficult to determine as that of -əm (Section 14.2). Like -əm, it appears to refer to a 'continued state.' In many occurrences, -t combines with total reduplications of roots CAC, e.g., qʷən-qʷán-t 'poor, destitute' (√qʷan 'to want'), kʷíw-kʷw-ət 'slippery' (kʷíʔəw 'to slip'), záw'-əzw'-ət 'getting you fed up, being a bother or a nuisance' (zá́ʔəw' 'fed up, tired, cranky'), líp'-əlp'-ət 'to be a nuisance' (líp'-in 'to squeeze smt., tr.), cáq-cq-ət 'Franklin's grouse, "foolhen"' (is caught easily; cf. cəq-cáq 'tame,' cáq-an' 'to tame, tr.), c'áx-c'x-ət 'shameful' (c'aʔx 'shy, embarrassed'), líx-əlx-ət 'slimy' (s-líx-il 'fish-slime'). Without simplex we have, for example, qʷám-qʷm-ət 'funny,' pạ́l-pə̣l-t/pạ́l-p̣l-ət 'stubborn,' k'ín-k'ən-t/k'ín-k'n-ət 'dangerous.'

Note that -t is largely in complementary distribution with -əm in that -əm mainly combines with total reduplications of roots CEC, whereas -t selects CAC. However, there are a few cases of -t combining with total re-duplications of roots CEC: ˁə́n'-ˁən'-ət 'getting mad easily' (ka-ˁə́n'‿a 'to get tough with smt., to get mad [angry] all of a sudden'), x̌ʷə́c'-x̌ʷc'-ət 'pushy' (x̌ʷə́c'-ən 'to force, coax smb. to do smt., tr.'), x̌ə́k-x̌k-ət 'bossy' (also n-s-x̌ə́k-x̌k-ət, cf. x̌ə́k-ən 'to correct smb., tr.').

There are a number of cases of -t after non-reduplicated roots, e.g., zaw'-t 'fed up, annoyed' (zá?əw' 'fed up, tired, cranky'), zax-t 'long' (cf. záx-al'qʷəm' 'tall,' -al'qʷəm' 'outward appearance'), s-k'ə́ɬ-t 'mud' (k'ə́ɬ-p 'to get muddy'). In a number of cases there are unreduplicated roots ending in t: these might historically contain the suffix -t, e.g., tayt 'hungry,' x̌ʷayt 'to die collectively (e.g., during an epidemic).'

Peculiar is the use of -t in may-t 'to make, fix, heal (like an Indian doctor)' (cf. máy-s-ən 'to repair, fix, tr. [-ən],' -s 'shape'), cu-t 'to say smt., intr.' (cf. cu-n 'to tell smb. smt., tr.'), c'niqʷ-t 'to fight' F (cf. c'níqʷ-ən 'to beat smb. up' F). Here -t behaves as though it were an intransitivizer.

14.4. The combination n-..-təm

The combination n- (Section 10.1.5) and -təm expresses in general 'ongoing or increasing development'; -təm is probably a combination of -t (Section 14.3) and -əm (Section 14.2). Examples are: n-x̌ʷúy-təm 'to go ahead' (x̌ʷuy 'go ahead!'), n-yíp-təm 'to grow up' (yi?p 'to grow [up]'), n-wúqʷ'il-təm 'heading down the valley, heading downstream (on water or land)' (wúqʷ'il 'to go downstream on water'), n-p'án'-təm 'to go backwards, to go down, to fall back after having been successful at first, to fail in health, to suffer a setback' (p'an't 'to return,' merges final t with -təm).

14.5. Conditioned suffixes

Three aspectual suffixes occur only when combined with various other operations: (1) -a: in ƛ'ə-ƛ'ák-a and p'iy-a-p'án't-a/p'ən'-a-p'án't-a (Section (12.2), and in the cases discussed in Section 12.5.2(1); (2) -aɬ: in, for example, k'ax 'dry' > k'á?k'x-aɬ 'dried out' (see Section 13.1.3); and (3) -im': co-occurs only with -aɬ above (see Section 13.1.3).

15
Lexical Suffixes

Lillooet has a large number of suffixes that are traditionally called lexical suffixes. Most of these suffixes refer to concrete objects or concepts; we call them primary lexical suffixes (see Section 15.2). The remaining suffixes comprise connectives (Section 15.3) and residual suffixes (Section 15.4). Connectives have no meaning of their own, but they may influence the meaning of a following lexical suffix (see Section 15.1.1). Residual suffixes are mainly formatives, devoid of a clear meaning.

Lexical suffixes are mostly attached to a bare root, or a root with another lexical suffix, or an aspectual suffix. In a few cases, however, a lexical suffix is attached to a stem with an (in)transitivizer, e.g., xʷík'-əm 'to butcher fish (xʷík'-), intr. (-əm)' > xʷik'-m-áɬxʷ 'shed for butchering fish' (-aɬxʷ 'house, place where smt. happens'); cf. the regular case in xʷík'-tən 'knife' (-tən 'instrument').

15.1. Lexical suffixes: combinations
In this section we discuss combinations of lexical suffixes with each other (Section 15.1.1) and combinations of lexical suffixes with the locative prefix n- (Section 15.1.2).

15.1.1. Combinations of lexical suffixes with each other
In terms of immediate constituents (IC), we have the following combinations of lexical suffixes:

1 The word is built up morpheme by morpheme from left to right, with each suffix commenting on the preceding complex, e.g., k'ʷúl'-c-tən 'instrument (-tən) for getting smt. to eat' (cf. k'ʷúl'-c-am' 'to get smt. to eat,' -am' intransitivizer, -c 'food,' √k'ʷul' 'to make').
2 The suffixes form a complex that in its entirety is added to a stem. There are two subtypes, the first involving connectives:

(a) The IC's form a new semantic unit, e.g., -l-aka? 'implement, instrument' (-l- connective, -aka? 'hand'), -al-us 'eye' (-al- connective, -us 'face'). Examples are: məc-l-áka? 'pencil' (méc-ən 'to write'), qam't-ál-us 'to get hit (qam't) on the eye.'

(b) The meaning of the first suffix limits that of the second, hence a sequence -X-Y means 'the X of Y,' e.g., -qin'-aka? 'finger(tip),' -qin'-xən 'toe(tip)' (-qin' 'head,' -aka? 'hand,' -xən 'foot'): q'ʷəx̌ʷ-qín'-aka? 'fingernail,' q'ʷəx̌ʷ-qín'-xən 'toenail' (q'ʷəx̌ʷ- only in these combinations).

15.1.2. Lexical suffixes and the prefix n-

The locative prefix n- (Section 10.1.5) may co-occur with some lexical suffixes. We have the following cases of IC's here:

(1) The prefix is one IC and the root-suffix combination another, e.g., q'áy-ləx 'to jump, run away' > n-q'áy-ləx 'to swim' (√q'ay UC, -ləx 'body'), káw-ləx 'to move away on land' > n-káw-ləx 'to move away on water' (√kaw 'far, away,' -ləx 'body').

(2) The prefix n- and the suffix form an 'ambifix,'[1] which enclasps the stem and expresses the setting for the referent of the stem, e.g., n-c'úl'l'-əc 'to have a bitter (√c'ul') taste in the mouth (-c)' (with final reduplication): the taste is here *in* the mouth, cf. x̌zum'-c 'to have a big (x̌zum) mouth,' where 'big' is characteristic *of* the mouth. From -tən 'implement, instrument' and -mən id., we derive n-..-tən 'setting,' n-..-mən id., e.g., n-qláw'-tən 'wallet' (s-qlaw' 'money'), n-k'íx̌-mən 'frying pan' (√k'ix̌ 'to fry') (cf. n-qláw'-tən with x̌ʷík'-tən, in the introductory remarks).[2]

As a rule, a number of lexical suffixes co-occur with n-. Besides n-..-iməm 'enclosed area' (Section 15.2[8]), where the idea of 'setting' is inherent, we have, for example, n-..-k 'back,' n-..-q 'buttocks,' n-..-l-əqs 'nose' (Section 15.2[92], [105], [107.1]), where the function of n- is less clear; n- is often dropped from these combinations in careless speech, but restored in more deliberate speech (in some cases a pronunciation without n- is regular, e.g., q'il'-q 'chair' [√q'il 'to set smt. down,' -q 'buttocks']). On the other hand, suffixes that normally do not take n- were recorded with n- in individual cases, e.g., n-qam't-ápqən 'to get hit (qam't) on the back of the head' (-apqən 'back of head') versus súp-apqn-am 'to scratch (sup-) oneself on the back of the head' (-am intransitivizer). The distribution of n- in this respect is far from clear: it seems to be a matter of idiolect, some speakers using n- more than others.

(3) The root and n- form one IC to which the suffixes are added. Here belong mainly a number of roots that refer to 'location': n-ʔal- 'concave or convex surface,' n-ʔac- id., n-záh-/n-zəh-ːˑ 'right (side),' n-c'íkʷ?-/n-c'əkʷ?-ːˑ 'left (side).' Examples are: n-ʔal-áka? 'shoulder' (-aka? 'hand, arm'; cf. qam't-áka?

'to get hit [qam't] on the hand, arm,' without n-), n-ʔác-ax̌an 'armpit' (-ax̌an '[upper] arm'), n-zəh-áka? 'right hand, right arm.' In some words, these roots were recorded without n-, e.g., s-ʔac-ápl'axən 'heel' (-apl'axən 'heel').

15.2. Primary lexical suffixes

Save for one verbalizing suffix (18c in the list below), primary lexical suffixes fall into nominalizing and neutral (neither nominalizing nor verbalizing) suffixes. Nominalizing suffixes generally refer to 'instrument, implement' or 'setting, location,' i.e., the instrument with which, or the location where, the activity referred to by the root is performed, e.g., -a+xʷ 'house, place where smt. happens' (48), as in ʔálk'ʷi+ 'to babysit' > ʔalk'ʷi+-á+xʷ 'place where one babysits, daycare centre' (see also -a+xʷ in the introductory remarks). Neutral suffixes generally refer to an object or concept that is qualified or commented on by the preceding stem, e.g., -alqʷ 'cylindrical object (tree, log, stick)' (85a) > pál?-aləqʷ 'one (pála?) log, stick'; -al'qʷəm' 'outward appearance' (86) > záx-al'qʷəm' 'tall' (cf. zax-t 'long'). Nominalizing suffixes are 9, 9.1, 10, 11, 16a, 16.1, 48, 51, 95.1, 104.1, 126.

The boundary between the nominalizing and neutral suffixes is blurred, however. In the first place, -az' 'plant, tree, bush' (126) occurs almost exclusively after nominal stems, so its nominalizing status is shaky. (However, it is classed with the nominalizing suffixes because it refers to a location for the referent of the stem.) Second, certain neutral suffixes are nominalizing in individual cases, e.g., -in'ak 'gun' (38), which does not change the verbal status of, for example, kʷúten 'to borrow' in kʷu+n-ín'ak 'to borrow a gun,' but is nominalizing in ʔáma 'good' > ʔamh-ín'ak 'good gun' (e.g., n-ʔamh-ín'ak 'my [n-] good gun'). Note also -al-ic'a? 'clothing' (20.1), normally neutral but nominalizing in ʔamh-ál-ic'a? 'good clothes.' Other suffixes are probably also nominalizing but have been classed with the neutral suffixes because we have too few examples to determine their status, e.g., 115. Hence the term 'neutral suffix' stands for suffixes that are truly neutral or whose status is somewhat dubious.

Within the neutral suffixes, there are somatic versus non-somatic suffixes. Most somatic suffixes are morphologically special in that they express 'to perform on one's own body part' when combined with an intransitivizer, but 'to perform on smb. else's body part' when combined with a transitivizer, as in sup-aká?-əm 'to scratch (sup-) one's own hand (-aka?)' (-əm intransitivizer) versus sup-aká?-ən 'to scratch smb. else's hand' (-ən transitivizer). Somatic suffixes that allow this possibility are 1.2, 1.3, 5.1, 18a, 22, 22.3, 34, 37, 37.1, 37.2, 40, 44, 45, 47, 49, 56, 90, 92, 95a, 98, 104a, 105a, 107, 107.1, 109.1, 109.2, 110, 112a, 113, 114, 116.2. Other somatic suffixes, usually unproductive ones, do not allow this possibility (or at least were not recorded with [in]transitivizers): 1.1, 3, 5, 19, 19.2, 46, 57b, 61b, 65, 82, 93.1, 94,

97, 100, 104.2, 105.1, 105.3, 107.2, 109, 109.4 to 109.7, 111, 121. For details on somatic suffixes and (in)transitivizers, see Section 18.2.

Non-somatic suffixes do not allow the morphological possibility that most somatic suffixes allow (i.e., one cannot combine non-somatic suffixes with intransitivizers and transitivizers to refer to 'performing on one's own object' versus 'performing on smb. else's object'; for details on non-somatic suffixes and [in]transitivizers, see Section 18.3).

A number of suffixes glottalize a resonant (or resonants) that follows the stressed vowel in the root. Here belong 18, 92, 105, 112.

A feature of most primary lexical suffixes is that they show no formal resemblance to the roots that have the same lexical content as themselves. For example, -aɬxʷ 'house, place where smt. happens' (48) and -alc 'house' bear no resemblance to citxʷ 'house' (root). However, some lexical items contain the pertinent suffix, e.g., s-kʷƛ̓-us 'face' (s- nominalizer, kʷƛ̓- UC, -us 'face').

In some cases, suffixes express generic concepts for which there is no free form, e.g., -alqʷ 'cylindrical object (tree, log, stick)' (85a): we have the free forms s-ɣap 'tree,' s-zik 'log,' and mulx 'stick,' but no free form that covers all three objects (in other words, the suffix is more abstract than the free forms here).[3]

Certain suffixes - 6, 7, 22.1, 22.2, 25, 32, 33, 50, 62, 75, 85a, 106, 109, 112.1, 120.3 - combine particularly easily (or almost exclusively) with numerals or numerical substitutes. See also Section 19.2.[4]

The primary lexical suffixes are listed below in an alphabetical order that is based on the place and manner of articulation of the consonants (labials first, laryngeals last) and that largely ignores the vowels.[5]

Combinations of primary suffixes and connectives are listed separately ('X' for the suffix, 'X.1' for the combination connective-suffix) if the combination comprises many cases (as in 20.1) or if there is a semantic shift (as in 95.1). In all other cases the combination connective-suffix is given together with the suffix (as in 126).

Some suffixes are formally, but not semantically, identical. They are listed as 'a,' 'b,' etc. under one number if it is clear, or at least plausible, that the various meanings result from semantic extension (as in 18a, b, c). Suffixes are listed separately where semantic extension does not seem plausible (as in 22 and 23).

Suffixes marked with the empty number (—) are variants of a suffix that is discussed elsewhere: see, for example, (—) -al̓nup between 71 and 72.

List of primary lexical suffixes

1   -ap 'back part': s-tq-ap '(beaver)dam' (√təq 'to touch,' s- nominalizer), tq-áp-əp 'to get jammed (logs or ice)' (with final reduplication), s-pl-ap

'buttocks' (cf.? s-pəl'-q 'penis'). Possibly also in n-qʷzápstən' '(back of) neck.'

1.1 -ap-l'əst 'limb': n-ʔəw't-áp-l'əst 'lower arm, lower leg' (recorded from CM only; for -l'əst see 24 in Section 15.4).

1.2 -ap-l'a-xən 'heel' (with connective -l'a-, and -xən 'foot, leg'): s-ʔac-áp-l'a-xən 'heel,' súp-ap-l'a-xn-am 'to scratch (sup-) one's heel.'

1.3 -ap-qən 'back of head' (with -qən 'head'): ʔac-áp-qən 'back of head,' (√ʔac 'concave or convex surface'), súp-ap-qn-am 'to scratch the back of one's head.'

2 -apaʔ '(part of) net': ckʷ-ápaʔ 'string to pull (√cəkʷ) dipnet,' X̌'ək̓ʔ-ápa? 'cross-piece on bow of dipnet' (X̌'ək̓ʔ-án 'to prop smt., tr.').

3 -upaʔ 'tail, backpart': łq̓'-úpaʔ 'wide-tailed' (łəq̓' 'wide'), X̌'qʷ-úpaʔ-tən 'beaver-tail' (√X̌'əqʷ 'to slap,' -tən 'implement'). Note also súspaʔ 'tail' (may be an [unusual] combination of the nominalizer s- and -upaʔ, plus consonant reduplication). There is a residual form, *-al-upaʔ (only in reduplicated form in c'əm-al-úlpaʔ 'point of land, foot of mountain [where it comes down in a point],' √c'əm 'pointed'; cf. also -ups [4]).

4 -ups 'tail, back part': see -qin-ups (109.2).

5 -apəl' 'cheek': kʷz-ápəl' 'cheek' (kʷz- UC), qam't-ápəl' 'to get hit (qam't) on the cheek.'

5.1 -aplaʔ 'cheek' (used only in F): sup-aplá?-əm 'to scratch one's cheek,' sk-ápəlʔ-an 'to hit smb. on the cheek with a stick or whip' (√sək 'to hit with stick or whip,' -ən transitivizer).

6 -upzaʔ 'young plant, root': ɣiʔp-úpzaʔ 'potatoes start growing (ɣiʔp 'to grow'), c'áq-upzaʔ/c'ác'q-upzaʔ 'to harvest root-vegetables (e.g., carrots) by pulling them out when the tops start to grow' (√c'aq 'to pull out'), cilkst-úpzaʔ 'five (cilkst) young plants, roots.'

7 -ám' 'row' (recorded only with numerals and numerical substitutes): kʷin-ám' 'how many (kʷin) rows (of potatoes)?,' pəlʔ-ám' 'one (pálaʔ) row,' ʔan'was-ám' 'two (ʔán'was) rows.'

8 n-..-iməm 'enclosed area': n-ʔúkʷ-iməm 'draw, pass in mountain' (s-ʔukʷ 'pass'), n-x̌zúm-iməm 'to be big (x̌zum) inside' (e.g., house, pot), n-k'əX̌'h-íməm 'rocky canyon' (k'éX̌'a 'rock, stone'), n-ʔal-íməm 'area inside house or cave' (n-ʔal- 'concave or convex area'),[6] n-X̌'p-íməm 'gulch' (X̌'əp 'deep').

9 -mən 'instrument, implement': sék-mən 'whip, stick used for hitting' (sék-ən 'to hit smb. with a whip or stick, tr.'), łáxʷ-mən 'patch, material for patching' (łáxʷ-an' 'to patch smt., tr.'), k'íp'-mən 'pair of tongs, tweezers' (k'íp'-in' 'to hold with tongs or tweezers, tr.'). Residual form: -amín (in səp'-amín 'windpipe'; √sup 'to breathe'), recorded from CM only.

9.1 n-..-mən 'setting, implement *in* which smt. is done' (versus -mən, which refers to an implement *with* which smt. is done): n-kʼíx̌-mən 'frying pan' (kʼíx̌-in' 'to fry smt., tr.'), n-qə́m-mən '(tea)kettle' (qə́m-ən 'to heat smt., tr.'), n-zúlʼ-mən 'rocker (for rocking gold)' (zúlʼ-xal 'to rock gold, intr.'; some speakers reject n-zúlʼ-mən in favour of zúlʼ-mən), n-ƛ̓ák-mən 'track, trail (i.e., setting where one goes)' (ƛ̓ak 'to go'; cf. s-ƛ̓ák-mən 'way of life [i.e., guidance instrument by which one goes, with an unusual combination of the nominalizer s- and -mən]'; however, many speakers use only one form, usually ƛ̓ák-mən, for both meanings: 'way of life' and 'trail, track').

10 -man (usually -mán) 'habitual performer, one who ...' (cf.? English 'man'): tiʕʷ-ay̓a-mán 'runner, footracer' (tiʕʷ-áy̓a 'to have a race'), q̓iƚil-mán 'runner, footracer' (q̓íƚil 'to run'), ʔuqʷaʔ-mán 'boozer, alcoholic' (ʔúqʷaʔ 'to drink'), tíntən-man 'bell-ringer' (tíntən 'bell'), sáti-man 'the one who leads the prayers' (sáti cf. English 'Saturday,' referring to prayers said on the eve of Sunday).

11 -min 'leftover matter': níkʼ-min 'sawdust' (níkʼ-in' 'to cut, saw smt., tr.'), ʔúx̌ʷ-min 'shavings, e.g., of wood' (√ʔux̌ʷ 'to shave [e.g., wood],' 'to peel, smoothen smt. by shaving it'), c̓ík-min 'cigarette butt' (√c̓ik 'to burn all up'), x̌əl-mín 'chips left by beaver when gnawing down a tree' (cf.? √x̌əl 'to build'). It is possible that -min is etymologically related to -mən (9).

12 -manst 'unmarried person': yaqcaʔ-mánst 'unmarried woman' M (s-yáqcaʔ 'woman' M), nəx̌ʷ-nəx̌ʷ-mánst 'unmarried woman' F (cf. s-nəx̌ʷ-n̓én̓x̌ʷ 'hen'), qayxʷ-mánst 'unmarried man, bachelor' (s-qayxʷ 'man'). This suffix might contain the reflexive suffix -st (see Section 17).

13 -im̓aƚ 'one who ...': kʷʼalʼ-ím̓aƚ 'person who makes nasty remarks' (kʷʼalʼ-ín 'to make nasty remarks about smb., tr.'), ʔucz-ím̓aƚ 'Transformer, mythical hero' (s-ʔúcəz 'good, okay').

14 -məx 'person' (often combined with the name of a place to indicate where a person is from; for allomorphs əmx, -amx see Sections 3.4 and 3.5): sáƛ̓-məx/sáƛ̓-əmx 'person from saƛ̓ (Lillooet),' s-xʷáp-məx 'Shuswap' (√xʷap UC), s-qátin-əmx 'person from s-qátin (Skookumchuck),' pankʷúph-amx 'person from pankʷúpa (Vancouver),' ƚəlcʔáh-məx 'person from here (ƚəlcʔá).' There is a residual form -amx (when not after ..? ..h) in sa-káw-amx 'Prairie Indian, Cree' (√kaw 'far'), c̓wán-amx 'Okanagan Indian' (cf.? c̓wan 'dried salmon').

15 -atməx 'ability, knowledge': ʔəmh-átməx 'to do things well, to be a perfectionist' (ʔáma 'good'), qḷ-átməx 'managing smt. improperly, not being able to do things right' (qəḷ 'bad'), zəw-átməx 'knowing how to do smt., skilled' (√zəw 'to know').

16   -tən

(a) 'implement, instrument': xʷík'-tən 'knife' (√xʷik' 'to butcher fish'), ʔíʔwʼəs-tən 'fishing rod' (ʔíʔwʼəs 'to fish with a rod'), kál'k-tən 'louse-comb' (kál'k-ən 'to delouse smb., tr.'). The difference between -tən and -mən is not clear; in some cases we have both -tən and -mən after the same root, e.g., xə́l-tən, x̌ə́l-mən 'wall' (√x̌əl 'to build'). However, -tən seems to be more productive (it occurs in more derivations than -mən). Also, -tən is more often combined with other lexical suffixes than -mən is (-tən always follows the other lexical suffixes), e.g., pə̣mʼp-c-tən 'Jew's harp' (pəmp 'fast,' -c 'mouth'), wíx-qʷ-tən 'comb' (wíx-qʷ-am 'to comb [wix-] one's hair [qʷ]'), zús-x-tən 'puttees, bandage on one's leg, hobble on a horse' (√zus 'to tie, bandage,' -x- variant of -xən 'foot, leg' before -tən), síx̌-x-tən 'way of walking' (√six̌ 'to move,' -x- 'foot, leg'), ɬʔ-áka?-tən 'cane, walking stick' (ɬa? 'close[by],' -aka? 'hand, arm'). Note also kʼʷə́x̌-mən 'rattle' versus kʼʷəx̌-m-áka?-tən 'stick for snare-drum' (-əm intransitivizer, -aka? 'hand'): here we have -mən immediately after the root, but -tən after the lexical suffix.

-tən appears in a fairly large number of combinations with UC's, e.g., qíx-tən 'elbow,' c̓ík-tən 'horn, antler.' This suffix is also possibly present (in the form tən') in pʼástən' 'false-azalea,' pʼústən' 'rye grass.'

We have a residual form (-atən) in xʷúxʷl-atən 'musical instrument, record player' (xʷúxʷl-am 'to make music').

(b) '-est' (forms superlatives; always combines with possessive affixes: with -s [3S poss.] it expresses in general '-est,' with possessive affixes 1P/2P/3P it expresses '-est of us, you folks, them'): títxa?-tən-s 'narrowest' (títxa? 'narrow'), s-niɬ ti‿ʕəlʕəl-tən-ɬkáɬ‿a 'he (s-niɬ) is the strongest of us' (ʕə́lʕəl 'strong,' -ɬkaɬ 1P poss., ti‿‿a composite article).

(c) 'able to ...': ?áz̓-tən 'to be able to buy (?az̓), afford,' máys-tən 'to be able to fix (mays-),' ník'-tən 'to be able to cut (nik'-).' This usage was recorded only in negative sentences and in combination with the transitivizer -s (see Section 18 for transitivizers), as in the following:

xʷ?aẓ	kʷa[s]‿stám'	kʷa‿s-ník'-tən-s-an
not	that there is‿what	that there is‿that which-cut-able to-tr.-1S subj.

'There isn't anything I can cut with; I don't have anything to cut with.'

(For kʷa‿ see Section 31.6.2; for s- expressing 'that which,' see Section 22.7).

16.1 n-..-tən 'setting, location, container; implement in which smt. is done' (no perceptible semantic difference with n-..-mən [9.1]): n-q'á?-tən 'trough, manger' M (q'a? 'to eat' M), n-qláw'-tən 'wallet' (√qlaw' 'money'), n-?úqʷa?-tən (1) 'container for drink,' (2) 'watering hole' (?úqʷa? 'to drink'), n-q'əlza?-tən 'sweat-lodge' (q'əlza? 'to take a sweat-bath'). In some cases we have -tən (without n-) in the meaning 'setting, container,' e.g., lámxal-tən 'church' F (lámxal 'to pray'), s-ʕáp-tən 'West' (ʕap 'evening'), s-psíl'-tən 'East' (psil' 'daylight'): note that lámxal-tən is a recently coined item, and that the same might hold for s-ʕáp-tən and s-psíl'-tən, which might explain the deviant use of -tən (without n-) here.[7]

17 -atqʷa?/-atkʷa? 'water' (-atkʷa? after roots with Q, but -atqʷa? after roots without Q): ʕəlʕəl-átkʷa? 'strong (ʕálʕəl) water, swift water,' ql-átkʷa? 'bad (qəl) water, booze,' p'an't-átqʷa? 'back eddy' (p'an't 'to return'), ?áḷṣəm-átqʷa? 'to have a hangover' M (?áḷṣəm 'sick' M). We have a residual form -tqʷa? in s-kʷís-tqʷ?-am 'waterfall' (kʷis 'to fall,' -am intransitivizer).

18 -c

(a) 'mouth, edge, opening': súp-c-am' 'to scratch one's mouth (lips),' qám't-əc 'to get hit (qam't) on the mouth,' x̌zum'-c 'to have a big (x̌zum) mouth,' s-k'əm'-c 'door' F (√k'əm 'area'), n-k'əm'-c 'edge of water, shore,' n-pət-c-án' 'to cover a door opening (with a piece of cloth), tr.' (√pət 'to cover').

(b) 'food': náqʷ'-c-am' 'to steal (naq'ʷ) food' (-am' intransitivizer), táw'-c-am' 'to buy food' (√taw 'to buy/sell'), cakʷ-c 'tablecloth' (√cakʷ 'to spread out').

(c) 'language, to speak': X̌'iq-c 'sound reaches over here' (X̌'iq 'to arrive here).' Usually, -c combines with words referring to certain people X, expressing 'to speak X language': ?uxʷalmíxʷ-c 'to speak Indian (?úxʷalmixʷ),' sám?-ac 'to speak a white man's (sáma?) language (esp. English),' líl'wat-əmx-əc 'to speak Mount Currie language' (líl'wat-əmx 'person from Mount Currie [líl'wat]'), sxʷápəmx-əc 'to speak Shuswap (sxʷápməx).' Note that in the cases of 'to speak X language,' we have nominal stems transposed to verbal ones.

18.1 -al'-c 'food' (with connective -al-, and 18b): cúkʷ-al'-c 'to finish (cukʷ) eating,' k'ʷít-al'-c 'to leave food, leftovers' (√k'ʷít 'to get left over'). Cf. 67.

19 -cin 'mouth': cú-cin 'mouth' (cu- cf.? cu-t 'to say'), X̌'əqəm-cín 'Lytton' (X̌'əqəm- UC; Lytton is situated at the spot where the Thompson River enters the Fraser). The combination X-cin-əm (-əm intransitivizer)

expresses 'to eat/drink X': c'i?-cín-əm 'to eat meat (c'i?),' piya-cín-əm 'to drink beer (píya).'

19.1 -acin' 'to eat': pal?-acín' 'to eat by oneself' (pála? 'one'), pan'-acín' 'to be just in time for a meal' (cf. pan'-c 'to have a meal with others').

19.2 -cin-xən 'ankle': qʷəm-cín-xən '(lump on) ankle' (√qʷəm 'to mound up'). For -xən see 104.

20 -ic'a? 'clothing, covering': səm?-íc'a? 'white man's (sáma?) clothing,' s-kt-íc'a? 'shirt' F (kt- UC), ˁi?i?-íc'a? 'blanket made out of magpie (s-ˁí?i?) skins,' cəsp-íc'a? 'sweater' (cəsp 'to stretch, get stretched,' ˁʷuy't-íc'a? 'pajamas, nightie' (ˁʷuy't 'to sleep').

20.1 -al-ic'a? 'clothing, covering': s-ƛ'p-ál-ic'a? 'undershirt' (√ƛ'əp '[under]clothing'), qḷ-ál-ic'a? 'dirty clothes' (qəḷ 'bad'), ?amh-ál-ic'a? 'good (?áma) clothes,' nəqʷ-ál-ic'a? 'warm (nəqʷ) clothes,' qʷ'ic'-al-íc'a? 'to wash clothes' (√qʷ'ic' 'to wash [clothes, not body]'). Residual form *-l-ic'a? in reduplicated form in w'əw'p-l-ílc'a? 'caterpillar' (√wəp 'hair').

21 -as 'flesh of fish': pq-as 'having white flesh' (about spawning salmon, pəq 'white'), cqʷ-as 'having pink flesh (before spawning)' (cf. cəqʷ-cíqʷ 'red'). Cf.? 27.

22 -us 'face, front, head, appearance': súp-us-əm 'to scratch (sup-) one's face,' c'aw'-ús-əm 'to wash (c'aw'-) one's face,' pəˁp-ús 'pale (pəˁp) in the face,' s-kʷˁƛ'-us 'face (√kʷˁƛ' UC), n-kl-us 'area (√kəl) in front,' k'ətxʷ-ús-ən 'to cut off (√k'ətxʷ) smb.'s head,' ?az-úy's 'handsome' (reduplication of *?az-ús; for *?az-úz's > ?az-úy's see Section 1.7.1; √?az 'nice'), n-q'áƛ'-us-əm 'to repair a net' (√q'aƛ' UC). We have the residual form -s 'appearance' in máy-s-ən 'to fix (may-) smt., tr.'

22.1 n-..-us '-fold': n-pál?-us 'single' (pála? 'one'), n-?án'was-us 'double' (?án'was 'two'), not with higher numerals; n-kʷ'ín-us 'how many (kʷ'in) layers?'

22.2 -us-əm 'kind, sort' (-əm intransitivizer, or aspectual suffix – see Section 14.2): pál?-us-əm 'group of the same kind of people' (pála? 'one'), kʷ'in-us-əm 'different kinds' (kʷ'in 'how many? several').

22.3 -al-us 'eye': sup-al-ús-əm 'to scratch one's eye,' kəxʷp-ál-us 'to have a bruised (kəxʷp) eye,' ciq-al-ús-əm 'to stab smb. in the eye' (cíq-in' 'to stab, tr.'). There are a few cases with -al'-us that generally refer to 'seeing, aiming': cíxʷ-al'-us 'to be able to see' (cixʷ 'to reach over there'; cf. also ti‿wa?‿cíxʷ-al'-us 'visionary, prophet' [wa? 'to be']), zəh-ál'-us 'good-sighted' (versus n-zəh-ál-us 'right [n-zəh-] eye'), n-c'n'-áḷ'-us-əm 'to take aim' (√c'n'- UC). There is a residual form -az'-us in n-c'ip'-az'-ús-əm 'to close one's eyes' (√c'ip' cf. √p'ic' 'to press down'). Another residual form is -al'-s, in ɬp-al'-s 'eyelashes' (√ɬəp 'to blink'). Cf. 69.

23 -us 'fire': ʔúcz-us 'to fix a fire' (ʔúcəz 'good, okay'), ˢʷəl-ús-əs 'fire going really well' (√ˢʷəl 'to burn'; note final reduplication). There is a residual form -s in pʼam-s-əm 'to make a fire,' s-pʼam-s 'fire, firewood' (pʼám-an 'to throw smt. into the fire, tr.').

24 -ús 'hill': sux̌ʷast-ús 'to come down a hill' (súx̌ʷast 'to go down, come down'), x̌aƛʼamʼ-ús 'to go up a hill' (x̌áƛʼ-əm 'to go up, ascend'; the change x̌áƛʼəm > x̌aƛʼamʼ-ús is unexplained), zənm-ús-ən 'to go around the top' (zánəm 'to go around'). This suffix is probably related to 22, but because of its stress-behaviour it is classed as a separate suffix.

25 -usaʔ 'round object, fruit, money': cicl-úsaʔ 'fresh fruit' (cícəl 'new'), ɬuɬqʼʷ-usáʔ-əm 'to peel fruit, potatoes' (ɬuɬqʼʷ- 'undressed, naked,' -əm intransitivizer), cwʼ-úwʼsaʔ/cʔ-úʔsaʔ 'to play soccer' (reduplication of *cwʼ-úsaʔ/cʔ-úsaʔ; √cuwʼ/cuʔ 'to kick'), pálʔ-usaʔ 'one (pálaʔ) piece of fruit, potato, dollar,' x̌ʷʔít-usaʔ 'expensive' (x̌ʷʔit 'much, many'). Cf. ʔúsaʔ 'huckleberry' F, ʔúʔsaʔ 'egg.'

26 -sup 'breath': qaʔəzʼ-súp 'to pant' (qáʔəzʼ 'tired'), cʼək-súp 'to be out of breath' (cʼək 'finished, all gone'). Cf. súpʼ-um 'to breathe.' Cases with -sup could also be considered as a unique type of compound; cf. also 31.

27 -ásuɬ/-suɬ 'fish': qəlʼq-ásuɬ 'spring salmon in June' (recorded from SM only; qəlʼq 'rose'), məqʔ-áʔsuɬ (1) 'any kind of salmon that arrives before the snow (máqaʔ) melts away,' (2) 'little fish that spawns as soon as the snow goes away' (different meanings given by different consultants; reduplication of *məqʔ-ásuɬ), səmʔ-ásuɬ 'Dolly Varden' (cf. sámaʔ 'white man'), s-ƛʼíqʼ-suɬ 'silver trout' (√ƛʼiqʼ 'white[ish], grey').

28 -úsləpʼ/-sləpʼ 'firewood': kʼətxʷ-úsləpʼ 'to cut (kʼətxʷ-) firewood,' ʔuɬxʷ-úsləpʼ 'to bring in firewood,' kʷám-sləpʼ 'to get firewood from the woodpile' (kʷam 'to take'), n-kámʼ-sləpʼ 'to gather firewood' (n-kámʼ-xal 'to pick up here and there').

29 -aslaq 'quantity of fruit': qx̌-áslaq 'many berries' (cf. Squamish qəx̌ 'much, many'), x̌ʷʔít-aslaq 'many berries, potatoes, fruit' (x̌ʷʔit 'much, many'), x̌ʷʔaz̦-aslaq 'few berries' (x̌ʷʔaz̦ 'not, no').

30 n-..-askʼaʔ 'song': n-xʷənaʔm-áskʼaʔ 'power song' (s-xʷnáʔəm 'Indian doctor'), n-ləmxal-áskʼaʔ 'hymn' (lámxal 'to pray').

31 -sqáx̌aʔ 'domesticated animal (esp. horse)': cʼ-sqáx̌aʔ/cʼ-qáx̌aʔ 'horse' (cʼ < cʼi? 'deer,' with a unique type of root reduction), kʷan-sqáx̌aʔ 'to get (kʷan) one's horse,' zuqʷ-sqáx̌aʔ 'to kill a domestic animal' (zuqʷ 'dead'), qəy-sqáx̌aʔ 'to round up horses, cows' (qəy- < √qaz 'to direct [traffic], to round up'). Cf. s-qáx̌aʔ 'dog' (formerly the only domesticated animal with the Lillooet). Cases with sqáx̌aʔ could be considered as compounds, but they are productive, in contrast to the operation of compounding as a whole (also, cases with sqáx̌aʔ lack the compound-former -aɬ-).

32   -asqʼət 'day': s-x̌əcp-ásqʼət 'week' F (√x̌əcp 'numerical unit'), palʔ-
     ásqʼət 'one (pálaʔ) day,' ʔanʼwas-ásqʼət 'Tuesday' (ʔánʼwas 'two'). Cf.
     sqʼit 'day.' The suffix -asqʼət is also found in a number of man's
     names, e.g., ʕit-ásqʼət (ʕítʕit 'snipe'), n-X̌ʼw-ásqʼət (√X̌ʼəw 'to crack'), ləʕp-
     ásqʼət (1) 'smt. is dragged' (ləʕ-ən 'to drag it along, tr.'), (2) 'sound of
     water in a creek.'
33   -aszanuxʷ 'year': kʼʷin-aszánuxʷ 'how old?' (kʼʷin 'how much? how
     many?'), palʔ-aszánuxʷ 'one (pálaʔ) year old,' s-xʷətp-aszánuxʷ 'year'
     (cf. n-xʷətp 'to go around').
34   n-..-anaʔ
     (a)   'ear': n-sup-anáʔ-əm 'to scratch one's ear,' n-x̌ə-x̌zúm-anaʔ 'to
           have big (x̌zum) ears,' n-təkʷ-tkʷ-ánaʔ 'deaf' (√təkʷ 'muted'),
           n-zəh-ánaʔ 'right (n-zəh-) ear.' Residual forms are -l-anaʔ and -al-
           anaʔ in n-cʼəm-l-ánaʔ 'pectoral fin, bone around gills' (√cʼəm
           'internal body part'), təx̌ʷ-p-al-ánaʔ 'to find smt. out' (√təx̌ʷ 'to
           straighten out,' -p aspectual suffix [Section 14.1]).
     (b)   'surface': n-ʔáxʷ-anaʔ 'to get covered up by a slide' (s-ʔaxʷ
           'slide'), n-kʼʷɬ-ánʔ-an 'to pour smt. out over smb., tr.' (kʼʷə́ɬ-ən 'to
           spill it, pour it out, tr.'), n-X̌ʼp-ánaʔ 'to get covered up' (X̌ʼəp
           'deep'). n-x̌ʷəs-x̌ʷís-anaʔ 'to smile (√x̌ʷis) all the time' probably
           belongs here also.
35   -anis
     (a)   'board': ɬqʼ-ánis 'wide board' F (ɬəq 'wide'), x̌p-ánis-əm 'to pile up
           (√x̌əp) lumber,' kʷz-ánis-əm 'to varnish boards' (√kʷəz 'smooth'),
           sak-anís-tən 'ripsaw' (sák-an 'to slice smt., tr.').
     (b)   'edge': s-X̌ʼákʷ-anis 'just about showing (e.g., an underskirt)'
           (s-X̌ʼakʷ 'showing'), pəlxʷ-ánis 'just about showing' (s-pəlxʷ 'to
           stick out'), kʼm-ánis 'edge' (√kʼəm 'area').
36   -anʼlup 'bed, floor': cz-ánʼlup 'to fix a bed, make a bed' (ʔúcəz 'good,
     okay'). The more usual form is -ayʼlup, as in cz-áyʼlup 'to fix a bed,
     make a bed,' X̌ʼxʷ-áyʼlup 'to sweep the floor' (X̌ʼə́xʷ-ən 'to shake, brush
     smt. in order to get dirt off'). The shape -alʼnup is found in ʔuʔcʼqʔ-
     ál̓nup/kʷuṣʔ-ál̓nup 'to wet one's bed (women/men)' (ʔúʔcʼqaʔ/kʷúṣə?
     'to urinate [women/men]').
37   -anʼak, -anʼk, -ank 'belly, inside, hillside': sup-anʼák-əm 'to scratch one's
     belly,' qʼʷl-álnʼak-əm 'to sunbathe' (reduplication of *qʼʷl-ánʼak-əm;
     qʼʷəl 'cooked'), s-wac-ánʼak 'manure' (s-wac 'excrement'), cʼm-anʼk
     'intestines' (√cʼəm 'internal body part'), s-qʷm-ə́mnʼək 'to be pregnant'
     (s-qʷm-ank id.; √qʷəm 'to mound up'), n-cʼíx̌ʷ-ank 'skin on belly is sore'
     (e.g., about a horse on which the saddle-strap is too tight; √cʼíx̌ʷ 'sore,
     worn out'), n-ʕʷəl-ánk-tən 'kindling' (√ʕʷəl 'to burn'), n-xʔ-ank 'deep
     bank' (xaʔ 'high'), n-cʼaʔɬ-ánk 'side-hill cools off when the sun goes

down' (c'aʔɬ 'to cool off'). Residual forms are -naʔk and -anáʔk in s-p'úm-naʔk 'smoked bear-gut' (√p'um 'to smoke'), x̌zum-anáʔk 'to have a big (x̌zum) belly.'

37.1 n-..-ank-akst 'palm of hand' (combination of 37 and 96): n-sup-ank-ákst-əm 'to scratch the palm of one's hand,' n-ʔac-ank-ákst 'palm of hand' (n-ʔac- 'convex or concave area'), n-x^was-ank-ákst '(to give or receive) Last Sacrament' (√x^was 'to rub on ointment').

37.2 n-..-an'k-xən 'sole of foot': n-súp-an'k-xn-am 'to scratch the sole of one's foot,' n-ʔac-án'k-xən 'sole of foot,' n-ƛ'áq'^w-an'k-xən 'horseshoe' (√ƛ'aq'^w 'to nail').

38 -in'ak 'gun': k^wuɬn-ín'ak 'to borrow (k^wúʔən) a gun,' ʔamh-ín'ak 'good (ʔáma) gun,' n-ʔaʔəz'm-ín'ak 'to trade (n-ʔáʔz'əm) a gun.' There is the residual form -in'k in s-wəl-m-ín'k 'gun' F (√wəl 'fire'). The suffix -in'ak (also -inak in a few cases) occurs in a number of woman's names, e.g., k^wəlamt-ín'ak (k^wəlamt- UC), k'^wwatm-ín'ak (k'^wwátəm 'to step [on smt.]').

39 -inx^w, -anx^w 'weather, wind': haw-haw-l-ánx^w 'warm wind' (√haw 'warm [atmosphere],' -l- connective), ʔaz-ínx^w 'warm weather, clear weather' (√ʔaz 'nice'), x̌'^wal-ánx^w 'sleet, freezing rain' (√x̌^wal UC).

40 n-..-anwas 'heart, inside, mind': n-ciq-anwás-ən 'to stab (ciq) in the heart,' n-qḷ-ánwas-min 'to dislike smt./smb., tr. (-min)' (qəḷ 'bad'), paʔq-ánwas 'heartburn' (paʔq 'red-hot'), n-cut-ánwas (also cut-ánwas) 'to think' (cut 'to say'), n-pəl'p-ánwas 'not feeling well (e.g., when a close relative dies)' (pəl'p 'lost'). Cf. 41 and 88-89. An etymological connection is also suggested with ʔán'was 'two,' via a shared concept of 'in half' (i.e., by splitting smt. in two/half, one obtains the inside).

41 n-..-in'was 'middle': n-k'x-ín'was 'island' (k'x < k'ax 'dry'), n-yəp-ín'was-tən 'centre pole in underground house' (√yəp 'upright'). Cf. 40.

42 -úɬ 'step-relative': sqacəzʔ-úɬ 'stepfather' (sqáczaʔ 'father'), skixəzʔ-úɬ 'stepmother' (skíxzaʔ 'mother'), k^wuzʔ-úɬ 'stepchild' (sk^wúzaʔ 'child, offspring'). This suffix is possibly related to -úɬ 'always' (Section 16[6]).

43 -áɬp/-ɬəp 'tree, bush, plant': sp'ac'n-áɬp 'Indian hemp plant' (sp'ác'ən 'Indian hemp, net made from Indian hemp'), qax^w-m'-áɬp 'white rhododendron' (the name refers to the fact that it is easy to break; √qax^w 'to break,' -əm intransitivizer, glottalization unexplained), pún-ɬəp 'Rocky Mountain juniper' (√pun UC), məlín-ɬəp 'balsam tree (both Amabilis fir and Alpine fir)' (məlín- cf. məlámən 'medicine'). The suffix -áɬp/-ɬəp resembles -az' (126) in function, but -aɬp/-ɬəp is unproductive.

44 -aɬməx 'belly, sack': súp-aɬməx-am 'to scratch oneself on the belly' M, cíq-aɬməx-an 'to stab smb. in the belly,' q^wáɬ'-aɬməx 'to have a belly-ache,' q'c'-áɬməx 'gunny sack' (√q'əc' 'to weave').

45 -aɬc'aʔ, -ɬc'aʔ 'meat, inside of body; mind, thoughts': zaxn-áɬc'aʔ 'to pack meat from a deer (or other game-animal)' (záxən 'to carry on

one's back'), kʷusuh-átc'aʔ 'pork' (kʷusú 'pig'), n-k'áx-a∤c'aʔ 'consti-pated' (k'ax 'dry'), k'áx-∤c'aʔ 'to dry meat,'ník'-∤c'aʔ 'to cut (nik'-) meat,' n-q!-ą́∤c'aʔ (also q!-ą́∤c'aʔ) 'mean(-spirited)' (qą! 'bad').

46   -a∤na∤ 'fish intestines': qʷʔ-á∤na∤ 'intestines of sturgeon' (√qʷuʔ 'string, line'), t∤-á∤na∤ 'intestines of fish' (√tə∤ 'to string across'). Both words recorded from CM only.

47   -a∤niw't, -∤niw't 'side of body': sup-a∤níw't-əm 'to scratch the side of one's body,' n-c'əkʷʔ-a∤níw't 'left (n-c'əkʷʔ-) side of body,' n-zəh-a∤níw't 'right (n-zəh-) side of body' (also recorded n-zah-∤níw't), n-pəs-pəs-∤níw't 'soft spot on side of body (between lowest rib and hip)' (√pəs UC). Note also n-∤niw't 'side of body.'

48   -a∤xʷ 'house, place where smt. happens, where smt. is': ʔalkʷi∤-á∤xʷ 'place for babysitting (ʔálkʷi∤), daycare centre,' xʷik'm-á∤xʷ 'shed for butchering fish (xʷík'əm),' xʷəman-á∤xʷ 'store' (xʷimán 'to run a store'), ʔalsm-á∤xʷ 'hospital' M (ʔálsəm 'sick' M), lamxal-á∤xʷ 'church' M (lámxal 'to pray'), say'sz'-á∤xʷ 'gym, gymnasium' (sáy'səz' 'to play'). In the meaning 'place where smt. happens/is,' -a∤xʷ overlaps with 9.1 and 16.1: cf. lamxal-á∤xʷ with lámxal-tən (16.1), and ∤x̌ʷəmx-á∤xʷ 'lodge for pubescent girl' (∤x̌ʷumx 'pubescent girl or boy,' usually in the re-duplicated form ∤x̌ʷə́x̌ʷm'əx) versus n-∤x̌ʷə́x̌ʷm'əx-tən 'lodge for pu-bescent girl.' There is a residual form -∤əxʷ in -qin-∤əxʷ (109.3), and in qʷúλ'-∤xʷ-am 'to chink a house' (√qʷuλ' 'to plug').

49   -a∤qʷəlt 'throat': súp-a∤qʷəlt-am 'to scratch one's throat,' n-cíq-a∤qʷəlt-an 'to stab smb. in the throat,' zəʔ-á∤qʷəlt-am 'to refuse food' (about a child or a grown-up when he is angry; √zəʔ 'fed up, dis-gusted'), k'áx-a∤qʷəlt 'to have a dry throat' (k'ax 'dry'). In a few cases we have -u∤qʷəlt: n-ʔucz-ú∤qʷəlt-am 'to clear one's throat' (ʔúcəz 'good, okay'), q'aʔz-ú∤qʷəlt 'Adam's apple' (recorded from SM only; q'aʔz- UC).

50   -i∤az' 'tree, bush, plant' (used mainly with numerals): pál?-i∤az' 'one (pála?) tree, bush, plant,' ʔan'was-í∤az' 'two (ʔán'was) trees, bushes, plants.' Note also p'un-í∤az' 'wormwood' (√p'un UC). Cf. 126 for the element az'.

51   -ala 'container': puxʷtn-ála 'mast, sail-pole' (púxʷtən 'sail'), s-ləm-ála 'bottle' M (lam 'liquor').

52   -álap/-lap 'form, shape': ∤q'-álap 'wide (object)' (∤əq' 'wide [person]'), n-cw-álap-ən 'to copy smt.' (√cəw 'design'), n-síx̌-lap-ən 'to copy smt.' (√six̌ 'to move').

53   -ílap, -lap 'floor': x̌l-ílap 'floor' F (√x̌əl 'to build'), qʷíx̌ʷ-lap 'floor' M (√qʷix̌ʷ cf. qʷíx̌ʷ-c-tən 'porch,' -c [18a]), zəx̌-láp 'to crawl on the floor' (√zəx̌ 'to move'), c'áw'-lap 'to wash (c'aw'-) the floor.'

54   -iĺap 'pants': cənəmən-íĺap 'denim pants' (cénəmən 'Chinese, "China-man"'), s-λ'p-íĺap 'undershorts' (√λ'əp 'clothing' or √λ'əp 'deep'), xʷəλ'min-íĺap 'buckskin (xʷəλ'min-) pants.'

55 -íl'əm 'load, firewood': ʔutxʷ-íl'əm 'to bring in firewood' (semantically virtually identical to ʔutxʷ-úsləp' [28]; ʔutxʷ 'to enter'), xaX̌'-íl'əm 'to unload a car, boat, or wagon' (√xaX̌' 'to take out').

56 n-..-al'im'at '(back of) neck': n-sup-al'im'át-əm 'to scratch one's neck,' n-ʔal-ál'im'at '(back of) neck' (n-ʔal- 'convex or concave surface'), n-xʷas-al'im'át-əm 'to rub one's neck with liniment' (√xʷas 'to rub on liniment').

57 -almixʷ

   (a) 'earth, land, soil': zax-almíxʷ-az' 'white pine' (√zax 'long'), yək-yík-almixʷ 'trees fall down to earth' (√yik 'tree falls down': special variant of √zik id., see n. 11 of Section 1). Probably also in ʔúxʷalmixʷ 'Indian, human being.' Cf. 58 and tmixʷ 'earth, land.'

   (b) 'udder, breast': p'ʔ-álmixʷ 'to milk' (√p'iʔ 'to squeeze smt. out'), x̌ə-x̌zúm-almixʷ 'to have big (x̌zum) breasts.'

58 -úlm'əxʷ/-lum'əxʷ 'earth, land, soil': qʷəcp-úlm'əxʷ 'earthquake' (qʷəcp 'to shake'), huʔqʷ-úlm'əxʷ 'land is freezing up' (huʔqʷ 'getting frozen'), hiʔ-úlm'əxʷ 'ground inhabited by hiʔ (a powerful spirit, supernatural being),' pús-lum'əxʷ 'wet (pus) land,' n-c'ám'-lum'əxʷ-tən 'deer-lick' (√c'am' 'to lick'). Cf. 57a.

59 -alt 'child, offspring': q'amaz'-ált 'young teenage girl' (q'ámaz' 'teenage girl'), s-k'zuz-ált 'twins' (k'zuz 'to have twins'), ʔamh-ált-əm 'to like smb. as a marriage partner for one's child' (ʔáma 'good'), tam-ált 'doe with antler (hermaphrodite)' (√tam UC). There are residual forms in s-cm-al't 'children, multiple offspring' (cm- UC) and kʷís-lət 'to give birth' (kʷis 'to drop'). Cf. 60.

60 n-..-il't 'child, offspring': n-x̌ʷz-íl't-əm 'to love (√x̌ʷəz) one's children,' n-ʔús-il't-əm 'sun-dog, ring around the sun' (literally 'he [the sun] throws his children out,' ʔus 'to be thrown out'), n-ʔaʔx̌ʔ-íl't 'child of an Indian doctor' (ʔáʔx̌aʔ 'spiritually powerful, supernatural'). Cf. 59.

61 -altəxʷ, -al'təxʷ, -əltxʷ

   (a) 'outside cover, skin': súx̌ʷ-altəxʷ 'outer redcedar bark' (√sux̌ʷ cf. √səx̌ʷ 'to take off'), kʷt-áltəxʷ 'cattails (botanical item)' (kʷt- UC), X̌'n-ál'təxʷ 'bulrushes' (X̌'n- UC), s-t-páˤ-əltxʷ 'grey (paˤ-) horse,' s-t-p'úm-əltxʷ 'buckskin-coloured horse' (√p'um 'to smoke'), s-t-q'ʷút-əltxʷ 'brown horse' (√q'ʷut 'scorched').

   (b) 'rib': qaxʷx̌ʷ-áltəxʷ 'to break one's rib' (qáxʷəxʷ 'to break'), c'k-ál'təxʷ (1) 'any rib' M, (2) 'lowest rib' F (c'ək 'all gone').

62 -alc 'house': líˤʷ-alc 'to tear down (líˤʷ-) a house,' s-zík-alc 'log (s-zik) house,' sil-álc 'tent' M (sil 'cloth'), nəqʷ-álc 'warm (nəqʷ) in the house,' pál?-alc-əm 'to visit' (pálaʔ 'one'). Cf. 105.2.

63 -al'c 'rock, hard matter, money (coins)': pq-al'c 'white (pəq) rock,' k'ím-al'c 'to freeze' (k'im- UC), qʷəsm-ál'c 'bullet, arrow' (qʷúsəm 'to shoot'),

n-ɫam'-áɬ'c 'loaded (gun)' (n-ɫam'-án 'to load it, tr.'), x̌k-áɬ'c-əm 'to count money (coins only)' (cf. x̌k-ús?-am 'to count money [paper or coins]'), n-ʔaʔz'əm-áɬ'c 'to change money' (n-ʔáʔz'əm 'to trade').

64   -alckzaʔ 'leaf': záx-alckzaʔ 'long (zax-) leaf,' pús-alckzaʔ 'wet (pus) leaf,' X̌'imin-álckzaʔ 'broad-leafed plantain' (referring to veins in leaf, X̌'ímin 'vein, sinew'), kaw-álckzaʔ 'yarrow' (kaw- UC). A residual form is -əlckzaʔ/-ləckzaʔ in wáw-əlckzaʔ/wáw-ləckzaʔ 'poplar' (√waw 'to shout').

65   -lac' 'penis': x̌zúm-lac' 'to have a big (x̌zum) penis,' ɫəxʷ-lác' 'conduit on baby-basket, for urinating through' (√ɫəxʷ 'to put on clothing'), paʔxʷ-lác' 'to get tired of having sexual intercourse' (paʔxʷ 'fed up'). There is a residual form -yac' in a few nicknames: kʷ'úc'-yac' 'crooked (kʷ'uc') penis,' wəp-yác' 'hairy (wəp-) penis.'

66   -ɬ'us '(saskatoon) berry': s-X̌'əx-ɬ'ús 'sweet (X̌'əx) saskatoon berry,' s-təx̌-ɬ'ús 'bitter (təx̌) saskatoon berry.' Cf.? 67.

67   -al's 'food': qʷc-áɬ's-əm 'to stir food' (√qʷəc 'to shake'), ph-áɬ's-əm 'to wind-clean berries, beans, etc.' (ph- UC, cf. Squamish √pəh 'blow'). Cf. 18.1.

68   -al'us 'colour': ʔixʷɫ-áɬ'us 'to be of a different (ʔixʷɫ) colour,' nak'-al'ús-əm 'to change (nak'-) the colour on smt., intr.' Combined with colour terms, -al'us refers to a lighter variant of that colour, or expresses 'almost': pq-áɬ'us 'almost white (pəq),' cəqʷ-cáqʷ-al'us 'sort of reddish, pinkish' (cəqʷ-cáqʷ 'reddish, pink'). Cf.? -al'us (22.3).

69   -al'us 'matter (in a wide sense)': s-X̌'úp-al'us 'tree is twisted' (s-X̌'up 'twisted'), q'íx̌-al'us 'hard to split (wood), timberbound' (q'íx̌ 'hard, firm'), s-X̌'p-áɬ'us 'bottom line on gillnet' (X̌'əp 'deep'), c'məʕʷt-áɬ'us 'fishnet is badly gone' (last item from CM only; c'məʕʷt- 'badly gone, worn out'), ɫkʷ'-áɬ'us '(to make a) basket' (√ɫək'ʷ 'to pierce': piercing a basket in progress to weave in new material is part of making the basket).

70   -al'st 'rock' (refers to rocks as material [cf. German *Gestein*] not to in-dividual rocks; like -al'c [63]: s-kʷ'ḷ-áɬ'st 'jade' (√kʷəḷ 'yellow, green'). We have the form -ḷ'əst in s-ḷiw-ḷ'əst 'sharp, little rocks' (√ḷiw UC).

71   -alín
   (a)   'basket': cəp-alín 'baby-basket, basket cradle' (√cəp UC), qʷəɫ-alín 'birchbark basket' (cf. qʷə́ɫ-ʔin 'birchbark').
   (b)   (in the shape -ạ́ḷin) 'container (?)': caʔk-ạ́ḷin 'metal cools off (caʔk),' k'əx̌m-ạ́ḷin (name of a mountain over which the wind [k'ə́x̌əm] is always blowing).

(—) -al'nup: see 36.

72   n-..-al'naq 'from the back': n-pkʷ-áɬ'naq 'to spill berries (from basket worn on back)' (√pəkʷ 'to spill').

73   -al'k 'surface': qɫ-áɬ'k-an' 'to cover smt. (with tarpaulin, canvas, dirt, hay)' (qə́ɫ-ən 'to put away, bury, tr.'), pt-áɬ'k-an' 'to cover smt. (with a

cloth or canvas)' (pə́t-ən 'to spread smt. out over smt. [like a cloth over a table], tr.'), záw'-al'k-an' 'to scoop smt. off (e.g., cream off milk)' (√zaw' 'scoop'), qʷ't-al'k 'other side (qʷ't-) of border.'

74 -l'íl'ik 'back' or 'water's surface': cəˤ-l'íl'ik-əm 'fish swimming just under the surface (so one can see its back)' (√cəˤ 'to tear'), x̌w'əs-l'íl'ik (also x̌w'əs-l'íl'ik-əm) = (√x̌w'is 'shallow').

75 -al'íkst 'sheet': paqʷ-al'íkst 'to read' (paqʷ 'to look'), pal?-al'íkst 'one (pála?) sheet (of paper),' p+u+-al'íkst 'thick (p+u+) sheet of paper, cardboard.'

76 -alk' 'string, rope': láw-alk'-ən 'to hang up (law-) a baby-basket on a vertical string, tr.,' n-sk-álk'-əm 'to make a phone call' (√sək 'to hit with whip or stick'; refers to hand-cranked phones), n-p'íx-alk'-ən 'to unravel (p'íx-) a rope, tr.' qʷ'l-alk' 'net gets warm and moist (if not properly dried before stored away)' (qʷ'əl 'cooked'), paqm-álk' 'net gets mouldy (if not properly dried before being stored away)' (páq-əm 'mouldy').

77 -ílx/-ləx 'body' (refers to 'body' in a more abstract sense than -al'íw's [90]; -ílx/-ləx in a sense functions also as a reflexive suffix – see Section 17): +qʷ-ílx 'to get on a horse' (s-+əqʷ 'to be on horseback'), xʷp-ílx 'to stand up from lying position' (xʷə́p-ən 'to put smb. on his feet'), ləˤʷ-ílx 'to hide (ləˤʷ-) oneself,' tá+-ləx 'to stand up from sitting position' (√ta+ 'upright'), +úqʷ'-ləx 'to take a blanket off oneself' (+uqʷ' 'naked'), c'áw'-ləx 'to wash (c'aw'-) oneself.'[8]

78 -al'xən 'tube, cylindrical object': p'?-ál'xn-an 'to squeeze out (√p'i?) a tube, to squeeze smt. out of a tube,' sl-ál'xən 'tumpline, headstrap for basket' F (səl 'string'). There is a residual form -ay'xən in q'əq'+?-áy'xən 'smt. braided (esp. a tumpline)' F (q'áq'+a? 'to braid').

79 -alxkən 'outward appearance, hulk, shape': ˤəlˤəl-álxkən 'strong (ˤə́lˤəl) looking,' x̌zúm-alxkən 'husky' (x̌zum 'big'), n-q'ʷz-álxkən 'black (q'ʷz-) hornet,' yəˤ-álxkən 'female mountain sheep' (yəˤ- UC). Semantically, -alxkən overlaps with -al'qʷəm' (86) and -aliwán' (91). A residual form is -ayxkən in k'ax-áyxkən 'tuberculosis' (k'ax 'dry').

80 -aləxʷ 'family': xʷ?ít-aləxʷ 'to have a big family' (xʷ?it 'much, many'). For ə in this suffix, see also Section 3.3.2.

81 -ul'axʷ 'land, earth, soil' (unproductive variant of 58): x̌'l-úl'axʷ 'to plough' (x̌'l- 'to cut into'), x̌ix̌'-úl'axʷ (a place close to Mount Currie, x̌ix̌' UC), nax̌ʷ-úx̌ʷ'l'axʷ 'coyote' (reduplication of *nax̌ʷ-úl'axʷ; nax̌ʷ-cf.? nux̌ʷ 'to gallop').

82 -alxʷca+ 'tongue': q'ʷə+p-álxʷca+ 'to burn one's tongue' (q'ʷə+p 'to get scorched'). Cf. təxʷc̣á+ 'tongue, part of the mouth.'

83 -al'aqs, -al'qs 'clothing': x̌'p-ál'aqs 'underskirt' (√x̌'əp '[under]clothing'), wac-al'áqs 'pocket watch' (not a commonly used word; wac- cf.

English 'watch'), xʷəX̌'min-ál'qs 'buckskin coat' (√xʷəX̌'min 'buckskin clothing').

84   n-..-alaqat 'surface of water': n-kəkaw'-aláqat 'wide body of water' (kəkáw' 'far'), n-təq'-aláqat id. (təq' 'wide'), x̌k'it-aláqat 'this side (x̌k'it) of the water,' tat?-aláqat 'other side (tatá?) of the water.'

85   -alqʷ
   (a)   'cylindrical object (tree, log, stick, etc.)': pál?-aləqʷ 'one (pála?) tree, stick, log,' sq'əm's-álqʷ 'fungus on tree' (sq'əm's 'mushroom'), páx̌-alqʷ-əm 'to scrape a stick or log, take the rough surface off' (páx̌-an' 'to scrape smt., tr.'). Cf. 105.3.
   (b)   'hulk, mass': kən'n'-álqʷ 'to bump (kén'ən') against smt. (like a car bumping into another car or tree, stump, horse),' qam't-álqʷ 'to get hit (qam't) on whole body by a big object (e.g., a car),' səm'p-álqʷ 'all skin and bones (as result of sickness)' (səm'p id., also 'drained out [liquid]').

86   -al'qʷəm' 'outward appearance': ?əmh-ál'qʷəm' 'good-looking' (?áma 'good'), q̓l-ál'qʷəm' 'ugly' (qə̓l 'bad'), ʕəlʕəl-ál'qʷəm' 'strong-looking' (about the same in meaning as ʕəlʕəl-álxkən [79]), záx-al'qʷəm' 'tall' (cf. zax-t 'long').

87   -ul'wat 'stuff, things': qəms-úl'wat 'to tidy up one's stuff, put it away' (qəms-án 'to put it away, clean it up, tr.'), kt-úl'wat 'to castrate' (kə́t-ən 'to take smt. off, apart').

88   -alwas 'lower part of body (below waist)': xʷuxʷX̌'-álwas 'having no pants on' (xʷuxʷX̌' 'naked'), s-X̌'p-álwas 'long underpants' (√X̌'əp '[under]clothing'). Cf. 40, 41, 89.[9]

89   -əl'was 'in half, in the middle, down the middle': cúqʷ-əl'was 'to add a piece (of rope) in the middle' (cúqʷ-xal 'to splice a rope, add on another piece, intr.'), -s-təq-əl'wás 'to have one's hands on one's hips' (√təq 'to touch'), sək'ʷ-əl'wás 'Cayoosh Creek' (refers to a rock there that is split [sək'ʷ-] in half), ti?tx̌ʷ-əl'wás 'midnight' (tí?təx̌ʷ 'right, correct'); -əl'was also allows the pronunciation -l'əwas. Cf. 40-41, 88.

90   -al'iw's 'body': n-zəh-ál'iw's 'right (n-zəh-) side of body,' c̓a?p-ál'iw's 'to have body odour' (c̓a?p 'sour, fermented'), cəx̌ʷ-p-ál'iw's 'to sweat' (cəx̌ʷ- cf. cíx̌ʷ-əx̌ʷ 'stream comes down'). -al'iw's is more concrete than -ílx/-ləx (77): cf. sup-al'iw's-əm 'to scratch one's body' versus súp-ləx 'to scratch oneself (e.g., a dog).'

91   -aliwan' 'size, hulk': x̌zum-aliwán' (also recorded x̌zúm-aliwan') 'husky' (x̌zum 'big'); -iwan' in ʕəlʕəl-iwán' 'husky-looking' (ʕə́lʕəl 'strong'): these items are also found with -alxkən (79), but x̌zum-aliwán' is more correct than x̌zúm-alxkən; qʷəqʷs-aliwán' 'smallish' (qʷiqʷs 'small').

92   n-..-k 'back': n-súp-k-am' 'to scratch one's back,' n-c'áw'-k-am' 'to wash one's back' (√c'aw 'to wash'), n-c'am'-k 'dorsal fin' (√c'am 'fishbone'),

n-c'ix̌ʷ-k 'to have a sore back, skin on back is damaged (like a horse when the saddle has been scraping its skin)' (√c'ix̌ʷ 'sore, worn out').

93 n-..-k 'middle': n-ʔíʔz'-ək 'to be in the middle (e.g., of three persons in a bed)' (ʔíʔəz' 'enough, sufficient, just right'), n-téx̌ʷ-tx̌ʷ-ək 'to be in the middle' (√təx̌ʷ '[to go] straight').

93.1 -k-əc 'jaw' (with -c [18a]): s-x̌áw'ən'-k-əc 'jaw, chin' (x̌áw'ən' 'low'), q'zúz'x̌ʷ-k-əc 'jaw, chin' (√q'zux̌ʷ 'cross, X'). Most speakers use only s-x̌áw'ən'-k-əc.

94 -k 'weeds, roots': c'áq-k-am' 'to weed, pull out (c'aq-) weeds,' ʔák'ʷ-k-am' 'to rake (ʔak'ʷ-) weeds,' máys-k-am' 'to fix roots before weaving them into a basket' (mays- 'to fix'), ʔúcəz'-k-am' = máys-k-am' (ʔúcəz 'good, okay'; glottalization of z in ʔúcəz'-k-am' may be a misrecording).

95 -akaʔ

(a) 'hand, arm, finger': sup-akáʔ-əm 'to scratch one's hand,' n-ʔal-ákaʔ 'shoulder' (n-ʔal- 'concave or convex surface'), ɬəsp-ákaʔ 'to have a rash (ɬəsp) on one's hand,' s-kəlʔ-ákaʔ 'index finger' (kélaʔ 'first'), qʷm-ákaʔ '(lump on) wrist.' Cf. also 109.4.

(b) 'wind': sutik-ákaʔ 'north wind' (sútik 'winter'), s-ʕəptn-ákaʔ 'west wind' (s-ʕáptən 'west').

95.1 -l-akaʔ 'instrument, tool': məc-l-ákaʔ 'pencil, pen' (méc-ən 'to write, tr.'), ƛ'əqʷ-l-ákaʔ 'hammer' (ƛ'áqʷ-an 'to hammer smt., hammer a nail into smt., tr.'), kʷzusəm-l-ákaʔ 'tool' (kʷzúsəm 'to work'). The difference between -l-akaʔ and -mən, -tən (9, 16) seems to be slight: cf. kʷʼəx̌-l-ákaʔ 'rattle, smt. to rattle with' and kʷʼəx̌-mən id. (√kʷʼəx̌ 'to rattle').

96 -akst/-kst

(a) 'hand, arm': ƛ'áq-əm-kst/ƛ'áq'-m-əkst 'six' (ƛ'aq' 'to cross over,' -əm intransitivizer; the word refers to crossing over to fingers of the other hand when counting), kʷəl-m-ákst 'yellow tree moss (*Evernia vulpina*)' (√kʷəl 'yellow, green'), kxm-akst 'tree-branch' (kxm- 'to walk along'). Note also s-kʷakst 'hand, arm' (with either -akst or -kst; the root might be related to kʷam/kʷan 'to take, intr./tr.'). Cf. 37.1, 109.5.

(b) 'wind': psx̌ix̌nəm-ákst 'northwest wind' (psx̌íx̌nəm 'Chilcotin Indian'; the Chilcotin inhabit a region northwest of the Lillooet), xʷapm
əx-ákst 'east wind' (s-xʷápməx 'Shuswap').

97 -íkən/-kən 'back': s-kɬ-íkən 'fat from an animal's back (deer, cow, etc.)' (√kəɬ 'to take off, apart'), sáx̌ʷ-kən 'dorsal fin, ridge on back' (√sax̌ʷ 'to pull smt. right off'), s-x̌ic'-kən' 'back' (√x̌ic' UC). A number of words ending in ikən' or kən' might contain this suffix, e.g., n-waníkən' 'fisher (animal)' (wan- not attested elsewhere).

98 n-..-kin'-us 'forehead' (combination of -kin' [limited to this combination],

and -us 'face'): n-sup-kin'-ús-əm 'to scratch one's forehead,' n-ʔáĺ-kin'-us 'forehead' (n-ʔal- 'concave or convex surface,' glottalization of I unexplained), n-təq-kin'-ús-əm 'to cross oneself, to make the sign of the Cross' (√təq 'to touch'), zus-kin'-ús-tən 'bandanna, ribbon on one's hair' (√zus 'to bandage, tie on').

99   -iknəx 'shoelace': ʕəc-íknəx-tən 'shoelace' (√ʕəc 'to tie'), ʕəc-íkənx-am 'to tie one's shoelaces' (-am intransitivizer). The variant -ikləx was also recorded, but seems to be substandard.

100   n-..-kilumaʔ 'eyebrow': n-wəp-kilúmaʔ 'eyebrow' (√wəp 'hair').

101   -kʷaʔ/-kʷa 'water': zél-kʷaʔ 'whirlpool' (√zəl 'to twist, go round'), n-kʷáw-kʷa F 'ice, coming down the river' (√kʷaw UC), n-ʔáxʷ-kʷa F = n-kʷáw-kʷa (s-ʔaxʷ 'slide').

102   -íkʷp/-kʷəp 'fire': c'x̌-ikʷp 'to see (c'x̌-) a fire somewhere,' xʷúĺ-kʷəp 'to drill (xʷul'-) fire.'

103   -kʷ 'around': zál-kʷ-ən 'to wrap smt. up' (√zal 'to twist'), xʷúl-kʷ-ən 'to roll smt. up (e.g., paper, a bedroll)' (xʷúl-un 'to drill, bore, tr.').

104   -xən

(a)   'foot, leg' (-x when before -tən 'implement, instrument'): súp-xn-am' 'to scratch one's foot, leg,' xʷúxʷx̌'-xən 'barefooted' (xʷuxʷx̌'- 'naked,' the reduplication glottalizes -xən), c'áʔp-xən 'to have smelly feet' (c'aʔp 'sour, fermented'), káʔp-xən 'to have sore feet (from walking too much, or from tight shoes),' síx̌-x-tən 'way of walking' (√six̌ 'to move'), zús-x-tən 'puttees, bandage on one's leg, hobble on a horse' (√zus 'to bandage, tie on'), n-múɫac-xən F 'leaf stem of cow parsnip ("wild rhubarb")' (literally 'woman-foot'; s-múɫac 'woman' F), n-qáyxʷ-xən 'bud stem of cow parsnip' (literally 'man-foot'; s-qayxʷ 'man'; the English terms 'woman-foot' and 'man-foot' are used by some speakers when talking in English). Residual forms are -aʔxən and -axən in s-qʷ|úl-aʔxən 'hoof,' s-c'-qʷúl-axən 'big toe' (both with √qʷul, cf. qʷul 'full').

(b)   (element in words referring to deprivation): zúqʷ-xən 'to starve' (also n-zúqʷ-xən; zuqʷ 'dead'), qəl-qəl-xn-án-cut 'to suffer from lack of help' (qəl 'bad'). Cf. also 105b.

104.1   -xín 'shoe': n'an'atxʷ-xín 'slipper' (s-n'án'atxʷ 'morning'), kʷuṣaʔ-xín 'nightslipper' (kʷúṣaʔ 'to urinate [about men]'), q'iɫil-xín 'runner' (q'íɫil 'to run'). There are probable residual forms in x̌əc'ixán' 'white man's shoe' and qʷɫíʔxən id. (both with unanalyzable roots).

104.2   -xín' 'foot': wac-xín' (a type of lizard, said to enter people through the anus and kill them that way; √wac 'excrement'), k'ʷəs-xín' 'poker' (√k'ʷəs 'to singe').

105 n-..-q
(a) 'buttocks, behind, bottom, leg/foot, shoe': n-súp-q-am' 'to scratch one's buttocks,' n-pus-q 'to have a wet (pus) bum (e.g., a baby),' n-kəl'-q 'to back up' (√kəl 'area), n-c'íkʷʔ-aq 'left (n-c'íkʷʔ-) leg, foot,' téxʷp-əq 'to buy (təxʷp) shoes.' This suffix is also used in nicknames (see Section 27.1).

(b) (used in one word referring to deprivation): n-qəl'-q 'to have bad (qəl) luck, to be out of luck (e.g., when hunting)' (cf. s-qəl'-q 'old shoes,' with 105a). Note also 104b: the common background of 104b and 105b might be comparable to English 'knee-deep in trouble.'

105.1 n-..-il'-q, n-..-il'-aq 'crotch': n-zəhaw's-íl'q-min 'to straddle smt., tr. (-min)' (zəháw's- 'middle'), q'ʷúX'-il'-aq 'too much pubic hair' (a nickname, √q'ʷuX' 'to plug').

105.2 -q-al'c 'part of house' (with -alc 'house' [62]; glottalization of -alc caused by -q): kisəm-q-ál'c 'back part (kísəm) of house,' X'aq'ʷ-q-ál'c-tən 'peg of tent' (√X'aq'ʷ 'to hammer, nail'), c'əq'-q-ál'c 'to drip from a leak on the outside of the house' (c'əq' 'to drip'; cf. c'q'-álc 'to drip from a leak on the inside of the house').

105.3 -q-al'qʷ 'penis' (with -alqʷ 'cylindrical object' [85a]; glottalization of -alqʷ caused by -q): sk'lap-q-ál'qʷ 'Coyote's Penis' (name of a rock close to Pavilion, officially known as Chimney Rock; sk'lap is the Shuswap word for 'Coyote').

106 *-aqaʔ 'barrel, cylindrical object' (found only with consonant reduplication of the preceding consonant): sk-ákqaʔ 'to flail things, to use a flail' (reduplication of *sk-áqaʔ; √sək 'to hit with whip or stick'), k'ʷwat-átqaʔ 'to thresh beans' (√k'ʷwat 'to step on smt.'), palʔ-áʔqaʔ 'one (pálaʔ)-year-old buck (has one spike on antler),' ʔan'was-ásqaʔ (1) 'two (ʔán'was)- year-old buck (has two spikes),' (2) 'double-barrelled gun.'

107 -qs 'nose, point, protruding part, direction': s̩-p'əs̩-qs 'nose' (√p'əs̩ UC; cf.? p'əs̩k'aʔ 'hummingbird'), nís-qs-am' 'to blow one's nose' (√nis UC), kʷámp-əqs 'blunt (point)' (kʷəmp 'dull [blade]'), xát-qs-an' 'to lift up (xat-) one end of a log, tr.,' X'iq-qs 'to reach over here (to the tip or end of smt.)' (X'iq 'to arrive here'). There is a residual form -aqs in cuɬ-áqs-ən 'to point a finger at smb. (esp. when angry), tr.' (√cuɬ 'to point at'), ɬxʷ-aqs 'halter for horse' (ɬəxʷ 'to put on clothing').

107.1 n-..-l-əqs 'nose, point, protruding part': n-súp-l-əqs-am' 'to scratch one's nose,' ka-n-péx̌ʷ-l-əqs‿a 'to get a bleeding nose all of a sudden' (√pəx̌ʷ 'to squirt out'), n-x̌zúm-l-əqs 'to have a big (x̌zum) nose,' n-ɬéx̌ʷ-l-əqs (also n-ɬéx̌ʷ-ɬəx̌ʷ-l-əqs) '"snot-nose," "punk," person who is still "wet behind the ears"' (ɬəx̌ʷ cf.? ka-ɬéx̌ʷ‿a 'to come up all of a sudden'). There are the following residual forms: -ul'-qs in n-px̌ʷ-ul'-qs 'to have a bleeding nose (keeps bleeding)' (cf. ka-n-péx̌ʷ-l-əqs‗a above), n-zəxʷ-zaxʷ-úl'-qs 'to have the sneezes' (√zaxʷ UC); -l-aqs in k'əm-l-áqs 'Bridge River' (a reserve situated on a point of land between two rivers; √k'əm 'area'); -y-əqs/-z-əqs in c'ə́k'ʷ-y-əqs/c'ə́k'ʷ-z-əqs 'downy woodpecker' (√c'ək'ʷ UC), túw'-y-əqs 'cucumber' (√tuw' 'to foam,' refers to foam that appears when the tip of a cucumber is cut off and rubbed against the rest of the cucumber to draw out acid), kə́m'xʷ-y-əqs 'truck, car' (√k'əm'xʷ 'to get cut off,' refers to upright radiator on old-style cars, which gives the impression of a cut-off tip).

107.2 -áqs-xən, -əqs-xín 'part of leg' (with 104a, 104.2); the function of -aqs/-əqs is not entirely clear: n-ʕəc-áqs-xən 'hip-joint' (recorded only from SM; √ʕəc 'to tie'), n-ʔal-áqs-xən 'shin' (n-ʔal- 'concave or convex surface'), zənm-áqs-x-tən 'garter' (zánəm 'to go around'; for -xən > -x see 104a), q'il-aqs-xín 'to have one's legs crossed' (√q'il 'to put down').

108 -aqs 'attitude, given to smt.': nukʷʔ-áqs 'friendly' (s-núkʷa? 'friend, relative,' núkʷʔ-am 'to help, intr.'), yaqcʔ-áqs 'chasing after women' M (s-yáqca? 'woman' M), n-mutac-áqs 'chasing after women' F (s-mútac 'woman' F), n-qayxʷ-áqs 'chasing after men (s-qayxʷ).'

108.1 -l-əqs, -y-əqs (hypocoristic suffix, found in proper nouns and pet-names) pípi-l-əqs (pet-name for a baby [pípi]), máh-y-əqs (a woman's name, cf. English 'Ma'), pạ́h-y-əqs (a man's name, cf. English 'Pa'). Note also s-ʔal'qs 'beloved person.'

109 -qin/-qin' 'head, antler': məlx-qín (unidentified type of mushroom; mulx 'stick'), cət-qín/st-qin 'pillow' (cət-/st- UC), s-c'əm-qín 'brains' (√c'əm 'internal body part'), cəm'p-qín 'to come to the end of the valley' (cəm'p 'to come to the end of smt.'), n-q'ʷwís-qin 'axe' M (q'ʷwis-UC), palaʔ-qín 'one (pála?)-year-old buck,' ʔan'was-qín 'two (ʔán'was)-year-old buck,' kat-qín 'three (katás)- year-old buck' (for elision of as, see Section 4.3).

109.1 n-..-la-qin' 'top of head': n-sup-la-qín'-əm 'to scratch the top of one's head,' n-túqʷ-la-qin 'bald-headed' (√tuqʷ 'naked'), n-x̌ətq-la-qín'-tən 'soft spot on baby's head' (s-x̌ətq 'hole'), n-ʔác-la-qin 'crown of head' (n-ʔac- 'concave or convex surface').

109.2 -qin-upa? '(tip of) tail' (with 3): n-pəq-qin-úpa? 'white-tailed' (pəq 'white'), n-qʷəc-qin-úpʔ-am 'to wag one's tail' (√qʷəc 'to shake'), ʕəc-qin-úpʔ-am 'to lead a horse by tying (ʕəc-) it to the tail of the horse in front,' n-ʔəx̌əc'-qin-úpa? 'tail bone' (ʔəx̌əc'-cf.? s-x̌íc'-kən 'back'). A residual form is -qin-ups in k'aʔ-qin-úps-əm = ʕəc-qin-úpʔ-am.

109.3 -qin-ɬəxʷ 'roof': kəc-qín-ɬəxʷ 'top log on roof of log house' (kic-
'to put down'), n-c-qín-ɬəxʷ 'roof' F (c- cf.? kəc- in preceding
item with possible aphaeresis of kə). Cf. 48.

109.4 -qin'-aka? '(tip of) finger' (with 95): qʼʷəx̌ʷ-qín'-aka? 'fingernail'
(qʼʷəx̌ʷ- UC).

109.5 -qin'-kst '(tip of) finger, nail' (with 96): s-cəcəw'-qín'-kst 'bear
cub (hypocoristic term)' (literally 'design [s-cə́cəw'] on claws'),
x̌əcp-qíqin'-kst 'hundred' M (x̌əcp-qíqən'-kst id. F; x̌əcp- cf.
s-x̌əcp-ásq'ət 'week' [-asq'ət 'day']).

109.6 -qin'-xən '(tip of) toe': qʼʷəx̌ʷ-qín'-xən 'toenail' (qʼʷəx̌ʷ- UC).

109.7 -qən 'head' (mainly after UC's): qʼʷúm-qən 'head' (qʼʷum- UC),
s-níɬ-qən 'sunflower root, when still in ground' (cf.? s-niɬ 3S
personal pronoun), s-níq'-qən 'sunflower root, when dug up
and cooked' (niq'- UC). There are the following residual forms:
-uɬ'-qən (in n-k'm-úɬ'-qn-am 'to dive' [k'əm- 'area']), -əɬ'-qən (in
wə́p-əɬ'-qən [a dog's name]; √wəp 'hair'). Note also 1.3, 116.3.

110   -qan'is 'tooth': c'aw'-qan'ís-əm 'to brush one's teeth' (√c'aw' 'to wash'),
qáx̌a?-qan'is 'eyetooth' (s-qáx̌a? 'dog'), qʷál'-qan'is 'to have a tooth-
ache' (qʷal' 'to ache').

111   -qnawɬ/-qniwɬ 'hip': s-ʕəc-qnáwɬ/s-ʕəc-qníwɬ 'to have smt. tied (ʕəc-)
to one's hip.'

112   -qʷ

(a)   'head, top, hair': súp-qʷ-am' 'to scratch one's head,' sək-qʷ-ám'
'to club smb. on the head' (√sək 'to hit with whip or stick'),
wíx-qʷ-am' 'to comb (wix-) one's hair,' qəɬ-qʷ-án' 'to put smt. on
top of smt.' (qə́ɬ-ən 'to put away, to bury'). There is the residual
form -iɬ'-aqʷ in s-X̌'əq'-íɬ'-aqʷ 'albino' (X̌'əq'- cf. s-X̌'iq'-t 'white
matter').

(b)   'animal': qʼʷəx̌-qʼʷíx̌-qʷ 'black (qʼʷəx̌-qʼʷíx̌) animal,' x̌zum'-qʷ
'big (x̌zum) animal' (cf. x̌zúm-us 'to have a big head,' with 22).
As a hypocoristic suffix in sáw't-əqʷ (pet-name for a boy; saw't
'slave').[10]

112.1 n-..-qʷ 'ball': n-?án'was-əqʷ 'two (?án'was) balls (of wool).' Note
pál?-aqʷ 'one (pála?) ball' without n-; n-..-qʷ combines with
'animal' reduplication of numerals and numerical substitutes
(Section 19.1) to express 'egg': n-pə́pəl?-aqʷ 'one egg,' n-x̌əx̌k-qʷ-
án' 'to count (√x̌ək) eggs.' Note also n-lílm'-əqʷ-tən 'eggshell'
(√lim' UC).

113   -ax̌an '(upper) arm': sup-ax̌án-əm 'to scratch one's arm,' wəp-áx̌an
'hair (wəp-) on arm,' n-?ác-ax̌an 'armpit' (n-?ac- 'concave or convex
surface').

114   -ax̌ʷac 'chest': sup-ax̌ʷác-əm 'to scratch one's chest,' kʷətp-áx̌ʷac

'heart is pounding (kʷətp),' qʷʷəqʷʷuʔɬ-áx̌ʷac 'breastbone' (qʷʷəqʷʷúʔɬ 'bone').

115   -awʹtəxʷ 'house': lam-áwʹtəxʷ 'liquor (lam) store.'

116   -awʹs 'middle': s-zəh-áwʹs 'area in between' (zəh- cf. n-zəh- 'right [side]'), s-cqʷ-awʹs 'loincloth, old-time belt' (cqʷ- UC).

   116.1   -awʹs-us 'middle of face' (with 22): X̌ʹəp-awʹs-ús 'racoon' (X̌ʹəp 'deep').

   116.2   -awʹs-xən 'knee': qʹpʹ-áwʹs-xən 'knee, kneecap' (√qʹəp' 'to cover'), ʔac-áwʹs-xən 'knee(cap)' (ʔac- 'concave or convex surface'), mikʹil-áwʹs-xən 'bannock, fry-bread' (kneaded on knees; s-míkʹil 'oil'). Cf. 104a.

   116.3   -awʹs-qən 'head in the middle': n-pʹəlkʹ-záwʹs-qn-am 'to somersault,' also pʹəlkʹ-n-áwʹs-qn-am; pʹəlkʹ-án 'to turn smt. over, tr.'). Cf. 109.7.

117   -awʹs 'group, collective': X̌ʹqʷ-awʹs 'together' (X̌ʹqʷ- UC), yaqcʔ-áwʹs 'man's female relatives (collectively)' (s-yáqcaʔ [1] 'woman' M, [2] 'man's female relative' M), kɬ-áwʹs-ən 'to split up people who are fighting' (kə́ɬ-ən 'to take off, apart, tr.'), mam-áwʹs 'couple' (cf. s-əmʔám 'wife').

118   n-..-awʹs

   (a)   'trail, road': zəwat-áwʹs 'to be a good rider' (√zəwát 'to know'), n-titxʔ-áwʹs (also titxʔ-áwʹs) 'narrow (títxaʔ) trail,' n-X̌ʹáqʹ-awʹs 'to cross (X̌ʹaq') a street' (also n-X̌ʹaqʹ-m-áwʹs with -m- intransi-tivizer), n-qʹayləx-m-áwʹs 'to skip a house (when selling smt.)' (qʹáyləx 'to jump, run away,' -m- intransitivizer),[11] n-ką́h-aw̓s 'railroad track' (kạh 'car, train').

   (b)   'to work during the ...': s-qʹit-áwʹs 'to do smt. during the day (s-qʹit), to work the daytime shift.'

119   -iwʹs 'day': zap-íwʹs (1) 'Sunday,' (2) 'week' (√zap UC; zap-iwʹs also al-lows the variant zəˤp-íwʹs [zəˤp- UC]), ptak-íwʹs 'Monday' (ptak 'to pass by'), cʹəqʷam'-íwʹs 'Saturday' (cʹəqʷam'- UC; cʹəqʷam'-íwʹs also has the variant cʹawʹqʷ-am'-íwʹs, from cʹáwʹqʷ-am' 'to wash [cʹawʹ-] one's hair [-qʷ],' which seems to be a popular etymology and is rejected by my main consultants).

120   -awɬ 'conveyance (car, wagon, boat, canoe)': məys-áwɬ 'to repair (mays-) a car, boat, etc.,' naqʹʷ-áwɬ 'to steal (naqʹʷ) a ride (e.g., on a train),' x̌ʷqʹʷ-awɬ 'to lighten the load on a wagon or truck' (x̌ʷəqʹʷ-xál 'to thin out, lower the price, intr.'), qaxʷxʷ-áwɬ 'car breaks down (qáxʷəxʷ),' n-ʔaʔəzʹm-áwɬ 'to trade (n-ʔáʔzʹəm) a car, canoe, wagon,' kʷuɬn-áwɬ 'to borrow (kʷúɬən) a car, canoe, etc.'

   120.1   -awiɬ

   (a)   'conveyance': ɬwəl-awíɬ 'to miss the train, boat, bus, etc.' (ɬwal 'to be left behind') x̌aqʹ-awíɬ 'to pay for the train, boat, bus, etc.'

(x̌áq'-ən 'to pay smb. for a service, tr.'), n-ʔiʔəz'k-awíɬ 'to be in the middle (n-ʔíʔz'ək) of a canoe,' ʔamh-áwiɬ 'good (ʔáma) car, canoe.'

(b) 'throat' (semantically connected to A through the notion 'container, hollow object'): ʔíq'-awiɬ 'to choke' (√ʔiq' 'to scrape').

120.2 -wiɬ 'conveyance': xíl-wiɬ 'to land a canoe, pull it ashore' (cf. xil-qs 'to land just the front end [-qs]'), ɬúkʷ-wiɬ 'to bail out (√ɬukʷ) a canoe,' p'akʷ-wiɬ 'to get in a boat and set out on a river or lake' (√p'akʷ 'to float'), cúkʷ-wiɬ 'to finish (cukʷ) making a canoe,' ɬəl'-wíɬ 'to make a canoe' (√ɬəl' 'to cut'), k'ʷəp'-wíɬ 'cross-piece of a canoe' (k'ʷəp'- UC), zə-wíɬ 'to make a canoe' (zə- UC).

120.3 -ul-wiɬ 'conveyance, container': məc-úl-wiɬ 'to paint (məc-) a canoe,' x̌'áɬ-ul-wiɬ 'to pitch a canoe, make it crack-resistant with pitch (x̌'aɬ-),' k'ʷás-ul-wiɬ 'to pitch a canoe' (k'ʷas- 'to singe': refers to the pitchwood that is burnt so the soot can cover the canoe), k'ə́ɬ-t-úl-wiɬ (also k'ɬ-úl-wiɬ) 'earthenware pot, crock' (s-k'ə́ɬ-t 'mud'), x̌zúm-ul-wiɬ 'big (x̌zum) bottle, canoe, car,' pálʔ-ul-wiɬ 'one (pála?) bottle, canoe, car,' ʔan'was-úl-wiɬ 'two (ʔán'was) bottles, canoes, cars.' There is a residual form -əl-wiɬ in k'əc'-əl-wíɬ-tən 'cross-piece in a canoe' (√k'əc' 'to fit across').

121 -aya/-ay'a 'body' (less productive than 77, 90): súp-aya 'itchiness, eczema' (√sup 'to scratch'), tiʕʷ-áy'a 'to have a footrace' (√tiʕʷ 'free'), taxʷ-áy'a 'to wrestle' F (may be a nursery variant of tiʕʷ-áy'a, with a semantic shift; taxʷ- UC), xʷic'am-aya 'teeter-totter' (√xʷic' 'one end of a board jumps up'; -am intransitivizer). Note also ɬə́nkaya 'cast-iron pot' and məxáy'a 'birchbark basket' F, which might contain this suffix.

122 -ayúʔ 'people together, crowd': cəkʷ-ayúʔ 'to have a tug-of-war' (√cəkʷ 'to pull'), məx̌'-ayúʔ 'people mixed together (e.g., all kinds of races or people at a gathering)' (√max̌' 'to mix').

(—) -yac': see 65.

123 -ayən 'net, trap': tɬ-áyən '(to put out a) gillnet' (√təɬ 'to string across'), c'x̌-áyən 'to inspect a net or trap (to see if one caught anything)' (c'x̌- 'to see'), məys-áyən 'to fix (mays-) a net.'

124 -ay'ɬ 'child, sympathetic person': zaxn-áy'ɬ 'to pack a baby on one's back' (záxən 'to pack on one's back'), ləqs-áy'ɬ 'favourite child, pet-child' (ləqs- < s-ʔal'qs 'beloved person'), muzmit-áy'ɬ 'charitable person' (múzmit 'pitiful'), nuk'ʷʔ-áy'ɬ 'to be of help' (s-núk'ʷaʔ 'friend,' núk'ʷʔ-am 'to help'), ʔum'n-áy'ɬ 'person who donates to a feast or gathering' (ʔúm'-ən 'to give smt. to smb., tr.').

(—) -ay'lup: see 36.

(—) -ayxkən: see 79.

125 -zaʔ (hypocoristic suffix, found in a number of terms for close relatives):

s-qác-za? 'father' (qac- cf.? qə́qcək 'elder brother'), s-kíx-za? 'mother' (√kix cf.? kə́x-kəx 'elder sister'), s-kʷú-za? 'child, offspring' (kʷu- UC; maybe *kʷuz-: cf. s-kʷaz-úz̓ 'doll' with -uz̓ 'play-'; Section 16[10]).

126 -az̓ 'tree, bush, plant' (usually combines with terms for fruits and vegetables and refers to the tree, bush, plant on which those fruits and vegetables grow): twán-az̓ 'salmonberry bush' (twan 'salmonberry'), xníz̓-az̓ 'gooseberry (s-xniz̓) bush,' pṣúṣ-az̓ 'bitter cherry (pṣuṣ) bush,' ʔápəls-az̓ 'apple tree' (based on a borrowing from English). In a fairly large number of words, we have -az̓ after UC's, e.g., tx̌áɬp-az̓ 'willow' (which might contain the suffix -aɬp 'tree, plant, bush' [43]), cáx̌-az̓ 'spruce,' qʷlít-az̓ 'jackpine.'

In the above examples we have -az̓ only after nominal stems or after UC's. With a verbal stem we have pakʷ-áz̓ (also pkʷ-az̓) 'cedar strips (used when making baskets)' (√pakʷ 'to slice'), also with a different semantic function than after nominal roots. There is one case of -l-az̓ (with the connective -l-), which follows a verbal stem: X̓ək̓ʷ-l-áz̓ 'balsam from balsam tree' (√X̓ək̓ʷ 'to burst open': the balsam is collected by bursting open the balls of pitch on the tree). With UC's we have k̓átl-az̓ 'devil's club' and q̓əm̓l-áz̓ 'broadleaf maple': these cases might contain -l-.

126.1 -az̓-al̓c 'stone' (with -al̓c 'rock, etc.' [63]). The function of -az̓ is unclear here; -az̓ may be the same element as in -az̓-us (22.3): s-pq-áz̓-al̓c 'quartz' (pəq 'white').

15.3. Connectives

Connectives are elements that link certain lexical suffixes to preceding stems. Semantically, connectives are empty, but in a few cases they influence the meaning of the following lexical suffix (see Section 15.1.1). Formally, connectives are C, VC, or CV, the C usually being l or l̓, in fewer cases y z or n (or their glottalized counterparts).[12] Combinations of connectives and lexical suffixes that are semantically special and/or attested in many cases are items 1.2, 18.1, 20.1, 22.3, 95.1, 105.1, 107.1, 108.1, 109.1, and 120.3 in Section 15.2: these cases all have l l̓ for C (also y in 108.1). In addition, connectives occur in a number of residual forms (see, for example, in Section 15.2[3]).

15.4. Residual suffixes

As mentioned at the beginning of Section 15, there are a number of residual suffixes that are devoid of a clear meaning. Historically, some of these suffixes do not seem to be lexical, but rather aspectual or abstract. However, they are classed here as a subset of lexical suffixes. The residual suffixes are as follows:

(1) -a: púl'h-am 'to collect (-am) nuts stashed away by squirrels' (< *púl'-a-am; s-pəl'-púl' 'nuts stashed away by squirrels'). There are a number of roots ending in a, e.g., ʔáma 'good,' pátkʷa 'needle': these might historically contain the suffix a.

(2) -aʔ: núx̌ʷ-aʔ 'sweetheart' (also n'ən'x̌ʷ-aʔ; cf. s-nəx̌ʷ-n'ən'x̌ʷ 'hen' F). A fairly large number of roots end in aʔ, e.g., s-qáx̌a? 'dog,' sáma? 'white person,' pála? 'one,' kə́la? 'first,' kʷúsa̠? 'to urinate (men or animals),' s-qʷsa? 'nephew.' Originally, -a? is probably a hypocoristic suffix. We also have a? as the final part of certain lexical suffixes, e.g., 17, 34, and 95 in Section 15.2.

(3) -i?: kʷl̩-i? 'green, yellow' (√kʷəl̩ id.).

(4) -ap: formative in a few words referring to berries, e.g., s-q'ʷl-ap 'strawberry' (q'ʷəl 'ripe'), c'q'-áp-ən 'to smash up berries, tr.' (√c'əq' 'to pound at smt.'). Possibly an ablaut form of -p (Section 14.1).

(5) -upst: formative in pál?-upst 'eight' (pála? 'one'; for derivation of 'eight' from 'one', cf. Shuswap nkʷ'?u?ps 'eight' and nkʷ'u? 'one,' -ups 'tail' [Kuipers 1974]). Cf.? Section 15.2(4).

(6) -im: doubtful common element in n-kál-im 'to wish to go (along with people on a trip), to feel left out' (√kal 'to follow, pursue'), pun-ím 'to find (pun) a whole bunch (e.g., berries, roots, mushrooms),' nak'-us-ím 'to change (nak'-) one's mind, to decide on one thing but do another thing' (-us 'face, head,' Section 15.2[22]).

(7) -at, -it, -ut: zəw-át-ən 'to know (√zəw),' ʔínw-at 'to say what? intr.' (cf. ʔínw-an 'to say what to him? tr.': for verbal substitutes like ʔínw-at, ʔínw-an, see Section 20), kʷl̩-it 'brass' (cf. kʷl̩-i? 'green, yellow'), qʷal'-út 'to speak, deliver a speech' (√qʷal' 'to speak'), k'c'-ut 'collarbone' (√k'əc' 'to go across [like latch]'). This suffix may be related to -t (Section 14.3).

(8) -atəm, -utəm: sxam-átəm 'stupid (like a young, inexperienced person who cannot do anything right)' (sxam 'foolish'), ləʕʷ-útəm 'Fountain Valley' (√ləʕʷ- 'to hide').

(9) n-..-til'qʷ 'upside down' (?): n-kʷəs-tíl'qʷ 'upside down' (cf. kʷis 'to fall'). Cf. -til'qʷ with -il'-aqʷ (Section 15.2[112a]).

(10) -tk: ʔus-tk 'to catch a fish with a net (esp., a dipnet),' ʔú?s-tək 'to catch a fish with a rod' (ʔus 'to be thrown out').

(11) -ac': formative in a number of animal names: s-əmc-ác' 'groundhog (of the type that occurs around Lillooet)' (cf. √məc 'to write,' refers to pattern on the animal). Without simplex we have txac' 'elk,' ləhác' 'otter,' x̌'úp'z'ac' 'flea.'

(12) -uc': s-q'ʷú+-uc' 'ashes' (√q'ʷu+ 'to burn').

(13) -s: doubtful common element in n-xáx-s-əm' 'to steam (e.g., like insoles or rubber boots that are being aired out)' (xax 'steam'), n-kʷíl'-s-tən (1) 'Creator,' (2) 'sweatlodge' (different meanings recorded from different consultants; √kʷil' 'to prepare'), tə́t-s-əm 'to pound sunflower root (in order to

remove skin)' (recorded from SM only; cf. tət-tət-tə́t 'sound of sunflower root being pounded').

(14) -ən, -ən': xʷít-ən 'to whistle' (cf. xʷit-aká?-əm 'to whistle on one's hands [-aka?]'), q'áx̌-ən' 'curled up' (cf. q'áx̌-ləx 'to curl up'; -ləx 'body'). Maybe also in x̌áw'ən' 'low.'

(15) n-..-an': n-muzmit-án' 'friendly, generous' (múzmit 'pitiful').

(16) -nuxʷ: zúqʷ-nuxʷ 'to kill game' (zuqʷ 'to die, dead'), qə̣l-qə̣l-núxʷ-min' 'to be unfriendly to smb., tr. (-min')' (qə̣l 'bad'). Cf.? Section 16(5). There is a residual form -nəxʷ in kʷíl'-nəxʷ 'to be ready' (kʷil'-ín 'to prepare smt., tr.'), which was recorded in F only (and rejected by M consultants, who prefer kʷəl'-kʷíl' 'all ready to go').

(17) -ənwa‡: muzmit-ənwá‡ 'to help others when they are having a hard time' (múzmit 'pitiful'); as -wa‡ in pzan-wá‡-ən 'to meet smb., to run into smb., tr. (-ən)' (pzan id.; cf. n-wá‡-ən 'to go and meet smb.': the latter form is interpreted as an aphaeresis form of pzan-wá‡-ən with a semantic shift).[13]

(18) -‡a?: hypocoristic suffix (?): n-cáqʷəm-‡a? (a man's name, cf. s-cáqʷəm 'saskatoon berry'). Maybe also in k'ák'‡a? (a type of bug found in dried salmon), n-c'úc'əm'‡a? 'deer fawn,' and (without ?) p'əˤ-p'íˤ'‡a 'frog.'

(19) -‡ən, -‡in': sáw-‡ən 'to ask a question' (√saw 'to ask'), saw-‡ín 'to ask a lot of questions' (for -‡ən ~ -‡ín' cf. sáw-ən 'to ask smb. smt., tr.' ~ saw-ín'-ən 'to question, interrogate smb., tr.').

(20) -a‡qʷaw't: pal?-a‡qʷáw't 'one (pála?) group of people (e.g., people walking together, or relatives).'

(21) -al': s-tup-ál' 'dried salmon pounded up' (√tup 'to punch').

(22) -il: doubtful common element in s-líx-il 'fish-slime' (cf. líx-əlx-ət 'slimy'), wúqʷ-il 'to go downstream in a canoe' (cf. wəqʷ 'to slip into the water, get carried away by water, to drown'). Maybe also in síkil 'tree bark,' s-mík'il '(fish)oil,' q'íⱡil 'to run,' záq'il 'to peek,' xíⱡ'il 'to kneel down,' məq'íl-ən 'to pass at a respectful distance.'

(23) -il': sək-íl'-ən 'to whip (√sək) a child, tr.' Cf.? Section 15.2(60).

(24) -l'əst: element in -ap-l'əst (Section 15.2[1.1]).

(25) n-..-alus: ka-n-tik-alús‿a 'to go to a darker place' (ka-tík‿a 'dusk, evening falls'), ka-n-ƛ'əp-alús‿a = ka-n-tik-alús‿a (ka-ƛ'ə́p‿a 'to get really dark'). The function of this suffix seems to be that of an aspectual suffix or an abstract suffix (cf. Sections 14, 16). However, because of a lack of sufficient examples, we class it with the residual suffixes.

(26) -aluˤʷ 'gall' (?): kʷ'ə‡-alúˤʷ 'to spill (√kʷ'ʷə‡) one's gall (e.g., when somersaulting).'

(27) -ulya?: mək'il-úlya? 'sticky matter' (s-mík'il '[fish]oil'). Since this is the only recorded instance of this suffix, it is impossible to tell whether the underlying shape of the suffix is -ulya?, as given here, or -uya?, with the

medial ! resulting from consonant reduplication. If the underlying form is -u̯ya?, a connection with -ya? ([40] below) is not excluded.

(28) -k: stám'-k-əmx 'to be from where?' (stam' 'what?,' -əmx 'person').

(29) -kal'c 'weeds' (?): s-wa?p-kál'c 'weeds' (wa?p- cf. √wəp 'hair'), ɣi?p-kál'c 'weeds' (ɣi?p 'to grow'). Cf. Section 15.2(94).

(30) n-..-kaw's 'part of a house' (?): n-xa?-káw's 'ceiling' (xa? 'high').

(31) -xʷ: sťəma̧lt-xʷ-íxʷəlt 'calf' F (s-ťəmá̧lt 'cow' F [borrowing from Shuswap]; -xʷ-íxʷəlt reduplication of *-xʷ-ilt, cf. Section 15.2[60]: l instead of the expected l' might be a misrecording).

(32) -axʷ: kʷ?íkʷl'-axʷ 'to dream' (cf. kʷ?íkʷl'-an 'to dream about smt., tr.').

(33) n-..-qalipa: n-təɬ-qalípa-tən 'spinal cord' (√təɬ 'to string across').

(34) -qʷus: wəl-wəl-qʷús-əm 'lightning' (√wəl 'fire'), ʕʷəl-ʕʷəl-qʷús-əm 'lightning' (√ʕʷəl 'fire, to burn'): the first form seems to be the more usual one.

(35) -x̌: formative in a few words referring to noise: ?íƛ'-x̌-c-am' 'to scream' (?íƛ'-əm 'to sing'), qʷəc-x̌-m-áz' 'buckbrush (which makes a rustling sound)' (√qʷəc 'to shake').

(36) -aw': qʷl-áw'-əm 'to pick berries' (qʷəl 'ripe'). Maybe also in s-qlaw' 'beaver,' haláw' 'golden eagle,' s-əmɣáw' 'lynx.'

(37) n-..-iwac: n-kxm-íwac 'to walk over a frozen river or lake' (cf. kxm-akst 'branch, limb' or n-kxm-áml'əqʷ 'stinking currant,' literally 'to walk along a stick [-alqʷ]).

(38) -iw'ən: s-ƛ'p-íw'ən 'shirt' (√ƛ'əp '[under]clothing').

(—) -waɬ: see (17) above.

(39) -wiltən: pəkʷ-wíltən 'part of salmon that is cut away when the fish is still fresh (to prevent the salmon from spoiling)' (pəkʷ- < √pakʷ 'to slice'). Also recorded pəkʷ-wíl'tən, pkʷ-íltən, although probably only one of the recorded variants is the correct one.

(40) -ya?: pə̧m-ya? 'spinning top' (pə̧m-p 'fast'). Cf.? Section 15.2(121) or -az' 'for fun,' Section 16(10).

(41) -?in: qʷəɬ-?in 'birchbark' (cf. qʷəɬ-alín 'birchbark basket').

16
Abstract Suffixes

Lillooet has 11 abstract suffixes that express notions such as 'real, the very one,' 'about to do smt.,' 'willing to do smt.,' 'for fun, playfully,' and so on. Most of them are somewhat aspectual in character. However, I do not list them with the aspectual suffixes (Section 14) because the suffixes here belong to a more 'outer layer' of the morphological system. Those in Section 14 operate immediately on the root, whereas the ones here, where they co-occur with lexical suffixes, are separated by these from the root (in a few cases we even have abstract suffixes preceded by [in]transitivizers). There is also a formal difference between the suffixes here and in Sections 14.1 to 14.4: the latter are of the shape -(ə)C or -CəC, whereas the ones here are more complex (all contain a vowel A, and most are 'strong,' i.e., always stressed; for stress, see also Section 2.1[6]).

The abstract suffixes are listed below in the alphabetical order used for the lexical suffixes (explained in Section 15.2).

(1) -ám, -ám 'almost, but not quite': nuʔqʷ-ám 'it gets a little warmer, after having been really cold' (nuʔqʷ '[weather] gets warm'), nəqʷ-nuqʷ-ám 'it is getting warm (weather)' (nəqʷ-núqʷ 'warm [weather]'), ka-siʕʷ-ám‿a 'to get better (in health)' (cf. səʕʷ-síʕʷ-ləx 'to get limbered up, do warm-up exercises,' -ləx 'body', √siʕʷ 'loose'), siʕʷ-ám-ən 'to loosen smt., make it looser, tr.' (√siʕʷ 'loose'), k̓ík̓t̓-ám 'closer' (k̓ík̓ta 'close'), ka-c̓aw̓-ám‿a 'it almost got clean (but there is still a stain in it)' (√c̓aw̓ 'to wash'), ka-n-k̓c̓-ám̓‿a 'it did not fall right in, it went sideways' (√k̓əc̓ 'to go across [like a latch]'). With a less clear function, we have ʔəmh-ám 'good (ʔáma) at smt.,' n-ƛ̓p-am 'deep (ƛ̓əp) pit, deep bottom,' sx-am 'foolish, silly' (sə́x-səx 'partly crazy').

(2) -mínst 'almost' (might contain the reflexive suffix -st [Section 17.1]): pəq-mínst 'almost white (pəq),' qʷəz-qʷaz-mínst 'almost blue (qʷəz-qʷáz)' (after colour terms, -mínst has about the same function as -al̓us, Section 15.2[68]]), ʕəlʕəl-mínst 'kind of strong (ʕə́lʕəl),' kʷís-minst 'drizzling' (kʷis 'to rain').

(3) -m'íx 'all the time, getting carried away doing smt.': ʕʷuy't-m'íx 'to sleep (ʕʷuy't) in,' nshaw-m'íx 'yawning (nshaw) all the time,' nq'san'k 'to get carried away laughing (nq'san'k),' matq-m'íx 'to walk (matq) and walk, without getting a ride,' szik-m'íx 'log (szik) fallen by itself (nobody felled it).'

(4) -sút 'out of control': q'íƛil-sút 'to run (q'íƛil) around, looking for help,' pǝmp-sút/pǝmp-ṣút 'to run out of control (e.g., a train going through its brakes, or a horse running wild)' (pǝmp 'fast'), qam't-sút 'to get hit (qam't) by accident,' matq-sút 'to wander around without a home' (matq 'to walk, to be on foot'), waz'am-sút 'to bark (wáz'am) for nothing,' zikt-sút 'tree falls by itself, windfall' (zikt 'tree falls'), papla?-sút 'to be all alone' (pápla? 'one person'). Originally, -sút is a reflexive suffix (it has part of that function in the last two examples above), but it has rearranged its function both semantically and formally. (As for the formal aspect: the reflexive suffix is -cut [Section 17.1]; -cut occurs only after transitive stems, whereas -sút occurs only after intransitive stems.) The suffix -sút has the shape -cút after s: kʷis-cút 'to drop, fall (kʷis) by accident.' With -sút following a stem with an intransitivizer, we have, for example, sǝk-xal-sút (1) 'to slug around, to swing a club or stick around,' (2) 'to jabber away (when not knowing the language one is trying to speak in)' (sǝk-xál 'to hit with whip or stick'), ptinus-ǝm-sút 'to ponder, worry' (ptínus-ǝm 'to think'). Cf. also -st, Section 17.1.

(5) -nuxʷ 'to get somewhere at a certain time' (the time is referred to by the stem): ʕáp-nuxʷ 'to get somewhere when it is dark already' (ʕap '[to be] evening'), psíl'-nuxʷ 'to get somewhere when it is already daylight (psil'),' wǝttam-núxʷ 'to be too late' (cf. wǝtatám' 'late,' recorded from different consultants), n?uc'qa?-núxʷ 'to make it through the winter' (n?úc'qa? 'spring [season]'). Cf.? Section 15.4(16).

(6) -úƛ 'always': ki?kl'-úƛ '(always) lazy' (kí?kǝl' 'unwilling to do smt.'), lulm'-úƛ 'always suspicious, suspecting one's partner of infidelity' (lúlǝm' 'jealous in matters of love'), ?ilal-úƛ 'always crying' (?ílal 'to cry'). In a number of cases this suffix occurs after stems that show total reduplication (with or without consonant reduplication): xǝƛ-xaƛ-úƛ 'diligent' (xǝƛ-xáƛ 'active'), s-qʷǝl'-qʷal'-úƛ 'tattle-tale' (s-qʷal' 'to report'), c'a?-c'a?x-úxƛ 'bashful, shy' (c'a?x 'shy'), pǝqʷ-pǝqʷ?-ú?ƛ 'afraid of everything' (páqʷu? 'to be afraid'), ƛǝp-ƛǝpn-ún'ƛ 'forgetful' (ƛáp-ǝn 'to forget, tr.').[1]

(7) -almǝn 'about to ...': psíl'-almǝn 'about to get light, dawn' (psil' 'daylight'), q'ǝm'p-álmǝn 'nine' (q'ǝm'p 'ten'), c'k-álmǝn 'almost gone, last quarter of moon' (c'ǝk 'finished, all gone'). A residual form is -almín in liʕʷ-almín 'almost falling apart, about to fall apart' (líʕʷ-in 'to take apart, tr.'). Cf. also 8.

(8) -al'mǝn 'to want to ...': q'?-ál'mǝn 'hungry' M (q'a? 'to eat'), ?uqʷ?-ál'mǝn 'thirsty' (?úqʷa? 'to drink'), ʕʷuy't-ál'mǝn 'sleepy' (ʕʷuy't 'to sleep'), kʷus?-ál'mǝn 'to want to urinate (men)' (kʷúṣa? 'to urinate [men]'). Cf. 7.

(9) -wíl'x 'to get into a certain state': ʔama-wíl'x 'to get better, to come back to life' (ʔáma 'good'), qəḷ-wíl'x 'to get spoiled' (qəḷ 'bad'), səx-wíl'x 'to get carried away by smt., to lose oneself in smt., to overdo it' (sə́x-səx 'partly crazy'), q'iǩ-wíl'x 'to get hard (q'iǩ),' qʷic-wíl'x 'to get rich (qʷic).'

(10) -uz', -az' 'for fun, playingly': xman'-úz' 'to play that one is smb.'s enemy' (xman' 'enemy'), səmʔam-úz' 'girlfriend, mistress, "blanketwife"' (səmʔám 'wife'), skʷaz-úz' 'doll' (cf.? skʷúzaʔ 'child, offspring'). With consonant reduplication we have the form ..CúCzaʔ: ləˤʷilx-úxzaʔ 'to play hide-and-seek' (ləˤʷ-ílx 'to hide oneself'), səmʔam-úmzaʔ = səmʔam-úz'. With -az' we have nq'əlx-áz' 'to swim (n-q'áyləx) around';[2] -az' occurs mainly in the combination -az'-am (-am intransitivizer), which expresses 'to pretend to be': ʔuxʷalmixʷ-áz'-am 'to pretend to be an Indian (ʔúxʷalmixʷ)' (also used as a joking reference to East Indians), kʷukʷpy'-áz'-am 'to pretend to be the chief (skʷúkʷpəy'),' ʔaḷsm-áz'-am 'to pretend to be sick (ʔáḷsəm)' M, ɬap-áz'-am 'to pretend to forget (ɬap-),' ləqsay'ɬ-áz'-am 'to pretend to be the pet, the favourite child (ləqsáy'ɬ).'

(11) -ʔúl 'real, original, par excellence, too much': məq'-ʔúl 'too full' (məq' 'full from eating'), sǩiq-ʔúl 'mallard' (sǩiq 'duck'), ʔuxʷalmixʷ-ʔúl 'a real Indian (ʔúxʷalmixʷ),' syəp-ʔúl 'Douglas-fir' (syap 'tree'), ʔaləlna[ʔ]-ʔúl 'youngest child in the family' (sʔalélnaʔ 'youngest in the family,' sʔalánaʔ id. [either child or grown-up]; glottalization of l in -ʔul' due to reduplication of preceding segment), szik-ʔúl 'just a log' (szik 'log'). Occasionally, -ʔúl is used to refer to the original meaning of a word that has acquired additional meanings in recent times, e.g., sqlaw'-ʔúl 'beaver' (versus sqlaw' 'beaver, gold, money': beaverskins were a means of exchange, functioning as money during the early contact period). However, such formations are rarely, if ever, used in conversations where the participants already know which meaning is intended.

17
Reflexive and Reciprocal Suffixes

Lillooet has a reflexive and a reciprocal suffix. Both occur only after transitive stems (i.e., stems with a transitivizer), although both leave at least one formally deviant residual type that occurs after intransitive stems. The productive reflexive and reciprocal suffixes convert the transitive stems on which they occur into intransitive stems (i.e., stems ending in a reflexive or reciprocal suffix select intransitive, rather than transitive, subject suffixes; see Section 22.5.5 for details). We deal with reflexive suffixes in Section 17.1, and with reciprocal suffixes in Section 17.2.

17.1. Reflexive suffixes
The productive reflexive suffix is -cut. Depending on the type of transitivizer that precedes -cut, this suffix may have various functions in addition to its reflexiveness, and it may be stressed or unstressed (see Section 18.6); -cut is purely reflexive when it is stressed and follows transitivizers of the type -Vn/-Vn', as in nuk'ʷʔ-an-cút 'to help (núk'ʷʔ-an) oneself,' x̌ʷəm-ən-cút 'to hurry' (x̌ʷəm 'fast, quick'), ɬuq'ʷ-un'-cút 'to undress (ɬúq'ʷ-un') oneself.'

As we have seen in Section 15.2(77), the suffix -ílx/-ləx 'body' also has a reflexive function (or at least one that often translates as a reflexive). The difference between -ílx/-ləx and -cút appears to be that -ílx/-ləx clearly refers to bodily actions and positions, whereas -cút operates on a more abstract level. There are a few cases of both -ílx/-ləx and -cút after the same root: wəq'ʷ-ílx 'to throw oneself into the water (in order to drown oneself)' versus wəq'ʷ-an-cút 'to drown oneself' (wəq'ʷ 'to get carried away by the water, to drown');[1] ɬuq'ʷ-ləx 'to take a blanket off oneself' (ɬuq'ʷ 'naked') versus ɬuq'ʷ-un'-cút above.

Etymologically, -cút is related to -sút (Section 16[4]).[2] There is a purely reflexive (not abstract) residual form of -sút: -st, in c'íx̌ʷ-st 'to spawn' (literally 'to wear oneself out'; √c'íx̌ʷ 'sore, skin is damaged, worn out'; the word c'íx̌ʷ-st refers to the fact that salmon die very shortly after spawning).

We may have -st in the suffixes -manst (Section 15.2[12]), and -minst (Section 16[2]).

17.2. Reciprocal suffixes

The productive reciprocal suffix is -twaɬ, as in núkʼʷʔ-an-twaɬ 'to help (núkʼʷʔ-an) each other.' There is a residual type -atwʼaxʷ, which is used in tup-atwʼáxʷ 'to box (sport)' (√tup 'to punch') and in təq-atwʼáxʷ 'to wrestle' (√təq 'to touch'), and perhaps also (in the shape -twaxʷ) in qʼəltwáxʷ '(to wage) war' (the element qʼəl is not attested in other derivations). Besides tup-atwʼáxʷ and təq-atwʼáxʷ, we have túp-unʼ-twaɬ 'to punch each other' and təq-ən-twáɬ 'to touch each other.'

18
Intransitivizers and Transitivizers

As we saw in Section 8.1.1, Lillooet stems fall into transitive and intransitive types. Transitive stems are always marked by a transitivizer, and are the only ones that may (in fact, must) take a reflexive, reciprocal, or object suffix. For example, from ʔác'x̌-ən 'to see smt., tr' (-ən transitivizer) we may form ʔac'x̌-ən-cí-ɬkan 'I (-ɬkan) see you' (-ci 2S obj. suffix). Intransitive stems fall into those that are marked by an intransitivizer (e.g., ʔác'x̌-əm 'to see, have vision'; -əm intransitivizer), and those that are unmarked (e.g., ʔac'x̌ 'to be seen'). Intransitive stems may not take reflexive, reciprocal, or object suffixes (hence *ʔac'x̌-əm-ci-ɬkan and *ʔac'x̌-ci-ɬkan are excluded).[1]

There are various types of intransitivizers and transitivizers, each with special functions. Moreover, the same (in)transitivizer may have different functions, depending on the type of stem to which it is attached, i.e., depending on whether it is attached to a plain stem (a stem without lexical or abstract suffixes), to a stem with a lexical or abstract suffix, or to a verbal or nominal stem.

Finally, with regard to the choice of transitivizer, we must (1) know whether or not the transitivizer is followed by the reflexive suffix -cut (Section 17.1); (2) know whether or not the stem already contains a transitivizer followed by a reflexive or reciprocal suffix; and (3) distinguish between stems that do not have the stative prefix s- or the resultative combination ka-..ʲa (see Sections 10.1.2 and 10.1.3), and stems that do have any of these markers.

The above parameters, together with the sections in which they are discussed, are as follows:

1 Stems without s- or ka-..ʲa
   (a) verbal plain stems: 18.1
   (b) verbal stems with somatic lexical suffixes: 18.2
   (c) verbal stems with non-somatic lexical suffixes: 18.3

(d) nominal stems (with or without nominalizing lexical suffixes): 18.4

(e) verbal or nominal stems with abstract suffixes: 18.5

(f) stems with -cut after the transitivizer: 18.6

(g) stems with a reflexive or reciprocal suffix followed by a transitivizer: 18.7

2 Stems with s- or ka-..._a: 18.8

To provide a frame of reference, the main types of (in)transitivizers are as follows. A complete list of all types and subtypes of (in)transitivizers, with references to their function in Sections 18.1 to 18.8, is given in Section 18.9.

1 Intransitivizers

(a) -xal

(b) m-intransitivizers (symbolized **M**): -əm -əm' -Am

(c) zero (unmarked stems)

2 Transitivizers

Type I

(a) -s

(b) -ən-s

Type II

(a) n-transitivizers (symbolized **N**): -ən -ən' -An -An' -an

(b) -nun/-nun'

(c) -min/-min'

(d) -xit

(e) -min-xit/-min'-xit

Transitivizers of type I require formally different object suffixes than transitivizers of type II (for details, see Section 22.3.2).

18.1. Plain stems

Here we discuss the function and distribution of (in)transitivizers after plain stems (stems without lexical or abstract suffixes). We discuss intransitivizers in Section 18.1.1 and transitivizers of types (Ia), (Ib), (IIa), and (IIb) in Section 18.1.2. In Section 18.1.3 we compare the functions of these four types, and in Section 18.1.4 we discuss types (IIc), (Iid), and (IIe). Overall remarks on the distribution of (in)transitivizers are made in Section 18.1.5, and in Section 18.1.6 we discuss special cases.

18.1.1. Intransitivizers

We have the following intransitivizers:

(a) -xal: k'áx-xal 'to dry smt.' (k'áx '[to be] dry'), púɫ-xal 'to boil smt.' (√puɫ 'to get boiled'),ník'-xal 'to cut (√nik') smt.,' q'ʷəl-xál 'to roast, cook smt.' (q'ʷəl 'cooked, done, ripe'), páqʷuʔ-xal 'to scare people' (páqʷuʔ 'to be afraid'), X̌'íq-xal 'to bring (here)' (X̌'iq 'to arrive [here]').

(b) m-intransitivizers (symbolized M): -əm, -əm' (the latter mainly after stems with consonant reduplication), e.g., ʔác'x̌-əm 'to see, have vision,' kʷzús-əm 'to work,' sáxʷ-əm 'to take a bath,' qʷúqʷs-əm' 'to hunt small animals' (reduplication of qʷús-əm 'to shoot'). Unstressed *Aʔ-əm yields ʔ-am (see Section 3.5), e.g., *núkʷʷaʔ-əm > núkʷʷʔ-am 'to help' (cf. s-núkʷʷaʔ 'friend'). There are a few unproductive cases with -Am (see Section 18.1.6).

(c) zero (unmarked stems): k'ax '(to be) dry,' qʷʷəl '(to be) ripe, cooked, done,' páqʷuʔ 'to be afraid,' X̌'iq 'to arrive (here),' x̌zum '(to be) big,' ʔac'x̌ 'to be seen,' qam't 'to get hit,' ʔúqʷaʔ 'to drink.'

Virtually all verbs with -xal, a number of those with -M, and some unmarked verbs imply reference to an undergoing object, e.g., k'áx-xal, ʔác'x̌-əm, ʔúqʷaʔ above. Such verbs may combine with an object complement (but not with object suffixes!), e.g., waʔ k'áx-xal ki̱ məxáz'‿a 'she is drying huckleberries (məxáz').'[2] The remaining verbs with M, and some unmarked verbs, are medial-reflexive in character, e.g., sáxʷ-əm, kʷzús-əm, X̌'iq. Remaining cases of unmarked verbs are passive in character, e.g., qam't, x̌zum. Neither the medial-reflexive nor the passive cases can take object complements.[3]

Remarkably, stems with -xal change -xal to -əm' when the root of such stems is subjected to consonant reduplication, e.g., n-síx̌-xal 'to put it from one pot into another' (√six̌ 'to move') > n-sísx̌-əm' 'to transfer it from one pot into different pots.'[4]

18.1.2. Transitivizers (Ia), (Ib), (IIa), and (IIb)

We have the following transitivizers:

Type I

(a) -s (-c after stems ending in s or ɬ): X̌'iq-s 'to bring (here)' (X̌'iq 'to arrive [here]'), qam't-s 'to hit' (qam't 'to get hit'), nas-c 'to take along' (nas 'to go'), x̌iɬ-c 'to do smt.' (√x̌iɬ 'to work out'), qʷal'út-s 'to speak to smb., to admonish, rebuke smb.' (qʷal'út 'to speak, hold a speech'), xʷítən-s 'to whistle (xʷítən) at smb.,' x̌zum-s 'to respect' (x̌zum 'big'), X̌'əx-s 'to like (food)' (X̌'əx 'sweet, tasty').

(b) -ən-s: unproductive, mostly found after bare roots that refer to an implied object, e.g., naqʷʷ-ən-s 'to steal (naqʷʷ) smt.,' qan'ím-ən-s 'to hear (qan'ím) smt.,' q'əm-ən-s 'to swallow' (q'əm-xál 'to swallow, intr.'), láx̌-ən-s 'to bring smt. up (as a topic, as smt. to be remembered)' (cf. ləx̌-láx̌-s 'to remember, tr.'). Unstressed *Aʔ-ən yields ʔ-an-s: ʔúqʷʷ-an-s 'to drink (ʔúqʷaʔ) smt., to drink it up.'

Type II

(a) n-transitivizers (symbolized **N**): these fall into the subtypes -ən, -ən', -An, -An', -an, with the following approximate distribution: (1) -An' (occasionally -An) after most stems CAC, CCAC, with -An'/-An copying the vowel of the stems, e.g., k'áx-an' 'to dry smt.' (k'ax 'dry'),ník'-in' 'to cut smt.' (√nik' 'to get cut'), púɬ-un' 'to boil smt.' (√puɬ 'to get boiled'), x̌zúm-un 'to make smt. bigger' (x̌zum 'big'), ɬút-ṇn' 'to squish smt. soft (esp. a bug)'; (2) -ən after stems CEC, e.g., q'ʷél-ən 'to roast, cook smt.' (q'ʷəl 'cooked, ripe'), mə́c-ən 'to write (√məc) smt. down,' and after a number of other stems, e.g., sáxʷ-ən 'to give smb. a bath' (cf. sáxʷ-əm 'to take a bath, intr.'), ʔác'x̌-ən 'to see smt./smb.' (ʔác'x̌ 'to be seen'), sqʷaɬ'-ən 'to report (sqʷaɬ) to smb.,' pták'ʷɬ-ən 'to tell a legend (ptak'ʷɬ) to smb.,' wəʔáw-ən 'to shout, holler (wəʔáw) at smb.'; *A?-ən yields ʔ-an: *núk'ʷa?-ən > núk'ʷ?-an 'to help smb.'; (3) -an in the remaining cases, e.g., páqʷ?-an 'to scare smb.' (páqʷu? 'to be afraid'),[5] záxt-an 'to make smt. longer' (zaxt 'long'), k'ʷík'ʷs-an 'to make smt. smaller' (kʷikʷs 'small'), x̌əlq'-án 'to roll smt. down' (x̌əlq' 'to roll down').

Stems with -An' change -An' to -ən' when the root of such a stem is subjected to consonant reduplication, e.g., ɬút-ṇn' 'to squish smt. soft' > ɬúɬt-ən' 'to squish it all up'; sák-an' 'to slice smt.' > sásk-ən' 'to slice smt. into thin pieces.' This change parallels the change -xal > -əm' (see Section 18.1.1, last paragraph).

(b) -nun/-nun': indicates that the subject nourishes a certain thought about the object (the content of the thought being expressed by the root). Only a limited number of cases were recorded: wənáxʷ-nun' 'to believe smb.' (wənáxʷ 'true'), kəkza?-nún 'to doubt smb.' (kákza? 'to tell a lie'), xʷ?úxʷ-nun' 'to smell smt.' (xʷ?uxʷ 'to give off smell'), sama?-nún 'to think smb. is a white person (sáma?)' (a rare case of -nun after a nominal stem). A special case is k'ʷís-nun' 'to drop smt. by accident' (kʷis 'to drop, fall'), where -nun' expresses 'by accident.' The distribution between -nun and -nun' seems to be: -nun when stressed, -nun' when unstressed.

18.1.3. Functions of transitivizers (Ia), (Ib), (IIa), and (IIb)

The transitivizer -s, (Ia), has three functions: (1) expressing causitivization, e.g., qam't-s 'to (cause to get) hit,' x̌'iq-s 'to bring' (= 'to cause to arrive here'); (2) referring to the object (addressee) of *verba declarandi*, e.g., qʷaɬ'út-s 'to speak to,' xʷítən-s 'to whistle at'; and (3) expressing that the subject nourishes a certain thought about the object, e.g., x̌zum-s 'to respect,' x̌'əx-s 'to like (food)': here -s forms transitive *verba sentiendi*.

The first two functions are also performed by n-transitivizers: (1) expression of causitivization: k'áx-an' 'to dry smt.' (= 'to cause it to get dry'), ʔác'x̌-ən 'to see smb./smt.' (= 'to cause it to be seen'); (2) referring to the object of *verba declarandi*: sqʷáɬ'-ən 'to report to,' pták'ʷɬ-ən 'to *tell* a legend to,' wə?áw-ən 'to shout at.' The third function, forming transitive *verba sentiendi,* is also performed by -nun/-nun'.

The difference between -s and N with regard to expression of causitivization appears to be that -s does not express control of the subject over the object, whereas N expresses that the subject is in control. For example, in X'iq-s 'to bring (here)' (= 'to cause to arrive here'), the subject causes the object to carry out an action over which the object is in control (i.e., the subject is not in full control, since it has to share control with the object). On the other hand, in qam't-s 'to (cause to get) hit,' the object is not in control over its being hit, but the subject is not in control over the hitting (one does not know in advance whether or not one will score a hit). Hence there is a total lack of control.

However, in k'áx-an' 'to dry smt.' (= 'to cause it to get dry'), the subject is in total control over the object (one can, for instance, put berries in the sun and keep them there until they are dried). Illustrative are the rare cases where we have both -s and N after the same stem, e.g., cuk^w-s 'to finish smt.' versus cúk^w-un' 'to put the finishing touches on smt.' (cuk^w 'to be finished, to quit'); cəm'p-s 'to get to the end of smt.' versus cəm'p-án 'to work on smt. until it is finished' (cəm'p 'finished, having gotten to the end'): one may not know in advance when one will finish smt. (cuk^w-s) or when one will get to the end of smt. (cəm'p-s), but one is more in control when putting on the finishing touches (cúk^w-un') or when working on smt. until it is finished (cəm'p-án). Note also cuk^w-un'-ɬkán̲kɬ 'I (-ɬkan) will (̲kɬ) put the finishing touches on it later,' besides which *cúk^w-s-kan̲kɬ was rejected: although ̲kɬ 'remote future' may be combined with verbs with -s, it apparently combines more naturally with N where there is a choice between -s or N, since N hints at the control that is necessary to make statements about one's future actions.

A final set of examples showing switching between -s and N on the same stem is provided by certain stems that allow final reduplication (Section 12.3). In addition to its aspectual function, this type of reduplication also conveys a certain lack of control. There are a few cases of stems that take N when not subjected to final reduplication, but -s when subjected to this type of reduplication: zəwát-ən 'to know smt.' versus zəwát-ət-s 'to have learned smt. (i.e., after some effort, having no pre-established control over the outcome)'; pták-ən 'to pass by smt.' (see also below for the function of the transitivizer here) versus ptak-ək-?úl-s 'to send smb. right by smt.' (-?úl 'too much,' Section 16[11]); ɬíl-in 'to sprinkle smt.' versus ɬíl-əl-s 'to sprinkle smt. too much, to overdo it when sprinkling smt.' (the last form was elicited after prompting and should therefore be treated with caution). Note also k^wán-ən-s 'to catch smt.,' from k^wán-ən 'to get caught,' itself derived from k^wan 'to catch smt., tr.' with an unusual detransitivizing function of the final reduplication (for kʷan see also Section 18.1.6). For switching between -s and N after the same stem, see also Sections 18.6 and 18.8.

The transitivizer -s may also follow intransitivizers in order to express causitivization, e.g., xáƛ'-xal-s 'to let smb. take things out' (xáƛ'-xal 'to take out [of a container]'), ptínus-əm-s 'to make smb. think' (ptínus-əm 'to think'). These cases show shared control between subject and object.[6]

The notion of control in verbs with n-transitivizers seems to convey that the natural result of the described action does not require a particular effort more than it conveys a notion of complete dominance of the subject over the action. Thus we also have N after certain verbs that by themselves indicate lack of control but do point at a rather easily achieved result, e.g., ɬáp-ən 'to forget smt.' (√ɬap 'to be forgotten, get extinguished') and xík'-ən 'to miss (a target).' Compare the latter example with qam't-s 'to hit smt.': missing a target is easier to achieve and more to be expected than hitting it (which requires a keen eye and a steady hand). In the same way, it is easier to forget something than to remember (ləx̌-láx̌-s) it (the latter sometimes requiring such laborious devices as calendars, agendas, or a piece of string tied around a finger).[7] Note also the n-transitivizer (merged with the root) in pun 'to find smt.,' and -ən in pun-sút-ən 'to find smt. by accident': although both verbs (for which see also Sections 18.1.6 and 18.5) refer to an action over which the subject has no control, finding something itself requires no particular effort. Interestingly, 'to lose smt.' is pəl'p-s, with non-control -s, possibly because from a Lillooet point of view to lose something requires a particular event.

As for referring to the object (addressee) of *verba declarandi,* I do not know why -s is used in some cases but N in others. (Remarkably, qʷal'út-s 'to speak to' and sqʷál'-ən 'to report to' both contain the root qʷal'- 'to speak'; compare qʷal'út > qʷal'út-s also with n-qʷal'ut-ána? 'to hint, drop hints' > nqʷal'ut-án?-an 'to hint to smb.') It is possible that again control is a factor in the choice between -s and N (it might be that from a Lillooet point of view, cases with N suggest that the message does get across to the addressee, while those with -s might suggest that the message may or may not get across).

I do not know why the third function, forming transitive *verba sentiendi,* is expressed by -nun/-nun' in some cases and by -s in others, although the cases with -s seem to suggest a greater subjectivity: it is a moot point whether somebody is worth respect (x̌zum-s 'to respect smb.'), but one can test objectively whether somebody is to be believed (wənáx̌ʷ-nun' 'to believe smb.'). For -s in this third function, see also Section 18.6(1).

There is also a fourth function, i.e., forming non-causative transitivizations of verbs that in general imply an object. This function is served by N

in a few verbs, and by all cases of -ən-s: c'aq' 'to throw' > c'aq'-ən 'to throw
smt. at smb., to bethrow smb.' (the person that smt. is thrown at is expressed by the object suffix following -ən); ptak 'to pass by' > pták-ən 'to
pass by smt.' (for cases with -ən-s, see Section 18.1.2). I do not know
whether -ən in -ən-s is the transitivizer -ən, or whether -ən is a unique
element, peculiar to this combination. The difference between -ən and
-ən-s in these cases may again be based on control; if so, the basis for such a
distinction eludes me.

The transitivizers (Ia), (Ib), (IIa), and (IIb), together with their functions,
are represented in Figure 6. The broken line indicates that the control cri-
terion is possibly invalid for functions 2 to 4.

Figure 6

Functions of transitivizers (Ia), (Ib), (IIa), and (IIb)

		Control	Non-control
1	Causativizing	N	-s
2	Referring to addressee *(verba declarandi)*	N	-s
3	Expressing a thought *(verba sentiendi)*	-nun/-nun'	-s
4	Non-causative transitivization	N	-ən-s

An interesting case of N versus -s is x̌zúm-un 'to make smt. bigger' (x̌zum
'big') versus x̌zézəm'-s 'to make smt. a little bit bigger' (x̌zézəm' 'a little bit
bigger'), with N and -s in function 1, and x̌zum-s 'to respect,' with -s in
function 3. It is not clear why x̌zúm-un and x̌zézəm'-s have different transitivizers (perhaps 'to make smt. a little bit bigger' is considered to be more
difficult than 'to make smt. bigger': hence, control might again be a factor
here). On the other hand, we have záxt-an 'to make smt. longer' (zaxt
'long') versus zəz'xt-án 'to make smt. a little bit longer' (both with N in
function 1). Besides záxt-an we also have zaxt-s id. (possibly with a different
control function than záxt-an). Compare also ƛ'əx-s 'to like food' (ƛ'əx
'tasty, sweet') with ƛ'əƛ'x-s 'to make smt. a little sweeter,' with -s in functions 3 and 1, respectively. Although ƛ'əƛ'x-s, zaxt-s, and x̌zézəm'-s are
problematic, I do not think they invalidate the schema above. I also recorded ƛ'éx-ən 'to sweeten smt.,' but I prefer to leave this case out of this
discussion because it was recorded after I suggested it.

18.1.4. Transitivizers (IIc) to (IIe)

These type II transitivizers are as follows.

(c) -min/-min' (for the distribution between -min and -min', see below): refers to an object that is affected less drastically than an object referred to by -s, -ən-s or N. Compare the following cases:

ʔiʔwaʔ-mín 'to go along (ʔíʔwaʔ) with'   ʔíʔwaʔ-s 'to take smb. along'
p'án't-min 'to return (p'an't) for smt.,   p'an't-s 'to return smt.'
    to return to get smt.'
kʷútən-min 'to borrow (kʷútən) smt.   kʷútən-s 'to lend smt. to'
    from'
ʔúqʷaʔ-min 'to drink (ʔúqʷaʔ) smt.   ʔúqʷʔ-an-s 'to drink smt. up'
    away, to lose it by drinking'
páqʷuʔ-min 'to be afraid (páqʷuʔ) of   páqʷʔ-an 'to scare smb.'
    smt.'
núk'ʷaʔ-min 'to accompany, go with'   núk'ʷʔ-an 'to help smb.'
ptákʷɬ-min 'to tell a legend (ptakʷɬ)   ptákʷɬ-ən 'to tell a legend to smb.'
    about smb.'
sqʷál'-min' 'to report on smb.'   sqʷál'-ən 'to report to smb.'
c'áq'-min' 'to throw smt.'   c'áq'-ən 'to throw smt. at smb.'
táw-min' 'to sell (taw-) smt.'   táw-ən 'to sell smt. to smb.'
ʔúl'l'us-min 'to join, go with smb.'   ʔúl'l'us-ən 'to gather, bring together'
    (ʔúl'l'us 'to get together')

A case like páqʷuʔ-min/páqʷʔ-an is typical: a person whom one fears (páqʷuʔ-min) is not affected by this fear, but a person whom one scares (páqʷʔ-an) is affected in that he has had fear put into him. In the same way, a person or animal about whom one tells a legend (ptákʷɬ-min) is not affected by the telling of the legend, but a person to whom one tells the legend (ptákʷɬ-ən) is affected in that he or she receives the information contained in the legend.

The distribution between -min and -min' is as follows: we have -min under the stress, and in those cases where it may attract the stress in subsequent extensions (see ʔiʔwaʔ-mín above, and note páqʷuʔ-min > paqʷuʔ-mín-as 'he is afraid of him'; for stress, see also Section 2.1). We have -min' where it cannot attract the stress, e.g., ƛ'íq-min' 'to arrive (ƛ'iq) for smt., to get smt.' > ƛ'íq-min'-as 'he arrived for it,' ƛ'iq-min'-ítas 'they arrived for it.'

With the exception of three-place verbs such as sqʷál'-ən 'to report to' or táw-ən 'to sell to' (see also the second to last paragraph of this section), transitivizers (Ia), (Ib), (IIa), and (IIb) refer to a direct object, i.e., a person or thing that is involved directly and not obliquely in the action (typically, direct objects undergo the action, but they are not beneficiaries or recipients). By generally referring to direct objects, the above transitivizers differ from the following two, (IId) and (IIe).

(d) -xit refers to an indirect object, i.e., a beneficiary or recipient, or the one from whom something is taken. Compare the following cases:

X̓íq-xit 'to bring smt. to smb.' X̓iq-s 'to bring smt.'
cúɬ-xit 'to point smt. out to smb.' cúɬ-un' 'to point at smt.'
q'ʷəl-xít 'to roast, cook smt. for smb.' q'ʷə́l-ən 'to roast, cook smt.'

The object suffix that follows -xit refers to the indirect object. Predicates with -xit may also refer to a direct object, which is then expressed by an object complement, as in cúɬ-xi[t]-c-as ti‿cítxʷ-s‿a 'he (-as) pointed out his (-s) house (citxʷ) to me (-c).' Where the indirect object is a third person, we may have two object complements, one referring to the indirect object, the other to the direct object (usually in this order): cúɬ-xit-kan ti‿sqáyxʷ‿a ti‿n-cítxʷ‿a 'I pointed out my house to the man (sqayxʷ).' Where we have a single object complement, it always refers to the direct object, e.g., cúɬ-xit-kan ti‿sqáyxʷ‿a 'I pointed out the man to him' (*not* 'I pointed it out to the man'; the latter can be expressed only by mentioning explicitly [in a direct object complement] what is pointed out [see cúɬ-xit-kan ti‿sqáyxʷ‿a ti‿n-cítxʷ‿a above]). For details on complement order, see also Section 36.1.1.

(e) -min-xit/-min'-xit (combination of [IIc] and [IId] transitivizers): implies an indirect object, but indicates that this indirect object is affected less drastically or less directly than when -xit is used. Thus the difference between -min-xit/-min'-xit and -xit parallels the difference between -min/-min' and (Ia), (Ib), (IIa), and (IIb). In particular, -min-xit/-min'-xit expresses 'to do smt. for smb. with regard to that person's possessions,' e.g., 'to arrive (X̓iq) here for smb. in order to get smt. belonging to that person,' c?ás-min'-xit 'to come (c?as) for smb. in order to get smt. belonging to that person,' txʷús-min'-xit 'to look out on smb.'s behalf for smt. belonging to that person' (txʷúsəm 'to look out').

The object suffix following -min-xit/-min'-xit refers to the indirect object, while the direct object is expressed by an object complement, as in txʷus-min'-xí[t]-c-kaxʷ ni‿n-c'qáx̌?‿a 'look out for my (n-) horse (c'qáx̌a?) for me (-c), (so you can tell me where it is or bring it to me).' We may also have two object complements when the indirect object is a third person, e.g., c?as-min'-xít-kan kʷ‿s-kíka? ?i‿xʷik'áy'-s‿a 'I am coming to get the prepared salmon that belongs to kíka? (so I can bring it to her)' (xʷik'áy'-s 'her prepared salmon').

The relationships between the various transitivizers is summarized in Figure 7 (using the term 'plain' for -s, N, -nun/-nun', -ən-s, and -xit; 'relational' for -min/-min' and -min-xit/-min'-xit; 'directive' for -s, N, -nun/-nun', -ən-s, and -min/-min'; and 'indirective' for -xit and -min-xit/-min'-xit).

Figure 7

Classification of transitivizers

	Directive	Indirective
Plain	-s N -nun/-nun' -ən-s	-xit
Relational	-min/-min'	-min-xit/-min'-xit

A number of exceptions apply here. First, the word qʷús-xit 'to shoot, tr.' refers to a direct object, and it may take only one object complement, e.g., qʷús-xit-kan ti‿c'í?‿a 'I shot the deer (c'i?).' On the other hand, a number of forms with directive transitivizers refer in fact to an indirect object, and they may take an object complement that is non-coreferential with the object suffix, e.g., ?úm'-ən 'to give smt. to smb.' (as in ?um'-ən-túmuɬ kʷu‿tíh 'give us [-tumuɬ] some [kʷu‿] tea [tih]'); sqʷəqʷl'-ən 'to tell smb. smt.' (as in húy'-ɬkan sqʷəqʷl'-ən-cín ti‿sx̌íləm-s‿a ti‿skʷúza?-sw‿a 'I will [huy'-] tell you [-cin] what your [-sw] child [skʷúza?] did' [sx̌íləm 'deed,' -s 'his']); kʷúɬən-s 'to lend smt. to smb.' (as in húy'-ɬkan kʷuɬən-s-túmin ni‿n-téx̌ʷ?ac‿a 'I will lend you [-tumin] my [n-] gun [téx̌ʷ?ac]': note also the difference between -cin and -tumin [both 2S obj.] after N [previous example] and -s [last example]; kʷúɬən-s-kán‿tu? ni‿n-téx̌ʷ?ac‿a kʷ‿swéta? 'I lent my gun to so-and-so [swéta?]'; ‿tu? refers to a past act); kʷúɬən-min 'to borrow from' (as in nás-kan kʷúɬən-min kʷ‿s-Bill ti‿kém'x'ʷyəqs-c‿a 'I am going [nas] to borrow Bill's car [kém'x'ʷyəqs]'; literally, 'I am going to borrow from Bill his [-c] car,' wa? kʷuɬən-mín-c-as ti‿n-téx̌ʷ?ac‿a 'he [-as] is [wa?] borrowing my [n-] gun [téx̌ʷ?ac]'); táw-ən 'to sell smt. to smb.' (as in táw-ən-ɬkan ?ayɬ ni‿n-c'qáx̌?‿a 'I sold him my horse [c'qáx̌a?]'; ?ayɬ 'and then, next').[8]

Lillooet does not allow the use of two object suffixes to refer to both the indirect and the direct object; hence, a sentence such as 'I will tell you about him' has to be expressed through one object suffix referring to the indirect object, and an object complement referring to the direct object, as shown by the example with sqʷəqʷl'-ən above. Also, Lillooet does not allow the use of causative constructions on transitive stems in order to express 'to make smb. do smt. to smb. else'; such sentences are expressed through constructions with 'to tell, order, force smb. to do smt. to smb.,' as in cún-c-as ni‿skíxza?-sw‿a kʷən‿x'ʷíl'ən-cin 'your (-sw) mother (skíxza?) told (cun) me (-c) that I (kʷən‿) look for (x'ʷíl'ən) you (-cin)' (for kʷən‿ see also Section 22.4.1).

18.1.5. Distribution of intransitivizers and transitivizers

The distribution of intransitivizers and transitivizers is partially predictable on semantic, syntactic, or morphological grounds (see Sections 18.1.1 to 18.1.4). In a number of cases, a stem combines with a zero intransitivizer, a marked transitivizer (referring to an implied object), and a -s or N transitivizer.

1 zero ~ M ~ N
   ʔac'x̌ 'to be seen'   ʔác'x̌-əm 'to see'   ʔác'x̌-ən 'to see smt.'

2 zero ~ -xal ~ N
   k'ax '(to be) dry'   k'áx-xal 'to dry things'   k'áx-an' 'to dry smt.'
   páqʷuʔ '(to be) afraid' páqʷuʔ-xal 'to scare   páqʷʔ-an 'to scare
                            people'   smb.'
   qʷ'əl '(to be) done,   qʷ'əl-xál 'to roast,   qʷ'əl-ən 'to roast, cook
   cooked'   cook'   smt.'

3 zero ~ -xal ~ -s
   ƛ'iq 'to arrive (here)' ƛ'íq-xal 'to bring   ƛ'iq-s 'to bring smt.
                            (here)'   (here)'

In most cases, only one intransitive (marked or unmarked) stem was recorded. Checking all recorded cases of (marked or unmarked) intransitives plus transitives will probably fill in a number of gaps. In a number of cases, a certain form was rejected. For example, besides qam't 'to get hit,' we have qam't-s 'to hit, tr.,' but *qám't-xal 'to hit, intr.' was rejected. In some cases we do not have the form with zero as such, but a derived form. Thus, besides púɬ-xal 'to boil smt.; intr.' and púɬ-un' 'to boil smt., tr.,' the form *puɬ was rejected, but we have púɬ-əɬ 'to be boiling' and s-puɬ 'boiled' (with final reduplication and the stative prefix -s, respectively).

We have a large number of pairs $C_1V_1C_2$-xal ~ $C_1V_1C_2$-V_1n' (or $C_1V_1C_2$-V_1n), e.g., k'áx-xal ~ k'áx-an', púɬ-xal ~ púɬ-un', qʷ'əl-xál ~ qʷ'əl-ən. This accords with the fact that C_1VC_2 is the favourite Lillooet root-shape, that -xal is a productive intransitivizer, and that -Vn/-Vn' is frequent after roots C_1VC_2.

Not all verbs that take -s or N also take -min/-min', -xit, or -min-xit/-min'-xit. On the other hand, some verbs do not take -s or N but take one or more of the other transitivizers, e.g., ptínus-əm 'to think' > ptínus-min 'to think about'; kʷ'zús-əm 'to work' > kʷ'zús-min 'to take care of.' Verbs of motion are most easily combined with the intransitivizers and transitivizers (see ƛ'iq ~ ƛ'íq-xal ~ ƛ'iq-s above, and ƛ'íq-min', ƛ'iq-xit, and ƛ'íq-min'-xit in Section 18.1.4).

18.1.6. Distribution of (in)transitivizers: special cases

In a few cases we have an intransitivizer -Am: máw-am 'to gossip,' ƛ'xʷ-um 'to win.' The transitives to these forms are máw-an 'to gossip about,'[9] ƛ'xʷ-un 'to beat smb. in a contest.' Some stems allow both M and -xal: qʷ'él-əm/qʷ'əl-xál 'to roast, cook,' kʷ'úl'-əm/kʷ'úl'-xal 'to make,' ƛ'əqʷ?-um/ƛ'əqʷ?u-xál 'to sew.' Transitives to these forms have N: qʷ'él-ən 'to roast, cook it,' kʷ'ul'-ún 'to make, create it,' ƛ'éqʷ?-un 'to sew it.' A few words have the combination -əm-xal, e.g., mán'x-əm-xal 'to have a smoke together, to get together for a good time' (mán'x-əm 'to smoke').

In a few stems, the n-transitivizer is merged with the root: pzan 'to meet, run into smb.' thin 'to admire' (mostly in the form thín-cut 'to brag about oneself [-cut], to show off'), cun 'to tell, order smb.' (cf. cut 'to say smt.'). For may-t/máy-s-ən and c'níqʷ-t/c'níqʷ-ən, see Section 14.3; for ?ínw-at/?ínw-an, see Section 15.4(7).

A special case is pun (1) 'to be found, intr.,' (2) 'to find, tr.' (cf. púpən' 'to find by accident, intr.,' with consonant reduplication). Also remarkable is kʷam 'to take, get, buy, intr.' versus kʷan 'to take, tr.,' but kʷán-ən 'to get caught, intr.' (with final reduplication; kʷán-ən-s 'to catch smt., tr.': for -s after forms with final reduplication, see also Section 18.1.3). From √ɬap 'extinguished, forgotten,' we have both ɬáp-ən 'to forget smt., tr.,' and ɬáp-an' 'to extinguish smt., tr.'

18.2. Somatic suffixes and (in)transitivizers

A combination of a verbal stem and a somatic suffix (without a marked intransitivizer) simply relates the stem to the suffix. In most of these combinations, the stem is passive in character, and the combinations express 'to have smt. (that is expressed by the stem) happen to one's body part,' e.g., n-qam't-ána? 'to get hit (qam't) on the ear (n-..-ana?),' n-x̌ə-x̌zúm-ana? 'to have big (x̌zum) ears' (with initial reduplication). However, in n-qʷal'ut-ána? 'to hint' (literally, 'to talk [qʷal'út] to smb.'s ears') we have a somatic suffix on a non-passive stem.

A combination of a verbal stem and a somatic suffix plus an m-intransitivizer expresses 'to perform on one's own body part,' e.g., n-sup-aná?-əm 'to scratch (√sup) one's ear.' A combination of a verbal stem and a somatic suffix plus -s or an n-transitivizer expresses 'to perform on smb. else's body part,' e.g., n-sup-aná?-ən 'to scratch smb. else's ear,' n-qam't-ána?-s 'to hit smb. on the ear.' As a rule, when a stem selects an n-transitivizer or -s when not combined with a somatic suffix (e.g., súp-un' 'to scratch,' qam't-s 'to hit'), it also selects an n-transitivizer or -s when combined with a somatic suffix (see examples above). However, the transitive counterpart of n-qʷal'ut-ána? (see above) is n-qʷal'ut-án?-an 'to hint to smb.,' although the transitive counterpart of qʷal'út 'to speak' is qʷal'út-s 'to speak to smb. seriously.'

Depending on the preceding somatic suffix, the intransitivizer appears in the shape -am′, -am, or -əm (and the corresponding n-transitivizer in the shape -an′, -an, or -ən). The following are the intransitive forms based on the root sup- 'to scratch':

'to scratch oneself on the ...'

'head'	súp-qʷ-am′
'top of head'	n-sup-la-qín′-əm
'back of head	súp-ap-qn-am
'face'	súp-us-əm
'eye'	sup-al-ús-əm
'nose'	n-súp-l-əqs-am′
'mouth, lips'	súp-c-am′
'cheek'	sup-aplá?-əm F
'ear'	n-sup-aná?-əm
'throat, front of neck'	súp-aɬqʼʷəlt-am
'back of neck'	n-sup-aɬim′át-əm
'forehead'	n-sup-kin′-ús-əm
'chest'	sup-ax̌ʷác-əm
'belly'	súp-aɬməx-am M, n-sup-an′ák-əm F
'side'	sup-aɬníw′t-əm
'back'	n-súp-k-am′
'buttocks'	n-súp-q-am′
'arm'	sup-ax̌án-əm
'hand'	sup-aká?-əm
'palm of hand'	n-sup-ank-ákst-əm
'leg, foot'	súp-xn-am′
'knee'	súp-aw′s-xn-am
'heel'	súp-ap-l′a-xn-am
'sole of foot'	n-súp-an′k-xn-am
'whole body'	sup-al′íw′s-əm

Suffixes ending in unstressed a? combine with -əm, -ən into ?-am, ?-an, e.g., c′aw′-ák?-am 'to wash (√c′aw′) one's hands,' c′aw′-ák?-an 'to wash smb. else's hands.'

The following suffixes do not combine with sup-:

'tooth'	c′aw′-qan′ís-əm 'to brush one's teeth' (√c′aw′ 'to wash')
'heart'	n-ciq-anwás-ən 'to stab (√ciq) smb. in the heart, tr.'
'inside'	n-c′x̌-áɬc′?-am 'to take a laxative' (√c′əx̌ 'to clean')
'tail'	n-qʷəc-qin-úp?-am 'to wag (√qʷəc) one's tail'

Not all somatic suffixes combine freely with (in)transitivizers. For example, the suffix -alxʷcaɬ 'tongue' was recorded only in q'ʷəɬp-álxʷcaɬ 'to burn (q'ʷəɬp) one's tongue.' Other suffixes are found only in fixed combinations that have largely the same meaning as the suffix itself, e.g., -cín-xən 'ankle,' only in qʷəm-cín-xən '(lump on) ankle' (√qʷəm 'to mound up'). Some suffixes show various forms, the choice of which in various derivations is somewhat unpredictable. For example, besides -l-əqs 'nose' in n-súp-l-əqs-am' (see above), we have -qs in nís-qs-am' 'to blow one's nose' (nis- UC). While the F suffix for 'cheek,' -apla?, allows (in)transitivizers, the M equivalent, -apəl', does not. Hence we have only cases like qam't-ápəl' 'to get hit (qamt) on the cheek' in M (both F and M have -apəl' in kʷz-ápəl' 'cheek').

A combination of the intransitivizer -xal and a stem with a somatic suffix generally expresses 'causing to be (referent of the stem),' e.g., c'a?x-ús 'ashamed' > c'a?x-ús-xal 'shameful, causing to be ashamed'; c'əx̌m-áml'us 'blinded (when facing the sun)' (reduplication of *c'əx̌m-álus; c'əx̌m- UC) > c'əx̌m-áml'us-xal 'blinding.'[10] A combination of the transitivizer -min/-min' and a stem with a somatic suffix expresses in general 'to do smt. with one's body part to smt.' e.g., kɬ-áka?-min 'to release one's grip on smt., to let go of smt.' (√kəɬ 'to take off, apart,' -aka? 'hand'), ɬút-xən-min 'to squish (√ɬuṭ) smt. with one's foot (-xən),' ʕəlʕəl-áka?-min (1) 'to give smb. a rough time, to be mean to smb.,' (2) 'to make smt. stronger (e.g., a chair that one is fixing)' (ʕə́lʕəl 'strong,' -aka? 'hand'). Somatic suffixes that require the shape -an' of the n-transitivizer (and -am' of the intransitivizer; see -qʷ, n-..-l-əqs, n-..-k, n-..-q, -xən in the list above) also require -min', rather than -min. (In stems where we do not have these somatic suffixes, the distribution of -min/-min' depends on the stress pattern; see Section 18.1.4.) In a number of cases where -min/-min' follows a stem with a somatic suffix, its use is not much different from that described in Section 18.1.4, e.g., c'a?x-ús-min' 'to be ashamed (c'a?x-ús) of,' n-qḷ-ánwas-min 'to dislike (n-qḷ-ánwas) smb., tr.'

For somatic suffixes that have lost their somatic meaning (e.g., -c 'food,' rather than 'mouth'), see Section 18.3.

The function of -xit and -min-xit/-min'-xit after somatic suffixes is similar to their function after stems without a somatic suffix, e.g., nás-aka?-xit 'to send smt. to smb.' (nas 'to go,' -aka? 'hand') (cf. nás-xit 'to give smt. to smb.').

I recorded one case of -s after a somatic suffix followed by M: c'aw'-ák?-am-s 'to enable smb. to wash (√c'aw') his hands (-aka?) (e.g., by getting water and a towel ready)': this case parallels ptínus-əm-s in Section 18.1.3.

18.3. Non-somatic suffixes and (in)transitivizers
A combination of a verbal stem and a non-somatic lexical suffix expresses in general 'referent of suffix is characterized or modified by referent of stem,' kʷík̓ʷs-aləqʷ 'small (kʷik̓ʷs) log (-alqʷ),' cicl-úsa? 'fresh (cícəl) fruit

(-usaʔ),' n-kə-kawʼ-aláqaɬ 'wide body of water' (kə-káwʼ 'far,' n-..-alaqaɬ 'body of water'), q̦-áḷʼqʷəmʼ 'ugly' (qəḷ 'bad,' -aḷʼqʷəmʼ 'outward appearance'). These cases parallel those where a stem combines with a somatic suffix (without a marked intransitivizer), e.g., n-qamʼt-ánaʔ above.

By adding an m-intransitivizer to a combination of a stem and a non-somatic suffix, we express 'to perform on the referent of the suffix,' or 'to perform on things with regard to the referent of the suffix,' e.g., páx̌-alqʷ-əm 'to scrape, smoothen (√pax̌ʷ) a stick (-alqʷ),' ɬuɬqʼʷ-usáʔ-əm 'to peel (√ɬuɬqʼʷ) fruit, potatoes (-usaʔ),' ʔamh-ált-əm 'to like smb. as a marriage partner for one's child' (ʔáma 'good,' -alt 'child'). Quite often, the intransitivizer is dropped, without a change in meaning, e.g., páx̌-alqʷ, ɬúɬqʼʷ-usaʔ, ʔamh-ált (= páx̌-alqʷ-əm, etc.).

A combination of a non-somatic suffix and a direct transitivizer (-s or N) simply indicates a direct transitivization, e.g., páx̌-alqʷ-ən 'to scrape (this particular) log, stick.' Some suffixes, e.g., -úlmʼəxʷ/-lumʼəxʷ 'land,' require -am, -an for M and N, e.g., n-ʕəc-úlmʼəxʷ-am/n-ʕəc-úlmʼəxʷ-an 'to stake (an animal), intr./tr.' (√ʕəc 'to tie'). The suffix -aḷʼk 'surface' requires -amʼ, -anʼ, e.g., qɬ-áḷʼk-anʼ 'to cover smt. (with a tarpaulin, canvas, dirt, or hay), tr.' The suffix -álap/-lap 'form, shape' takes the transitivizer -ən in n-cw-álap-ən 'to copy smt.' and n-síx̌-lap-ən 'to copy smt.,' but it takes -an in ɬqʼ-álap-an 'to widen smt.' (ɬqʼ-álap 'wide'): the use of -an in the latter form parallels that of -an in záxt-an 'to make longer' and kʷíkʷs-an 'to make smaller' (Section 18.1.2).

Not all non-somatic suffixes combine freely with marked (in)transitivizers. For example, no marked (in)transitivizers were recorded with -aḷʼqʷəmʼ 'outward appearance.' In the same way, no intransitivizers follow -ílx/-ləx 'body' except for a few cases where -ílx/-ləx itself is followed by a lexical suffix (see n-qʼay-ləx-m-áwʼs, Section 15.2[118]). For the special status of -ílx/-ləx, see also Section 17.1. For transitivizers on -ílx/-ləx, see below.

Somatic suffixes that have lost their somatic meaning behave like non-somatic suffixes in combinations with (in)transitivizers, e.g., náqʼʷ-c-amʼ 'to steal (naqʼʷ) food' (-c 'food,' derived from -c 'mouth'). Semantically, this word is on the same line as páx̌-alqʷ-əm, etc. above in that it refers to 'to perform on the referent of the suffix' (versus súp-c-amʼ 'to scratch [√sup] one's mouth').

The transitivizers -min/-minʼ, -xit, and -min-xit/-minʼ-xit have the same function after non-somatic suffixes as after plain stems. We have a fair number of cases of -min after -ílx/-ləx 'body,' the combination expressing 'to apply one's body to,' e.g., ləʕʷ-ílx-min 'to hide (ləʕʷ-) oneself (-ílx) from smb.,' qʼáy-ləx-min 'to run away (qʼáy-ləx) from smb.,' tx̌ʷ-ílx-min 'to come straight (tx̌ʷ-ílx) at smb.' (cf. the last form with tx̌ʷ-ílx-an 'to straighten smt. out [e.g., a road],' with the direct transitivizer -an).

18.4. Nominal stems and (in)transitivizers

Nominal stems combine productively with the intransitivizer -am to express 'to get, pick, hunt the referent of the stem,' e.g., púʔy'axʷ 'mouse' > puʔy'axʷ-ám 'to hunt mice'; míx̌aɬ 'bear' > mix̌aɬ-ám 'to hunt bear' (stress possibly a misrecording; one would expect it on i), twan 'salmonberry' > twán-am 'to pick salmonberries'; pípa 'paper, check, mail' (from English 'paper') > píph-am 'to get the mail.' Nominal stems with s- (nominalizer) drop s- when combined with -am, e.g., s-x̌iq 'duck' > x̌íq-am 'to hunt ducks,' s-p'ams 'firewood' > p'áms-am 'to get firewood' (cf. the last case with p'áms-əm 'to make a fire,' Section 9[3]).

Semantically and morphologically unique are the cases sitst-ím 'to do smt. at night (sitst)' and n'an'atxʷ-ám 'to do smt. in the morning (s-n'án'atxʷ), to get up early to do smt.' The vowel of the intransitivizer repeats the vowel of the stem. The words ʕap '(to be) evening' and s-q'it 'day' do not allow this derivation.

Combinations of nominal stems and the transitivizer -an express 'to infest with the referent of the stem, to apply the referent of the stem to smt.' Such forms are usually in the passive, e.g., puʔy'axʷ-án-əm 'it is infested with mice (púʔy'axʷ)' (-əm passive suffix, not to be confused with the intransitivizer -əm [Section 22.3.4]), məkn'-án-əm 'it is infested with lice (mə́kən'),' puɬ'h-án-əm 'it is infested with púɬ'a (maggots when still in the egg), k'ak'ɬ?-án-əm 'it is infested with k'ák'ɬa? (bugs in dried salmon).'

When combined with -min, nominal stems express various notions, e.g., stqín-min 'to use smt. for a pillow (stqin),' c'áz'q-min 'to use smt. for a cushion (c'az'q)' (the use of -min, rather than -min', in stqín-min is remarkable with regard to the stress [see Section 18.1.4]; in the same way one would expect -min' after -q contained in c'az'q [cf. Section 18.2]), száytən-min 'to carry out, execute' (száytən 'business, what one does'), saw't-mín-əm 'he was taken slave' (saw't 'slave'). When combined with names of animals, -min expresses 'animal destroys, eats, meets smt.' (-min' was not recorded here). Such forms are usually in the passive, e.g., mix̌aɬ-mín-əm 'it was eaten by a bear (míx̌aɬ), he was met by a bear, ran into a bear,' wuw'a-mín-əm 'it was eaten by a cougar (s-wúw'a),' puʔy'axʷ-mín-əm 'it was eaten by mice.'

I recorded only a few cases of nominal stems with other transitivizers: száytən-s 'to do smt. to smb.' (cf. száytən-min above), x̌ʷʔít-ən 'to wedge smt., to use the wedge on smt.' (x̌ʷʔit 'wedge'), samaʔ-nún 'to think (-nun) that smb. is a white man (sámaʔ).'

For verbalized nominal stems, see also Sections 18.5 and 18.6.

In principle, the above rules should also apply to stems with nominalizing suffixes, but examples are hard to come by. One possible case is p'ústn'-am 'to collect rye grass (p'ústən'),' which possibly contains a residual form

-tən' of -tən 'instrument' (Section 15.2[16a]). We also have cases based on száytən (see above), which is analyzed as containing -tən (√zay UC).

18.5. Abstract suffixes and (in)transitivizers

The position of abstract suffixes is peculiar in that in rather many cases, abstract suffixes follow (in)transitivizers, e.g., k'ay'-c-am'-úɬ 'always (-úɬ) denying' (√k'ay' UC, -c 'to speak,' -am' intransitivizer), ɬəm'-c-am'-úɬ 'always hanging on to one's food, always stingy with one's food' (√ɬəm' 'to hang on to,' -c 'food,'), ɬəp-ɬəp-n-ún'ɬ 'forgetful' (ɬáp-ən 'to forget, tr.,' -úɬ 'always'), nas-us-ən-ʔúl 'really (-ʔúl) looking like one of one's parents' (nás-us-ən 'to look like one of one's parents, to inherit smb.'s features,' nas 'to go,' -us 'face,' -ən transitivizer), sək-xal-sút (1) 'to slug around, to swing a stick or club around,' (2) 'to jabber away (if you don't know the language you are trying to speak in)' (-sút 'out of control,' √sək 'to hit with stick, whip, or club,' -xal intransitivizer), ptinus-əm-sút 'to ponder, worry' (ptínus-əm 'to think').

A special case here is -qʷ-am'-sút 'helplessly, desperately' (-qʷ 'head,' -am' intransitivizer), in cəs-qʷ-am'-sút 'to feel around in the dark' (√cas 'to feel'), ƛ'am'-qʷ-am'-sút 'to struggle to get onto smt. (e.g., when one has fallen into the water and is trying to get out)' (√ƛ'am' 'to grab'). Note also pun-sút-ən 'to find smt. by accident (e.g., smt. that one did not know one had lost),' with N merged with the stem before -sút, and -ən following -sút.

Where (in)transitivizers occur after an abstract suffix, the function of the (in)transitivizer is usually not different from when it occurs after plain stems, e.g., kʷukʷ-sút 'to be fortunate' > kʷukʷ-sút-xal 'to help, out, to provide smt. that is needed' (cf. -sút-xal in this word with sək-xal-sút above). However, -az' 'for fun, playingly' (Section 16[10]) combines with the intransitivizer -am into -az'-am with the specialized meaning 'to pretend' (for examples, see Section 16[10]; note that in kʷukʷpy'-az'-am, ʔuxʷalmixʷ-áz'-am, and ləqs-ay'ɬ-áz'-am the combination -az'-am occurs on nominal stems and is verbalizing).

When stems ending in an abstract suffix are transitivized, they generally select the same transitivizer as the stem without abstract suffix, e.g., qam't-sút 'to get hit by accident' > qam't-sút-s 'to hit by accident' (cf. qam't 'to get hit' > qam't-s 'to hit'). Note also pun-sút-ən, as discussed above. We do have the case ptak-ək-ʔúl-s 'to send smb. right by it' (ptak 'to pass by') with pták-ən, while ptak is parallelled by transitive -ən 'to pass by it,' but here -s and -ən have different functions.

18.6. The reflexive suffix -cut

The reflexive suffix -cut (Section 17.1) influences the shape of the preceding transitivizer. There are three sets of formal semantic cases here. In the first two, -cut is stressed.

(1) -s-cút (with -s, transitivizer [Ia]): expresses 'to pretend to be, to act as though one were such-and-such, to act like': sama?-s-cút 'to pretend to be a white person (sáma?), to act as though one were a white person,' kʷʷukʷʷm'it-s-cút 'to act like a child (s-kʷ'ʷúkʷʷm'it),' ləqs-ay'ɬ-cút 'to act as though one were the pet, the favourite (ləqs-áy'ɬ)' (for dropping of -s, see Section 22.3.2), kʷʷukʷpəy'-s-cút 'to pretend to be the chief (kʷʷúkʷpəy'),' xa?-s-cút 'to brag' (xa? 'high'), ʕəlʕəl-s-cút 'to act tough' (ʕə́lʕəl 'strong'). Here the function of the transitivizer -s is 'expressing a thought' (cf. Section 18.1.3). Note that in the first four cases -s occurs after nominal stems.[11]

The difference between -s-cút and -az'-am (Section 18.5) is slight: both suffixes overlap to a great degree in function; cf. kʷʷukʷpəy'-s-cút above with kʷʷukʷpy'-áz'-am (Section 16[10]), and cf. also kʷʷukʷʷm'it-s-cút above with kʷʷukʷʷm'it-áz'-am 'to behave like a child' (for the latter pair, see also [3] below).

(2) -ən-cút, -an-cút, -An'-cút: makes straightforward reflexive forms, without further connotations. The distribution between the three sub-forms of this combination is not entirely predictable. In a few cases, -ən is changed to -an before -cút, e.g., xə́k-ən 'to correct smb.' > xək-an-cút 'to be stubborn, bossy, to do smt. against smb.'s advice'; mays-ən 'to fix smt.' > mays-an-cút 'to make oneself up.' Examples with -ən-cút are: ma?-ən-cút 'to blame (má?-ən) oneself,' x̌ʷəm-ən-cút 'to hurry' (x̌ʷəm 'fast, quick'), cuw'-cw'-ən-cút 'to kick around (like smb. having a fit)' (cúw'-ən 'to kick smb., tr.'), nukʷ'ʷ?-an-cút 'to help (nukʷ'ʷ?-an) oneself' (with underlying -ən).

Examples with -an-cút other than the ones given above are: xəɬ-an-cút 'to volunteer, to offer help' (√xəɬ 'active'), c'x̌-us-an-cút 'to look at one's face' (c'x̌-ús-ən 'to look smb. in the face, tr.'). A special case is kʷʷul'-an-cút 'to make smt. for oneself' (kʷʷul'-ún' 'to make smt., tr.'): cf. this form with kʷʷul'-xi[ɬ]-cút below. With -An'-cút we have ɬuq'ʷ-un'-cút 'to undress (ɬúq'ʷ-un') oneself.'

Stems with the transitivizer -s change -s to -an before -cút, e.g., X̌'ak-s 'to take along' (X̌'ak 'to go' > X̌'ak-an-cút 'to take oneself along, to take care of one's own transportation'; nas-c 'to bring along' (nas 'to go') > nas-an-cút 'to take care of one's own transportation'; qam't-s 'to hit' (qam't 'to get hit') > qam't-an-cút 'to hit oneself'; zuqʷ-s 'to kill' (zuqʷ 'dead') > zuqʷ-an-cút 'to kill oneself.' The suffix -cút converts the preceding stem into one where the subject is in control of the action (since the subject is performing it on himself or herself), and this control is indicated by -an (stems with -an-cút may be secondarily marked for non-control by ka-..._a; see Section 18.8).[12]

Stems with -min/-min' are extended with -an before -cút (i.e., -cút is not attached immediately to -min/-min'): páqʷu?-min 'to be afraid of' > paqʷu?-min-an-cút 'to be afraid of oneself'; nkʷʷzánwas-min 'to worry about' > nkʷʷzanwas-min-an-cút 'to worry about oneself'; k'al'an'-min' 'to listen to' >

k'al'an'-min'-an-cút 'to listen to one's own advice'; k'ʷzús-min' 'to work for, to look after' > k'ʷzus-min'-an-cút 'to look after oneself.'

The transitivizer -xit merges t with -cút: mays-xi[t]-cút 'to fix (mays-) smt. for oneself,' qʷʷəl-xi[t]-cút 'to cook (qʷʷəl-) smt. for oneself,' k'ʷul'-xi[t]-cút 'to make (k'ʷul'-) smt. for oneself.' (There seems to be a semantic difference between the last word and k'ʷul'-an-cút above, but my consultants could not pin it down).

(3) -án-cut (unproductive): expresses 'to pretend to be, to act like': it overlaps semantically with -s-cút (see [1] above) and -az'-am. Examples are: qayxʷ-án-cut 'to act like a man, to do it the man's way (e.g., a man doing woman's work in a clumsy manner)' (s-qayxʷ 'man'), k'ʷukʷʷm'it-án-cut 'to act like a child (s-k'ʷúkʷʷm'it)' (no perceptible difference with k'ʷukʷʷm'it-s-cút; see [1]), ʕəlʕəl-án-cut 'to want to act tough, to want to be brave (when one is not), to force oneself to do smt.' (ʕélʕəl 'strong,' cf. ʕəlʕəl-s-cút [1]), qəlqəl-xn-án-cut 'to suffer from lack of help' (qəl 'bad,' -xən 'deprivation,' Section 15.2[104b]), x̌ʷəst-án-cut 'to make a big effort' (x̌ʷəst- 'smt. needed, worth an effort'). Residual cases that belong here are k'ʷaz-án'-cut 'to train oneself' (k'ʷáz-ləx id.) with -an'-cut, and thín-cut 'to show off, brag about oneself' (thin 'to admire'; see also Section 18.1.6).

18.7. Reflexive and reciprocal suffixes: detransitivization and retransitivization

Stems ending in the reflexive suffix -cut or the reciprocal suffix -twal' (Section 17.2) are formally intransitive. This means (1) that such stems take intransitive, rather than transitive, subject suffixes (see Section 22.5.5), and (2) that such stems may be retransitivized by adding a transitivizer after -cut or -twal'.

With -cut I recorded the following retransitivizations: ʕəlʕəl-s-cút-min' 'to act tough (ʕəlʕəl-s-cút) on smb.,' x̌ʷəst-án-cut-min 'to make an effort (x̌ʷəst-án-cut) for smt.,' thín-cut-min 'to brag (thín-cut) about smt.' The transitivizer -min/-min' is the only one recorded after -cut: its use resembles that of -min/-min' after -ilx/-ləx (Section 18.3). With -twal' we have max̌'-min'-twál'-ən 'to mix (max̌'-) things together,' cuqʷ-min'-twál'-ən 'to add several pieces of rope together.' (I did not record *max̌'-min' *cuqʷ-min' without -twal', but I did record máx̌'-an' 'to mix, tr.' and cúqʷ-un' 'to add smt., to splice a rope, tr.'):

18.8. Stative and resultative forms

When stems with an n-transitivizer are combined with the stative prefix s- (Section 10.1.2) or the resultative combination ka-..ˌa (Section 10.1.3), the n-transitivizer is replaced with the transitivizer -s: ʔác'x̌-ən 'to see smt., tr.' > s-ʔac'x̌-s 'to watch over, look after,' ka-ʔác'x̌-sˌa 'to catch sight of'; téq-ən 'to touch smt., tr.' > s-təq-s 'to hold on to,' ka-téq-s‿a 'to catch smt. (e.g., a ball)'; ʕʷél-ən 'to light smt., set fire to smt., tr.' > s-ʕʷəl-s 'to keep lit,' ka-ʕʷél-s‿a 'to manage to light it.' Note that ka-..‿a implies lack of control, either in the form of smt. that happens suddenly ('to catch sight of') or in the form of smt. that requires a certain effort ('to manage to light it'). As for s-, the stative in Lillooet apparently also carries a notion of lack of control in the sense that it will require an effort (with no guarantee of success) to keep something lit, or to maintain a watch over something. This then would explain the use of -s after both s- and ka-..‿a, which are diametrically opposed in their aspectual functions.[13]

The markers s- and ka-..‿a do not influence the choice of N before -cút: s-ʔac'x̌-an-cút 'to look after oneself' (also ʔac'x̌-an-cút with aphaeresis), ka-λ'ak-an-cút‿a 'to manage to provide one's own transportation' (λ'ak-an-cút 'to provide one's own transportation'). Remember that stems ending in -cut are intransitive (see Section 18.7), which explains the fact that s- and ka-..‿a do not influence the choice of transitivizer before -cut: they operate only on transitivizers that conclude a stem.

Transitivizers other than N do not change in stative or resultative forms, e.g., ka-ɬəx̌ʷ-min-ɬkán‿a 'I (-ɬkan) sneaked (ɬəx̌ʷ-) up to it.'

18.9. Summary of (in)transitivizers
The following is a list of (in)transitivizers, with references to their functions described in Sections 18.1 to 18.8.

1   Intransitivizers
   (a) -xal
      1)   expressing 'with object' after plain stems: 18.1.1
      2)   replaced with -əm' in forms with consonant reduplication: 18.1.1
      3)   relation to transitivizers: 18.1.5
      4)   in combination with -əm: 18.1.6
      5)   after somatic suffixes: 18.2
   (b) m-intransitivizers (M)
      1)   -əm, -əm' expressing 'with object' or 'medial-reflexive' after plain stems: 18.1.1
      2)   -əm' replacing -xal: 18.1.1
      3)   relation of -əm, -əm' to transitivizers: 18.1.5
      4)   -əm in combination with -xal: 18.1.6
      5)   residual form -Am: 18.1.6
      6)   -əm, -am, -am' after somatic suffixes, expressing 'to perform on one's own body part': 18.2
      7)   -əm, -am, -am' after non-somatic suffixes, expressing 'to perform on the referent of the suffix': 18.3

8) -am after nominal stems, expressing 'to get, pick, hunt the referent of the stem': 18.4

9) -Am after nominal stems referring to time, expressing 'to do smt. during that time': 18.4

10) -am in -az'-am 'to pretend': 18.5

(c) zero (unmarked stems)

1) expressing 'with object,' 'medial-reflexive,' or 'passive' after plain stems: 18.1.1

2) relation to other intransitivizers and to transitivizers: 18.1.5

3) expressing 'referent of suffix is characterized or commented on by referent of root,' after somatic and non-somatic suffixes: 18.2, 18.3

2 Transitivizers

Type I

(a) -s

1) expressing causitivization and transitive *verba sentiendi et declarandi* after plain stems: 18.1.2, 18.1.3

2) expressing causitivization after marked intransitivizers: 18.1.3

3) relation to intransitivizers: 18.1.5

4) expressing 'to pretend to be, to act like,' in combination with reflexive -cút: 18.6

5) replacing N in forms with stative s- or resultative ka-..‿a: 18.8

(b) -ən-s

1) non-causative transitivization: 18.1.2, 18.1.3

Type II

(a) n-transitivizers (N)

1) -ən, -ən', -An, -An', -an expressing causativity, transitive *verba declarandi*, and non-causative transitivizations (-ən): 18.1.2, 18.1.3; also used in a few three-place verbs: 18.1.4 (last paragraph)

2) -ən' replacing -An' in forms with consonant reduplication: 18.1.2

3) relation to intransitivizers: 18.1.5

4) -An corresponding to the intransitivizer -Am, plus special cases: 18.1.6

5) -ən, -an, -an' expressing 'to perform on smb. else's body part,' after somatic suffixes: 18.2

6) -ən, -an, -an' expressing 'to perform on referent of suffix,' after non-somatic suffixes: 18.3

7) -an expressing 'to infest with referent of stem,' after nominal stems: 18.4

8) -ən-cút, -an-cút, -An'-cút expressing reflexiveness: 18.6; -an-cút after -min/-min': 18.6

9) -án-cut expressing 'to pretend': 18.6

(b) -nun/-nun'
1)   forming transitive *verba sentiendi:* 18.1.2, 18.1.3
(c) -min/-min'
1)   expressing that the object is affected indirectly: 18.1.4
2)   after somatic and non-somatic suffixes: 18.2, 18.3
3)   expressing various notions after nominal stems: 18.4
4)   extended with -an before -cút: 18.6
5)   after -cút: 18.7
6)   before -twal': 18.7
(d) -xit
1)   implies indirect objects: 18.1.4;[14] irregularly a direct object in q^{w}ús-xit: 18.1.4
2)   cases with -cút: 18.6
(e) -min-xit/-min'-xit
1)   expressing a less drastic effect than -xit: 18.1.4

19
Numerals and Numerical Substitutes

Here we discuss first cardinal numerals and numerical substitutes (Sections 19.1 to 19.3), and then ordinals, numerical adverbs, and numerical-distributive adverbs (Section 19.4).

19.1. Cardinals and numerical substitutes

Lillooet has separate cardinal numerals for the units 1 to 10 and for 100. Multiples of 10 are expressed by 'two, three, four, etc., times ten.' Numerical units between multiples of 10 are expressed by 'ten and one, ten and two,' etc. (using wi or múta? 'and'). In the same way, 200 is 'two times hundred,' 101 is 'hundred and one,' etc. The numerals 1 to 10, the numerical interrogative, and the root x̌ək- 'to count' have separate forms for counting objects, persons, and animals.

	Objects	Persons	Animals
1	pála?	pápla?	pépla?
2	?án'was	n-?án'was	?á?ən'was
3	kaɬás	n-kə-kaɬás	kaɬə́ɬs
4	x̌ʷ?úcin	n-x̌ʷə-x̌ʷ?úcin	x̌ʷ?ú?cin'
5	cil-kst	n-cíl-cl-əkst	cə́cl'-əkst
6	ƛ'áq'-əm-kst	n-ƛ'áq'-ƛ'q'-əm-kst	ƛ'áƛ'q'-əm'-kst
7	cúɬ-aka?	n-cúcɬ-aka?	cúcɬ-aka?
8	pál?-upst M	n-pál-pəl?-upst M	pápəl?-upst M
	pəl?-ú?pst F	n-pəl-pəl?-ú?pst F	pəl?-ú?pst F
9	q'əm'p-álmən	n-q'əm'-qəm'p-álmən	q'əm'p-ápəl'mən
10	q'əm'p	n-q'ém'-q'm'əp	q'éq'm'əp
how much, how many?	kʷin	n-kʷ'ín-kʷ'ən	kʷ'ə́kʷ'ən'
to count, tr.	x̌ə́k-ən	n-x̌ə́k-x̌k-ən	x̌ə́x̌k-ən'

11	q'əm'p wi pála? (q'əm'p múta? pála?)
12	q'əm'p wi ?án'was (q'əm'p múta? ?án'was)
20	?án'was kw‿s-q'əm'p-s
21	?án'was kw‿s-q'əm'p-s wi (múta?) pála?
30	kaɬás kw‿s-q'əm'p-s
100	x̌əcp-qíqin'-kst M, x̌əcp-qíqən'-kst F
101	x̌əcp-qíqin'-kst wi (múta?) pála?
111	x̌əcp-qíqin'-kst wi (múta?) q'əm'p wi (múta?) pála?
121	x̌əcp-qíqin'-kst wi (múta?) ?án'was kw‿s-q'əm'p-s wi (múta?) pála?
200	?án'was kw‿s-x̌əcp-qíqin'-kst-s
1,000	q'əm'p kw‿s-x̌əcp-qíqin'-kst-s

19.1.1. Formation

The numerals 1 to 4 call for no comment, except for ?án'was 'two': see 40, 88, and 89 in Section 15.2 and n. 9 of Section 15. The element cil- in cil-kst 'five' means 'new' (cf. cícəl id.), while -kst means 'hand' (Section 15.2[96a]), with the whole complex referring to having to use a new hand after counting the five fingers. In X̌'áq'-əm-kst 'six' we have X̌'aq' 'to cross over' and an m-intransitivizer; see Section 18.1.1(b) and n. 11 of Section 15.

In cúɬ-aka? 'seven' we have √cuɬ 'to point at' and -aka? 'hand, finger' (Section 15.2[95a]). For pál?-upst 'eight,' see Section 15.4(5). The numeral q'əm'p-álmən 'nine' consists of q'əm'p 'ten' and -almən 'about to' (Section 16[7]). The word for 'hundred,' x̌əcp-qíqin'-kst/x̌əcp-qíqən'-kst, contains the suffix for 'finger(tip),' -qin'-kst, in reduplicated form (Section 15.2[109.5]): the root x̌əcp- is probably the same as in x̌əcp-ásq'ət 'week' (-asq'ət 'day'), probably meaning 'unit' or 'filled out.' Multiples of 10 and 100 employ a kw-construction (see Section 22.3.1).

19.1.2. Prefixation, reduplication, and alternative forms

All forms for 'persons,' except pála?, have the prefix n- (see Section 10.1.5[2]).[1] All forms in the category 'persons,' except n-?án'was, also show some kind of reduplication: consonant reduplication in 1 and 7, initial reduplication in 3 and 4, and total reduplication in 5, 6, 8, 9, and 10, and in kw'in and x̌ək-ən. The form n-?án'was may have resisted reduplication because it already has n-?an'.. (phonetically [ŋ?ɛn', ?ŋ?ɛn']; see Section 3.1).

The forms for 'animals' all show consonant reduplication (with or without change A > E). Forms with RəK following the stressed syllable also allow əRK and vice versa (e.g., besides X̌'áq'-əm-kst one also hears X̌'áq'-m-əkst, and besides q'éq'm'əp, also q'éq'əm'p; the forms in Section 19.1 appear to be the most commonly used). For 'nine animals' I also recorded q'əq'əm'p-álmən, q'əq'əm'p-ál'mən, q'əm'-q'əq'əm'p-ál'mən, q'əm'p-ápəl'm'ən', q'əm'pépəl'mən, and q'əq'əm'p-ápəl'mən. For 'six animals' I also recorded X̌'əX̌'q'-m'-əkst, and for 'six people' also n-x̌'áx̌'q'-əm'-kst. However, the forms in Section 19.1 are those that are used most of the time.[2]

Note that in F, the form for 'eight objects' and 'eight animals' are the same: pəl?-ú?pst.

19.1.3. Complex numerals and reduplication

When the numerals 11 to 19 refer to persons or animals, we may reduplicate both numerals in the complex, e.g., n-q'ém'-q'm'əp múta? n-cíl-cl-əkst '15 persons,' q'éq'm'əp múta? céct'-əkst '15 animals.' However, usually only the last numeral is reduplicated (this seems to be more common with 'animals' than with 'persons'), e.g., q'əm'p múta? n-cíl-cl-əkst, q'əm'p múta? céct'-əkst. In other complex numerals (i.e., multiples of 10 or 100, or such multiples plus a numeral from 1 to 9), usually only the last numeral is reduplicated, e.g., ?án'was kʷ‿ən-q'ém'-q'm'əp-s '20 persons,'[3] ?án'was kʷ‿s-q'éq'm'əp-s '20 animals' (with two-member complexes, reduplication throughout is still allowed, e.g., ?á?ən'was kʷ‿s-q'éq'm'əp-s '20 animals').

19.2. Suffixation

Numerals and numerical substitutes may combine with certain lexical suffixes. These combinations usually express 'X objects' or 'the Xth object.' Lexical suffixes that combine particularly easily (or exclusively) with numerals are summarized in Section 15.2 (see comments preceding the list of suffixes). For the morphophonemics of such combinations, see also Section 4.3. One set of examples, with -alqʷ 'tree, log, stick' will suffice here: pál?-aləqʷ 'one tree, log, stick,'[4] ?an'was-álqʷ 'two trees, logs, sticks,' kał-álqʷ 'three trees, logs, sticks.' ML often extends the 'animal' forms with -qʷ 'head, animal' when the animals are mentioned by name, e.g., kałéłs-əqʷ cíkən 'three chickens,' q'éq'əm'p-əqʷ ?i‿c'q'ažʔ-s‿a 'ten are his (-s) horses (c'qážaʔ) = he has ten horses.' In complex numerals, suffixes combine with the last member: q'əm'p wi pál?-iłaz' 'eleven trees, bushes' (-iłaz' 'tree, bush').

19.3. Special questions

Indefinite quantifiers are xʷʔit 'much, many,' kʷʷík'ʷna? 'little, a few' (reduplication of kʷʷin; see Section 12.4), tákəm 'all,' zí?zəsʕ 'every, each,' put 'enough, just right,' nukʷ 'some.'[5] We may combine xʷʔit with lexical suffixes, e.g., xʷʔít-usa? 'much money, expensive.' The numeral pála? allows the reduplication pi-pála? 'one at a time' (Section 12.2), also with lexical suffixes, e.g., pi-pál?-usa? '(to take, peel) one piece of fruit at a time.'

We also have ?i-?án'was 'two at a time,' but other numerals do not allow this reduplication. The word mit 'dime' requires the 'animal' form of all numerals except pála?, hence pála? mit 'one dime,' ?á?ən'was mit 'two dimes,' kałéłs mit 'three dimes,' etc. (However, some speakers reject the reduplicated forms here and use the basic 'object' forms.) The word cuk^w 'finished' allows the 'person' reduplication in n-cúk^w-cək^w 'a number of people are finished.'

19.4. Ordinals, numerical adverbs, and numerical-distributive adverbs

Here we discuss ordinals (Section 19.4.1), numerical adverbs ('once, twice,' etc.; Section 19.4.2), and numerical-distributive adverbs ('in two,' 'in three,' etc.; Section 19.4.3). These numerical elements require certain morpho-syntactic constructions that are discussed in Section 22.3.1. (The reader may want to skip Sections 19.4.1 to 19.4.3 for now, until after familiarizing himself or herself with the contents of Section 22.3.1.) For the Lillooet equivalent of the English numerical-distributive adjectives 'single, double,' see n-..-us (Section 15.2[22.1]).

19.4.1. Ordinals

Except for kéla? 'first' (and ?aw't 'last [late, behind]'), Lillooet has no special forms for ordinals. English phrases with ordinals are generally parallelled in Lillooet by constructions of the type 'this way (that way) that it is two (= it is the second),' as in the following:

(a) ?əc?á X'ɬ   (ɬ)?án'was-as   k^wu pún-an
     this way now   (that)two-it is   the one find-I
     'this is the second one I find'
(b) ?áti? X'ɬ   (ɬ)kaɬás-as   nzaw'áksttən k^wu ?úq^w?ans-an
     that way now   (that)three-it is cup   the one drink-I
     'this is the third cup I am drinking'
(c) ?áti? X'ɬ   (ɬ)kaɬ-úlwiɬ-as   k^wu ?úq^w?ans-an
     that way now   (that)three-container-it is   the one drink-I
     'this is the third bottle I am drinking'
(d) plan X'ɬ   ?áti?   ɬ kaɬás-as   k^w s-?ác'x̌n-an   ɬk^wúnsa
     already now that way that three-it is that fact.-see (him)-I today
     'this is already the third time I see him today'

The parentheses in (ɬ) mean that ɬ usually merges with ɬ of preceding X'ɬ, but that it is present in deliberate speech.

19.4.2. Numerical adverbs

English numerical adverbs ('once,' 'twice,' etc.) are parallelled in Lillooet by constructions expressing 'X that it is done' (with a k^w-construction, Section 22.3.1), as in the following:

(a) kałás   kʷ‿s-q'áyləx-s
    three   that‿fact.-jump-his
    'he jumped three times'

(b) x̌ʷʔúcin   kʷ‿s-q'əlxánʔan-əm
    four that   fact.-jump over-3S passive
    'he was jumped over four times'

19.4.3. Numerical-distributive adverbs

In order to express 'in two, in three,' etc., we use a cardinal numeral in combination with a t-construction (Section 22.3.1), as in the following:

(a) kałás   t‿s-qəxʷqaxʷan'-án‿a
    three   the‿fact-break all up-I‿reinf.
    'I broke it in three' (qəxʷqáxʷan' 'to break up anything, tr.')

(b) kałás   t‿s-ləm'ləm'n-án‿a
    three   the‿fact-break all up-I‿reinf.
    'I broke it in three' (lém'əlm'ən 'to break up dry, brittle stuff, tr.')

20
Verbal Substitutes

Lillooet has two types of verbal substitutes for which there are no direct equivalents in English: interrogative verbs (Section 20.1), and relator-verbs (Section 20.2). For other substitutes see Sections 24, 25, and 26.

20.1. Interrogative verbs

Interrogative verbs translate as phrases where the complement or predicate head is an interrogative pronoun or an interrogative phrase: kánəm 'to do what? be in what state? what is the matter with? to have what happening to oneself?', s-kən-kán 'to be of what size, amount?' (partially overlaps in meaning with kʷʷin, also a verbal substitute; see Section 19.1), s-kən-kán-s 'to make it how much? to ask what price for smt.? tr.,' kas 'to do it how? intr.,' kas-c 'to do it how to smt.? tr.,' ʔínw-at 'to say what? intr.,' ʔínw-an 'to say what to smb.? tr.' A few examples will suffice to show the function of these verbs.

With kánəm we have, for example:

(a) kaxʷ kánəm 'how are you doing?' (kaxʷ 2S subj. [Section 22.1])

(b) kánəm ti‿kⁿáh-sw‿a 'what happened to your car (kạh)? what is the matter with your car?'

(c) húy'-ɬkaɬ‿qaʔ kánəm 'what are we going to do now?' (huz' 'to be about to' > huy' before -ɬkaɬ 1P subj., ‿qaʔ 'now, after all')

Examples of s-kən-kán and s-kən-kán-s include:

(d) s-kən-kán kʷu‿s-qʷíqʷs-c 'how small is it?' (literally, 'how much is its smallness [s-qʷiqʷs]?')

(e) s-kən-kán-s-kaxʷ ti‿ɬkⁿʷál'us-cw‿a 'how much are you asking four your (-sw) basket (ɬkⁿʷál'us)?'

The word s-kən-kán is also used as an invariable adverb (like those discussed in Section 28), with xʷʔaz 'not' expressing 'not at all, no way':

(f) xʷʔáz‿kʷuʔ mútaʔ s-kən-kán kʷas‿cút 'Butcherknife,' 'no way that he would say (cut) "Butcherknife" again (mútaʔ)'

With ʔínw-at, ʔinw-an we have, for example:

(g) ʔinw-at-wít‿kɬ 'what will they (-wit) say?' (‿kɬ remote future)

(h) ʔinw-an-ítas   ti‿kʷúkʷpy'‿a 'what did they (-itas) say to the chief (kʷúkʷpəy')?'

With kas, kas-c we have, for example:

(i) wa? kas ɬəxʷ‿máysən ʔi‿ɬkʷʼáľus‿a 'how do you make (máysən) baskets (ɬkʷʼáľus)?' (literally, 'how is it done when you make baskets?')

(j) xʷʔạz kʷas‿zəwátn-as ɬəs‿kás ɬəs‿qʼʷə́l 'she did not (xʷʔạz) know (zəwátən) how it was cooked (qʼʷəl)'

(k) kas-c-káxʷ‿tu? 'what did you do to it?' (‿tu? 'smt. is over and done with'; stress is suspect: one would expect it on the root)

(l) kás-c-kaxʷ ɬ‿máysn-axʷ 'how did you fix it?' (literally, 'what did you do to it when you fixed it?')

(m) xʷʔáy‿X'u? káti? kʷ‿s-kás-c-an 'I (-an) did not do anything to him'

Besides kas we also have kás-ləx (-ləx 'body,' Section 15.2[77]), which is mainly used in expressions for 'going, getting there':

(n) kas-ləx-káɬ‿kɬ ɬ‿nás-at 'how are we going to go?' (-kaɬ, -at 1P subj., nas 'to go,' ‿kɬ 'remote future')

Besides kas, kas-c we also have s-kas, s-kas-c (s- stative prefix [Section 10.1.2]); s-kas-c has the same meaning as kas-c. However, s-kas is used mainly to mean 'to come how? to get (t)here how?'

(o) s-kás-kaxʷ 'how did you come? how did you get (t)here?'

(p) s-kás-kaxʷ‿kɬ 'how are you going?' (‿kɬ 'remote future')

(q) s-kas-c-káxʷ‿kɬ 'how are you going to do it?' (for stress see [k] above)

For the use of kʷ‿s- and ɬ‿ (ɬəxʷ‿, ɬəs‿) in the above sentences, see Section 22.

20.2. Relator-verbs

Relator-verbs[1] generally translate as phrases where the complement or the predicate head is a preposition or prepositional phrase: c'íla 'to be like, to be such,' c'íla-s 'to do it like, tr.,' xíləm 'to act, do like, intr.,' xiɬ 'to work out (in a certain way), intr.,' xiɬ-c 'to do it in a certain way, tr.,' lak 'to be in, at, around,' ʔak 'to be in that direction,' ɬlak 'to be from.' Relator-verbs may occur with or without complements, i.e., the thing likened to (in the case of c'íla, c'íla-s, xíləm, xiɬ, xiɬ-c) or the thing that is the setting (in the case of lak, ʔak, ɬlak). Where there are complements, these may be, but need not be, preceded by prepositions. Where there is no complement, the use of relator-verbs resembles the use of English 'alike' or 'in,' as in 'we are alike' or 'the doctor is in.' Examples of use are:

(a) ʔáma ɬ‿c'ílh-as 'it is good (ʔáma) if (ɬ‿) it is (-as) such' (expression of 'Amen'; note absence of complement)

(b) c'əl-c'íla-ɬkáɬ‿X'u? skʷʷəmkʷʷúkʷʷm'it 'we (-ɬkaɬ) were   children (skʷˀəmkʷˀúkʷˀmʾit) of the same size and age' (no complement; note reduplication in c̓əl-c̓íla)

(c) c̓ila‿X̌ʾuʔ wi‿sníɬ kʷ‿s-ˁəlˁəl-ɬkáɬ 'we are just as strong (ˁəlˁəl) as they (wi‿sníɬ) are' (wi‿sníɬ complement without preposition; cf. [p] below)

(d) níɬ‿X̌ʾuʔ s-c̓əq̓ʾpán-axʷ l‿ti‿nkʷˀX̌ʾústən̓-sw‿a ti‿núkʷ‿a, c̓íla ti‿núkʷ‿a 'so (níɬ‿X̌ʾuʔ) you (-axʷ) stick (c̓əq̓ʾpán) one (ti‿núkʷ‿a) on (l‿) your (-sw) eye (nkʷˀX̌ʾústən̓), the other (ti‿núkʷ‿a) goes likewise' (or 'you stick one piece on one eye, and the other piece on the other eye')

(e) huʔ c̓ila-s-twítas ti‿cúwaʔ-sw‿a sqʷal̓út 'they will do according to your (-sw) word (sqʷal̓út)' (translation of 'Thy will be done,' cúwaʔ 'possession, own' [see Section 24.4])

(f) x̌íləm‿X̌ʾuʔ mútaʔ, zúqʷ‿tuʔ 'he did the same thing (or: the same thing happened), he died (zuqʷ)' (‿tuʔ 'over and done with')

(g) x̌íləm-ɬkan ni‿s-cún-c-axʷ‿a, ʔáz̓ʾən-ɬkan 'I (-ɬkan) did like you (-axʷ) told (cun) me (-c), I bought (ʔáz̓ʾən) it'

(h) x̌íɬ-c-kan l‿t‿s-cunam̓ʾən-c-ás‿a 'I did it the way he (-as) taught (cunám̓ʾən) me (-c)' (l‿ 'in')

(i) lcʔa ɬ‿lák-as 'it is here (lcʔa) that it is'

(j) lak ltʔu 'it is over there (ltʔu)' (according to SM, only used for non-humans, whereas waʔ ltʔu 'it is over there' refers to humans; waʔ 'to be busy with, involved in, to stay')

(k) lak l‿snímuɬ ɬəs‿wáʔ 'it is here with us (snímuɬ) that he is staying (waʔ)'

(l) lak ʔi‿X̌ʾíq-as 'it is then (lak) that he (-as) came (X̌ʾiq)' (note the use of lak as a temporal deictic; according to ML, this sentence is virtually the same in meaning as láni? ʔi‿X̌ʾíq-as 'it is then that he came'; lániʔ 'then, at that time' [see Section 26.2])

(m) xʷʔaz kʷasu‿lák l‿s?ənc 'don't be with me!' (expresses 'it is none of your business what I [s?ənc] am doing'; xʷʔaz 'not,' kʷasu‿ 'you' [Section 22.4.1])

(n) ti‿pépəlʔ‿a ɬlák‿ʔiz̓ 'one (animal) from those, one of them' (literally, 'the one being from those,' pépla? 'one animal,' ʔiz̓ 'those' [Section 25.1])

Relator-verbs are sometimes used in positions other than the predicate position. In such cases they resemble English prepositions in function and in position.

(o) ʔáma ɬ‿cəkʷən-túmuɬ-axʷ ʔak ti‿ʔámh‿a sxʷákʷək̓ʷ-su 'it is good (ʔáma) if (ɬ‿) you (-axʷ) pull (cékʷən) us (-tumuɬ) to (ʔak) your (-su) good heart (sxʷákʷək̓ʷ)'

(p) ˁəlˁəl-ɬkáɬ X̌ʾit, cíla ʔə‿wi‿sníɬ 'we (-ɬkaɬ) are strong too (X̌ʾit), just like them' (ʔə‿ 'towards')

21
Summary of Stem Formation

This section summarizes stem formation under four headings: formal operations (Section 21.1), aspect (Section 21.2), control (Section 21.3), and transposition (Section 21.4). For a brief introductory discussion of aspect, control, and transposition, see also Section 8.1 (seventh paragraph).

21.1. Formal operations

Below, we demonstrate the function of reduplication and non-personal affixation, basing our examples on the root qʷal/qʷal' 'to speak, talk.' The form qʷal is used in only two cases (see ka-qʷál‿a and qʷəl-qʷál below), while qʷal' is used in all other formations. From qʷal' we form two basic stems: qʷal'-út 'to speak seriously, to deliver a speech,' and s-qʷal' 'to bring news.'[1] From these two stems we derive other forms through reduplication and affixation.

Lillooet	English	Morphological comments
ka-qʷál‿a	'to be able to speak'[2]	ka-..‿a resultative, 'suddenly, to be able to' (10.1.3)
qʷəl-qʷál	'to speak'[3]	total reduplication (12.1[4]; 12.5), lexicalized
qʷal'-út	'to deliver a speech, to speak seriously	√qʷal' plus unproductive formative -ut (15.4[7])
qʷal'-út-s	'to speak seriously to, to admonish, tr.'	-s transitivizer (18.1.2, 18.1.3)
qʷal'-út-min'	'to ask about, to complain about, to ask a woman's hand in marriage'[4]	-min' indirect transitivizer (18.1.4[c])

Lillooet	English	Morphological comments
qʷalʼ-ut-sút	'to talk nonsense, to talk away (e.g., when trying to cover up a lie')'	-sút 'out of control' (16[4])
s-qʷalʼ-út	'speech'	s- nominalizer (9)
qʷalʼ-út-tən, n-qʷalʼ-út-tən	'language, word, telephone, microphone'	-tən 'instrument,' (15.2[16a]), n-..-tən 'setting' (15.1.2 and 15.2[16.1])[5]
n-qʷalʼ-ut-ána?	'to hint, drop hints'	n-..-ana? 'ear' (15.2[34a])
n-qʷalʼ-ut-án?-an	'to hint to, tr.'	-an transitivizer (< -ən) (18.2)
qʷə-qʷalʼ-út	'to talk loud, to bawl out'	initial reduplication (12.1[1a]; 12.2)
qʷə-qʷalʼ-út-s	'to bawl smb. out, tr.'	-s transitivizer (18.1.2, 18.1.3)
qʷə-qʷalʼ-út-c-amʼ	'to mumble, to make lots of noise without saying'	-c 'mouth' (15.2[18c]), -am' intransitivizer (18.2)
qʷəlʼ-qʷalʼ-əlʼt	'to talk, have a conversation'	qʷalʼ-út plus total reduplication and consonant reduplication (12.1[5c]; 12.5)
qʷəlʼ-qʷalʼ-əlʼt-s	'to talk to, tr.'	-s transitivizer (18.1.2, 18.1.3)
qʷəlʼ-qʷalʼ-əlʼt-min	'to talk about, tr.'	-min indirect transitivizer (18.1.4[c])
qʷəlʼ-qʷalʼ-əlʼt-sút	'chatterbox'	-sút 'out of control' (16[4])
qʷəlʼ-qʷalʼ-əlʼt-úɬ	'chatterbox'	-úɬ 'always' (16[4])
s-qʷalʼ	'to bring news'	s- stative prefix (10.1.2), here with partial loss of meaning
s-qʷálʼ-ən	'to report to, tr.'	-ən transitivizer (18.1.2, 18.1.3)
s-qʷálʼ-minʼ	'to report on, tr.'	-min' indirect transitivizer (18.1.4[c])
s-qʷəlʼ-qʷalʼ-úɬ	'tattletale'	total reduplication (12.5) plus -úɬ 'always' (16[6])
səqʷ-sqʷálʼ	'to squeal, to spread news or gossip around'	total reduplication comprising s- (see 12.5, last paragraph)
s-qʷə́qʷəlʼ	'(to tell a) story'[6]	consonant reduplication (12.1[3]; 12.4)
s-qʷə́qʷlʼ-ən	'to tell a story to, tr.'	-ən transitivizer (18.1.2, 18.1.3)
s-qʷəqʷəlʼ-mín	'to tell a story about, tr.'	-min indirect transitivizer (18.1.4[c])

21.2. Aspect

Following Comrie (1981:3), we may state that aspects 'are different ways of viewing the internal temporal constituency of a situation.' This broad definition also holds for the various Lillooet aspectual operations, even though Lillooet differs from most of the languages discussed by Comrie in that Lillooet does not distinguish tenses, at least not on the morphological level,[7] and the Lillooet word class 'verb,' to which aspectual operations are limited, includes categories that in many languages would not be included within 'verb' but rather, for example, in 'adjectives' (see also Section 8.1.1 for word classes). Here we will briefly compare the aspectual operations that are employed in Lillooet. An exhaustive treatment of aspect remains a task for the future.[8]

Lillooet has the following productive (or at least amply attested) aspectual operations (the sections where these are covered are also indicated):

(1) resultative ka-..ˍa: 10.1.3

(2) stative s-: 10.1.2

(3) final reduplication, type (2a): 12.3

(4) final reduplication, type (2b): 12.3

(5) interior glottalization and -p: 13 and 14.1

(6) -əm: 14.2

(7) -t: 14.3

(8) n-..-təm: 14.4

(9) -a, -aɬ, -im': 14.5

(10) total reduplication, type (4d): 12.6

(11) A doubtful case is represented by the large number of lexicalized forms with total reduplication, e.g., cəq^w-cíq^w 'red' (see also Section 12.5). These forms might contain an aspectual notion (of a rather elusive character). Note also the initial or total reduplications that combine with -a (Section 14.5).

Unproductive aspectual operations include initial reduplication of type (1b) (Section 12.2) and initial reduplication C_1i-C_1V.. (Section 12.2). These are not considered further here.

Cases 1 to 11 do not form an integrated system, i.e., there are no roots or stems to which we may apply all operations listed above. We do have some cases that allow both (2) and (3), e.g., s-puɬ 'boiled' versus púɬ-əɬ 'to boil,' or s-qáx^w 'broken' versus qáx^w-əx^w 'to break, break down.' There are also a number of cases of (11) and (5), e.g., nəq^w-núq^w 'warm (atmosphere)' versus nu?q^w 'to get warm' (see also Section 13.1). For cases of (1) and (2) on the same stem, see Section 18.8. Other selections are rarer. For example, besides s-nə́m'-nəm' 'blind' (with [2] combined with [11]), we have nə́m'-ənm'-əp 'going blind' (with [5] and [11]). From the root √kaw 'far (away)' we have ká?əw 'to go farther,' with (5), and káw-əw 'to fall away (like an addition to a house tilting away from that house),' with (3). Note also ʔúʔca⁴ versus ʔucá⁴-p (Section 14.1).

Combinations of aspectual operations on the same stem are relatively rare. Some operations clearly exclude each other, e.g., (1) and (2). On the other hand, (9) occurs exclusively in combination with other types, while (11) does so often, e.g., with (6) or (7) (see Sections 14.2 to 14.3 for examples). See also s-nə́m'-nəm' and nə́m'-ənm'-əp above for combined operations.[9]

21.3. Control

Control - the degree to which a state or action is controlled by the one involved in it - is a major morphological/semantic category in Salish (see Thompson 1979a, 1981, 1985). In Lillooet, control manifests itself mainly through the choice of transitivizer (see Sections 18.1.2, 18.1.3, and 18.8). As pointed out in those sections, control in Lillooet does not imply complete dominance of the actor over the act, but rather that the process, state, or action does not require a special effort or some special happening. (Thus, 'to dry it,' 'to miss it,' and 'to find it' are controlled events, because these actions require no unusual effort or special event to lead to a result, whereas 'to hit it,' 'to make smb. take it out,' or 'to lose it' are not controlled, in that they require either a particular skill ['to hit it'], or a certain effort to overcome possible resistance from the causee ['to make smb. take it out'], or a particular accident ['to lose it'].)

We have also seen that at least some morphological operations - resultative ka-..ₐa, stative s-, and final reduplication - mark a stem as not controlled (with the consequence that such stems are transitivized with -s; see Sections 18.1.3 and 18.8). Interestingly, the suffix -sút indicates 'out of control,' but apparently more on a lexical level than on a grammatical one, in that in at least one form, pun-sút-ən (Section 18.5), there is a control transitivizer following -sút.

The control system ties in with the aspectual system in that the resultative and stative markers and final reduplication (marking continuative aspect) also have a control function (see above).[10]

21.4. Transposition

As we saw in Section 8.1.1, stems fall into three classes: transitive verbs, intransitive verbs, and nouns. Transposition from noun to intransitive verb takes place through the intransitivizer -am (Section 18.4), ʔəs- 'to have' (Section 10.1.1), -c 'to speak' (Section 15.2[18c]), and some cases of total reduplication (Section 12.5).

Transposition from intransitive verb to noun takes place mainly through the prefix s- (see Sections 8.1.1 and 9), while certain lexical suffixes are also nominalizing (see Section 15.2). Transposition from noun to transitive verb takes place through certain transitivizers (Section 18.4). Transposition from transitive verbs to nouns is a special problem of personal affixation (see Section 22.7). Transposition from intransitive to transitive verbs or vice versa is a matter of shifting from intransitivizer to transitivizer or vice versa (see Sections 18.1 to 18.3). Reflexive and reciprocal suffixes also transpose a transitive stem to an intransitive one (see Sections 17 and 18.7).

22
Personal Affixation

As we saw in Section 8.1, Lillooet distinguishes three types of personal affixes: possessive affixes, object suffixes, and subject suffixes. Personal affixes distinguish three persons in singular and plural. With these affixes, we have three basic paradigms: (1) a possessive paradigm: possessive affixes on nominal stems; (2) an intransitive paradigm: subject suffixes on intransitive stems; (3) a transitive paradigm: object suffixes and subject suffixes (in this order) on transitive stems (for the difference between nominal, intransitive, and transitive stems, see Section 8.1.1).

The transitive paradigm falls into two subtypes (with partially different object suffixes), depending on the type of transitivizer involved. The intransitive paradigm distinguishes a declarative paradigm from an imperative paradigm (e.g., 'I help' versus 'help!'), while the transitive paradigm distinguishes an active from a passive paradigm within the declarative paradigm, besides an (active) imperative paradigm (e.g., 'I help him' and 'I am helped' versus 'help him!'). The passive paradigm has a non-personal passive suffix instead of subject suffixes, while the imperative paradigms have special imperative suffixes in the subject slot. The forms with 1P transitive subject are borrowed from the passive (e.g., 'we help you' is 'you are helped').

The intransitive and transitive paradigms also fall into indicative and subjunctive paradigms. The indicative forms are marked by an element, -(ɬ)k-, before the subject suffixes 1SP and 2SP (ɬ being present after vowels and resonants but absent elsewhere). In addition, there is a factual paradigm, which combines the nominalizer s- plus possessive affixes (expressing the subject) in the intransitive paradigm, and s- plus subject suffixes (the latter taken from either the indicative or the subjunctive paradigm) in the transitive paradigm. As we saw in Sections 8.1.2 and 8.1.3, indicative and subjunctive forms form full independent predications, whereas factual forms form dependent (subordinate) clauses (see also Section 22.3.1 for a further discussion of the functions of the indicative, subjunctive, and factual forms).

Finally, all paradigms have simple and complex forms. In the latter, the verb base is preceded by an auxiliary that generally attracts the subject suffixes. The auxiliary is a full word in the indicative paradigm and in two subsets of the subjunctive paradigm, but a proclitic construction in the remaining subsets of the subjunctive and in the factual paradigm.

All possibilities of the intransitive and transitive paradigms are summarized in Figure 8, which also shows the sections in which the various paradigms are discussed (the possessive paradigm is discussed in Section 22.2; tables of the various affixes are given in Section 22.1).

Figure 8

Classification of verbal paradigms

			Indicative	Factual	Subjunctive
Intransitive	Declarative	Simple		22.3.1	
		Complex		22.4.1	
	Imperative	Simple		22.3.5	
		Complex		22.4.4	
Transitive	Declarative Active	Simple		22.3.2 to 22.3.3	
		Complex		22.4.2	
	Declarative Passive	Simple		22.3.4	
		Complex		22.4.3	
	Imperative	Simple		22.3.5	
		Complex		22.4.4	

In Section 22.5 we discuss special questions pertaining to the matters dealt with in Sections 22.3 and 22.4. As we saw in Section 8.1.2, certain predicates may also occur as subject or object complements. These cases are discussed in Sections 22.6 to 22.8.

22.1. Survey of affixes

The possessive affixes, object suffixes, and subject suffixes are as follows:

(1) Possessive affixes (Figure 9)

(2) Object suffixes (Figure 10). Most object suffixes have more than one shape, depending on (a) whether the object suffix is preceded by a transitivizer of type I or II (see also the opening remarks in Section 18), and (b)

Figure 9

Possessive affixes

	Singular	Plural
1	n-	-(ł)kał[2]
2	-su -cu[1]	-lap
3	-s -c[1]	-i

[1] -cu -c after ł s; -su -s elsewhere.
[2] -łkał after vowels and resonants; -kał elsewhere.

which person is referred to by the subject suffix following the object suffix. 1P and 2P object overlap in -tumuł. As Figure 10 shows, certain object markers consist of two morphemes: these combinations are discussed in Section 22.3.

(3) Subject suffixes (Figure 11). Most subject suffixes have various shapes. The choice between them depends on (a) whether the form in question is indicative or subjunctive, or intransitive or transitive; and (b) in the case

Figure 10

Object suffixes

		Transitivizer		Subject suffix
		II	I	
Object suffixes	1S	-c-al	-tumx-al	3P
		-c	-tumx	2SP, 3S
	2S	-ci(n)[1]	-tumi(n)[1]	1S
		-cih	-tumih	3SP
	3S	zero		all
	1P	-tumul		3P
		-tumuł		2SP, 3S
	2P	-tumuł		1S
		-tam-al'ap		3SP
	3P	-tan-i(h)[2]		1S
		-wit		2SP, 1S
		zero		3SP

[1] For distribution of -ci ~ -cin and -tumi ~ -tumin, see Section 22.3.2.
[2] -tan-i in indicative, -tan-ih in subjunctive.

Figure 11

Subject suffixes

		Intransitive	Transitive			
1S	Indicative	-(ɬ)k-an				
	Subjunctive	-an				
2S	Indicative	-(ɬ)k-axʷ				
	Subjunctive	-axʷ				
3S	Indicative	zero				
	Subjunctive	-as				
1P	Indicative	-(ɬ)kaɬ	(see Section 22.3.4)			
	Subjunctive	-at				
2P	Indicative	-(ɬ)k-aɬʼap				
	Subjunctive	-aɬʼap				
3P	Indicative	-wit	-as-wit	-it-as		-twit-as
	Subjunctive	-wit-as				
			2SP	1SP	II	I
						3SP
			Object suffixes			

of 3P subject, also on which person is referred to by the preceding object suffix (where the object suffix is 3SP, the object suffix is zero [see above], and the choice of 3P subject suffix depends on the type of transitivizer, which now immediately precedes 3P subject).

22.2. The possessive paradigm
On the basis of tmixʷ 'land' we have:

n-tmixʷ	'my land'	tmíxʷ-kaɬ	'our land'
tmíxʷ-su	'your land'	tmíxʷ-lap	'the land of you folks'
tmíxʷ-s	'his land'	tmíxʷ-i	'their land'

Examples with -cu, -c are: skʷx̌ʼus 'face' > skʷx̌ʼús-cu 'your face,' skʷx̌ʼus-c 'his face'; pʼáqʼʷuɬ 'cache' > pʼáqʼʷuɬ-cu 'your cache,' pʼáqʼʷuɬ-c 'his cache.' An example with -ɬkaɬ: slamála 'bottle' M > slamála-ɬkaɬ 'our bottle.' Note that -su (-cu) is changed to -sw (-cw) before a vowel, and that -i 'their' is extended to -ih before a vowel (see Section 4.1): ti‿tmíxʷ-sw‿a 'your land,' ti‿skʷƛ̓ús-cw‿a 'your face,' ti‿tmíxʷ-ih‿a 'their land' (for the article ti‿..‿a, see Section 31).

22.3. Simple intransitive and transitive paradigms
In the following subsections, we discuss the simple paradigms, i.e., those that do not employ auxiliary constructions: the simple intransitive declarative paradigm (Section 22.3.1), the simple transitive declarative paradigm (Section 22.3.2), special cases with transitivizers of type I (Section 22.3.3), the simple passive paradigm (Section 22.3.4), and the simple imperative (intransitive and transitive) paradigm (Section 22.3.5).

22.3.1. The simple intransitive declarative paradigm
The factual paradigm coincides with the possessive paradigm. Comments on the use of the various conjugations follow. The examples are based on the stem cut 'to say smt.'

	Indicative	Factual	Subjunctive
1S	cút-k-an	n-s-cut	cút-an
2S	cút-k-axʷ	s-cút-su	cút-axʷ
3S	cut	s-cut-s	cút-as
1P	cút-kaɬ	s-cút-kaɬ	cút-at
2P	cút-k-al'ap	s-cút-lap	cút-al'ap
3P	cút-wit	s-cút-i	cút-wit-as

After stems ending in a vowel or resonant, the indicative marker k has the shape ɬk: qan'ím 'to hear' > qan'ím-ɬk-an, qan'ím-ɬk-axʷ, qan'ím-ɬkaɬ, qan'ím-ɬk-al'ap (in the factual paradigm, also s-qan'ím-ɬkaɬ). In the form for 1P indicative, we do not split off -ɬk from aɬ, since this subject marker is not parallelled by a suffix *-aɬ in the subjunctive paradigm (in the way that the forms for 1S and 2SP are parallelled in the subjunctive by forms that result from omitting -ɬk).

Indicative forms are used as full predications with an objective (non-optative) mood: cút-k-an 'I say (said),' cút-k-axʷ 'you say (said),' etc. For 'optative' predications, see also subjunctive (1) below.

Factual forms are used only in subordinate clauses:

(a) As such after níɬ‿ƛ̓u? 'and so, and then,' or kánəm 'why?,' e.g., níɬ‿ƛ̓u? s-cut-s 'and then he said.' For details, see Section 37.2.

(b) After kʷ‿, which roughly corresponds to English 'that' (kʷ‿s-cut-s 'that he says [said]'). Constructions with kʷ‿ are mainly used after *verba sentiendi et declarandi* and after xʷ?az '(it is) not (the case),' e.g., xʷ?az kʷ‿s-cut-s 'he did not say.' See also Section 19.4.2. For further details, see Section 37.1.

(c) Embedded in t̯...̯a (t̯ is a remnant of the article ti̯ [Section 31]) and expressing various notions, e.g., 'because' (in this case often preceded by nit, Section 29.1[8]: nit t̯s-cút-s̯a 'because he said'); also used to express numerical-distributive adverbs (Section 19.4.3); for further details, see Section 37.3.

The three subgroups of the factual paradigm are called s-constructions, kʷ-constructions, and t-constructions, respectively. Factual forms may not be confused with nominalized forms with possessive affixes (although they are formally the same); see the last paragraph of Section 22.4.1.

Subjunctive forms are first of all used as full (independent) predications:

(a) As such with an 'optative' mood: cút-an 'may I say, let me say,' cút-axʷ 'may you say,' etc. Such forms are only rarely used by themselves: more often we find them in combination with certain adverbial enclitics (Section 32), which then modify the optative meaning, e.g., ʔínwat 'to say what?' > ʔínwat-wít-as̯kt 'I wonder what they will say' (̯kt 'remote future'), cf. ʔinwat-wít̯kt 'what will they say?' (indicative).

(b) Obligatorily in combination with the adverbial enclitic ̯an' 'it seems that' (Section 32.1.3), e.g., tayt-áxʷ̯an' 'you look hungry (tayt)' (cf. indicative táyt-kaxʷ 'you are hungry').

Subjunctive forms are also used in subordinate clauses:

(c) After the proclitic conjunctions t̯ 'if, when' and ʔi̯ 'when,' e.g., ʔi̯cút-an 'when I said.' For details see Sections 37.4.1 and 37.4.2.

For a discussion of main and subordinate predications, see also Section 35.

22.3.2. The simple transitive declarative paradigm

The examples are based on cun 'to tell, order smb.' (type II transitivizer) and xʷítən-s 'to whistle at' (type I transitivizer), and are organized around the subject suffixes. Forms with 1P subject are discussed in Section 22.3.4. As the examples show, the factual and subjunctive paradigms coincide where 1S and 2SP are subject, except in the case 1S-2S, and the paradigms all coincide where 3S and 3P are subject. (However, the factual forms are always preceded by s-, hence cún-an [1S-3S], cun-tumút-an [1S-2P], etc., are in fact s-cún-an, s-cun-tumút-an in the factual paradigm.) In the indicative 1S-2S relationship, we have both -ci-tk-an and -cin-tk-an (in about equally frequent use). In the factual and subjunctive 1S-2S forms, we have -cin for 2S object (note that in factual 1S-2S there is no overt marker for 1S subject).

cun 'to tell, order smb., tr.'

	Indicative	Factual		Subjunctive
1S-2S	cún-ci(n)-tk-an	s-cún-cin		cún-cin-an
1S-3S	cún-tk-an		cún-an	
1S-2P	cun-tumút-k-an		cun-tumút-an	

	Indicative	Factual	Subjunctive
1S-3P	cun-tan-í-ɬk-an		cun-tan-íh-an
	cún-wit-k-an[1]		cún-wit-an
2S-1S	cún-c-k-axʷ		cún-c-axʷ
2S-3S	cún-ɬk-axʷ		cún-axʷ
2S-1P	cun-tumúɬ-k-axʷ		cun-tumúɬ-axʷ
2S-3P	cún-wit-k-axʷ		cún-wit-axʷ
2P-1S	cún-c-k-alʼap		cún-c-alʼap
2P-3S	cún-ɬk-alʼap		cún-alʼap
2P-1P	cun-tumúɬ-k-alʼap		cun-tumúɬ-alʼap
2P-3P	cun-wit-k-álʼap		cun-wit-álʼap
3S-1S		cún-c-as	
3S-2S		cún-cih-as	
3S-3SP		cún-as	
3S-1P		cun-tumúɬ-as	
3S-2P		cun-tam-álʼap-as	
3P-1S		cun-c-al-ít-as	
3P-2S		cun-cih-ás-wit	
3P-3SP		cún-it-as	
3P-1P		cun-tumúl-it-as	
3P-2P		cun-tam-alʼap-ás-wit	

The forms with xʷítən-s are different from those with cun only where we have 1S or 2S object and in the case of 3P-3SP. However, I give all forms of xʷítən-s for easy reference. Forms with 1S or 2S object and 3P-3SP are indicated by the symbol ◊.

xʷítən-s 'to whistle at, tr.'

	Indicative	Factual	Subjunctive
1S-2S	◊ xʷitən-s-túmi(n)-ɬk-an	◊ s-xʷitən-s-túmin	◊ xʷitən-s-túmin-an
1S-3S	xʷítən-s-k-an	xʷítən-s-an	
1S-2P	xʷitən-s-túmuɬ-k-an	xʷitən-s-túmuɬ-an	
1S-3P	xʷitən-s-tán-i-ɬk-an	xʷitən-s-tán-ih-an	
	xʷitən-s-wít-k-an	xʷitən-s-wít-an	
2S-1S	◊ xʷitən-s-túmx-k-axʷ	◊ xʷitən-s-túmx-axʷ	
2S-3S	xʷítən-s-k-axʷ	xʷítən-s-axʷ	
2S-1P	xʷitən-s-túmuɬ-k-axʷ	xʷitən-s-túmuɬ-axʷ	
2S-3P	xʷitən-s-wít-k-axʷ	xʷitən-s-wít-axʷ	
2P-1S	◊ xʷitən-s-túmx-k-alʼap	◊ xʷitən-s-túmx-alʼap	
2P-3S	xʷitən-s-k-álʼap	xʷitən-s-álʼap	
2P-1P	xʷitən-s-tumuɬ-k-álʼap	xʷitən-s-tumuɬ-álʼap	
2P-3P	xʷitən-s-wít-k-alʼap	xʷitən-s-wít-alʼap	

	Indicative	Factual	Subjunctive
3S-1S	◊ xʷitən-s-túmx-as		
3S-2S	◊ xʷitən-s-túmih-as		
3S-3SP	xʷítən-s-as		
3S-1P	xʷitən-s-túmuɬ-as		
3S-2P	xʷitən-s-tam-ál'ap-as		
3P-1S	◊ xʷitən-s-tumx-al-ít-as		
3P-2S	◊ xʷitən-s-tumih-ás-wit		
3P-3SP	◊ xʷitən-s-twít-as		
3P-1P	xʷitən-s-tumul-ít-as		
3P-2P	xʷitən-s-tam-al'ap-ás-wit		

The transitivizer -s, which has the shape -c after ɬ s (see Section 18.1.2), is dropped when it occurs after ɬ or s and before a suffix starting with t, hence x̌iɬ-c 'to do, carry out, tr.' > x̌iɬ[-c]-twít-as 'they did it'; nas-c 'to bring, tr.' > nas[-c]-twít-as 'they brought it.' In the same way, the combination -s-cút (Section 18.6[1]) drops -s- after ɬ (we have no examples after s): ləqsay'ɬ-cút 'to act as though one were the pet' < *ləqsay'ɬ-s-cút.

Since the indicative and subjunctive transitive paradigms merge where 3SP is subject (the factual paradigm still has the nominalizer s- here to keep it separate from indicative and subjunctive), we have to rely on the context to determine whether a transitive form with 3SP subject is indicative or subjunctive. An example of a transitive (3S subject) subjunctive form is provided by c'aqʷan'-ás ƛ'uʔ in plán ƛ'uʔ waʔ ʔáma kʷ s-palʔacmin'-as ƛ'úʔ ti?, c'aqʷan'-ás ƛ'uʔ sniɬ 'it is okay (ʔáma) already (plan) that he eats that (ti?) all by himself, let him eat (c'áqʷan') it' (pálʔacmin' 'to eat smt. all by oneself,' sniɬ 3S personal pronoun, ƛ'uʔ 'well, so'): here c'aqʷan'-ás ƛ'uʔ is obviously in the subjunctive although formally identical with the indicative form, c'aqʷan'-ás ƛ'uʔ 'he eats it.'

22.3.3. Special cases with transitivizers of type I

When we have stems with the transitivizer -s combined with the object suffixes -tumx(al), -tumi(n)/-tumih, -tumuɬ/-tumul, or -tan-i, these object suffixes glottalize m or n if according to the rules set out in Section 2.1(1) to (4), the stress falls on the stem or on the first vowel after m or n. Cases that deviate with regard to the stress from the cases with xʷítən-s in Section 22.3.2 are given below (only indicative forms are listed).

ƛ'iq-s 'to bring (here), tr.'

1S-2S	ƛ'iq-s-tum'í(n)-ɬk-an
1S-2P	ƛ'iq-s-tum'úɬ-k-an
1S-3P	ƛ'iq-s-tan'-í-ɬk-an

2S-1S	X̣'íq-s-tum'x-k-axʷ	2P-1S	X̣'íq-s-tum'x-k-ál'ap
2S-1P	X̣'íq-s-tum'úł-k-axʷ	2P-1P	X̣'íq-s-tum'úł-k-al'ap

3S-1S	X̣'íq-s-tum'x-as	3P-1S	X̣'íq-s-tum'x-ál-it-as
3S-2S	X̣'íq-s-tum'íh-as	3P-2S	X̣'íq-s-tum'íh-as-wit
3S-1P	X̣'íq-s-tum'úł-as	3P-1P	X̣'íq-s-tum'úl-it-as

22.3.4. The simple passive paradigm

The passive forms 1SP, 2S, and 3S are made by placing a passive suffix after the object suffixes for these persons.[2] In the case of 1SP passive, we have the same object suffixes as in 3P-1SP; the passive suffix is -əm here. In 2S the passive suffix is -m; in 3S it is -əm with type II transitivizers and -tum with type I transitivizers.

The passive endings 2P and 3P are -tam-łk-al'ap and -tan-əm-wit, respectively (cf. the first with -tam-al'ap 2P object, and the second with -tan-i 3P object). The passive forms 2SP and 3SP also express the relationships 1P-2SP and 1P-3SP, respectively (e.g., 'you are told' is also 'we tell you').

Factual forms are the same as indicative forms, except that factual forms have s- (e.g., 1S passive is s-cún-c-al-əm in the factual paradigm). Subjunctive forms are made by adding -as (3S subjunctive) to the indicative forms.

	Indicative	Factual	Subjunctive
1S	cún-c-al-əm		cun-c-al-ə́m-·as
2S	cún-ci-m		cún-ci-m-as
3S	cún-əm		cún-m-as
1P	cun-tumúl-əm		cun-tumúl-m-as
2P	cun-tam-łk-ál'ap		cun-tam-łk-ál'ap-as
3P	cún-tan-əm-wit		cun-tan-əm-wít-as
1S	xʷitən-s-túmx-al-əm		xʷitən-s-tumx-al-ə́m-as
2S	xʷitən-s-túmi-m		xʷitən-s-túmi-m-as
3S	xʷítən-s-tum		xʷitən-s-túm-as
1P	xʷitən-s-túmul-əm		xʷitən-s-tumul-ə́m-as
2P	xʷitən-s-tam-łk-ál'ap		xʷitən-s-tam-łk-ál'ap-as
3P	xʷitən-s-tán-əm-wit		xʷitən-s-tan-əm-wít-as

Note that in the subjunctive forms, -əm retains ə before -as when -əm can attract the stress (as in cun-c-al-ə́m-as; for stress see Section 2.1[2], [8]). When -əm cannot attract the stress, it drops ə here (cún-m-as, cun-tumúl-m-as). We have the alternate treatment of -əm in forms with, for example, cułun' 'to point at': cułun'-c-ál-m-as, cułun'-ə́m-as, cułun'-tumul-ə́m-as. The object suffixes -tumx/-tumx-al, -tumi(n), -tumuł/-tumul, and -tum (3S passive) glottalize m in the passive forms under the same stress conditions under which they glottalize m in the active forms (Section 22.3.3).

	Indicative	Factual	Subjunctive
1S	ƛ̓iq-s-tum̓x-ál-əm		ƛ̓iq-s-tum̓x-ál-m-as
2S	ƛ̓íq-s-tum̓i-m		ƛ̓iq-s-tum̓í-m-as
3S	ƛ̓íq-s-tum̓		ƛ̓íq-s-tum̓-as
1P	ƛ̓iq-s-tum̓úl-əm		ƛ̓iq-s-tum̓úl-m-as

The transitivizer -c (< -s after ɬ s) is dropped before -tum̓ (no cases with -tum recorded): nas-c 'to bring' > nás[-c]-tum̓ 'we brought him.'

22.3.5. The simple imperative (intransitive and transitive) paradigm

The indicative imperative forms either are the same as the declarative ones with 2SP subject (e.g., cún-ɬk-axʷ 'you tell him!') or have the following shapes:

Intransitive

2S	cut
2P	cút-wi

Transitive

2S-1S	cun-c	xʷítən-s-tumx
2S-3S	cun	xʷítən-s
2S-1P	cún-tumuɬ	xʷitən-s-túmuɬ
2S-3P	cún-wit	xʷítən-s-wit
2P-1S	cún-c-al-i	xʷítən-s-túmx-al-i
2P-3SP	cún-i	xʷítən-s-twi
2P-1P	cun-tumúl-i	xʷitən-s-túmul-i

The make-up of these forms is as follows. In the intransitive we have the bare stem for 2S, and the stem plus -wi for 2P. In the transitive we have the transitive stem plus the object suffixes 1S, 1P, 3S, or 3P for a command to 2S, but for a command to 2P we have the transitive stem plus the object suffixes as required by 3P subject, followed by -i or -twi. The imperative forms for 2P are apparently derived from the declarative forms with 3P subject by dropping the portion after i in the declarative suffix 3P, e.g., cút-wit 'they say' > cút-wi 'say, you folks!'; cún-it-as 'they tell him' > cún-i 'tell him, you folks!' Imperative forms often combine with the adhortative enclitic ˏmaɬ (Section 32.1.1), e.g., xʷitən-s-túmuɬˏmaɬ 'whistle at us!'

The factual and subjunctive imperative forms are identical to the declarative forms with 2S or 2P subject (only cases of factuals [b] and subjunctive [c] were recorded as imperatives): xʷʔạ̈z-as kʷˏs-q'ʷə́ɬp-su 'don't get burnt!' (qʼʷətp 'to get burnt'), xʷʔáz-as kʷ‿s-cún-axʷ 'don't tell him!' (xʷʔaz 'not,' -as 3S 'optative' [Section 22.3.1]), lcʔa ɬ‿kícin'-axʷ 'put it down (kícin') here (lcʔa)!' (for the use of ɬ‿ here, see Section 37.4.1[2]).

22.4. Complex forms

The general make-up of complex forms is discussed in the introductory remarks to Section 22. The paradigms in Section 22.4.1 to 22.4.4 give further details. Virtually every intransitive stem that is temporal, aspectual, or modal in character may be used as an auxiliary, e.g., waʔ 'to be busy with, involved in,' huzʼ 'to be about to,' plan '(to have) already (done),' stəx̌ʷ 'really.' In the lists in Section 22.4.1 to 22.4.4, we use waʔ, which has special proclitic forms in the factual and subjunctive. The use of waʔ corresponds to the English progressive tense.

22.4.1. Complex declarative intransitive forms

Within the factual paradigm, the s-, t-, and kʷ-constructions yield different proclitic forms, sometimes even more forms for one subject. For subjunctive (a) and (b) forms (as discussed in Section 22.3.1), see below.

Figure 12

Complex declarative intransitive forms

		Auxiliary				
	Indicative	Factual			Subjunctive (c)	Verb-base
		s-	t-	kʷ-		
1S	wáʔ-ɬkan	nswa‿ / sən‿	tənswa‿	kʷənswa‿ / kʷən‿	ɬ‿wan‿	cut
2S	wáʔ-ɬkaxʷ	saxʷ‿ / su‿	tsaxʷa‿ / tswa‿ / tsəswa‿	kʷasu‿	ɬ‿waxʷ‿	
3S	waʔ	səs‿	tsa‿ / tsəsa‿	kʷas‿	ɬ‿was‿	
1P	wáʔ-ɬkaɬ	sat‿ / skaɬ‿	tsata‿ / tskaɬa‿	kʷat‿ / kʷaɬkaɬ‿	ɬ‿wat‿	
2P	wáʔ-ɬkalʼap	salʼap‿	tsalʼapa‿	kʷalʼap‿	ɬ‿walʼap‿	
3P	wáʔ-wit = 3S	= 3S	= 3S	= 3S	= 3S	cút-wit

Examples of complex forms include: wá?-ɬk-an cut 'I am saying,' ɬ‿wan‿cút 'if, when I am saying.' Except for 3P, the verb base has no subject markers. It yields them to the auxiliary in the indicative, whereas in the other paradigms the auxiliary is otherwise defined for person and number. The indicative 3P is the only case where -wit may be combined with the auxiliary. The factual forms show remnants of various elements, e.g., of the article ti‿ in the t-forms, or -su in kʷasu‿ (2S), but I do not posit morpheme boundaries within these proclitic constructions. The subjunctive forms clearly show the subjunctive endings and the remnant of wa?. Instead of ɬ‿, as in the above forms, we may also have ?i‿ 'when' (?i‿wan‿ 'when I was,' etc.). The proclitic forms are often reduced in rapid speech, e.g., ɬən‿, ɬəxʷ‿, for ɬ‿wan‿, ɬ‿waxʷ‿ (the fact that proclitics are by definition unstressed accounts for their unstable phonetic status).

In addition to wá?-ɬk-an, wá?-ɬk-axʷ, wá?-ɬkaɬ, and wá?-ɬk-al'ap, we also have kan, kaxʷ, kaɬ, and kal'ap (without perceptible difference in meaning from the forms with wa?), e.g., kan cut 'I am saying.' Forms with kan, etc. (rather than wá?-ɬk-an) are frequently used in M but rarely in F.

Auxiliaries other than wa? behave like wa? in the indicative, e.g., húz'-ɬk-an cut 'I will (huz') say.' In the factual and subjunctive (c) paradigms, these auxiliaries are fully stressed factual and subjunctive (c) forms, as discussed in Section 22.3.1 (e.g., kʷ‿ən-s-húz' cut, t‿ən-s-húz'‿a cut, n-s-huz' cut, ɬ‿húz'-an cut).

We may also have two auxiliaries, the first of which takes the subject markers, e.g., plán-ɬk-an wa? cukʷ 'we are finished (cukʷ) already (plan),' ?i‿wan‿wá? skʷúkʷʷm'it 'when I was a child (skʷúkʷʷm'it).' See also n. 1 of Section 32.

Complex subjunctive (a) and (b) forms consist of a full-word auxiliary (like indicative complex forms) plus subjunctive suffixes, followed by a verb base: (a) wá?-as‿X'u? ?íX'əm 'let him (be) sing(ing)' (?íX'əm 'to sing,' ‿X'u? 'well, but, so'); cf. indicative wá?‿X'u? ?íX'əm 'he is singing.'

(b) plan-at‿ká‿tu? wa? cixʷ 'I wish we were there already' (plan 'already,' cixʷ 'to get there,' ‿ka 'should, would,' ‿tu? 'definite past'); cf. indicative plan-ɬkaɬ‿ká‿tu? wa? cixʷ 'we should have been there already.'

(c) plán-at‿an' wa? pəl'p 'it looks like (‿an') we are lost (pəl'p) already (plan)'; cf. indicative plán-ɬkaɬ wa? pəl'p 'we are lost already.'

As is the case in the indicative, the suffix 3P subject may occur after the auxiliary or on the verb base: (d) wa?-wit-ás‿maɬ‿X'u? ?íX'əm (= wa?-as‿máɬ‿X'u? ?íX'əm-wit) 'let them sing (?íX'əm), they might as well sing' (‿maɬ adhortative: in combination with ‿X'u? and an 'optative' it usually expresses 'might as well').

In Section 22.3.1 we remarked that (intransitive) factual forms may not be confused with nominalized forms that have possessive affixes. In the simple paradigm we have, for example, the factual form t‿ən-s-cút‿a 'the fact that I say' (formally very close to the nominalized form ti‿n-s-cút‿a 'that what I say' (with the noun s-cut 'what one says'; ti‿ is often collapsed into t‿ and in that case ti‿n-s-cút‿a formally completely coincides with t‿ən-s-cút‿a). However, in the complex paradigm, factuals and nominals are quite different: nominals are made complex by putting waʔ between the article and the noun (waʔ is then proclitic, and ‿a is dropped). Such forms are quite different from complex factuals:

(e) ti‿waʔ‿ən-s-cút 'what I am saying' (nominal)

(f) tənswa‿cút 'the fact that I am saying' (factual)

22.4.2. Complex declarative transitive forms

The auxiliaries are the same as in the intransitive (Figure 13), with the exception of 1P subject (discussed in Section 22.4.3).

Figure 13

Complex declarative transitive forms

	Indicative	Auxiliary			Subjunctive (c)	Verb-base	Object
		Factual					
		s-	t-	kʷ-			
1S	wáʔ-ɬkan	nswa‿ sən‿	tənswa‿	kʷənswa‿ kʷən‿	ɬ‿wan‿	cún-cin cun cún-tumuɬ cun-taníh-an cún-wit	2S 3S 2P 3P
2S	wáʔ-ɬkaxʷ	saxʷ‿ su‿	tsaxʷa‿ tswa‿ tsəswa‿	kʷasu‿	ɬ‿waxʷ‿	cun-c cun cún-tumuɬ	1S 3S 1P
2P	wáʔ-ɬkaɬap	saɬap‿	tsaɬapa‿	kʷaɬap‿	ɬ‿waɬap‿	cún-wit	3P
3S	waʔ	səs‿	tsa‿	kʷas‿	ɬ‿was‿	cún-c-as cún-cih-as cún-as cun-tumúɬ-as cun-tamáɬap-as	1S 2S 3SP 1P 2P
3P	waʔ	səs‿	tsəsa‿	kʷas‿	ɬ‿was‿	cun-cal-ítas cun-cih-áswit cún-itas cun-tumúl-itas cun-tamaɬap-áswit	1S 2S 3SP 1P 2P

The 3SP subject suffixes occur in the verb base, so that the verb-base forms here are identical to those in the simple paradigm. In 1S and 2SP subject we have no subject suffixes in the verb base except in 1S-3P (-an in -tan-ih-an: note that 1S is also marked in the auxiliary). The other verb-base forms with 1S and 2SP consist of a stem plus object suffix.[3]

With 'to whistle at' we have the following forms in the base:

1S-2S	xʷitən-s-túmin	2SP-1S	xʷítən-s-tumx
1S-3S	xʷítən-s	2SP-3S	xʷítən-s
1S-2S	xʷitən-s-túmuɫ	2SP-1P	xʷitən-s-túmuɫ
1S-3P	xʷitən-s-tán-ih-an	2SP-3P	xʷitən-s-wit
	xʷítən-s-wit		

The forms with 3SP subject are the same as in the simple paradigm (waʔ xʷitən-s-túmx-as 3S-1S, etc.). With verbs of the type ƛ'iq-s we have regular glottalization in ƛ'íq-s-tum'in, etc.

22.4.3. The complex passive paradigm

This paradigm is formed by placing the same auxiliaries that are used for 3S subject before the simple indicative passive forms (Figure 14).

With xʷítən-s we have waʔ xʷitən-s-túmx-al-əm (1S), etc. 2SP and 3SP are also used to express the relationship 1P-2SP and 1P-3SP (waʔ cún-ci-m 'we are telling you' besides 'you are being told'). The suffixes -ɫk-al'ap and -wit in 2P and 3P are part of larger suffix complexes, and they do not move to the auxiliary (there is no *wáʔ-ɫk-al'ap cún-tam, or *wáʔ-wit cún-tan-əm). I did not record any cases of subjunctive (a) and (b) complex passive forms.

Figure 14

Complex passive forms

	Auxiliary				Verb-base
	Indicative	Factual		Subjunctive (c)	
		s-	t-	kʷ-		
1S						cún-cal-əm
2S						cún-ci-m
3S			tsa˰			cún-əm
	waʔ	səs˰		kʷas˰	ɫ˰was˰	
1P			tsəsa˰			cun-tumúl-əm
2P						cun-tamɫkáľap
3P						cún-tanəmwit

22.4.4. Complex imperative forms

Indicative imperative complex forms are as follows.

Intransitive

2S	wá?ˍmaɬ cut
2P	wá?-wiˍmaɬ cut
	wá?ˍmaɬ cút-wi

The intransitive paradigm consists of an auxiliary plus ˍmaɬ (adhortative) and the intransitive simple forms. With 2P addressee, the suffix -wi may appear after the auxiliary or on the verb base.

Transitive

2S-1S	wá?ˍmaɬ cun-c	wá?ˍmaɬ xʷítən-s-tumx
2S-3S	wá?ˍmaɬ cun	wá?ˍmaɬ xʷítən-s
2S-1P	wá?ˍmaɬ cún-tumuɬ	wá?ˍmaɬ xʷitən-s-túmuɬ
2S-3P	wá?ˍmaɬ cún-wit	wá?ˍmaɬ xʷítən-s-wit
2P-1S	wá?ˍmaɬ cún-c-al-i	wá?ˍmaɬ xʷitən-s-túmx-al-i
	wá?-wiˍmaɬ cun-c	wá?-wiˍmaɬ xʷítən-s-tumx
2P-3SP	wá?ˍmaɬ cún-i	wá?ˍmaɬ xʷítən-s-twi
	wá?-wiˍmaɬ cun	wá?-wiˍmaɬ xʷítən-s
2P-1P	wá?ˍmaɬ cun-tumúl-i	wá?ˍmaɬ xʷitən-s-túmul-i
	wá?-wiˍmaɬ cún-tumuɬ	wá?-wiˍmaɬ xʷitən-s-túmuɬ

Like the intransitive ones, the transitive complex forms are composed of an auxiliary plus ˍmaɬ before the corresponding simple forms. With 2P addressee we may replace -i (-twi) in the verb base with -wi after the auxiliary. Note that with 2P addressee there is no distinction between 3S and 3P object.[4]

In the facultative paradigm, I recorded only imperative complex forms with kʷ-constructions (these are the same as in the declarative paradigm):

xʷ?az kʷasuˍcút	(1) 'you don't say'	(2) 'don't say!'
xʷ?az kʷal'ap̓ˍcút	(1) 'you folks don't say'	(2) 'don't say, you folks!'
xʷ?az kʷasuˍcún-c	(1) 'you don't tell me'	(?) 'don't tell me!'

As a rule, xʷ?áz-as (Section 22.3.5) is not used in the complex imperative paradigm. Subjunctive imperative complex forms (of type [c]) are identical to the declarative forms.

22.5. Special questions

Here we discuss the following issues: imperatives 1P (Section 22.5.1), imperative stems (Section 22.5.2), expression of 1P transitive subject (Section

22.5.3), -ɫk suffixes after obstruents (Section 22.5.4), and reflexive and reciprocal forms (Section 22.5.5).

22.5.1. Imperatives 1P

Besides the indicative intransitive imperative form xʷuy 'come on!' (see also Section 22.5.2), we have transitive xʷúy-s‿maɫ and xʷuy-s-twí‿maɫ (both with the transitivizer -s). Although xʷúy-s‿maɫ and xʷuy-s-twí‿maɫ are formally commands to 2S and 2P, respectively, they are in fact used to express 'let *us* (go, do it)!'; xʷúy-s‿maɫ is used for a smaller group within a larger group, whereas xʷuy-s-twí‿maɫ is used for the whole group. We therefore have a case of 1P exclusive versus 1P inclusive here, the only case where this difference is formally expressed in Lillooet.

22.5.2. Imperative stems

There are a few stems in Lillooet that are used exclusively in imperative expressions, never in declarative ones. Besides xʷuy, xʷúy-s‿maɫ, and xʷuy-s-twí‿maɫ (Section 22.5.1), we have síma? 'come!' (as in síma?‿ƛ'u? 'come in! come right over!' ƛ'u? 'well, but, so'), or síma?‿qa? 'come then!' (for ‿qa? see Section 32.1.11), and hú?‿maɫ 'good-bye' (to one), hú?-wi‿maɫ 'good-bye, you folks.' Declarative formations based on these stems are incorrect (hence we do not have *síma?-ɫk-an or *hú?-ɫk-an).

22.5.3. Expression of 1P transitive subject

As pointed out in Sections 22.3.4 and 22.4.3, the forms for 2SP and 3SP passive also express 1P-2SP and 1P-3SP. One can bring out the 1P subject function in the indicative paradigm by using wá?-ɫkaɫ instead of wa? (other auxiliaries do not seem to allow this possibility). Compare:

(a) wa? núkʲʷ?an-əm (1) 'he is being helped,' (2) 'we are helping him,' but wá?-ɫkaɫ núkʲʷ?an-əm '*we* are helping him' (as answer to the question 'is nobody helping him?').

(b) wa? nukʲʷ?an-tán-əm-wit (1) 'they are being helped,' (2) 'we are helping them,' but wá?-ɫkaɫ nukʲʷ?an-tán-əm-wit '*we* are helping them' (as answer to 'is nobody helping them?').

The suffix ɫkaɫ is used only when there is some doubt as to the involvement of 1P in the action. Hence we often have the enclitic combination ‿a‿qa? 'well, as you can see, as you should know' after -ɫkaɫ in these cases: wa?-ɫkaɫ‿á‿qa? núkʲʷ?an-ci-m 'but we *are* helping you' (if somebody complains that nobody is helping him).

22.5.4. -ɫk suffixes after obstruents

In a few words some speakers use the endings -ɫk-an, ɫk-axʷ, -ɫkaɫ, -ɫk-al'ap (instead of -k-an, -k-axʷ, -kaɫ, -k-al'ap) after obstruents, e.g., ƛ'íq-ɫk-axʷ 'you arrived' (also 'there you are!' – used as a greeting) instead of ƛ̓íq-k-axʷ. The usage of -ɬk- here is not incorrect. However, it appears to be limited to monomorphemic (hence intransitive) stems. The suffix -(ɬ)kaɬ 1P possessive does not allow ɬ after obstruents.

22.5.5. Reflexive and reciprocal forms

As mentioned in Sections 17 and 18.7, reflexive and reciprocal suffixes convert transitive stems to intransitive ones. This means that stems with such suffixes select intransitive rather than transitive subject suffixes, e.g., nukʷˀʔan-cút 'to help (núkʷˀʔan) oneself' > nukʷˀʔan-cút-kaɬ 'we help ourselves,' nukʷˀʔan-cút-wit 'they help themselves'; núkʷˀʔan-twal' 'to help each other' > nukʷˀʔan-twál'-ɬkaɬ 'we help each other,' nukʷˀʔan-twál'-wit 'they help each other.'

22.6. Object- and subject-centred forms

Lillooet verbal complexes where the third person is object or subject may fill the slot of subject or object complement in a sentence. The best translation for verbal forms in these cases is that of a relative clause with the antecedent enclosed ('one who says,' 'one who tells me'). In the intransitive paradigm we only have the cases where 3SP is subject, whereas in the transitive paradigm we have the possibilities 1SP/2SP/3SP-3SP ('object-centred forms') and 3SP-1SP/2SP/3SP ('subject-centred forms').

These forms are exemplified in the paradigms below. The examples are only of cases where 3S is the centre of the construction, the expression of 3P being discussed later. The article used (ti‿…‿a) expresses 'present, known, singular.' Comments follow.

Intransitive
ti‿cút‿a   'the one who says (said)'[5]

Transitive 1 (object-centred)

ti‿cún-an‿a	ti‿xʷitən-s-án‿a	'the one I told, whistled at'
ti‿cún-axʷ‿a	ti‿xʷitən-s-áxʷ‿a	'the one you told, whistled at'
ti‿cún-as‿a	ti‿xʷitən-s-ás‿a	'the one he told, whistled at'
ti‿cún-m‿a	ti‿xʷitən-s-túm‿a	'the one we told, whistled at'
ti‿cun-al'áp‿a	ti‿xʷitən-s-ál'ap‿a	'the one you folks told, whistled at'
ti‿cun-it-ás‿a	ti‿xʷitən-s-twít-as‿a	'the one they told, whistled at'

Transitive 2 (subject-centred)

ti‿cún-c-as‿a	'the one who told me'
ti‿cuncih-ás‿a	'the one who told you'
ti‿cun-talíh‿a	'the one who told him'

tiˏcun-tumúɬ-asˏa	'the one who told us'
tiˏcun-tam-aɬ'ap-ásˏa	'the one who told you folks'
tiˏcun-tan-əm-wít-asˏa	'the one who told them'
tiˏxʷitən-s-túmx-asˏa	'the one who whistled at me'
tiˏxʷitən-s-tumih-ásˏa	'the one who whistled at you'
tiˏxʷitən-s-tálihˏa	'the one who whistled at him'
tiˏxʷitən-s-tumuɬ-ásˏa	'the one who whistled at us'
tiˏxʷitən-s-tam-aɬ'ap-ásˏa	'the one who whistled at you folks'
tiˏxʷitən-s-tan-əm-wít-asˏa	'the one who whistled at them'

The object-centred forms are the same as the ones used in the factual paradigm for 1SP/2S/3SP-3S, but without s- here. The subject-centred forms with 1SP/2SP/ object are the same as the ones used in all paradigms for 3S-1SP/2SP. Where 3S is object, we have -tali, which is used exclusively in subject-centred (not in declarative) forms. The form for 3P is that of the 3P passive subjunctive.

The suffix -tali glottalizes l under the same conditions under which other suffixes glottalize their resonants (see Sections 22.3.3 and 22.3.4), e.g., tiˏx̌'iq-s-taɬ'íhˏa 'the one who brought it.'

By using plural articles with these forms, we make reference to 3P subject or object, e.g. (with ʔiˏ..ˏa 'present, known, plural'), ʔiˏcútˏa 'the ones who say (said),' ʔiˏcún-anˏa 'the ones I told,' ʔiˏcún-c-asˏa 'the ones who told me.'

We also have complex object- and subject-centred forms. These consist of an object- or subject-centred form preceded by an auxiliary, which attracts the article but not the subject suffixes, e.g., tiˏhúz'ˏa cún-an 'the one I will tell.'

22.7. Indirect object-centred forms (nominalized transitives)

Some transitive forms imply not only a subject and a direct object but also an indirect object, e.g., cun 'to tell, order smb. smt.,' ʔúm'ən 'to give smb. smt.,' and virtually all cases with -xit (Section 18.1.4[d]), e.g., cúɬ-xit 'to point smt. out to smb.' The simple factual forms (Section 22.3.2) of such forms may combine with articles, fill the slot of subject or object complement, and refer to what is told, given, etc. to the indirect object, i.e., what one tells, gives, or points out to smb., as in tiˏs-cún-anˏa 'what I told him' (cf. tiˏcún-anˏa 'the one I told' [Section 22.6]), tiˏs-cún-c-axʷˏa 'what you told me.'

Note that indirect object-centred forms may contain a non-third person object suffix and a non-third person subject suffix in the same form, as in the last example. Object- or subject-centred forms (Section 22.6) must contain a third person object or subject suffix.

Where indirect object-centred forms combine with the article ti‿··‿a, such forms are phonetically close to simple transitive t-constructions (e.g., t‿s-cún-an‿a 'the fact that I tell him'). As is the case with intransitive forms (Section 22.4.1), there is no ambiguity in the complex paradigm:

(a) ti‿wa?‿s-cún-an 'what I am telling him' (nominal)

(b) tənswa‿cún 'the fact that I am telling him' (factual)

Although indirect object-centred forms are nominal, they are the only type of noun that may not take possessive affixes (see Section 8.1.1), because they are already marked for person.

22.8. Summary of complements, nominal forms, and factual forms

To summarize what we have said about complements and nominal versus factual forms, we arrive at the following six-point system: intransitive stems parallelled by transitive stems, and both the intransitive stems and the transitive stems having the possibility of (1) occurring as subject or object complement (in this case containing an overt or covert person marker), (2) being nominalized and then occurring as a complement, and (3) being factualized and occurring in a t-construction (Figure 15).

Figure 15 lists only the simple forms. Complex forms are discussed in the sections referred to in the figure.[6]

Figure 15

Complements, nominal forms, and factual forms

	Complement		Factualized
	Verbal	Nominalized	(t-constructions)
Intr.	ti‿cút‿a 'the one who said' (22.6)	ti‿n-s-cút‿a 'what I said' (22.4.1)	t‿ən-s-cút‿a 'the fact that I said' (22.3.1, 22.4.1)
Tr.	ti‿cún-an‿a 'the one I told' (22.6: object-centred) ti‿cún-c-as‿a 'the one who told me' (22.6: subject-centred)	ti‿s-cún-an‿a 'what I told him' (22.7)	t‿s-cún-an‿a 'the fact that I told him' (22.3.2, 22.7)

23
Invariable Words: General Remarks

For basic observations on invariable words, see Section 8.2. As mentioned there, some invariable words have limited affixing or reduplicating possibilities. Pronominal elements (Sections 24 to 26), proper nouns (Section 27) and sentence-equivalents (Section 29) may take 3S intransitive markers and occur as predicates. For example, xʷʔaz 'not' (sentence-equivalent) occurs with 3S indicative (zero) to express 'it is not the case,' or with -as 3S subjunctive in xʷʔáz-as 'let it not be the case' (see Sections 22.3.1 and 22.3.5 for examples).

Personal pronouns, demonstrative pronouns, and proper nouns may also occur as object or subject complements. Interrogative pronouns (Section 24.2) and so-called 'pivoting' local deictics (Section 26.1) may take the full set of intransitive subject suffixes. However, they are discussed with the invariables because the overall system to which they belong, the pronominal elements, is largely invariable. For the status of proper nouns with regard to affixation, see Section 27. Greetings, exclamations, and interjections often contain personal affixes, but may not be changed further (see Section 30).

A number of deictic roots occur both in the system of demonstrative pronouns and in that of demonstrative adverbs (Sections 25 and 26, respectively), and (often in abbreviated form) as articles (Section 31).

24
Personal Pronouns and Related Substitutes

In this section we discuss first the personal pronouns (Section 24.1), then interrogative and indefinite pronouns (Section 24.2), so-called evasive pronouns (Section 24.3), possessive substitutes (Section 24.4), the anticipatory pronoun niɬ (Section 24.5), and remaining personal substitutes (Section 24.6).

24.1. Personal pronouns
Figure 16 shows the personal pronouns found in Lillooet.

Figure 16

Personal pronouns

	Singular (S)	Plural (P)
1	s-ʔənc 'I'	s-nímuɬ 'we'
2	s-núwa 'you'	s-nuláp 'you folks'
3	s-niɬ 'he, she, it'	wi‿sníɬ 'they'

Note the partial resemblance between s-núwa 2S and s-nuláp 2P. For s-nuláp cf. -lap 2P possessive (Section 22.1). The pronoun s-nímuɬ 1P partially resembles -tumuɬ 1P object (Section 22.1). For s-niɬ 3S cf. the anticipatory pronoun niɬ (Section 24.5). The element wi‿ in 3P is the plural article for proper nouns (see Section 31.1). The pronouns 1P and 2P may also be combined with wi‿ (without a perceptible difference in meaning from forms without wi‿): wi‿snímuɬ and wi‿s-nuláp. The pronoun 1S s-ʔənc is often combined with the reinforcing enclitic ‿a (Section 32.2): s-ʔénc‿a. The other pronouns combine with ‿a only when ‿a itself is followed by another enclitic, e.g., s-nimuɬ‿á‿qaʔ 'well, it's us' (also s-nímuɬ‿qaʔ; for ‿qaʔ

see Section 32.1.11). The pronoun s-núwa is also pronounced s-nu, but this usage is not considered correct by some speakers.[1]

24.1.1. Use of personal pronouns

In the first place, personal pronouns may occur as predicates, i.e., with a 3S intransitive subject marker of the indicative, subjunctive, or factual paradigm. Such predicates express 'it is me, you, him, us, etc.' (or 'I am, you are, etc., the one [who ...]'), as in:

(a) s-ʔə́nc‿a ti‿qʷusxi[ɬ]-tálih‿a 'I am the one who shot (qʷúsxit) him'

(b) cúkʷ‿X̌'uʔ s-ʔənc ti‿cíxʷ‿a ʔákʷuʔ 'it was only (cúkʷ‿X̌'uʔ) me who went (cixʷ) there (ʔákʷuʔ), I was the only one who went there'

(c) s-ʔənc-ás kʷu‿nás 'let me be the one to go (nas)' (kʷu‿ article 'potential' [Section 31.1])

(d) s-núwa‿ha 'is it you?' (‿ha question-marker [Section 32.1.12])

(e) s-nuwh-ás kʷu‿maysən-táli 'you'd better be the one to fix (máysən) it'

(f) paqʷuʔ-ɬk-áxʷ‿ha‿ka ka‿ɬ‿s-nuwh-ás 'would you be afraid (páqʷuʔ) if (ɬ‿) it were you?' (‿ka, ka‿ irreal-markers [Sections 32.1.6 and 32.5.1(d)])

(g) xʷʔaz kʷas‿snít 'it is not (xʷʔaz) him'

(h) s-níɬ-as kʷu‿maysən-táli 'let him be the one to fix (máysən) it'

(i) wi‿s-nímuɬ-as kʷu‿cukʷun'-táli 'let us be the ones to finish (cúkʷun') it'

(j) s-nuláp-as kʷu‿nukʷʔan-tan-əm-wít-as 'you folks better help (núkʷʔan) them'

(k) wi‿s-níɬ-as kʷu‿x̌íɬ[-c]-taľi 'let them be the ones to do (x̌iɬ-c) it'

(l) wi‿s-níɬ‿tuʔ nəɬ‿X̌'ák‿a 'they are the ones who went by (X̌'ak)' (‿tuʔ 'definite past' [Section 32.1.2]; nəɬ‿...‿a article 'absent, plural' [Section 31.1])

In the second place, personal pronouns may fill the slot of subject or object complement. Since grammatical persons are already indicated through subject and object suffixes in the predicate, the use of personal pronouns as subject or object complements puts a certain emphasis on a person, as in:

(m) cún-əm wi‿s-nímuɬ 'pəľaɬcítxʷ' 'we call it (cun) "newcomer" (pəľaɬcítxʷ)'

(n) nk'yáp-ɬk-an, pəplaʔ-ɬk-áxʷ s-núwa 'I (-ɬk-an) am a coyote (nk'yap), but you are just one animal' (pə́plaʔ 'one animal')[2]

(o) níɬ‿X̌'uʔ mútaʔ n-s-ka-q'sə́sn'ək‿a s-ʔənc 'so I burst out (ka-..‿a) giggling (q'sə́sn'ək) again (mútaʔ)'

(p) tqíɬ‿X̌'uʔ X̌'it nq'san'k s-niɬ 'he almost (tqíɬ‿X̌'uʔ) laughed (nq'san'k) too (mútaʔ)'

(q) stə́x̌ʷ‿maɬ muzmits-túmuɬ wi‿snímuɬ ʔúxʷalmixʷ 'do have pity (múzmits) on us people (ʔúxʷalmixʷ)' (stə́x̌ʷ 'really, truly')[3]

It is possible to have personal pronouns both in the predicate and in the complement in the same sentence:

(r) ka‿ɬ‿s-ʔənc-ás s-núwa 'if (ɬ‿) I were you' (ka‿ irreal-marker)

Personal pronouns may also be the object of a preposition (for prepositions, see Section 34), as in:

(s) xʷʔaz kʷas‿ənlíʕʷc l‿wi‿s-nuláp 'it is not (xʷʔaz) allowed (nliʕʷc) to (l‿) you folks'

(t) swat ɬəl‿wi‿s-nuláp kʷu‿x̌íɬ[-c]-tal'i 'who (swat) of you folks is the one who did it?' (ɬəl‿ 'of, from')

24.1.2. Personal pronouns and predicates with a possessive marker

English sentences such as 'you are my friend,' where the subject is a personal pronoun and the predicate-head is marked with a possessive pronoun, are rendered in two different ways in Lillooet.

Combination of possessive and subject suffixes. We have this solution where 1S is the possessor: subject suffixes 2SP and 3SP are placed after the form that contains the possessive prefix 1S n-:

(a) n-snúk'ʷaʔ-ɬk-axʷ 'you are my friend (snúk'ʷaʔ)'

(b) n-snúk'ʷaʔ‿ti? 'that one (‿ti?) is my friend' (with 3S intransitive indicative subject suffix zero)

(c) n-snək'ʷnuk'ʷaʔ-ɬkál'ap 'you folks are my friends' (for the reduplication, see Section 12.5)

Any possessive affix may combine with the 3S intransitive indicative (zero) or subjunctive (-as) subject suffix:

(d) n-cuwaʔ‿ká‿ti? séna? 'that (‿ti?) should (‿ka) be mine' (cúwa? 'own, possession' [see Section 24.4]; for séna? see Section 28.2.2)

(e) n-cuw?-ás‿ka‿ti? 'I wish that were mine'

(f) cuwa?-sú‿ka‿ti? 'that should be yours'

(g) cuwa?-sw-ás‿ka‿ti? 'I wish that were yours'

(h) cuw?-íh‿ka‿ti? 'that should be theirs'

(i) cuw?-ih-ás‿ka‿ti? 'I wish that were theirs'

(j) snuk'ʷaʔ-ɬkáɬ‿ti? 'that one is our friend'

(k) snuk'ʷaʔ-láp‿ha‿ti? 'is that one the friend of you folks?'

(l) qəqcək-sú‿ha‿ti? 'is that your elder brother (qə́qcək)?'

All other combinations of possessive and subject markings are expressed through a personal pronoun in the predicate and a form with a possessive affix in the complement:

(m) s-ʔənc ti‿snúk'ʷaʔ-sw‿a 'I am your friend'

(n) s-ʔənc ti‿snuk'ʷaʔ-láp‿a 'I am the friend of you folks'

(o) snúwa ti‿snuk'ʷaʔ-ɬkáɬ‿a 'you are our friend'

Cases of the second type also serve as an alternative to cases of the first type. For example:

(p) s-núwa ti‿n-snúk'ʷ?‿a 'you are my friend'; cf. (a)

(q) s-niɬ ti‿snuk'ʷaʔ-ɬkáɬ‿a 'he is our friend'; cf. (j)

24.2. Interrogative and indefinite pronouns

The interrogative pronouns are swat 'who?' and stam' 'what?' The indefinite pronouns are based on swát-as and stám'-as (-as 3S subjunctive intransitive subject) in combination with various enclitics (discussed in Section 32). These combinations express 'somebody(thing),' 'anybody(thing),'
'who(what)ever.' The interrogative and indefinite pronouns are found
first of all in predicates:

(a) s-wát‿ti? 'who is that?'

(b) s-wát-kaxʷ 'who are you?'

(c) s-tám'‿ti? 'what is that?'

(d) s-wát-as‿k'a 'it is somebody; I wonder who it is' (‿k'a 'apparently')

(e) swát-as‿k'a múta? kʷu‿?um'ən-cíh-as ti‿qḷám‿a 'I wonder who it is who
gave (?úm'ən) you (-cih) that ugly (qḷạm) thing' (múta? 'again' [Section 28.2.1])

(f) s-tám'-as‿k'a núkʷun' kʷu‿száytən-su 'you must have done something again' (száytən 'what smb. does'; núkʷun' 'again' [Section 28.2.3])

(g) s-tam'-as‿k'á‿ti? kʷu‿huz'‿kʷtámc-s 'I wonder what the husband
(kʷtamc) of that one (‿ti?) will be' (-s 3S possessive)

For another example, see Section 24.1.1(t). Interestingly, s-wat is used in
inquiries about smb.'s name:

(h) s-wat kʷu‿skʷácic-su 'what (literally 'who') is your name (skʷácic)?'

The interrogative and indefinite pronouns are also used as subject or
object complements. (The difference between complements based on interrogative pronouns and those based on indefinite pronouns is semantically opaque.) The choice of article determines the degree of familiarity of
the speaker with the thing meant (for articles, see Section 31): pronouns
combined with 'unknown-absent' articles roughly correspond to Russian
xtó-nibudʸ, štó-nibudʸ, while combinations with other articles roughly correspond to Russian xtó-to, štó-to. Examples are:

(i) xə́ləncám' káti? ki‿s-tám'‿a 'he begged for all kinds of food'
(xə́ləncám' 'to beg for food'; for káti? see Section 26.1.2)

(j) xʷ?áz-as kʷaľap‿ɬwálən káti? kʷu‿s-tám' 'don't you folks leave
(ɬwálən) anything!'[4]

(k) púpən' ti‿s-tam'-as‿á‿k'a 'he found (púpən') something' (also s-tám'-
as‿k'a ti‿s-púpən'-s‿a)

(l) ns?á?z'əm kʷu‿s-tám'-as‿ƛ'u? 'he traded (ns?á?z'əm) for anything'

(m) qan'ím-xən-s-kan kʷu‿s-wat-as‿á‿k'a 'I heard (qan'ím) somebody's
footsteps (-xən)'

Cases of xʷ?ạz 'not' plus s-wat or s-tam' in the clause subordinated to
xʷ?ạz correspond to English 'nobody, nothing'; see (j) above.

24.3. Evasive pronouns

The pronouns swat and stam' are matched by the pronouns swə́ta? and wéna?, respectively. The pronoun swéta? 'so-and-so' is used when the speaker does not remember or does not want to reveal smb.'s name. When swéta? occurs as a complement, it combines with the proper noun article kʷ (cf. Section 31.1):

(a) ka ɫ wá?-as kənc?á kʷ swéta?, plán ka ti? wa? máysn-as 'if (ɫ) so-and-so would (ka) have been (wa?) around here (kənc?á), he would (ka) have fixed (máysən) that (ti?) already (plan)'

(b) ?u, kʷ swéta?, niɫ a xʷíɫ k'a ?i scmal't-káɫ a s-q'ʷəl-xi[t]-túmuɫ-as 'Oh, that so-and-so. It turns out that it is our (-kaɫ) children (scmal't) that she has cooked (q'ʷəl-) for (-xit) us (-tumuɫ)' (niɫ anticipatory pronoun [Section 24.5]; xʷiɫ 'it turns out' [Section 32.1.10]; s-q'ʷəl-xi[t]-túmuɫ-as indirect object-centred form [Section 22.7])

The word wéna? 'what's-it-again' is used if the speaker does not remember, or does not want to use, the right word. For instance, wéna? may be used as a euphemism for private parts:

(c) ti wéna?-sw a 'your you-know-what'

One also uses wéna? as an interjection, when searching for the right word:

(d) plan wa?, wéna?, ka méx̌ʷ a ti máq? a 'already (plan) the snow had, uhm, come down quite a bit (ka méx̌ʷ a)'

(e) kʷán kʷu? ?ayɫ káti? ?i , wéna?, zúc'mən-s a 'then (?ayɫ) he took (kʷan) her, uhm, paint (zúc'mən)' (?i... a article [Section 31.1]; the absence of -as after transitive kʷan is unexplained)

(f) n-p'ukʷ-alus-n-ás kʷu? ?ayɫ ki síkil a, ki , wéna?, q'ʷal'íɫ a 'so she poured (p'ukʷ-) tree bark (síkil) and, uhm, pitch (q'ʷal'íɫ) into his eyes (-alus)'

We may also combine wéna? with resultative ka...a, as in:

(g) plán X̌'u? wa? lil'q kʷas ka-wén? a 'it was already (plan) easy (lil'q) to ... uhm' (the word wanted was ka-céss a 'to get stretched')

We also have ka wén? a in expressions referring to offence:

(h) ka-wən?-áxʷ a 'excuse me!' (said when passing smb. at close range; -axʷ 2S subjunctive intransitive)

(i) xʷ?áz-as kʷ s-ka-wéna?-sw a, húy'-ɫkan sqʷəqʷl'ən-cín ti s-x̌íləm-s a ti skʷúza?-sw a 'I hope you don't mind, but I (-ɫkan) will (huy'-) tell (sqʷəqʷl'ən) you (-cin) what your (-sw) child (skʷúza?) did' (s-x̌íləm 'deed, what one does')

With the stative prefix s- we have s-wéna?-xal 'to nag, bother, intr. (-xal),' s-wéna?-s 'to nag, bother smb., tr. (-s), be a bit against smb.':

(k) wá? həm' X̌'u? s-wəna?-xál 'he is nagging, bothering (həm', Section 32.1.13)

(l) wa? s-wəna?-stúmx-as 'he is a little bit against me'

We also have transitive wən?-án with the meaning 'to do what-was-it-again to smt.' and 'to look after smb./smt.' (in the latter meaning it might be a misrecording of wə?án 'to keep, hold smb./smt.' or it may result from confusion with wə?án by the consultant):

(m) nít‿λ̓'u? s-wən?-án-axʷ I‿ti‿nkʷλ̓'ústən'-sw‿a 'so you, uhm, do whatever it is to (I‿) your (-sw) eye (nkʷλ̓'ústən')' (the word wanted was c'əq'p-án 'to stick on')

(n) wá?‿maɬ‿ti? wən?-án 'look after that one (‿ti?)' (e.g., when telling smb. to look after a baby; ‿maɬ adhortative [Section 32.1.1])

24.4. Possessive substitutes

The word for 'whose' is swán'uɬ, as in:

(a) swán'uɬ‿ti? sqáx̌a? 'whose dog (sqáx̌a?) is that (‿ti?)?'

(b) swán'uɬ c?a sk'ʷul' 'whose product (sk'ʷul') is this (c?a), who made this?'

24.5. The anticipatory pronoun niɬ

The pronoun niɬ 'it is the one' is used to draw attention to a following item, as in:

(a) niɬ ti‿sqácza?-sw‿a núk'ʷ?an-c-as 'it is your (-sw) father (sqácza?) who helped (núk'ʷ?an) me (-c)'

See also Section 24.3(b). For details of use, see Section 38.5.

24.6. Remaining non-local substitutes

For the expression of 'which,' see Section 26.1.4(c). For relative pronouns with antecedent enclosed ('I know who, what, whose ...'), see Section 37.4.1(3). The word nukʷ expresses '(an)other,' e.g.:

(a) qʷnux̌ʷ ?ayɬ múta? ti‿núkʷ‿a 'so (?ayɬ) another one fell ill (qʷnux̌ʷ) again (múta?)'

(b) ɬ‿x̌ʷíc'xi[ɬ]-c-axʷ k'ʷu‿núkʷ ɬáx̌ʷmən, ɬumun-ɬkán‿kɬ lc?a 'if (ɬ‿) you (-axʷ) give (x̌ʷíc'xit) me (-c) another patch (ɬáx̌ʷmən), I will (‿kɬ) put it on (ɬúmun) here (lc?a)'

(c) nít‿λ̓'u? s-c'əq'pán-axʷ I‿ti‿nkʷλ̓'ústən'-sw‿a ti‿núkʷ‿a, c'íla ti‿núkʷ‿a 'so (nít‿λ̓'u?) you stick (c'əq'pán) one piece on one eye (nkʷλ̓'ústən'), and the other piece on the other eye' (literally 'so you stick one on your [-sw] eye, likewise the other'

The word nukʷ also expresses 'some':

(d) ?i‿núkʷ‿a ɬəl‿kizá 'some of (ɬəl‿) these (kizá)'

25
Demonstrative Pronouns

We discuss the main facts about demonstrative pronouns in Section 25.1. In Section 25.2 we discuss the suffix -wna/-na 'right on the spot,' and in Section 25.3, special forms of demonstrative pronouns after prepositions.

25.1. Demonstrative pronouns: basic information

Lillooet employs twelve demonstrative pronouns, which are listed in Figure 17. The following comments refer to Figure 17.

Figure 17

Demonstrative pronouns

	Visible			Invisible		
	This	That	That (farther)	This	That	That (farther)
Singular	cʔa	tiʔ	tʔu	kʷʔa	niʔ	kʷuʔ
Plural	ʔizá	ʔizʼ	ʔizú	kʷɬa	nəɬ	kʷɬ
	These	Those	Those (farther)	These	Those	Those (farther)

Formal aspects: the pronouns for 'this' and 'these' (visible and invisible) have the shape C(V)Ca, while the pronouns for 'that (farther)' and 'those (farther)' (visible) are C(V)Cu. All other demonstrative pronouns are C(V)C. Note also the formal similarity between the plural pronouns in the 'visible' category, and between the plural pronouns in the 'invisible' category (the latter all having ɬ for C_2). All singular pronouns have ʔ for C_2. Within the 'invisible' category, the pronouns for 'this' and 'these' are distinguished from the pronouns for 'that (farther)' and 'those (farther)' by the presence of final a in 'this' and 'these' and by the dropping of u in kʷuʔ.

> kʷ?a. The pronouns ti?, ni?, and kʷu? resemble the articles ti‿, ni‿, and kʷu‿, respectively, while nə+ and kʷ+ are identical to the articles nə+‿ and kʷ+‿ (see Section 31 for articles); kʷu? is also identical to the quotative marker ‿kʷu? (Section 32.1.9), while c?a, ti?, t?u, kʷ?a, and kʷu? also occur as the roots of local deictics (see Section 26.1). Demonstrative pronouns may fill the slot of (a) predicate, (b) subject or object complement, and (c) attribute, as in the following:

(a) c?a 'this is the one, it is the one'

(b) sqayxʷ c?a 'this is a man'

(c) c?a kʷu‿sqáyxʷ 'this man' (kʷu‿ 'attribute-connector' [see Section 33.2; also for attributes in general])

Pronouns C(V)C may yield their stress and occur as clitics. This frequently happens with pronouns of the shape CAC, and always with those of the shape C(ə)C. For example, with CAC:

(d) sqáyxʷ‿ti? 'that is a man'

(e) ti?‿kʷu‿sqáyxʷ 'that man'

When deictics occur as attributes, they may also be linked to the head through an article, rather than through kʷu‿ (I have not been able to find a consistent functional difference between forms that employ kʷu‿ and those that employ articles):

(f) c?a ti‿sxʷápməx‿a 'this Shuswap (sxʷápməx)'

25.1.1. Semantics and examples

The division 'visible' versus 'invisible' hinges on whether or not the thing meant is visible to the speaker in the situation of speech. The pronouns for 'this/these' (visible and invisible) are used for an object in the speaker's immediate vicinity, whereas 'that/those (farther)' (visible and invisible) are used for objects in the periphery of the speaker's range of perception. The pronouns for 'that/those' (visible and invisible) refer to objects between these two extremes.[1] Examples (with stam' 'what?') include:

(a) stam' c?a 'what is this?' (e.g., when holding smt.)

(b) stam' ?izá 'what are these?' (e.g., when holding some things)

(c) stám'‿ti? 'what is that?' (e.g., when pointing at smt. at some distance)

(d) stám'‿?iz 'what are those?' (e.g., when pointing at some things at some distance)

(e) stam' t?u 'what is that (way over there)?'

(f) stam' ?izú 'what are those (way over there)?'

(g) stam' kʷ?a 'what is this?' (e.g., when touching smt. in the dark)

(h) stam' kʷ+a 'what are these?' (e.g., when groping around in a box in the dark)

(i) stám'‿ni? 'what was that?' (e.g., when smt. whizzed by and you did not see it)

(j) stám'‿nəɬ 'what were those?' (e.g., when some things whizzed by and you did not see them)

(k) stám'‿kʷu? 'what is that?' (e.g., when hearing a noise)

(l) stam'‿kʷɬ 'what are those?' (e.g., when hearing different noises)

Compare also (m) and (n):

(m) níɬ‿ti? kʷu‿citxʷ ʕʷəlp 'that is the house (citxʷ) that burned down (ʕʷəlp)' (when pointing at the ruins; niɬ anticipatory pronoun [Section 24.5])

(n) ʕʷə́lp‿tu? ni?‿kʷu‿cítxʷ 'that house burned down' (when talking about the house when it is completely absent from the situation of speech; ‿tu? 'definite past')

Different demonstrative pronouns may be combined to indicate (apparently) midpoints between their respective points of reference, as in:

(o) ɬ‿X̌'íq-as ti? c?a ti‿sxʷápməx‿a 'when this Shuswap came (X̌'iq)'

25.2. Suffixation with -wna/-na

The pronouns ending in V may be extended with the suffix -wna/-na 'right on the spot' (-wna after a; -na after u): c?á-wna 'this one right here,' t?ú-na 'that one right there.'

25.3. Special forms after prepositions

After the prepositions l‿ 'in, on, at,' ɬəl‿ 'from,' ?ə‿ 'towards, along,' kən‿ 'around, via,' we have kizá, kiz', kizú instead of ?izá, ?iz', ?izú: ɬəl‿kizá 'from these,' etc. (see Section 34 for prepositions).

26
Demonstrative Adverbs

Lillooet demonstrative adverbs consist of local adverbs ('here, there, below,' etc.) and temporal adverbs ('then, soon,' etc.). These groups consist of deictics ('here, there, then') and non-deictics ('below, soon'). Here we discuss mainly local deictics (Section 26.1) and temporal deictics (Section 26.2). Non-deictics are briefly discussed at the end of each subsection (local non-deictics in Section 26.1.6 and temporal non-deictics in Section 26.2.1).

26.1. Local deictics

The system of local deictics distinguishes eight points of reference (Figure 18). Local deictics consist of a deictic root plus one of four local prefixes. Forms with the prefix l-/lá- 'in, on, at' are given in Figure 18.

Figure 18

Demonstrative adverbs

		Pivoting	Non-pivoting
Visible	Proximal 'here'	l-cʔa	lá-tiʔ
	Distal 'there'	l-tʔu	lá-taʔ
Invisible	Proximal 'here'	l-kʷʔa	lá-kʷuʔ
	Distal 'there'	l-kʷʔu	lá-kʷʔa

Formal aspects: the roots in the 'pivoting' category have the shape CʔV, while the non-pivoting roots have CVʔ (except for lá-kʷʔa). The roots in the 'visible' category have c or t as C_1, while the 'invisible' roots have kʷ as C_1. The prefix has the shape l- in the 'pivoting' category and lá- in the 'non-pivoting' category: lá-kʷʔa combines the characteristics of pivoting deictics (root C?V) and non-pivoting deictics (prefix lá-; note that l-kʷ?a and lá-kʷ?a share the same root). For details on affixation, see Section 26.1.2.

26.1.1. Semantics and use

The division 'visible' versus 'invisible' hinges on whether the thing or place meant is visible or invisible to the speaker. The categories 'proximal' versus 'distal' express that the thing or place meant is (relatively) close to the speaker versus (relatively) far from the speaker. The categories 'pivoting' versus 'non-pivoting' indicate whether or not a certain place or object is considered to be the centre or orientation point of an area. Compare (a) and (b):

(a) l-c?a   ɬ‿was‿qʷálʼqʷəlʼt 'it is here that (ɬ‿) it is hurting (qʷálʼqʷəlʼt)' (when speaker points at spot on own body)

(b) lá-ti?   ɬ‿was‿qʷálʼqʷəlʼt 'it is here that it is hurting' (said to smb. who points at the same spot on speaker's body, e.g., a doctor investigating that spot)

In (a) the spot itself is the orientation point, whereas in (b) it is identified through the addressee.

Within the 'invisible' category we have:

(c) l-kʷ?a   ɬ‿was‿qʷálʼqʷəlʼt 'it is here that it is hurting' (speaker indicates an invisible [to him/her] spot on own body, e.g., on back)

(d) lá-kʷu?   ɬ‿was‿qʷálʼqʷəlʼt 'it is here that it is hurting' (said to smb. who indicates an invisible [to speaker] spot on speaker's body)

The distal deictics were all rejected in the examples above, which gives an idea of the minimal range of 'proximal.' In the distal category, it is on the whole more difficult to pinpoint the difference between pivoting and non-pivoting than in the proximal category, where non-pivoting lá-ti?, lá-kʷu? are generally associated with the addressee (distal/non-pivoting lá-ta?, lá-kʷ?a do not have such a natural orientation point).[1] The difference between l-t?u and lá-ta? is shown by (e) versus (f):

(e) swat l-t?u ti‿wá?‿a ti‿cəqʷcíqʷ‿a ti‿cəspícʼa?-s‿a 'who (swat) is the one in the red (cəqʷcíqʷ) sweater (cəspícʼa?) there?' (wa? 'to be')

(f) swat   lá-ta?   ti‿wa?‿cəqʷcíqʷ   ti‿cəspícʼa?-s‿a   ti‿wa?‿s?úlʼlʼus l‿ki‿wa?‿sʕəwʼp 'who is the one in the red sweater in the crowd (sʕəwʼp) over there?' (s?úlʼlʼus 'to be among people')

In (e) the man himself is the orientation point, whereas in (f) the man is identified through another orientation point (the crowd).

In the distal/invisible category, matters are complicated by the fact that lá-kʷ?a generally refers not to a location but to a smell, a sound, or some other sensation (i.e., refers to something that not only is invisible but, un-like l-kʷ?a, lá-kʷu?, l-kʷ?u, cannot even be made visible). Examples include:

(g) ƛʼiq lá-kʷ?a kʷ‿s-A 'I think A has arrived (ƛʼiq)'

(h) huz̓ lá-kʷʔa kʷis 'I think it is going to (huz̓) rain (kʷis)' (e.g., when my scar is aching)

(i) npəʕʷcám' lá-kʷʔa 'smb. is knocking on the door' (npəʕʷcám' 'to knock on the door')

(j) xʷʔuxʷ lá-kʷʔa 'smt. is stinking (xʷʔuxʷ)'

(k) məq̓-kán lá-kʷʔa 'I feel full (from eating)' (məq̓ 'to be full from eating')

(l) ƛ̓əx-ʔúl lá-kʷʔa ti‿tíh-sw‿a 'your (-sw) tea (tih) is too (-ʔúl) sweet (ƛ̓əx)'

(m) wənaxʷ-c-ʔúl lá-kʷʔa ti‿radioh‿a 'the radio is too loud (wənáxʷ-c)'

The vagueness of lá-kʷʔa is directly related to the nature of the categories distal, invisible, and pivoting. The deictic lá-kʷuʔ often takes over the function of lá-kʷʔa as the non-pivoting counterpart of l-kʷʔu. Compare (n) and (o):

(n) l-kʷʔu pankʷúph‿a 'there in Vancouver (pankʷúpa)' (for ‿a see Section 26.1.3)

(o) lá-kʷuʔ pankʷúph‿a ɬ‿was‿wá? ɬkʷúns‿a 'he is there in Vancouver right now (ɬkʷúns‿a)': the non-pivoting function of lá-kʷuʔ is described by ML as 'lá-kʷuʔ is where it's at, where they were, where it happened.'

Although lá-kʷuʔ often replaces lá-kʷʔa when it comes to expressing the distal/invisible/pivoting dimension in terms of physical distance, lá-kʷʔa may be used for this function. Compare (p) and (q):

(p) lá-kʷʔa pankʷúph‿a ɬ‿pún-an ti‿púkʷ‿a 'I found (pun) the book (pukʷ) there in Vancouver' (according to LW, this sentence has an 'idea of past')

(q) lá-kʷuʔ pankʷúph‿a ɬ‿pún-an ti‿púkʷ‿a 'I found the book there in Vancouver' (without 'idea of past')

For lá-kʷʔa see also Section 26.1.3(f).

26.1.2. Affixation

Besides the prefixes l-/lá-, we also have the prefixes ʔə-/ʔá- 'towards, along,' ɬəl-/ɬlá- 'from,' and kən-/kná- 'around, via.' The first member of each pair is used in pivoting devices, the second one in non-pivoting ones: ʔə-cʔá 'this way,' ʔá-ta? 'that way,' etc. Instead of kná-ti? and kná-kʷuʔ, one frequently uses ká-ti? and ká-kʷuʔ. The form ká-ta? for kná-ta? is more unusual. The forms *ʔá-kʷʔa, *ɬlá-kʷʔa, and *kná-kʷʔa were rejected, and I have only one example of ká-kʷʔa: wa? ká-kʷʔa npəʕʷcám' 'smb. is knocking at the door' (cf. Section 26.1.1[i]).

The word ʔə-kʷʔú 'that way (invisible/distal/pivoting)' is often proclitic kʷu‿ in quick speech. The pivoting deictics allow suffixation with -wna/-na 'right on the spot' (-wna after a; -na after u): l-cʔá-wna 'right here,' l-tʔú-na 'right there,' ʔə-cʔá-wna 'right to this place,' etc. The prefixes l-, ʔə-, ɬəl-, and kən- are the prefix counterparts of the proclitic prepositions l‿, ʔə‿, ɬəl‿, and kən‿ (see Section 34).

26.1.3. Special questions

English phrases like 'here in the house' (deictic-preposition-article-noun) are matched exactly in Lillooet, e.g., l-c?a l̲ti̲cítxʷ̲a (l̲ 'in, on, at,' ti̲..̲a article, citxʷ 'house'). However, the preposition and the proclitic article are often dropped from such phrases, e.g., lc?a cítxʷ̲a. Local deictics are used more often in Lillooet than in English, as shown by (a) through (d):

(a) húy'-ɬkan míca?q ?á-ti? sqʷʼút-sw̲a 'I am going to (huy'-) sit down (míca?q) at your (-sw) side (sqʷʼut)'

(b) húy'-ɬkan ləp'xál ?á-ti? sqʷʼút-s̲a ti̲n-cítxʷ̲a 'I am going to make a garden beside my (n-) house' (ləp'xál 'to plant, make a garden')

(c) húy'-ɬkan nas cə́qən ti̲n-ką́h̲a ?á-kʷu? sqʷʼút-s̲a ti̲cítxʷ-sw̲a 'I am going to go and park (cə́qən) my car (kąh) beside your house'

(d) ka-?ac'x̌sás̲a l-t?u x̌?íɬ̲a ?i̲wa?̲záwəm 'he caught sight (ka-?ac'x̌sás̲a) of people who were fishing (záwəm) on the other side' (x̌?íɬ 'other side')

Note the absence of preposition-article constructs in the above sentences. Although 'here' and 'there' can be used in the English versions, they are not as necessary as in the Lillooet versions, which would sound odd without the deictics.

The local deictics may occur in combinations that usually give a more general location than single deictics:

(e) wa? ?á-kʷu? ká-ti? 'he was over there, somewhere'

(f) c?as lá-kʷ?a ɬá-kʷu? kʷu̲sx̌'atálm̲a 'there was a grizzly (sx̌'atáləm) coming (c?as) from somewhere'

A speaker may use various deictics to designate one and the same spot as his focus shifts:

(g) cixʷ ?á-kʷu? l̲t̲swá?-s̲a ?i̲wa?̲záwəm, níɬ̲x̌'u? s-súx̌'xal-s lá-ti? 'he arrived (cixʷ) at the spot where they were fishing (záwəm), so (níɬ̲x̌'u?) he smoked a few puffs there' (súx̌'xal 'to smoke a few puffs'; swá?-s 'spot-his/their'; for the coreference between -s 'his' and plural ?i̲wa?̲záwəm, see Section 38.4)

The word ká-ti? 'around (t)here' is also used in the meaning 'at all, any,' as in:

(h) xʷ?ạz ká-ti? 'not at all'

(i) skan ká-ti? kʷas̲lák kʷu̲k'ʷíɬaľc 'are there any leftovers (k'ʷíɬaľc)?' (skan question marker [see Section 29]; lak 'to be there' [see Section 20])

The words ?ə-c?á 'this way,' ?á-ti? 'that way,' and ?á-kʷu? 'that way' are also used with c'íla '(to be) like,' x̌íləm 'to do like,' and cut 'to say,' as in:

(j) c'íla ?ə-c?á 'like this'

(k) c'íla ?á-ti? 'like that/this'

(l) x̌íləm ?ə-c?á '(to do) like this'

(m) x̌íləm ?á-ti? '(to do) like that/this' (x̌íləm-ɬkan ?á-ti? 'this is what I did')

(n) cut ?á-kʷu? 'to say that'

26.1.4. Interrogative and indefinite local deictics

The interrogative local deictic is n-ka? (1) 'where?' (2) 'whither?' (in the latter meaning it probably results from *?ə-n-ká?, with the same prefix ?ə- as in ?ə-c?á, etc.). Examples include:

(a) n-ka? ɬ‿waxʷ‿wá? 'where are you staying (wa?)?'

(b) n-ka? ɬ‿nás-axʷ 'where are you going?'

One also uses n-ka? where English uses 'which (one),' as in:

(c) n-ka? kʷu‿cúwa?-s   s-A   cəspíc'a? 'which one is A's sweater (cəspíc'a?)?' (cúwa? 'own' [Section 24.4])

Indefinite local deictics are derived from the interrogative ones by adding -as 3S intransitive subjunctive subject suffix. Various adverbial enclitics (see Section 32) may be added to express various shades of meaning ('somewhere, anywhere, wherever'):

(d) n-ka?-as‿k'á‿tu? (ɬ‿)ɬwáln-an 'I left it (ɬwálən) somewhere, I wonder where I left it' (‿k'a 'apparently,' ‿tu? 'definite past')

(e) n-ká?-as‿X'u? (ɬ‿)ɬwáln-axʷ 'leave it anywhere' (‿X'u? 'well, but, so'); the parentheses in (ɬ‿) indicate that ɬ is present in slow, but absent in fast, speech.

By combining xʷ?ạz 'no(t)' with n-ka?, we express 'nowhere, not anywhere':

(f) xʷ?ạz‿X'u? kən‿[n-]ká? kʷən‿pún 'I can't find (pun) it anywhere' (for kən‿ see Section 34)

The form kən‿tákəm expresses 'everywhere' (tákəm 'all'). There is also an 'evasive' deictic ?í?luqʷ (also recorded ?í?tuɬ) 'somewhere (none of your business where),' used when the speaker does not want to reveal the location of smt., as in:

(g) lá-kʷu? ?í?luqʷ‿a 'over there (none of your business where)'

See Section 37.4.1 for relative local deictics ('I know where ...').

26.1.5. Morphosyntactic comments on local deictics

Pivoting deictics and the interrogative deictic are affixing, i.e., they can attract, among other affixes, personal suffixes, as in:

(a) l-c?á-ɬkan 'I (-ɬkan) am here'

(b) n-ká?-ɬkaxʷ 'where are you?'

(c) n-ká?-wit‿tu? 'what route did they take?' (‿tu? 'definite past')

(d) l-c?áh-as‿maɬ ɬ‿wá?-at 'let us stay here' (literally 'let it be here that we stay')

(e) l-t?úh-as 'let it be there'

(f) n-ka?-as‿k'á‿həm'‿tu? ni‿pú?y'axʷ‿a 'the mouse (pú?y'axʷ) must have gone somewhere': note that n-ka? here does not refer to an impersonal state as in Section 26.1.4(d) and (e), but to an action ('to go where?') performed by the mouse.

Pivoting deictics and n-ka? also combine with -məx 'people, person' (and usually at the same time with ɬəl-) to express 'to be from here, where?': ɬəl-cʔáh-məx 'to be a person from here,' ɬəl-ən-káʔ-məx 'to be from where?'

26.1.6. Local non-deictics
Local non-deictics ('below, above, under,' etc.) are based on words with a local reference (e.g., x̌áwʼən' 'low') as in:
   (a) x̌ʷáyt‿kʷu? l-kʷʔa kʷɬ‿wáʔ‿a x̌áwʼnʼ‿a 'those who are (waʔ) here below are all dying, I hear' (x̌ʷayt 'to die collectively'; ‿kʷu? quotative; for ‿a in x̌áwʼnʼ‿a, cf. Section 26.1.3[a] to [d])
   For the use of local non-deictics as prepositions, see Section 34.2.

26.2. Temporal deictics
Lillooet has the following temporal deictics: lá-ni? 'at that time, then,' ɬlá-ni? 'from that time,' piná-ni? 'about that time.'[2] Examples include:
   (a) lá-ni? ?i‿pún-an 'that is when I found (pun) it'
   (b) September‿kʼa piná-ni? 'round about September' (‿kʼa 'apparently')
   (c) pina-ni?‿kʼá‿wi? ɬ‿x̌ánʼ-as 'he must have gotten hurt (x̌anʼ) about that time' (for ‿wi? see Section 32.1.14)
   The interrogative temporal deictic is kánmas-as 'when?'[3] as in:
   (d) kánmas-as ɬ‿ƛ̓íq-as 'when did he arrive (ƛ̓iq)?'
   (e) kánmas-as ɬ‿húzʼ-as ƛ̓iq 'when will he arrive?'
   For past events we may also use ?i‿kánmas-as (?i‿ 'when' [see Section 37.4.2]):
   (f) ?i‿kánmas-as ɬ‿ƛ̓íq-as 'when did he arrive?'
   Combinations of kánmas-as and various adverbial enclitics express 'sometime, anytime, whenever,' as in:
   (g) kanmas-ás‿kʼa 'oh, sometime' (‿kʼa 'apparently')
   (h) kanmas-ás‿qa? ɬ‿húzʼ-as ƛ̓iq 'I wonder when he'll come' (for ‿qa? see Section 32.1.11)
   For relative 'when' ('I know when ...'), see Section 37.4.1(3e).

26.2.1. Temporal non-deictics
Temporal non-deictics are ɬkʷun 'now' (also ɬkʷúnsa, probably from *l‿ti‿s‿ɬkʷún-s‿a 'in [l‿] its nowness'), ɬ‿núkʷ-as 'once in a while' (nukʷ '[an]other' [Section 24.6]), kalál 'soon,' and ɬ‿kalál-as 'after a while.' The idea of 'never' is rendered through various combinations with x̌ʷʔaz 'no(t),' such as x̌ʷʔaz skənkán 'never, no way' (see Section 20.2 for skənkán), x̌ʷʔay-s 'not in a while.'[4]
   Note that the expressions given above are as such invariable. We also have the variable word papt 'always,' which is used as an auxiliary (see Section 22.4 for use of auxiliaries). Other references to time make use of variable words referring to particular time units, as in:

(a) ʔi‿sítst-as 'last night' (sitst 'night')

(b) ʔi‿nátxʷ-as 'yesterday' (natxʷ 'tomorrow'; note the semantic shift when used in ʔi‿nátxʷ-as)

(c) zánuxʷ-əm 'next year' (√zánuxʷ 'year'; -əm intransitivizer or aspectual suffix)

(d) ʔi‿zánuxʷ-m-as 'last year'

27
Proper Nouns

Proper nouns form a special category in Lillooet. On the one hand, they may contain lexical suffixes and (in the predicate position) intransitive subject suffixes; on the other hand, they do not take (in)transitivizers, or personal affixes other than intransitive subject suffixes. Because of these limitations, we class them with the invariable words. In Section 27.1 we discuss the make-up of proper nouns, and in Section 27.2, the use of proper nouns. In Section 27.3 we deal with generic pet-names.

27.1. Make-up of proper nouns
From a formal point of view, proper nouns are basically of two kinds: unanalyzable terms, e.g., kʷə́z'psa? (a woman's name), or derived terms, which may be either borrowed or derived from Lillooet proper nouns or Lillooet variable words. Borrowings may be taken from other Salish languages or from English (e.g., pạh 'Pa,' mah 'Ma'). We may derive proper nouns from Lillooet stems through retraction or through lexical suffixation. With retraction we have, for example, sxam 'foolish, irresponsible' > sạxạ́m (a man's name); súspa? 'tail' > sụ́ṣpạ? (a man's name). See also Section 5.4.

There are no special lexical suffixes for deriving proper nouns. Some suffixes are used in nicknames or pet-names, e.g., -qʷ (Section 15.2[112b]), as in saw't 'slave' > sáw't-əqʷ (a boy's pet-name), -l-əqs/-y-əqs (see Section 15.2[108.1] for examples). The suffix -q 'buttocks, behind' (Section 15.2[105a]) is used with humoristic effect to form nicknames: -q is suffixed either to a word that describes a person's proclivity or to a person's real name, e.g., twan'-q 'given to eating salmonberries (twan),' cəm'-q 'Jim (cəm)' (the latter also has the humoristic connotation 'scorched bottom': cəm 'to get scorched').

Other suffixes used to form names do not seem to have a humoristic or hypocoristic connotation, but are used in official names, e.g., -asq'ət 'day'

(Section 15.2[32]) in men's names, or -in'ak 'gun' (Section 15.2[38]) in women's names.

For anthropological information on Lillooet names, see also Hill-Tout (in Maud 1978:124-132) and Teit 1906:294-295. I have not made any detailed anthropological study of Lillooet name giving, and I do not venture any assessment of the correctness of Hill-Tout's and Teit's descriptions.

27.2. Use of proper nouns

Proper nouns may be used as predicates or as subject or object complements. When used as complements, proper nouns usually take different articles than variable words (see Section 31.1). Proper nouns are extended with the nominalizer s- when they are used as predicates or complements, although s- is occasionally dropped in less careful speech (s- is categorically absent in quotations of proper nouns out of context, or in direct address, e.g., 'Joe!'). Examples of proper nouns as predicates include:

(a) s-Belinda-ɬkan 'I am Belinda'
(b) Joe-ɬkan 'I am Joe'

These examples may also be rendered through s?ənc 'I' in the predicate position and the proper nouns in the complement position (see Section 31.6.2[g], [h]; Section 31.5 also lists further examples of the use of proper nouns.

27.3. Generic pet-names

Lillooet has a number of generic pet-names, i.e., terms of endearment for certain classes rather than for individuals. Here belong ?ápa? (term of endearment for men or boys, roughly corresponding to English 'mate' or 'buddy') and kíka? (term of endearment for women and girls, roughly corresponding to English 'dear'). When used as complements, these terms are extended with the nominalizer s-, and they take the same articles as the proper nouns. There is also a special pet-name for bear cubs, which was recorded only in complements: s-cəcəw'qín'kst (from the s-cə́cəw' 'design' that bear cubs have on their -qin'-kst 'nail, claw'). For examples of generic pet-names in sentences, see Section 31.5(c) to (f).

28
Full-Word Conjunctions and Adverbs (Particles)

Lillooet has a number of invariable full words that correspond in function to English conjunctions and non-demonstrative adverbs. We deal separately with conjunctions (Section 28.1) and adverbs (Section 28.2). For demonstrative adverbs, see Section 26; for adverbial enclitics, see Section 32; and for proclitic conjunctions, see Section 33. Remaining elements that function as conjunctions and adverbs are discussed in Section 29.

28.1. Conjunctions
Of the conjunctions discussed here, 28.1.1 to 28.1.3 link sentences (i.e., predicates with or without complements), whereas 28.1.4 and 28.1.5 link components within complements. All conjunctions in Sections 28.1.1 to 28.1.5 are coordinating, i.e., they do not indicate a hierarchy between the elements they link (unlike the subordinating conjunctions discussed in Section 33).

28.1.1. The conjunction ƛ'uʔ 'but'
The conjunction ƛ'uʔ is formally the same as the enclitic ˌƛ'uʔ (Section 32.1.4), and historically it is doubtless the same element. However, unlike the enclitic adverb ˌƛ'uʔ, it occurs clause-initially and has full word-stress. The conjunction ƛ'uʔ generally introduces information that was unexpected on the basis of earlier information (in this respect it resembles Russian no; cf. also més ˌƛ'uʔ and zámas ˌƛ'uʔ in Section 36.2). Examples of ƛ'uʔ 'but' include:

   (a) stəx̌ʷ-kán ˌƛ'uʔ waʔ ʔama-mín-cin, ƛ'uʔ papt-káx̌ʷ ˌƛ'uʔ waʔ qlíl-min'-c 'I am really (stəx̌ʷ) good (ʔáma) to (-min') you, but still you are always (papt) angry (qlil) at (-min') me'
   (b) x̌ʷʔux̌ʷ ʔi ləp'aɬk'ʷún ʔ ˌa, ƛ'uʔ wáʔ-ɬkan ƛ'əx-s 'the cured salmon eggs (ləp'aɬk'ʷúnaʔ) stink (x̌ʷʔux̌ʷ), but still I like (ƛ'əx-s) them'

(c) X̌'ənam'-ílx-kał ʕʷəln-ə́m c?a ti_sp'áms_a, X̌'u? pus-?úl 'we tried (X̌'ənam'-ílx) to light (ʕʷélən) this (c?a) wood (sp'ams), but it is too (-?úl) wet (pus)' (ʕʷəln-ə́m < kʷ_s-ʕʷəln-ə́m with irregular dropping of kʷ_s-)

(d) wa? sə́na? kəns-k'ʷatan'-túmuł-as, X̌'u? plán-łkał_X̌'u? tákəm wa? k'ʷzúsəm 'he wanted (kəns-) to hire (k'ʷátan') us, but all (tákəm) of us are working (k'ʷzúsəm) already (plan)'

(e) kəns-q'ʷúsxit-kan sə́na?, X̌'u? stə́x̌ʷ_X̌'u? kəkaw'-?úl 'I wanted to shoot it, but it was really (stəx̌ʷ) too (-?úl) far (kəkáw')'

28.1.2. The conjunction k'á_mał 'but'

The conjunction k'á_mał is composed of k'a (cf. the enclitic _k'a [Section 32.1.8]), and the enclitic _mał (Section 32.1.1). This conjunction generally introduces information that is contrary to what has been said about something else (comparable to Russian a). Examples include:

(a) xʷ?az kʷ_s-x̌əł-c łkʷúnsa, k'á_mał ?i_nátxʷ-as 'it is not (xʷ?az) cold (x̌əł) today (łkʷúnsa), but then yesterday (?i_nátxʷ-as)!'

(b) nu?qʷ-ám łkʷúnsa, k'á_mał ?i_nátxʷ-as kə́la?_X̌'u? x̌əł 'it is warming up (nu?qʷám) today, but yesterday it was really cold'

(c) tákəm_X̌'u? swat wa? zəwatən-cál-itas kʷənswa_nk'yáp, k'á_mał xʷ?az snúwa kʷasu_nk'yáp 'everybody (tákəm swat) knows (zəwátən) that I am a coyote (nk'yap), but you are not a coyote'

28.1.3. The conjunction X̌'u 'until'

The conjunction X̌'u corresponds directly to English 'until,' as in:

(a) húy'-łkan cukʷ X̌'u natxʷ 'I am going to quit (cukʷ) until (it is) tomorrow (natxʷ)'

(b) matq-kát_X̌'u? X̌'u cíxʷ-kał 'we walked (matq) until we got there' (cixʷ 'to get there')

(c) wá?_kʷu? ?aył láti? s-təq-s-ás X̌'u ka-ʕʷuy't_á_X̌'u? 'he was holding (s-təq-s) it there (láti?) until he fell asleep (ka-ʕʷúy't_a)'

(d) húy'-łkan k'ʷzúsəm X̌'u X̌'aləl-łkán_kł 'I will work until I drop' (X̌'áləl 'to stop, grind to a halt, drop from fatigue')

(e) k'aləm-łkát_kł X̌'u nq'íq'əl' ti_máq?_a ?əł_nás-kał_kł ?aył q'ámqʷ?-am 'we will wait (k'áləm) until the snow (máqa?) freezes before we go (nas) to get cattail tops (q'ámqʷa?)' (nq'íq'əl' 'top layer of snow freezes'; for -am in q'ámqʷ?-am see Section 18.4; for ?əł_ see Section 33.1)

The conjunction X̌'u is often followed by a construction consisting of cixʷ 'it gets to that point' plus a t-construction:

(f) k'ʷzusəm-łkát_X̌'u? X̌'u cixʷ t_s-X̌'aləl-łkát_a 'we worked until we could not work any more' (cf. [d] above)

(g) ?ax̌ʷxal-łkán_X̌'u? X̌'u cixʷ t_s-qʷáľqʷəľt-s_a ti_n-sx̌íc'kn'_a 'I kept digging (?áx̌ʷxal) until my back (sx̌íc'kən') got sore (qʷáľqʷəľt)'

(h) say'səẑ-wít‿λ̓'uʔ λ̓'u cixʷ t‿s-paʔxʷ-íh‿a 'they played (sáy'səẑ') until they got tired of it' (paʔxʷ 'to get tired of, fed up with')

Literally, the constructions with cixʷ in (f) to (h) mean 'until it got to our stopping,' '... to the aching of my back,' '... to their being fed up.'

28.1.4. The conjunction mútaʔ 'and'

This conjunction, formally identical to the adverb mútaʔ 'again' (Section 28.2.1), connects components within subject or object complements, as in:

(a) waʔ k'ʷzúsəm-wit ti‿n-sqácəʔ‿a mútaʔ ti‿n-sísqʔ‿a 'my father (sqácza?) and my uncle (sísqa?) are working'

(b) huẑ' q'aʔ-wít wi‿s-máhyəqs mútaʔ s-páhyəqs 'Máhyeqs and Páoh-yeqs were about to eat (q'aʔ)' (huẑ' 'to be about to do smt.')

We also have mútaʔ in composite numerals (between multiples of ten):

(c) q'əm'p mútaʔ pálaʔ 'eleven' ('ten and one')

28.1.5. The conjunction wi 'and'

The conjunction wi has the same function as mútaʔ (Section 28.1.4). However, its use is restricted to numerals:

(a) q'əm'p wi pálaʔ 'eleven'

28.2. Adverbs

Full-word adverbs usually appear after the first word in a sentence, like adverbial enclitics (see Section 32). Unlike the enclitics, however, they do not enter into one stress unit with the word they follow, but they retain their own stress.

Semantically, full-word adverbs are about as heterogeneous as the adverbial enclitics, expressing modal or temporal-aspectual notions. For the adverb s-x̌ək 'maybe,' see Section 36.1.

28.2.1. The adverb mútaʔ 'again'

This adverb, formally identical to the conjunction mútaʔ (Section 28.1.4), expresses a reversal or a repetition of an action. Examples include:

(a) p'an't mútaʔ ʔúx̌ʷal' 'he returned (p'an't) home (ʔúx̌ʷal') again'

(b) súx̌ʷast, ʔúqʷaʔ, λ̓'ak mútaʔ x̌áλ̓'əm 'he went down (súx̌ʷast), he drank (ʔúqʷaʔ), and he went (λ̓'ak) uphill (x̌áλ̓'əm) again'

(c) cukʷ, nít‿λ̓'uʔ [s-]sʔixʷɬ-c ti‿waʔ‿száytən-s 'she was finished (cukʷ), and then she did something different (sʔixʷɬ) again' (száytən 'what one does, one's business')

28.2.2. The adverb sénaʔ 'unfulfilled'

This adverb is used when the subject nurtures an unfulfilled wish or indicates that he has changed his mind or that his plans have changed:

(a) X̓iq-as‿ka‿X̓u? sə́na? 'I hope he will come (X̓iq)' (‿ka in combination with the subjunctive expresses 'to hope,' Section 32.5[a] to [l])

(b) ka-ʕʷə́l-s-kan‿a sə́na? 'I lit it (but I don't know if it will burn)' (cf. ka-ʕʷə́l-s-kan‿a 'I managed to light it')

(c) nás-kan sə́na? 'I was going (nas), but I changed my mind'

(d) nás-kan sə́na?, xʷ‿az-wíĺx múta? kʷ‿ən-s-nás 'I was going, but then I changed my mind about going' (xʷ‿az-wíĺx 'mind or plans are changed')

(e) zuhən-c-ás‿X̓u? sə́na? 'he told me to be careful (but I did not obey him)' (zúhən 'to tell smb. to be careful')

See also Section 24.1.2(d) and (f), and Section 28.1.1(d) and (e).

28.2.3. The adverb núkʷun' 'again'

This adverb generally expresses 'again,' but often with a connotation of amusement or annoyance. It is also used when something happens that one more or less expected to happen (as a result of somebody's clumsiness, for instance). Examples include:

(a) My, c?a núkʷun' 'My, now it's this (c?a) again!' ('what next?!')

(b) kʷ̓is-c-kaxʷ núkʷun' 'well, you dropped (kʷ̓is-c) it (like I thought you would)'

(c) wa? núkʷun' ?ə[s]-s?úqʷa? 'he's got (?əs-) a drink (s?úqʷa?) again'

(d) níɬ‿k̓a‿həm´ núkʷun' s-Peter 'that is Peter at it again' (niɬ anticipatory pronoun [Section 24.5])

(e) húy̓-ɬkaxʷ núkʷun' sqyax̌ 'you are going to be drunk (sqyax̌) again'

(f) ʕʷuy̓t láti?, plán‿kʷu?‿X̓u? núkʷun' X̓iq ti‿ʕʷuy̓t-min-talíh‿a 'she slept (ʕʷuy̓t), and the one who slept with her came (X̓iq) again'

(g) lán‿X̓u? núkʷun' wa? ka-k̓ə́m'‿a 'he is going too far again' (ka-k̓ə́m'‿a 'to go too far,' lan 'already')

(h) snúwa núkʷun' 'you (snúwa) again!'

(i) lan núkʷun' wa? wə?áw kʷ‿?ápa? təm 'Apa7 Tem (a man's name) is inviting people to the gathering again' (wə?áw 'to shout,' here referring to the function of town crier)

28.2.4. The adverb nukʷɬ '(not) a bit'

This adverb was recorded only in combination with xʷ?az 'no(t)'; nukʷɬ has a reinforcing function here. It is apparently only used in F, and is probably a borrowing from Shuswap. Examples include:

(a) xʷ?az nukʷɬ 'not a bit'

(b) xʷ?az káti? kʷas‿k̓ə́k̓x̌əm' nukʷɬ láti? kʷas‿?úɬxʷ 'there was not a bit of a draft (k̓ə́k̓x̌əm') coming in (?úɬxʷ) there (láti?)'; the expression xʷ?az nukʷɬ is reinforced here by káti? (see also Section 26.1.3[h])

28.2.5. The adverb X̓it 'also, too'

This adverb parallels English 'also, too' exactly. Examples include:

(a) nk'yáp-kan‿X̌'u? X̌'it 'I am also a coyote (nk'yap)'

(b) tqíɬ‿X̌'u? X̌'it nq'san'k sniɬ 'he (sniɬ) almost (tqíɬ‿X̌'u?) laughed (nq'san'k) too'

(c) nás-kan‿kɬ, kʷám-ɬkan‿kɬ kʷu‿sqáwc 'I will (‿kɬ) go (nas), I will also get (kʷam) some potatoes (sqawc)'

(d) ʕʷuy't ?ayɬ ti‿?í?mac-s‿a, níɬ‿X̌'u? s-ʕʷuy't-s X̌'it sniɬ 'her grandchild (?í?mac) fell asleep (ʕʷuy't), so (níɬ‿X̌'u?) she fell asleep too'

(e) xʷ?az X̌'it kʷas‿x̌ʷəm kʷənswa‿ka-ptínusm‿a 'I cannot think (ptínusəm) fast (x̌ʷəm) either'

28.2.6. The adverb ka?ɬ 'for a while, once more, again'

This adverb indicates a continuation or a repetition of an action. Examples include:

(a) húy'-ɬkan ka?ɬ cukʷ 'I am going to quit (cukʷ) for a while'

(b) X̌'álləx ka?ɬ 'stop! (I want to talk with you)' (X̌'álləx 'to stop')

(c) zám'əm' ka?ɬ 'take it easy (zám'əm') for a while!'

(d) nX̌'ák'ʷ-xi[t]-c ka?ɬ 'pour (nX̌'ak'ʷ-) me (-c) another one!' (-xit 'for')

(e) sək-qʷ-án' ka?ɬ 'give him another blow (sək-) on the head (-qʷ)!'

(f) núwa ka?ɬ kʷu‿zaxn-áy'ɬ 'it's your turn to carry the baby' (-ay'ɬ 'baby,' záxən 'to carry on back,' núwa 'you' [usually s-núwa], kʷu‿ article)

28.2.7. The adverb zam' 'after all, as things are now, as things turned out to be'

As a general rule, this adverb accompanies commands or information that are given as an afterthought. Examples include:

(a) xʷúy‿qa? zam' 'okay, go ahead then!' (xʷuy 'go ahead!,' for ‿qa? see Section 32.1.11)

(b) nás‿maɬ zam' 'go (nas) then!' (‿maɬ adhortative [Section 32.1.1])

(c) ?íkəna zam' ?izáwna 'my, oh, my, now these things again!' (?íkəna exclamation of surprise, Section 30.2[1]; ?izáwna 'these')

(d) ka-xál-almən‿a ?ákʷu?, Lillooet‿a zam', ti‿wa?‿Lillooet ɬkʷúnsa 'he got close (-almən) to the brow of the hill, that is at Lillooet, at what is Lillooet now (ɬkʷúnsa)' (ka-xál‿a 'to get to the brow of a hill')

(e) níɬ‿kʷu? wa? cún-itas ?i‿sám?‿a 'smallpox,' wín'axʷ‿X̌'u? zam' ti‿wa?‿s-nah-n-ém wi‿snímuɬ ?úxʷalmixʷ, 'smallpox' cút-kaɬ 'that (kʷu?) is what the white people (sáma?) call "smallpox," so we (wi‿snímuɬ) Indians (?úxʷalmixʷ) call (náhən) it the same (wín'axʷ), we (wi‿snímuɬ) say (cut) "smallpox"'

(f) ka‿ɬ‿?əmhám-as‿X̌'u? zam', (ɬ‿)s?ixʷɬ-ás‿ka ɬláti?, wá?-ɬkan‿ka lúləm', xʷ?az zam' 'if (ɬ) it would have (ka‿) been somebody better (?əmhám), or somebody else (s?ixʷɬ) than that one (ɬláti?), I would have been jealous (lúləm'), but now I am not (xʷ?az)'

(g) ka‿ɬ‿nas[-c]-tum'x-áxʷ‿X̌'uʔ ʔəkʷʔú pankʷúph‿a, xʷaz'wíl'xs-káxʷ‿ha zam' 'I thought (ka‿ɬ‿, Section 32.5.1) that you were bringing (nas-c) me to Vancouver (pankʷúpa); did you change your mind after all?' (xʷaz'wíl'xs 'to change one's mind')

28.2.8. The adverb ʔayɬ 'next, this time, and then'

The adverb ʔayɬ indicates that the speaker supplies some new information. As such, it is used mainly when a new event is introduced, as in (a) to (e), and in speculations or explanations of what has happened, as in (f) to (g).

(a) X̌'ak, qʷax̌t ʔayɬ ʔi‿ʔuxʷalmíxʷ‿a 'he went along (X̌'ak), and then the people (ʔúxʷalmixʷ) noticed (qʷax̌t) him'

(b) húy'-ɬkan ʔayɬ ʔuxʷalmíxʷ-c-min' cʔáwna ti‿nk'yáp‿a 'this time I am going to tell a story in Indian about this coyote' (-c 'to speak,' -min 'about,' ʔúxʷalmixʷ 'Indian')

(c) kʷám‿kʷuʔ ʔi‿qʷal'íɬ‿a, qíqc'əm‿kʷuʔ ʔayɬ 'he took (kʷam) some pitch (qʷal'íɬ), and then he chewed (qíqc'əm) it, as I was told (‿kʷuʔ)' (qíqc'əm probably a misrecording for qíqc'əm')

(d) níɬ‿X̌'uʔ s-ʔác'x̌-s-as ti‿skʷʷúkʷʷm'it‿a, X̌íq-wit ʔayɬ ʔi‿waʔ‿qʷʷláw'əm 'so (níɬ‿X̌'uʔ) she watched over (s-ʔac'x̌-s) the child (skʷʷúkʷʷm'it), and then the berry-pickers (ʔi‿waʔ‿qʷʷláw'əm) came (X̌iq)'

(e) níɬ‿X̌'uʔ s-ʔúc'qaʔ-s ti‿skʷúzaʔ-s‿a, waʔ ʔayɬ láti smícaʔq ʔílal 'so her daughter (skʷúzaʔ) went out (ʔúc'qaʔ), but she [the mother] stayed (waʔ) there (láti), sitting (smícaʔq) and crying (ʔílal)'

(f) naʔq' sqawc ti‿kʷanən-s-ás‿a, nkaʔ-as‿ƙá‿həm'‿tuʔ ʔayɬ ni‿púʔy'axʷ‿a 'it was a rotten (naʔq') potato (sqawc) that she had caught (kʷánən-s), but the mouse (púʔy'axʷ) had apparently gone off somewhere' (for nkaʔ-as see also Section 26.1.5[f]; for the text from which this sentence is taken, see Section 39)

(g) zikt‿kʷuʔ‿túʔ‿X̌'uʔ, lán-s‿kʷuʔ ʔayɬ n-c'aqʷ-q-án'-əm ʔə‿ki‿sxʷúxʷz̓‿a 'she toppled over (zikt), because the ants (sxʷúxʷəz̓) had already (lan) eaten (c'aqʷ-) her bum (n-..-q)'

The adverb ʔayɬ is used very frequently. ʔayɬ is also used as an auxiliary, meaning 'to have just done smt.' (variable word) as in:

(h) ʔayɬ-wit‿ʔíz'‿X̌'uʔ kʷán-twal' 'they (‿ʔiz') had just started to go together' (kʷan 'to take,' -twal' 'each other')

Hence, ʔayɬ straddles the boundary between variable and invariable words.

29
Sentence-Equivalents

Lillooet has a number of invariable full words that, like the words discussed in Section 28, correspond to English conjunctions and non-demonstrative adverbs. However, whereas the words in Section 28 are linked paratactically to the sentences they modify, the words discussed in this section occur as full predicates (with 3S subject suffixes), and they require the sentences they modify to appear as a subordinate clause. (A subordinate clause is a clause whose predicate is a factual [kʷ-, s-, t-]construction, or a subjunctive [c] construction; see also Section 22.3.1.)

We use the term 'sentence-equivalent' for these conjunctional and adverbial terms.[1] In Section 29.1, we organize the sentence-equivalents according to the type of subordinate clause they require: kʷ-clauses (1 to 5), s-clauses (6, 7), t-clauses (8), and kʷ-clauses or ɬ (subjunctive [c]) clauses (9). In Section 29.2 we discuss variable words that may function as sentence-equivalents.

29.1. List of sentence-equivalents
The group of sentence-equivalents has the following members:

1 xʷʔaz 'not, it is not the case (that)': when followed by a subordinate clause, xʷʔaz expresses negative sentences (by negating the content of the subordinate clause). It is also used by itself, without a subordinate clause, to express 'no!' As we saw in Section 8.2, xʷʔaz has limited affixing possibilities. Examples of xʷʔaz include:
   (a) xʷʔaz kʷ˰s-ƛ'íq-i 'they did not come (ƛ'iq)'
   (b) xʷʔaz kʷ˰s-núkʷʷʔan-c-as 'he (-as) did not help (núkʷʷʔan) me (-c)'
2 s-kan 'is it the case?': question marker, cf. Polish *czy*. The function of s-kan seems to be exactly the same as that of ˰ha (Section 32.1.12), although s-kan might express a greater degree of puzzlement ('I wonder whether ...'):
   (a) s-kan kʷ˰s-ƛ'íq-i 'did they come?'

3 swáts‿ka 'it is to be hoped, I hope': expresses the speaker's wish with regard to a (usually future) happening. This word probably contains swat 'who?' and -s 3S possessive; ‿ka expresses 'should' (Section 32.1.6). Examples include:

(a) swáts‿ka kʷ‿s-X̣'iq-s ɬkʷúnsa kʷ‿s-Bill 'I hope Bill will come (X̣'iq) today (ɬkʷúnsa)'

(b) swáts‿ka kʷ‿s-ka-mays-c-án‿a ɬkʷúnsa 'I hope I will be able (ka-..‿a) to fix (mays-c) it today'

4 cəsutá‿ka 'it is to be wished, I wish': expresses that the speaker wishes that such-and-such might be the case. Contains ‿ka 'should,' and is possibly an altered version of swáts‿ka (although swáts‿ka and cəsutá‿ka are used as, and considered to be, two different expressions). An example is:

(a) cəsutá‿ka kʷ‿s-ka-ʔac'x̣-s-án‿a 'I wish I could (ka-..‿a) see (ʔac'x̣) it'

5 ləp‿X̣'uʔ 'suddenly': contains ləp (peculiar to this construction) and ‿X̣'uʔ (adverbial enclitic [Section 32.1.4]):

(a) ləp‿X̣'uʔ kʷ‿s-ka-qlíl-s‿a 'he suddenly got angry'

6 niɬ‿X̣'uʔ 'and so, and then (it came to pass that ...)': contains niɬ anticipatory pronoun (Section 24.5) and the adverbial enclitic ‿X̣'uʔ (Section 32.1.4). Instead of niɬ‿X̣'uʔ, we sometimes have X̣'uʔ‿s-niɬ-c (without perceptible difference in meaning). Examples of niɬ‿X̣'uʔ include:

(a) nás‿kʷuʔ ʔámləx ʔákʷuʔ cípun-s‿a, niɬ‿X̣'uʔ s-X̣'ák-s-as ti‿x̌láka?-s‿a 'allegedly (‿kʷuʔ), she went (nas) that way (ʔákʷuʔ) to get food from her root-house (cípun), so she took along (X̣'ak-s) her (-s) bucket (x̌láka?)' (ʔámləx 'to get food from store or cellar')

(b) plán‿kʷuʔ waʔ pɬ'ukʷ ti‿np'ámstn‿a, niɬ‿X̣'uʔ s-ʔác'x̣n-as ɬəs‿kánəm 'allegedly (‿kʷuʔ), the stove (np'ámstən) was smoking (pɬ'ukʷ), so she [went to] see (ʔác'x̣ən) what was happening (kánəm)'

Occasionally, ‿X̣'uʔ is dropped:

(c) cixʷ say'səz'-s-túmx-as, niɬ s-wáʔ-ɬkaɬ sáy'səz' 'he came (cixʷ) to play (sáy'səz') with (-s) me (-tumx), so we played'

7 wiʔ 'and so': recorded only in F. This is the full-word variant of the enclitic ‿wiʔ (Section 32.1.14):

(a) xʷ?áz‿k'a‿wiʔ put kʷ‿s-kə-káw'-s kʷu‿tmíxʷ-s, wiʔ s-x̌ʷəm-s kʷ‿s-cixʷ-s ʔúx̌ʷal' 'her land (tmixʷ) was not far (kə-káw'), so she got home (ʔúx̌ʷal') fast (x̌ʷəm)' (put 'enough, sufficient,' 'at all' when in combination with xʷ?əz)

8 niɬ 'because (?)': anticipatory pronoun (Section 24.5), combined with t-constructions to express 'because.' However, t- is fairly often dropped, in which case it is the t-construction that carries the meaning 'because':

(a) xʷ?əz kʷənswa‿ka-c'uqʷaz'ám‿a, niɬ t‿s-nik'in'-ítas‿a ni‿n-sp'ác'n‿a 'I cannot fish (c'úqʷaz'am), because they cut (ník'in') my (n-) net (sp'ác'ən)'

(b) plan xʷ?əz kʷas‿k'ʷzúsəm kʷ‿s-Bill, niɬ t‿s-plán-s‿a waʔ

qəɬməmən'-ʔúl 'Bill does not work (kʷzúsəm) any more, because he is too (-ʔúl) old (qəɬmémən') already (plan)'

9 ʔuc 'it is not so-and-so': indicates that the identification of a person or object is incorrect. Usually ʔuc takes a kʷ-construction, but in one case I recorded a ɬ-construction:

(a) plán‿X̌'u? ʔuc kʷasu‿ʔúxʷalmixʷ 'you look really bad' (literally 'you are not human [ʔúxʷalmixʷ] any more')

(b) ʔuc‿a‿xʷíɬ‿ti? kʷas‿cúwaʔ-s 'that (‿ti?) is not his' (cúwaʔ 'own' [Section 24.4], -s 3S possessive; ‿xʷíɬ 'after all' [Section 32.1.10])

(c) ʔúc‿ti? ɬ‿níɬ-as ni‿n-skíʕʷ‿a 'that (‿ti?) is not my skiʕʷ (female friend)'

29.2. Variable words as sentence-equivalents

A number of variable words may also occur in adverbial or conjunctional functions (in these cases they combine with a 3S subject suffix into an impersonal construction requiring a subordinate clause). For instance, we may combine numerals or words referring to a quality with kʷ-constructions to express 'it is done X times, in an X way.' For examples with numerals, see Section 19.4.2; for a term referring to quality, see x̌ʷəm kʷ‿s-cixʷ-s in Section 29.1(7a). This matter is discussed further in Section 37.1(2).

30
Greetings, Exclamations, and Interjections

In this section we discuss two residual types of utterances: greetings and related expressions (Section 30.1), and exclamations and interjections (Section 30.2). The difference between these two types is that in the former the speaker usually requires some reaction from the addressee or reacts to the addressee, whereas in the latter the speaker gives vent to his or her own emotions or is preoccupied with his or her own utterances.

30.1. Greetings and related expressions

Some greetings are based on common variable words; other greetings and related expressions employ words that are exclusively used in this function.

1 ƛ̓íq-kan 'here I am' (literally 'I [-kan] arrived [ƛ̓iq]'), ƛ̓íq-kaɬ 'here we are' (greetings used by arrivers), ƛ̓íq-kaxʷ 'there you are,' ƛ̓íq-kalʼap 'there you folks are' (said to arrivers).

2 k̓a‿ɬ‿wáʔ-axʷ 'how are you?' k̓a‿ɬ‿wáʔ-alʼap 'how are you folks?' (waʔ 'to be,' ‿k̓a 'apparently' [Sections 32.1.8 and 32.5.1]). The literal meaning of these expressions is 'apparently there you (folks) are.' Besides k̓a‿ɬ‿wáʔ-axʷ I also recorded wáʔ-axʷ‿k̓a.

3 wənáxʷ‿ha 'is it true (wənáxʷ)?' (‿ha question marker [Section 32.1.12]): a general greeting recorded only in M, apparently hardly different in meaning from kánəm (4), although wənáxʷ might have an ironic tinge that is absent from kánəm.

4 kánəm 'what's up, how are things, what's the matter?' (kánəm 'to do what? to be in what state?' [Section 20.1]). This greeting may also specify the addressee: kaxʷ kánəm 'how are you?' kálʼap k̓ánəm 'how are you folks?'

5 ʔáma sq̓it 'good (ʔáma) day (sq̓it),' ʔáma sʕap 'good evening (sʕap)': calques from English and not too much appreciated by many fluent speakers who prefer the typically Lillooet greetings.

6   ʔac'x̌ən-cí(n)-ɬkan̓ kɬ múta? 'I shall (͜kɬ) see (ʔác'x̌ən) you (-ci[n]) again (múta?),' ʔac'x̌ən-tumuɬ-kán̓ kɬ múta? 'I shall see you folks (-tumuɬ) again': common formulae when somebody leaves (used both by person leaving and by person staying).

7   hú?͜maɬ 'good-bye' (to one), hú?-wi͜maɬ 'good-bye, you folks': used both by person(s) leaving and by person(s) staying. The stem hu? is used exclusively in these forms (see also Section 22.5.2); ͜maɬ adhortative (Section 32.1.1).

8   síma? 'come!' (to one), síma?-wi 'come!' (to more). See also Section 22.5.2. For examples, see also Sections 32.1.1(c), 32.1.4(g), 32.1.11(f).

9   x̌ʷuy 'come on!' (to one), x̌ʷúy-wi 'come on!' (to more) (see also Section 22.5.2); x̌ʷúy-s͜maɬ 'let us (exclusive) go, do it!' x̌ʷúy-s-twí͜maɬ 'let us (inclusive) go, do it!': see also Section 22.5.1.

10   ka-wən?áx̌ʷ͜a 'excuse me!' See also Section 24.3.

11   kʷúkʷ-s-tum'x-kaxʷ 'thank you' (one to one), kʷukʷ-s-tum'x-kál'ap id. (one to more), kʷukʷ-s-tum'úɬ-kaxʷ id. (more to one), kʷukʷ-s-tum'úɬ-kal'ap id. (more to more); kʷukʷ-s 'to save, help out smb., tr.'

12   ʔi 'yes.'

13   x̌ʷ?ạz 'no': use of x̌ʷ?ạz (Section 29.1[1]) without subordinate clause; x̌ʷ?ạz 'no' is also pronounced x̌ʷ?ạ? (one speaker also says ʔa?x̌). There is also a nursery variant tạ?, used exclusively with children ('don't!').

14   wənc 'isn't it?': might historically be an allegro form of wənáx̌ʷ͜ha c?a 'is this (c?a) true (wənáx̌ʷ)?' The frequent use of 'innit?' (for 'isn't it?') by many Lillooets when speaking English might be caused by the frequent use of wənc in Lillooet parlance.

15   x̌ʷit͜a͜qá?͜a 'whistle!': used in hide-and-seek game, as a command to identify oneself to those who are hiding (√x̌ʷit 'to whistle').

16   niwí: greeting used when entering a place (comparable to 'anybody home?') or when meeting people (said to be anonymous with s-nuláp͜ha 'is that you guys?'); also an expression used to show amazement or amusement. In both meanings, niwí seems to be rather archaic: as an expression of amusement or amazement, one consultant remarked that 'the old ladies used to use it.'

17   tust 'I got it!': used when somebody drops something and the speaker catches (and claims) it.

18   ʔá?han 'see?! so there! didn't I tell you?': used when proving to the addressee that he or she was wrong; also ʔá?hancu; ʔá?han might historically be an allegro form of ʔác'x̌ən 'see!'

19   ʔi?áy 'come on, tell us more!': used by listeners to a story, to prompt the storyteller and to indicate that the audience has not fallen asleep yet (the storyteller will occasionally interrupt the story and wait for the audience to call out ʔi?áy).

20 **tay** 'say! hey': used to attract somebody's attention, as in:
(a) tay, n-snúkʷʷaʔ, ʔáma ti‿n-sxʷákʷkʷ‿a t‿s-xʷʔáy-s‿a kʷasu‿qʷúsxi[t]-c
'say, my (n-) friend (snúkʷʷaʔ), I am glad that you did not shoot (qʷúsxit) me' (ʔáma ti‿n-sxʷákʷkʷ‿a 'I am glad,' literally 'my heart is well').

30.2. Exclamations and interjections
We have the following exclamations and interjections:

1 **ʔíkəna** 'my goodness!': expression of amazement, often in the form ʔíkəna ʔákəna:
(a) ʔíkəna ʔákəna 'my, oh, my!'
(b) ʔíkəna zam' ʔizáwna 'my goodness, what next?!' (cf. Section 28.2.7[c])
2 **ʔəs** (also ʔis): expression of disbelief, apparently mainly used by young girls; also used to shrug off someone's teasing.
3 **wa̱ʔ**: expression of disbelief, tinged with slight ridicule, mainly used by men. Possibly a retracted form of waʔ 'to be (busy with).'
4 **ʔísta̱ʔ**: expression of disbelief, apparently stronger than ʔəs above; also used when smb. does smt. silly).
5 **ʔaxáʔ**: 'swear word'; no adequate translation recorded. According to one consultant, 'If you say this to the old ladies, you'd better be ready to run.' Cf.? ʔáʔxaʔ 'sacred, supernatural.'
6 **ʔáycuɬ ʔáycuɬ** 'my, oh, my': expression used to show that one is impressed.
(a) ʔáycuɬ ʔáycuɬ, xʷʔit wi‿s-kíkaʔ 'my, oh, my, lots of girls' (from a traditional dancing song)
7 **ʔananáh** 'ouch!': expression of pain.
(a) ʔananáh, ʔananáh, wáyt-kan lákʷʔa, ʔananáh, wáyt-kan 'ouch, ouch, something is wrong with me, ouch, something is wrong with me' (wayt 'smt. is wrong with smb.'; for lákʷʔa see Section 26.1.1[g] to [m]).
8 **ʔú‿X̌'u̱ʔ‿tiʔ**: expression of anger or annoyance, e.g., when noticing that smb. is cheating. For ʔu see 9 below; X̌'u̱ʔ retracted variant of X̌'uʔ adverbial enclitic (in this variant limited to this expression); ‿tiʔ 'that.'
9 **ʔu** 'oh': expression of surprise, also used to accept or acknowledge information, as in:
(a) ʔu kíka? ʔu 'is that so? (I presume you're right)' (to a woman)
(b) ʔu ʔápa? ʔu id. (to a man)
10 **si̱** 'kiss my a--!': expression of strong disapproval.[1]
11 **qaʔ**: interjection, like English '... uhm'; see Section 32.1.11(j) to (l).
12 **wə́naʔ**: interjection; see Section 24.3(d) to (f).

31
Articles

Lillooet has nine identificatory proclitics (articles) that combine with variable words and proper nouns when these fill the slot of subject or object complement. Formal aspects of the articles are discussed in Section 31.1. Semantics and use are discussed in Sections 31.2 to 31.6.

31.1. Formal aspects

The articles are listed in Figure 19.

Figure 19

Articles

	Variable words					Proper nouns
	Known			Unknown		
	Present		Absent	Present	Absent	
	Collective	Individual				
Sing.	ki‿	ti‿	ni‿	kʷu‿		kʷ‿
Plur.		ʔi‿	nəɬ‿	kʷɬ‿		wi‿
	With ‿a				Without ‿a	

As Figure 19 shows, five articles (ki‿, ti‿, ʔi‿, ni‿, nəɬ‿) require an enclitic element ‿a (which occurs after the first word preceded by these articles). With the articles kʷu‿ and kʷɬ‿, the presence versus absence of ‿a indicates the presence versus absence of the thing meant. Note the presence of ɬ in two plural articles (nəɬ‿ and kʷɬ‿). The F dialect has ta‿, na‿ instead of ti‿, ni‿, which are characteristic of the M dialect (in the examples given in this book, ti‿ and ni‿ are written throughout, even in sentences recorded in the F dialect).

In rapid speech, the articles ti‿ (ta‿), ni‿ (na‿), ki‿, and kʷu‿ tend to drop their final vowel or have it reduced to schwa. The articles ti‿ (ta‿) and, less often, ni‿ (na‿) are occasionally dropped. For dropping of preposition-article combinations, see Section 26.1.3. The article nəɬ‿ is sometimes pronounced ɬ‿ before words starting in n- (1) 'my,' (2) 'in, on, at.' For formal aspects of the proper noun articles, see Section 31.5. For the formal overlapping between ki‿ and ʔi‿ after prepositions, see Section 31.3.1.

31.2. Semantics of the articles: general information

For the proper noun articles, see Section 31.5. Within the articles for variable words, the division 'known' ~ 'unknown' hinges on whether or not the thing meant is known to the speaker. The speaker is the sole arbiter here, hence the use of ti‿ in the following:

(a) ʔác'x̌ən-ɬkan ti‿sqáyxʷ‿a 'I saw (ʔác'x̌ən) a man (sqayxʷ)': note that English uses the indefinite article here, since the man is not yet identified to the addressee. Compare this with:

(b) nká?‿tu? kʷu‿sqácza?-su 'where did your (-su) father (sqácza?) go?' (nka? 'to go where?,' ‿tu? 'definite past'): here 'unknown' kʷu‿ is used to indicate that the addressee's father is unknown to the speaker (although known to the addressee; see also [i] and [j] in Section 31.4).

The concepts 'present' versus 'absent' are discussed in Sections 31.3 and 31.4.

31.3. The category 'known': 'present' versus 'absent'

Within 'known,' the distinction between 'present' and 'absent' depends on whether or not the thing meant is present (i.e., can be pointed out) in the situation of speech, and also, if it is absent, on whether its absence is relevant in the given situation: compare (a) and (b), (c) and (d), and (e) and (f):

(a) pún-ɬkan ti‿n-ɬkʷáɬ'us‿a 'I found (pun) my (n-) basket (ɬkʷáɬ'us)' (when just mentioning the fact, or when showing the basket to the addressee)

(b) pún-ɬkan ni‿n-ɬkʷáɬ'us‿a 'I found my basket' (when the basket is absent from the situation of speech, and the addressee wonders whether it has been found yet)

(c) wa? xʷil'ən-cíh-as ti‿sísqa?-sw‿a 'your (-sw) uncle (sísqa?) is looking for (xʷíl'ən) you (-cih)' (when just mentioning the fact)

(d) wa? xʷil'ən-cíh-as ni‿sísqa?-sw‿a 'your uncle was looking for you' (i.e., he was here not too long ago, but now he is gone again)

(e) ʔác'x̌ən-ɬkan ti‿skíxza?-sw‿a 'I saw your mother (skíxza?)' (i.e., at a certain unspecified moment)

(f) ʔác'x̌ən-ɬkan ni‿skíxza?-sw‿a 'I saw your mother (just a minute ago, while I was at the store, etc.)' (said to smb. who is looking for his mother)

While the basket or the addressee's uncle or mother need not be present in situations (a), (c), and (e), they are definitely absent in situations (b), (d), and (f). It also follows that 'absent' is the marked category.

The articles for 'absent' are obligatory where the absence of smt. or smb. is explicitly stated, as in:

(g) sʷə́lp‿tuʔ ni‿cítxʷ-s‿a 'his (-s) house (citxʷ) burned down (sʷəlp)' (‿tuʔ 'definite past')

The article ni‿ is also used in expressions that refer to a past time:

(h) ni‿pálʔ‿a X̣'ánam'tən 'one (pálaʔ) month (X̣'ánam'tən) ago, last month'

The 'absent' articles are generally used when reference is made to a permanently absent object or person (e.g., deceased relatives or lost possessions), but again the 'absent' articles are used only when the speaker finds it relevant to remark that these persons or objects are absent, as in (i) and (j). We use 'present' articles to refer to absent objects or persons when we do not judge their absence to be relevant, as in (k):

(i) nił   waʔ   sqʷəqʷ'l'ən-c-ás   ni‿n-kʷə́kʷ?‿a   ʔi‿wan‿skʷúkʷ'm'it 'this is what my (n-) grandmother (kʷə́kʷaʔ) told (sqʷə́qʷ'l'ən) me (-c) when (ʔi‿) I was a child (skʷúkʷ'm'it)' (nił anticipatory pronoun [Section 24.5])

(j) níł‿tiʔ   száytən-łkał   sʔənc   mútaʔ   ni‿n-kʷə́kʷ?‿a 'that (‿tiʔ) is what happened to me (sʔənc) and (mútaʔ) my grandmother' (száytən 'business,' -łkał 'our')

(k) ksnán-c-as   ti‿n-kʷə́kʷ?‿a 'my grandmother sent me on an errand (ksnan)': the grandmother in (k) is the same one as in (j), and both sentences are from the same story.

With the plural article ʔi‿ we have, for example:

(l) lcʔa   ʔi‿kapúh-lap‿a 'here (lcʔa) are the coats (kapúh) of you folks (-lap)'

(m) cʔás-wit   ʔi‿xmán'‿a 'the enemies (xman') are coming (cʔas)'

With nəł‿ we have, for example:

(n) pəl'p-s-kán‿tuʔ   nəł‿ən-sqʷ'láw'‿a 'I lost (pəl'p-s) the berries that I had picked' (pəl'p-s 'what one has picked,' ‿tuʔ 'definite past')

(o) zúqʷ‿tuʔ   nəł‿slal'íl'təm-s‿a 'his (-s) parents (slal'íl'təm) died (zuqʷ)'

31.3.1. The category 'known': use of ki‿

Within 'present-known,' the distinction 'collective' ~ 'individual' hinges on whether the thing meant is seen as an unspecified quantity or mass (collective, marked with ki‿) or as one or more individual objects. Forms with ki‿ often translate as forms without article in English:

(a) waʔ   nsʔáʔz'əm   ki‿smán'x‿a 'he is trading (nsʔáʔz'əm) tobacco (sman'x)'

(b) ł‿X̣'íq-as ti? cʔa ti‿sxʷápməx‿a, waʔ tawəm, táwəm ki‿smán'x‿a 'when this Shuswap (sxʷápməx) came (X̣'iq), he used to be selling, selling (táwəm) tobacco'

The use of ki‿ in (a) and (b) contrasts with cases where we have ti‿smán'x‿a 'the tobacco (= one particular quantity of tobacco),' or ʔi‿smán'x‿a 'more particular quantities of tobacco,' as in:

(c) c'əks-ás ti‿smán'x‿a 'he had finished (c'əks) his tobacco (sold it all out)'

(d) kʷʷin láti? kʷ‿s-súX̆'xal-s ǀ‿ti‿smán'x‿a 'he had a few (kʷʷin) puffs of the tobacco' (súX̆'xal 'to have a few puffs')

All recorded forms with ki‿ function as objects to intransitive verbs; see (a) and (b), and also compare (e) and (g) with (f) and (h):

(e) wá?-ɬkan ɬúɬxʷxal ki‿sk'ək'xús‿a 'I am stringing on (ɬúɬxʷxal) beads'

(f) wá?-ɬkan ɬúɬxʷən' ?i‿sk'ək'xús‿a 'I am stringing on *the* beads'

(g) wa? k'áxxal ki‿məxáz'‿a 'she is drying (k'áxxal) huckleberries (məxáz')'

(h) wa? k'áxan'-as ?i‿məxáz'‿a 'she is drying *the* huckleberries'

After prepositions (see Section 34), the article ?i‿ is ki‿ (formally identical to ki‿ collective). Compare (i) and (j):

(i) ?i‿?uxʷalmíxʷ‿a 'the Indians'

(j) ǀ‿ki‿?uxʷalmíxʷ‿a 'among (ǀ‿) the Indians'[1]

31.4. The category 'unknown'

Within 'unknown,' the categories 'present' versus 'absent' coincide with the notions 'evidential' versus 'potential.' The 'unknown-present' ('evidential') articles are typically used for something that is smelled, heard, or sensed but not seen, whereas the 'unknown-absent' ('potential') articles are used for an unknown object or person that might materialize (e.g., by meeting him, by buying it). Compare (a) and (b):

(a) xʷ?úxʷnun'-ɬkan kʷu‿smán'x‿a 'I smelled (xʷ?úxʷnun') tobacco (sman'x)'

(b) húy'-ɬkan ?az' kʷu‿sman'x 'I am going to (huy') buy (?az') tobacco'

Further examples with 'present' kʷu‿...‿a include:

(c) ka-xʷál's-kan‿a kʷu‿ná?q'‿a sc'úqʷaz' 'I smelled a rotten (na?q') fish (sc'úqʷaz')' (ka-xʷál's‿a 'to get a whiff of smt.')

(d) wa? wáz'am kʷu‿sqáx̆?‿a 'there is a dog (sqáx̆a?) barking (wáz'am)'

(e) ?əkʷ?á ǀ‿tsa‿sɬéc ?i‿sp'áms‿a ɬ‿was‿X̆'iqc kʷu‿nkxʷáns‿a 'it is this way (?əkʷ?á) where (ǀ‿tsa‿) the firewood (sp'ams) is piled up (sɬəc) that we heard the ghost-owl (nkxʷans)' (X̆'iqc 'sound reaches over here')

Compare also (f) and (g):

(f) c?as lákʷ?a ɬlákʷu? kʷu‿sX̆'aɬálm‿a 'there is a grizzly (sX̆'aɬáləm) coming (c?as) from there (ɬlákʷu?)' (used by a person who hears a grizzly)

(g) ?əm?ímnəm‿kʷu? ti?‿ti‿sX̆'aɬálm‿a ɬlákʷu? 'that (ti?‿) grizzly was growling (?əm?ímnəm) from there' (used by storyteller describing the same event)

The following is an example of kʷɬ‿...‿a:

(h) wa? lákʷ?a sáy'səz' kʷɬ‿skʷʷəmkʷúkʷʷm'it‿a lákʷu? ləp'xáltn‿a 'there are children (skʷʷəmkʷúkʷʷm'it) playing (sáy'səz') in the garden (ləp'xáltən)' (when the children are heard but not seen)

For the function of 'absent' kʷu‿, compare (i) and (j), and (k) and (l):

(i) nká?‿tu? kʷu‿sqácza?-su 'where (nka?) did your (-su) father (sqácza?) go?' (when the speaker does not know the addressee's father)

(j) nká?‿tu? ni‿sqácza?-sw‿a 'where did your father go?' (when the speaker knows the addressee's father)

(k) pún-ɬkaxʷ‿ha kʷu‿slamálh-i 'did you find (pun) their (-i) bottle (slamála)?' (when the speaker does not know the bottle)

(l) pún-ɬkaxʷ‿ha ni‿slamalh-íh‿a 'did you find their bottle?' (when the speaker knows the bottle)

Further examples of kʷu‿ include:

(m) húy'-ɬkaľap kʷámǝm kʷu‿s?ál̦sǝm 'you folks are going to (huy'-) catch (kʷámǝm) a disease (s?ál̦sǝm)'

(n) síma?xi[t]-c kʷu‿pála? 'give (síma?xit) me (-c) one (pála?)'

(o) ɬ‿xʷíc'xi[t]-c-axʷ kʷu‿núkʷ ɬáxʷmǝn, ɬumun-ɬkán‿kɬ lc?a 'if (ɬ‿) you give (xʷíc'xit) me (-c) another (nukʷ) patch (ɬáxʷmǝn), I will (‿kɬ) put it on (ɬúmun) here (lc?a)'

The article kʷu‿ may also refer to a potential quality of something or somebody while that very object or person is present, as in:

(p) s?ǝnc‿a‿kɬ kʷu‿nuk'ʷ?an-táli 'I (s?ǝnc) will (‿kɬ) be the one to help (núk'ʷ?an) him'

Compare (p) with (q):

(q) s?ǝnc‿a ti‿nuk'ʷ?an-tálih‿a 'I am the one who helped him'

The function of 'absent' kʷɬ‿ is shown by (r) versus (s), (t) versus (u), and (v) versus (w):

(r) nká?‿tu? kʷɬ‿stǝm'tǝ́tǝm'-su 'where (nka?) are your (-su) belongings (stǝm'tǝ́tǝm')?' (when the speaker does not know the addressee's belongings)

(s) nká?‿tu? nǝɬ‿ǝn-stǝm'tǝ́tm'‿a 'where are my (n-) belongings?' (the belongings are known to the speaker)

(t) pǝľps-kaľap‿há‿tu? kʷɬ‿sq'ʷláw'-lap 'did you folks lose (pǝľps) your (-lap) berries (sq'ʷlaw')?' (when the berries are unknown to the speaker)

(u) pǝľps-túm‿tu? nǝɬ‿sq'ʷláw'-ɬkaɬ‿a 'we have lost our berries'

(v) nk'ʷínk'ʷǝn‿tu? káti? kʷɬ‿X̌'ak 'how many (nk'ʷínk'ʷǝn) did go by (X̌'ak)?'

(w) nk'ʷínk'ʷǝn káti? nǝɬ‿plán‿a X̌'ak 'several (nk'ʷínk'ʷǝn) went by already (plan)'

31.5. The articles kʷ‿ and wi‿

The articles kʷ‿ and wi‿ are used first of all with proper nouns. As we saw in Section 27.2, proper nouns take the nominalizer s- when they occur as predicates or complements. The article kʷ‿ occurs with single proper nouns, as in:

(a) wa? k'ʷzúsǝm kʷ‿s-John 'John is working (k'ʷzúsǝm)'

The combination kʷ‿ is often reduced to k‿, especially in the speech of younger people, e.g., waʔ kʷzúsəm kˍJohn.[2] The article wiˍ occurs before the first of two or more different proper nouns, as in:

(b) waʔ kʷzúsəm-wit wiˍs-John múta? s-Pete 'John and Pete are working'

For the use of wiˍ with personal pronouns, see Section 24.1. We also have kʷˍ and wiˍ in combination with generic pet-names such as s-kíkaʔ (for women or girls), s-ʔápaʔ (for men or boys), and s-cəcəw'-qín'kst (for bear cubs; s-cécəw' 'mark, design,' -qín'kst 'finger[nail]'), as in:

(c) waʔ lcʔa kʷˍs-kíkaʔ 'here is kíkaʔ' ('here is our darling little girl')

(d) xʷʔit wiˍs-kíkaʔ 'lots (xʷʔit) of girls'

(e) xʷʔit wiˍs-ʔápaʔ 'lots of boys'

(f) wáʔ-ɬkan lcʔa ʔalkʷ'ən-tánih-an wiˍscəcəw'-qín'kst 'I am babysitting (ʔálkʷ'ən) the cubs here (lcʔa)'[3]

For the combination of proper nouns with tiˍ, see Section 31.6.2(g) and (h).

31.6. Special questions

Here we discuss the merging of *ˍaˍa into ˍa (Section 31.6.1), and the issue of complex complements (Section 31.6.2).

31.6.1. Merging of *ˍaˍa into ˍa

When the enclitic ˍa (required by most articles [Section 31.1]) should follow another instance of ˍa, it merges with the first ˍa, as in niˍka-xʷáz'ˍa 'the deceased one' (< *niˍka-xʷáz'ˍaˍa; ka-xʷáz'ˍa 'he disappeared [for good]'). Note that here the categories 'unknown-present' and 'unknown-absent' coincide, e.g., kʷuˍka-xʷáz'ˍa (1) 'the deceased one' (unknown-present; *kʷuˍka-xʷáz'ˍaˍa), (2) id. (unknown-absent). The enclitic ˍa does not merge with non-enclitic stem-final a: slamála 'bottle' M > tiˍslamálhˍa 'the bottle' (for a > h see Section 4.1).

31.6.2. Complex complements

When a complement consists of two lexical items and it is preceded by an article that requires ˍa, we have ˍa after the first item, as in:

(a) tiˍx̌zúmˍa citxʷ 'the big (x̌zum) house (citxʷ)'[4]

This also holds for cases where the first lexical item is an auxiliary, as in:

(b) tiˍhúz'ˍa ƛ'iq 'the one who will (huz') come (ƛ'iq)'

However, when the first lexical item in a complex complement is waʔ 'to be (busy with, involved in),' the enclitic ˍa is not used and waʔ enters into a proclitic construction with the article, as in:

(c) tiˍwaʔˍzúsxal 'the policeman' (zúsxal 'to tie')

(d) tiˍwaʔˍməcməcxál 'the secretary' (məcməcxál 'to write a lot')

(e) tiˍwaʔˍnúkʷʔan-c-as 'the one who helps (núkʷʔan) me'

Where we have proclitic waʔ, the formal distinction between 'unknown-present' and 'unknown-absent' disappears, as in kʷuˍwaʔˍzúsxal (1) 'the policeman' (unknown-present), (2) id. (unknown-absent). The proclitic sequences ti‿wa?‿ and kʷu‿wa?‿ are generally pronounced twa and kʷa, respectively. When wa? occurs by itself as a complement, the enclitic ‿a is not dropped:

(f) nka? ɬláta? ɬəl‿ki‿wá?‿a kʷu‿sqácza?-su 'which one (nka?) out of those people is your father (sqácza?)?'

We may also have an article plus proclitic wa? before proper nouns, but in such cases we do not use the special proper noun articles:

(g) s?ə́nc‿a ti‿wa?‿s-Joe 'I (s?ə́nc‿a) am Joe' (literally 'I am the one who is Joe'); cf. Section 27.2(b)

(h) s?ə́nc‿a ti‿wa?‿s-Belinda 'I am Belinda'; cf. Section 27.2(a)

I do not know whether there is any semantic difference between the above sentences and those given in Section 27.2(a) and (b).

32
Enclitics

Lillooet has a number of enclitic elements, i.e., elements that are never used by themselves as stressed units but rather form one stress unit with the preceding full word. Enclitics generally follow the first word in a sentence; in this respect they are different from suffixes, which stay on one and the same word regardless of the position of that word in the sentence (see Section 8.3[b]). Enclitics also behave differently from suffixes with regard to the stress (see Section 2.2). Semantically, enclitics are adverbs, expressing modal-aspectual notions such as 'irreal,' 'evidential,' 'definite past,' etc.

In this section we first discuss the enclitics individually (Section 32.1), with special attention to ‿a (Section 32.2). Next, we discuss combinations of enclitics (Sections 32.3 and 32.4), and enclitics after indicative versus subjunctive forms (Section 32.5).

32.1. Individual enclitics

32.1.1. The enclitic ‿maɬ 'adhortative'
This enclitic is used mainly in commands, as an adhortative element:

(a) cúkʷ‿maɬ 'quit!'

(b) wá?‿maɬ kʼʷzúsəm 'you'd better work!'

(c) síma?‿maɬ 'come here, keep coming this way!' (for síma? see Section 22.5.2)

I also recorded ‿maɬ in a few non-imperative sentences, in which it seems to suggest 'well, as you should know, please note that ...' Not all speakers accept this usage of ‿maɬ, however. Examples include:

(d) qʷacác-kan‿maɬ, húy'-ɬkan nas kʼʷzúsəm 'well, I'm on my way, I am going (nas) to work' (qʷacác 'to set out')

(e) nx̌ʷəx̌ʷ?úcin‿maɬ ?i‿sqáyqəyxʷ‿a scmaɬ't 'lo and behold, she had four (nx̌ʷəx̌ʷ?úcin) sons' (sqáyqyəxʷ 'men,' scmaɬ't 'offspring')

32.1.2. The enclitic ‿tuʔ 'definite past'
The enclitic ‿tuʔ indicates that something is over and done with, that a time period has definitely been concluded:
(a) c'ə́k‿tuʔ 'it is all gone, finished (c'ək)'
(b) ʕʷə́lp‿tuʔ ni‿cítxʷ-s‿a 'his (-s) house (citxʷ) burned (ʕʷəlp) down'
This enclitic also indicates that a person or object was here recently but has now gone to perform the action referred to in the predicate. Compare (c) and (d), and (e) and (f):
(c) ʕʷəw'p-wít‿tuʔ 'they went to the meeting' (ʕəw'p 'to meet, gather')
(d) ʕəw'p-wít 'they are (were) at the meeting'
(e) nkáʔ‿tuʔ ni‿máw‿a 'where (nkaʔ) did the cat (maw) go?'
(f) nkaʔ ni‿máw‿a 'where is the cat?'

32.1.3. The enclitic ‿an' 'evidential'
This enclitic indicates that the speaker concludes something from circumstantial evidence. As pointed out in Section 22.3.2, ‿an' requires subjunctive suffixes in the predicate it follows:
(a) tayt-áxʷ‿an' 'you must be hungry (tayt)'
(b) plán-at‿an' waʔ pəl'p 'it looks like we are lost (pəl'p) already (plan)'
(c) xʷʔáz-as‿an' kʷas‿huy'‿X̌'íq 'it looks like he won't come (X̌'iq)'[1]

32.1.4. The enclitic ‿X̌'uʔ 'well, but, so'
This is one of the most frequently used enclitics. Its meaning is difficult to define, but it generally expresses notions such as 'still, well, but, so.' Often it is best left untranslated in English. Examples include:
(a) wáʔ‿X̌'uʔ ʔáma 'he is (still) okay' (ʔáma 'good')
(b) stəx̌ʷ-kán‿X̌'uʔ waʔ ʔálsəm 'I am really (stəx̌ʷ) sick (ʔálsəm)'
(c) pápt‿X̌'uʔ waʔ ʕʷuy't 'she used to sleep (ʕʷuy't) always (papt)'
(d) cúkʷ‿tiʔ‿X̌'uʔ 'well, that (‿tiʔ) is all' (cukʷ 'finished')
The enclitic ‿X̌'uʔ is also used in commands to somebody to keep doing what he or she is already doing or is about to do:
(e) wáʔ‿X̌'uʔ, wáʔ‿X̌'uʔ 'oh, heck, keep on doing that!' (said to somebody who is doing something foolish)
(f) X̌'ák‿X̌'uʔ X̌'ak 'just keep on going (X̌'ak)!' (said, for example, to somebody who is going from door to door with merchandise that you are not interested in buying)
(g) síma‿X̌'uʔ 'come right over, come in!' (said to somebody who is quite close already, e.g., at the door); cf. Section 32.1.1(c)
This enclitic also occurs in a number of adverb-like and conjunction-like constructions, such as nít‿X̌'uʔ 'and so, and then' (Section 29.1[6]), tqít‿X̌'uʔ 'to almost have done smt.'

32.1.5. The enclitic χ'ɬ 'demarcation of time'

This enclitic indicates that 'the time is stopped.' It is used with events that interrupt or terminate other events, as in (a) to (e), or when mention is made of how long something has been going on, as in (f) and (g). The English adverb 'presently' corresponds fairly well to χ'ɬ. Examples include:

(a) xʷʔáz‿kʷuʔ‿χ'uʔ láti? kʷ‿s-xin'-s, c?ás‿kʷuʔ‿χ'ɬ ti‿skalúl?‿a 'it did not (xʷʔaz) take long, and then the owl (skalúla?) came (c?as)' (‿kʷuʔ quotative marker [Section 32.1.9])

(b) húy'-ɬkaɬ‿χ'uʔ múta? q'a?, lan‿χ'ɬ múta? ka-q'sán'k‿a kʷ‿s-Thom 'we were just (‿χ'uʔ) about to (huy'-) eat (q'a?) again (múta?), and then Thom burst out (ka-..‿a) laughing (nq'san'k) already (lan)'

(c) xʷʔáy‿χ'uʔ kʷ‿s-pála?-s máqa?, lan‿χ'ɬ múta? χ'iq ʔi‿cuwʔ-íh‿a scmaɬt 'not before one (pála?) year (máqa?) had passed, they got children (scmaɬt) themselves' (máqa? literally 'snow,' χ'iq 'to arrive,' cúwa? 'own,' -i 'their')

(d) χ'iq‿χ'ɬ ʔi‿wa?‿?əc'?ác'xnəm 'the ones we were waiting for (?əc'?ác'xən) arrived (χ'iq)'

(e) qʷacác‿χ'ɬ 'he is leaving (qʷacác) now' (note that the interrupted or terminated event does not need to be mentioned)

(f) plan‿χ'ɬ ʔán'was zapíw's kʷənswa‿?ális̓əm 'I have been sick (?ális̓əm) for two (?án'was) weeks (zapíw's) already (plan)'

(g) kʷʷin‿χ'ɬ 'what time is it?' (kʷʷin 'how much?')

See also Section 19.4.1(a) to (d).

32.1.6. The enclitic ‿ka 'obligation, expectancy'

This enclitic expresses 'would' or 'should.' Examples include:

(a) ɬ‿xʷʔáz-as‿ka kʷ‿s-ʕʷúy't-su, lán‿ka‿tu? wa? xzum ʔi‿nkʷχ'ústən'-sw‿a 'if (ɬ‿) you would not (xʷʔaz) have slept (ʕʷuy't), your eyes (nkʷχ'ústən) would have been big (xzum) already (plan)'

(b) cukʷun'-ɬkán‿ka‿ti? 'I should finish (cúkʷun') that (‿ti?)'

(c) xzúm‿ka‿həm' kʷu‿kəm'xʷyəqs-káɬ 'we should have a big (xzum) car (kém'xʷyəqs)' (literally 'big should be our [potential] car'); for ‿həm' see Section 32.1.13

(d) xʷʔáz‿ka kʷasu‿pápt wa? ?úqʷa? 'you shouldn't be drinking (?úqʷa?) always (papt)'

32.1.7. The enclitic ‿kəɬ 'remote future, possibility'

This enclitic refers to a (possible) future event. It is often translatable with 'might':

(a) qlil-min'-cih-as‿kéɬ‿tu? 'he might get angry (qlil) at (-min') you' (‿tu? Section 32.1.2)

(b) ka-cət‿a‿kə́ɬ‿a 'he will sober up (ka-cə́ɬ‿a), at some point' (for ‿a₂ see Section 32.4.1)

When ‿kəɬ is unstressed, it is pronounced ‿kɬ:

(c) ʔac'x̌əncín-ɬkan‿kɬ   múta? 'I shall see (ʔác'x̌ən) you again (múta?)' (used as a greeting; cf. English 'I'll be seeing you')

(d) X̌'aḷan-c-ás‿kɬ   ti‿sqax̌a?-láp‿a 'the dog (sqáx̌a?) of you folks (-lap) might bite (X̌'áḷan) me'[2]

32.1.8. The enclitic ‿k'a 'possibility, surmise'

This enclitic indicates that the speaker surmises something, as in:

(a) wá?‿k'a   láti?   ʔəs-cítxʷ   ti‿skíxza?-s‿a   ti‿syáqc?‿a 'I guess that the mother (skíxza?) of the woman (syáqca?) had (ʔəs-) a house (citxʷ) there (láti?)'

(b) sáma?‿k'a   kʷu‿sqʷal'ən-táli 'it must have been a white man (sáma?) who told (sqʷál'ən) her'

(c) xʷ?áz‿k'a   kʷas‿xʷ?ít   kʷu‿wa?‿stəm'tə́təm'-s 'apparently she did not (xʷ?az) have many (xʷ?it) belongings (stəm'tə́təm')'

The enclitic ‿k'a shares the idea of conjecture with ‿an' (Section 32.1.3). However, ‿k'a refers to a possibility only, whereas ‿an' refers to an almost inevitable conclusion. Compare (d) and (e):

(d) wá?‿k'a   k'ʷzúsəm 'he must be at work (that's why he is not here)'

(e) wá?-as‿an'   k'ʷzúsəm 'it looks like he is working'

32.1.9. The enclitic ‿kʷu? 'quotative'

This enclitic expresses that the speaker relays information that was given to him or her, that the speaker did not witness the talked-about events personally:

(a) X̌'ák‿kʷu?   káti? 'he was going along (X̌'ak), as I was told'

(b) plán‿kʷu?   ʔayɬ   wa?   ʕáp-almən 'so (ʔayɬ) it got evening, as I was told' (ʕap 'evening,' -almən 'to be about to,' plan 'already')

Compare also (c) and (d):

(c) c?as   lák'ʷ?a   ɬlák'ʷu?   kʷu‿sX̌'aɬálm‿a 'there is a grizzly (sX̌'aɬáləm) coming (c?as) from there (ɬlák'ʷu?)': used by the person who hears the grizzly

(d) ʔəm?ímnəm‿kʷu?   ti?‿ti‿sX̌'aɬálm‿a   ɬlák'ʷu? 'that (ti?‿) grizzly was growling (ʔəm?ímnəm) from there (ɬlák'ʷu?), as I was told': used by the story-teller describing the same event

The enclitic ‿kʷu? is understandably widely used in legends, since these deal exclusively with events that were not witnessed by the story-teller.

32.1.10. The enclitic ‿xʷiɬ 'after all, it turned out to be'

This enclitic expresses that the speaker just remembered the information he or she is giving, or that the speaker is giving the information as an afterthought.

The enclitic ˌxʷi‡ is always combined with ˌa (Section 32.2), which precedes ˌxʷi‡:[3]

(a) ní‡ˌaˌxʷi‡   niˌn-sqácəzʔˌa   núkʷˑʷʔan-c-as 'it is my father (sqácza?) who helped (núkʷˑʷʔan) me' (used when the speaker just remembers who helped him or her; ni‡ anticipatory pronoun (Section 24.5)

(b) ka-ƛ'ək'ˌaˌkʷúʔˌtuʔ   ʔay‡   tiˌskʷˑʷúkʷˑʷm'it̯ˌa,   t̯ˌs-plán-sˌaˌxʷi‡   ʔay‡ kʷánəmˌtuʔ   ʔəˌtiˌskalúlʔˌa 'the child (skʷˑʷúkʷˑʷm'it) had fallen silent (ka-ƛ'ək'ˌa), but then she had already (plan) been taken (kʷan) by the owl (skalúla?)'

(c) ʔucˌaˌxʷí‡ˌtiʔ   kʷasˌsní‡   tiˌkʷúkʷpy'ˌa 'that (ˌti?) one is not the chief (kʷúkʷpəy')' (ʔuc 'to be not so-and-so'; sni‡ 'he')

The combination ˌaˌxʷi‡ often co-occurs with (and in that case precedes) ˌk'a (Section 32.1.8):

(d) ƛ'əpˌaˌkʷúʔˌa   tiˌsʔístknˌa,   ni‡ˌaˌxʷí‡ˌk'a   ‡ˌʔú‡xʷ-as   tiˌskalúlʔˌa tiˌsʔístknˌa 'the underground house (sʔístkən) got dark (ƛ'əpˌa), because the owl (skalúla?) entered (ʔu‡xʷ) the underground house after all' (ƛ'əpˌa 'to get dark' < ka-ƛ'əpˌa)

(e) waʔˌaˌxʷí‡ˌk'a   n‡am'ál'c 'apparently it was loaded (n‡am'ál'c) after all'

(f) tiˌsqáyxʷˌa waʔ ncutanwasmín-an kʷasˌniˌn-sqácəzʔˌa, nsisqʔˌaˌxʷí‡ˌk'a 'the man (sqayxʷ) I thought (ncutánwasmin) to be my father (sqácza?) turned out to be my uncle (sísqa?)'

In combinations with ˌk'a, the sequence ˌaˌxʷi‡ is often extended to ˌaˌxʷi‡ˌa (i.e., ˌa is repeated after ˌxʷi‡ but before ˌk'a):

(g) planˌaˌxʷí‡ˌaˌk'a   waʔ   cíxʷalmən   kʷasˌzúqʷ 'it was already (plan) getting close (cíxʷalmən) to the time that he would die (zuqʷ)'

(h) stə́x̌ʷˌƛ'uʔ   ʔaʔx̌aʔ-witˌaˌxʷí‡ˌaˌk'a   ʔiˌwaʔˌk'zúz 'those who are twins (k'zuz) are really (stəx̌ʷ) spiritually powerful (ʔáʔx̌aʔ), after all'

(i) ni‡ˌaˌxʷí‡ˌaˌk'a   ʔiˌcíclˌa   qʷ‡íʔxən-s   tiˌkʷtámc-sˌa 'those turned out to be her husband's (kʷtamc) new (cícəl) shoes (qʷ‡íʔxən)' (ni‡ anticipatory pronoun [Section 24.5])

(j) waʔ-‡kaxʷˌaˌxʷi‡ˌáˌk'a   ʔákʷuʔ   cut 'so that is what you have been saying (cut)' (for the function of ʔákʷuʔ here, see Section 26.1.3[n])

(k) ní‡ˌkʷuʔˌƛ'uʔ   ʔay‡   s-k‡akaʔmín-asˌkʷuʔ   láti? tiˌsqawcˌaˌxʷi‡ˌáˌk'a 'and then (ní‡ˌƛ'uʔ) she let go her hand (k‡áka?min) of what turned out to be a potato (sqawc)'

32.1.11. The enclitic ˌqaʔ 'presupposed knowledge'

This enclitic puts a certain emphasis on an utterance. It also indicates that the speaker presupposes a certain knowledge on the part of the addressee: 'as you (should) know, as you can see.' Examples include:

(a) ʔámaˌƛ'uʔ   ʔizá, wáʔ-‡ka‡ˌqaʔ, xʷʔəz kʷasˌxʷʔít ʔiˌwaʔˌstám'-‡ka‡ 'these (ʔizá) things are good (ʔáma), and here we are (wa?), our belongings (stam') are not (xʷʔəz) much (xʷʔit)' ('so we'd better take these things')

(b) ʔu, húy'-ɬkaɬ‿qaʔ kánəm 'oh, what are we going to do? (now that you have messed things up)' (kánəm 'to do what?,' huy'- 'to be about to')

(c) níɬ‿qaʔ s-kxiʔúɬ ti‿ʔum'ən-c-ás‿a 'well, it is Kci7ólh who gave (ʔúm'ən) it to me (as you should know)'

(d) waʔ kánəm su‿sxát-s ti‿x̌ʷuláka?-sw‿a - ʔu, wáʔ-ɬkan‿qaʔ ʔəs-yálməc 'why (waʔ kánəm) are you holding up (sxats) your finger (x̌ʷuláka?)? - oh, I have (ʔəs-) a ring (yálməc) here (as you can see)'

(e) húz'‿qaʔ zam' ʔác'x̌nəm 'okay, we will (huz') see (ʔác'x̌ən)' ('and you will see for yourself that you're wrong')

The enclitic ‿qaʔ also gives a pleading connotation to commands:

(f) símaʔ‿qaʔ 'come here (símaʔ), please' (if one is not sure whether the addressee is inclined to come; cf. Section 32.1.1[c] and 32.1.4[g])

The enclitic ‿qaʔ often combines with ‿a (Section 32.2), as in:

(g) waʔ-ɬkan‿á‿qaʔ ncutánwas kʷas‿ʔiz'‿níɬ nəɬ‿ʔáyn‿a 'well, I thought (ncutánwas) that those (ʔiz') were the irons (ʔáyən)' (níɬ anticipatory pronoun [Section 24.5])

(h) waʔ-ɬkaɬ‿á‿qaʔ núk'ʷʔan-ci-m 'but we *are* helping (núk'ʷʔan) you'

(i) wi‿sníɬ‿a‿qaʔ 'but it was them!' (wi‿sníɬ 3P personal pronoun)

The enclitic ‿qaʔ is also formally identical to qaʔ, an interjection used when the speaker corrects himself or herself (like English 'no' in 'a man, no, a woman'). However, the interjection qaʔ can occur anywhere in a sentence, and forms an independent stress unit (as such, it is not a clitic):

(j) wáʔ‿kʷuʔ‿x̌'uʔ wáʔ-wit sx̌'qʷaw's, ʔu, qaʔ, nkəkaɬás-wit 'they were together (sx̌'qʷaw's), oh, uh, there were three (nkəkaɬás) of them'

(k) ɬəl‿t‿s-ləsp-s‿a‿k'a‿túʔ‿tiʔ, qaʔ, ləsn-ítas ʔi‿ʔuxʷalmíxʷ‿a ti?‿ti‿s?ístkn‿a 'since that (tiʔ) got caved in (ləsp), uh, since the people (ʔúxʷalmixʷ) caved that (tiʔ‿) underground house (s?ístkən) in'

(l) ti?‿ti‿syapʔú..., qaʔ, ti‿s?apɬqʷáz'‿a 'that Douglas-fir (syapʔúl), no, bull pine (s?ápɬqʷaz')'

32.1.12. The enclitic ‿ha 'interrogative'
This enclitic forms interrogative sentences, like Russian li. Examples include:

(a) wáʔ-ɬkaxʷ‿ha k'ʷzúsəm 'are you working?'

(b) sqayxʷ‿há‿tiʔ 'is that (‿tiʔ) a man (sqayxʷ)?'

By placing ‿ha after each one of a series of predicates, one expresses 'or':

(c) sc'úqʷaz'‿ha, c'íʔ‿ha 'is it a fish (sc'úqʷaz') or meat (c'iʔ)?'

32.1.13. The enclitic ‿həm' 'antithesis'
This enclitic may accompany information that is contrary to earlier information or to expectations:

(a) xʷʔaz kʷas‿xʷʔit ɬ‿wan‿ʔíɬən, xʷʔít‿həm' tənswa‿ʔúqʷaʔ 'I do not (xʷʔạz) eat (ʔíɬən) much (xʷʔit), but I drink (ʔúqʷaʔ) lots'

(b) ʔác'x̌ən-ɬkan ti‿sqáyxʷ‿a skʷúzaʔ-s, xʷʔạz‿həm'‿x̌'uʔ kʷ‿sʔác'x̌n-an ti‿smúɬac‿a skʷúzaʔ-s 'I saw (ʔác'x̌ən) his son (sqayxʷ skʷúzaʔ), but I did not see his daughter (smúɬac skʷúzaʔ)'

(c) Harry Carey ti‿səmʔám-s‿a, ɬapən-ɬkan‿maɬ‿hám'‿tuʔ zam' ni‿skʷácic-s‿a 'it was Harry Carey's wife (səmʔám), but I have forgotten (ɬápən) her name (skʷácic)' (zam' 'after all' [Section 28.2.7])

(d) ʕəcn-ás‿həm' ti‿sél‿a l‿ti‿sq'ʷáx̌t-s‿a 'she tied (ʕécən) a string (səl) on (l‿) her foot (sq'ʷax̌t)' ('and that is how she solved the problem')

(e) húz'‿həm'‿x̌'uʔ x̌'íq-min'-as cʔa ti‿sm'ám'ɬac‿a 'he will still come (x̌'iq) for (-min') this (cʔa) girl (sm'ám'ɬac)' ('don't think we have beaten him yet')

(f) xʷʔạz‿həm'‿ti? kʷas‿wənáxʷ, sptakʷɬ‿ti? 'after all, that (‿ti?) is not true (wənáxʷ), it is a legend (sptakʷɬ)'

The enclitic ‿həm' is also often used in expressions of annoyance, such as:

(g) wá?‿həm'‿x̌'uʔ 'there you go again! oh, you! see what happened now?!' (wa? 'to be')

(h) wá?‿həm'‿x̌'uʔ snúwa 'oh, you! (don't act like that; don't be so stuck-up!)' (snúwa 2S personal pronoun)

(i) wá?‿həm'‿x̌'uʔ núkʷun' snúwa səxnám 'boy, are you dumb (səxnám)' (núkʷun' 'annoyance' [Section 28.2.3])

(j) nká?‿həm'‿tuʔ ni‿sqáx̌aʔ-sw‿a 'where (nka?) did that dog (sqáx̌a?) of yours go?'

(k) nká?‿həm'‿tuʔ núkʷun' ni‿sisqaʔ-ɬkáɬ‿a 'where did our uncle (sísqa?) go?' ('he must be up to something ridiculous again')

The instances of ‿həm' in (a) to (f) and in (g) to (k) share an idea of 'what it boils down to, what is really the case.' My consultants translate this semantically difficult enclitic with 'for sure, the real thing.'

32.1.14. The enclitic ‿wi? 'emphasis'

The meaning of this enclitic is difficult to define. It puts a certain emphasis on an utterance, and often co-occurs with ‿k'a (Section 32.1.8). Examples include:

(a) kánəm‿wi? s-qʷacác-su '*why* (kánəm) did you leave (qʷacác)?'

(b) stám'-as‿k'a múta? kʷɬ‿wa?‿s?íɬən-s ?i‿scmáɬt-s‿a, sqəx̌qəqx̌a?‿wí?‿?iz' 'I wonder what (stám'-as‿k'a) the food (s?íɬən) of her children (scmaɬt) was, they were pups (sqəx̌qə́qx̌a?), after all' (‿?iz' 'those')

(c) pinani?‿k'á‿wi? ɬ‿x̌án'-as 'he must have gotten hurt (x̌an') about that time (pináni?)'

(d) tayt‿k'á‿wi? 'he must be hungry (tayt)'

(e) wá?‿k'a‿wi? ?əs-kʷəzkʷák̓ʷza? 'apparently she had (?əs-) kids'

See also ‿wən (Section 32.1.15).

32.1.15. The enclitic ˍwən 'emphasis'

This enclitic is not perceptibly different from ˍwi? (Section 32.1.14). It also puts a certain emphasis on an utterance, and it was recorded only in combination with ˍk'a (Section 32.1.8).

(a) ɬənka?məx-ás ˍk'a ˍwən 'I wonder where he is from' (ɬənká?məx 'to be from where?,' -as 3S subjunctive intransitive subject, often used in indefinite pronouns and adverbs; see, for example, Section 26.1.4[d], [e])

(b) skan-as ˍk'á ˍmaɬ ˍwən   kʷ ˍs-X̌'iq-s 'I wonder if he came (X̌'iq)' (skan question marker, Section 29.1[2])

The enclitic ˍwən was recorded only in the M dialect, whereas instances of ˍwi? were almost all recorded in the F dialect. Therefore, we probably have dialectal variants of the same enclitic here.

32.1.16. Position of enclitics

In the examples given in Sections 32.1.1 to 32.1.15, most enclitics follow the first word in a sentence. When they follow a word that occurs later in a sentence, the speaker wants to make the enclitic refer especially to this word. See ˍX̌'u?₂ in (a), ˍk'a in (b), and ˍX̌'u? ˍtu? in (c):

(a) níɬ ˍX̌'u?   ?ayɬ nləsạn?an-ítas ˍX̌'u?   ti? ˍti ˍs?ístkn ˍa 'so they caved in (nləsạn?an) that (ti?) underground house (s?ístkən)'

(b) plán ˍkʷu? ˍti?   wa?   ?an'w[as]-aszanuxʷ-ás ˍk'a 'apparently he was already (plan) two (?án'was) years (-aszanuxʷ) old' (note also the position of -as 3S subjunctive subject after the main verb, rather than after the auxiliary plan; for ˍk'a in combination with subjunctive forms, see also Section 32.5)

(c) níɬ ˍX̌'u?   láti?   s-lə̣ṣ-c ˍX̌'u? ˍtu?   ?ákʷu?   ti ˍs?ístkn ˍa 'and so (níɬ ˍX̌'u?) the underground house caved in (lə̣ṣ) there (láti?)'

See also ?a?x̌a?-wit ˍa ˍxʷíɬ ˍa ˍk'a in Section 32.1.10(h) and ti ˍsqawc ˍa ˍxʷíɬ ˍá ˍk'a in Section 32.1.10(k).

32.2. The enclitic ˍa 'reinforcement'

Lillooet has an enclitic ˍa, which is used in three ways:

(1) In combination with certain enclitics, mainly ˍqa? (Section 32.1.11[g] to [i]) and ˍxʷiɬ (Section 32.1.10). Note that ˍxʷiɬ does not occur without ˍa. Occasionally we also have ˍa without other enclitics, e.g., s?énc ˍa 'I' (Section 24.1).

(2) With certain articles that require them (see Section 31.1)

(3) In the combination ka-.. ˍa 'suddenly, out of control' (see Section 10.1.3)

In the last two cases, ˍa does not necessarily follow the first word in a sentence (e.g., wa?   kʷzúsəm   ti ˍsqáyxʷ ˍa 'the man [sqayxʷ] is working').[4] However, it is an enclitic rather than a suffix in these cases because ˍa is mobile when required by articles (see Section 8.3[a]), and ˍa in ka-.. ˍa may be separated from the preceding word by ˍan' (Section 32.1.3), as in ka-qʼʷus-axʷ‿án’‿a 'you look (‿an') frightened' (ka-qʼʷús‿a 'to get frightened').

The overall function of ‿a in these three cases is not entirely clear. In the second case, it is associated with the notion 'known' or (in the category 'unknown') with 'present.' Hence it might suggest a certain concreteness of information. We use the term 'reinforcing' for ‿a because its presence is limited to the elements described above, and because ‿a, by its presence, draws attention to these elements.

See also Section 31.6.1 for the merging of various instances of ‿a.

32.3. Combinations of enclitics

When enclitics follow each other, they appear in a more or less fixed order. Figure 20 reflects the relative order of the enclitics insofar as it could be established. Enclitics separated by horizontal lines could not be elicited in combination with each other. Enclitics separated by vertical lines follow each other from left to right, i.e., ‿an’ occurs first in those combinations where it is found, and ‿tu? and ƛ’u? occur last. Note that ‿a (which always precedes ‿xʷiɬ) is sometimes repeated after ‿xʷiɬ (see Section 32.1.10). The enclitic ‿tu? may precede or follow ƛ’u? (for details see Section 32.3.13). The enclitics ‿wən and ‿wi? are probably dialectal variants of each other (see Section 32.1.15), and further research will probably place them in the same box. Enclitics from non-adjacent boxes also occur in various combinations, but the order is the one shown in Figure 20 (e.g., ‿an’‿tu?).

Figure 20

Order of enclitics

an’	a	xʷiɬ	kʷu?	ka	ƛ’ɬ			
		qa?			maɬ	wən		
		ha		k’a	wi?	həm’	kəɬ	tu?/ƛ’u?

The following subsections (32.3.1 to 32.3.13) list the various enclitic combinations under the enclitic that heads each combination.

32.3.1. Combinations with ‿an’

(a) ‿an’‿a: ka-qʼʷus-axʷ‿án’‿a 'you look frightened (ka-qʼʷús‿a)'

(b) ‿an’‿tu?: wa?-as‿án’‿tu? kənc?á kʷu‿wá? 'somebody (kʷu‿wá?) must have been around here (kənc?á)'

(c) ˌan'ˌX̉'uʔ: stx̌ʷ-áxʷˌan'ˌX̉'uʔ q'ʔáĺmən 'you really (stəx̌ʷ) look hungry (q'ʔáĺmən)'

32.3.2. Combinations with ˌa

(a) ˌaˌxʷiɬ: see Section 32.1.10

(b) ˌaˌqaʔ: see Section 32.1.11(g) to (i), and Section 32.3.4(a)

(c) ˌaˌha: ka-paqʷuʔ-ɬkáxʷˌaˌha 'did you get scared (páqʷuʔ)?'

(d) ˌaˌkʷuʔˌtuʔ: ka-xim'ˌaˌkʷúʔˌtuʔ 'he disappeared (ka-xím'ˌa), I heard'

(e) ˌaˌka: ka-qʷusxit-ánˌaˌka 'I wish I could shoot (qʷúsxit) it' (for 'I wish,' expressed by the subjunctive ending -an plus ˌka, see Section 32.5)

(f) ˌaˌk'a: npzán-ɬkan látiʔ tiˌnukʷˈʷʔan-tanəmwitasˌáˌk'a 'I met (npzan) the one who apparently helped (núkˈʷʔan) them'

(g) ˌaˌmaɬ: ka-X̉'ə́k'ˌaˌmaɬ 'keep quiet (ka-X̉'ə́k'ˌa)!'

(h) ˌaˌkɬ: ka-məc'-s-kaxʷˌáˌkɬ 'you will smother, crush it (with your weight)'

(i) ˌaˌtuʔ: ka-qz'əx̌-s-kanˌáˌtuʔ 'I saw a glimpse of it'

(j) ˌaˌX̉'uʔ: ʔiˌtakmˌáˌX̉'uʔ 'all (tákəm) of them'

32.3.3. Combinations with ˌxʷiɬ

Disregarding ˌa, which always precedes ˌxʷiɬ, we have:

(a) ˌxʷiɬˌkʷuʔ: niɬˌaˌxʷíɬˌkʷuʔ niˌn-sqácəzʔˌa nukˈʷʔan-cíh-as 'well, it is my father (sqácza?) who helped (núkˈʷʔan) you (I was just told)'; cf. Section 32.1.10(a)

(b) ˌxʷiɬˌk'a: see Section 32.1.10(d) to (f); for ˌxʷíɬˌaˌk'a see Section 32.1.10(g) to (k)

(c) ˌxʷiɬˌaˌk'aˌX̉'uʔ: waʔˌaˌxʷiɬˌaˌk'áˌX̉'uʔ látiʔ waʔ sX̉'ix̌áx̌ən' 'he was just sitting there with his wings spread out'

32.3.4. Combinations with ˌqaʔ

(a) ˌqaʔˌkʷuʔ: wiˌsniɬˌaˌqáʔˌkʷuʔ 'well, it was them, as I was told'; for ˌa before ˌqaʔ, see also Section 32.1.11(g) to (i)

(b) ˌqaʔˌmaɬˌkəɬ: kasˌqaʔˌmáɬˌkɬ niɬ s-ɬax̌-s 'how (kas) is he going to get better (ɬax̌)'

(c) ˌqaʔˌk'a: stam'ˌqaʔˌk'áˌti? 'I wonder what that (ˌti?) is'

32.3.5. Combinations with ˌha

(a) ˌhaˌkʷuʔ: wiˌsníɬˌhaˌkʷuʔ 'was it them (that did it)?' (according to ML, wiˌsníɬˌhaˌkʷuʔ is 'about the same' as wiˌsníɬˌha)

(b) ˌhaˌk'a: xʷˈʔaz kʷənˌzəwátən ɬˌníɬ-asˌháˌk'aˌti? s-John, ɬˌniɬ-asˌháˌk'aˌti? s-Bill 'I don't know (zəwátən) whether (ɬˌ...ˌha) that is John or Bill'

(c) ˌhaˌkəɬ: kˈʷzusəm-ɬkáxʷˌhaˌkɬ natxʷ 'are you going to work (kˈʷzúsəm) tomorrow (natxʷ)?'

(d) ‿ha‿kəɬ: nuk'ʷ'ʔan-cih-as‿há‿kɬ 'is he going to help (núk'ʷ'ʔan) you?'

(e) ‿ha‿tuʔ: ʔal̕səm-ɬkáxʷ‿ha‿tuʔ 'were you sick (ʔál̕səm)?'

(f) ‿ha‿X̌'uʔ: kaxʷ‿ha‿X̌'uʔ wa? ʔáma 'are you still okay (ʔáma)?'

(g) ‿ha‿ka‿X̌'uʔ: waʔ-ɬkan‿há‿ka‿X̌'uʔ 'should I stay (wa?)?'

32.3.6. Combinations with ‿kʷuʔ

(a) ‿kʷuʔ‿k'a: láns‿kʷuʔ‿k'a ʔayɬ n-c'aqʷ-q-án'-əm ʔə‿ki‿sxʷúxʷz'‿a 'her bum (n-..-qʷ) had already been eaten (c'aqʷ-) by (ʔə‿) the ants (xʷúxʷəz')'

(b) ‿kʷuʔ‿k'a‿tuʔ: qʷacac‿kʷuʔ‿k'á‿tuʔ ʔi‿waʔ‿ʔəs-cmál't 'the parents had left apparently, as I was told' (ʔəs- 'to have,' scmal't 'offspring')

(c) ‿kʷuʔ‿maɬ: expresses 'guess what?': kanəm-ɬkán‿kʷuʔ‿maɬ núkʷun' 'guess what I did?' (kánəm 'to do what?'; núkʷun' 'annoyance' [Section 28.2.3]; in the story from which this sentence is taken, the speaker has just done something stupid)

(d) ‿kʷuʔ‿maɬ: stám'‿kʷuʔ‿maɬ ti‿n-s-púpn'‿a 'guess what I found (púpən')?'

(e) ‿kʷuʔ‿X̌'ɬ: cút‿kʷuʔ‿X̌'ɬ ti‿núkʷ‿a: 'tay, k'al'án'-wi' 'and then the other (nukʷ) said (cut): "hey (tay), listen (k'al'án'), you folks'"; see also Section 32.1.5(a) for ‿kʷuʔ‿X̌'ɬ

(f) ‿kʷuʔ‿X̌'uʔ: wáʔ‿kʷuʔ‿X̌'uʔ ʔáti? x̌íləm 'he was doing (x̌íləm) that'

(g) ‿kʷuʔ‿X̌'uʔ: wáʔ‿kʷuʔ láti? ti‿s?á?a?‿a, c'ila‿kʷúʔ‿X̌'uʔ kʷu‿zúqʷalmən 'there was the crow (s?á?a?), just as if (c'íla) he was dying (zúqʷalmən)'

32.3.7. Combinations with ‿ka

(a) ‿ka‿X̌'ɬ: ni‿n-sqácəz?‿a ka‿ɬ‿zəwátn-as, səkən-c-ás‿ka‿X̌'ɬ 'if (ɬ‿) my father (sqácza?) would have known (zəwátən) it, he would have whipped (sékən) me' (for proclitic ka‿ see Section 32.5.1[d])[5]

(b) ‿ka‿həm': x̌iɬc-kaxʷ‿ká‿həm' ʔəc?á 'you should do (x̌iɬc) it this way'

(c) ‿ka‿tuʔ: plan-ɬkaɬ‿ká‿tuʔ wa? cixʷ 'we should have arrived there already (plan)' (cixʷ 'to arrive there')

(d) ‿ka‿X̌'uʔ: xʷ?áz‿ka‿X̌'uʔ kʷ‿s-nas-c 'he should not (xʷ?az) go (nas)'

32.3.8. Combinations with ‿k'a

(a) ‿k'a‿maɬ: stam'-as‿k'á‿maɬ kʷu‿wa?‿?ilal-mín-as 'whatever she was crying (?ilal) for (-min)'

(b) ‿k'a‿maɬ‿tuʔ: nka?-as‿k'á‿maɬ‿tuʔ 'I wonder where (nka?) he could be'

(c) ‿k'a‿wi?: see Section 32.1.14(c) to (e)

(d) ‿k'a‿wi?‿həm': niɬ‿k'a‿wí?‿həm' ti‿s-əm?am-min-ás‿a ti‿sm'ém'ɬac‿a 'that was what he had made the girl (sm'ém'ɬac) into by keeping her as a wife' (niɬ anticipatory pronoun [Section 24.5]; m?ám-min 'to keep as a wife [səm?ám]')[6]

(e) ‿k'a‿wən: see Section 32.1.15(a); for ‿k'a‿maɬ‿wən see Section 32.1.15(b)

(f) ˌk'aˌƛ'ɬ: ƛ'aq'əmkstˌk'áˌƛ'ɬ   máqaʔ   ɬəlˌniˌsʔac'x̌n-ánˌa 'it must be six (ƛ'áq'əmkst) years (máqaʔ 'snow') since (ɬəlˌ) I saw (ʔác'x̌ən) him'

(g) ˌk'aˌhəm'ˌtuʔ: nkaʔ-asˌk'áˌhəm'ˌtuʔ   ʔayɬ   niˌpúʔy'ax^wˌa 'the mouse (púʔy'ax^w) must have gone somewhere' (ʔayɬ 'and then' [Section 28.2.8])

(h) ˌk'aˌtuʔ: sk'əlˌk^wuʔ   ʔiˌqmút-ihˌa   ɬˌxin'-asˌk'áˌtuʔ 'apparently, their hats (qmut) were (made of) buckskin (sk'əl) a long time (xin') ago'

(i) ˌk'aˌƛ'uʔ: sxin'sˌk'aˌƛ'uʔ   k^wasˌzúq^w 'he had been dead (zuq^w) for a long time (sxin's)'

32.3.9. Combinations with ˌmaɬ

(a) ˌmaɬˌkəɬ: skan-asˌmáɬˌkɬ   k^wˌs-ƛ'íq-i 'I wonder whether they will come (ƛ'iq)' (skan question marker, Section 29.1[2])

(b) ˌmaɬˌhəm': ʔáma ti sqáyx^wˌa,   qə́lˌmaɬˌhəm'   tiˌsəmʔám-sˌa 'the man (sqayx^w) is good (ʔáma), but his wife (səmʔám) is bad (qə́l)'

(c) ˌmaɬˌhəm'ˌtuʔ: see Section 32.1.13(c)

(d) ˌmaɬˌƛ'uʔ: paplaʔ-sútˌmaɬˌƛ'uʔ 'you go by yourself!'

32.3.10. Combinations with ˌwiʔ

(a) ˌwiʔˌkəɬ: x^wʔáyˌƛ'uʔ   k^wˌs-zəwátn-an skan-asˌwíʔˌkɬ k^wˌən-s-nás 'I do not (x^wʔáyˌƛ'uʔ) know whether I shall go (nas)'

(b) ˌwiʔˌƛ'uʔ: x^wʔázˌwiʔˌƛ'uʔ   k^wənswaˌka-ʕ^wúy'tˌa 'I cannot sleep (ʕ^wuy't)'

32.3.11. Combinations with ˌhəm'

(a) ˌhəm'ˌkəɬ: waʔ-ɬkanˌhəm'ˌkɬˌƛ'uʔ   lc'ʔa, wáʔˌmaɬ wáʔ-wi 'I am going to stay (waʔ) here (lc'ʔa), but you folks go right ahead'

(b) ˌhəm'ˌtuʔ: nɬɬˌƛ'uʔ   s-nák'ləx-kaɬ   ʔúx^walmix^w, sqax̌aʔˌhəm'ˌtuʔ   ɬəlˌtˌs-kəlaʔ-ɬkáɬ a 'so (níɬˌƛ'uʔ) we changed (nák'ləx) into human beings (ʔúx^walmix^w), but we were dogs (sqáx̌aʔ) before' (kélaʔ 'first')

(c) ˌhəm'ˌƛ'uʔ: húy'-ɬkanˌhəm'ˌƛ'uʔ   ka-máys-cˌa 'I will (huy'-) be able (ka-..ˌa) to fix it (mays-c) after all'

(d) ˌhəm'ˌƛ'uʔ: stəx̌^wˌhəm'ˌƛ'úʔˌtiʔ   sq^wéq^wəl' 'that is a true (stəx̌^w) story (sq^wéq^wəl'), you know' (for ˌhəm'ˌƛ'uʔ see also Section 32.1.13[g] to [i])

32.3.12. Combinations with ˌkəɬ

Combinations with ˌkəɬ as first member comprise, first, cases of ˌkəɬˌtuʔ. These generally express a more remote possibility than ˌkəɬ by itself. Besides Section 32.1.7(a) we have, for example:

(a) ʔáḷsəm-ɬkáɬ kɬ ˌtuʔ 'we might get sick (ʔáḷsəm)'

(b) qyax̌-kal'ápˌkɬˌtuʔ 'you folks might get drunk (qyax̌)'

Next, we have cases of ˌkəɬˌƛ'uʔ, e.g.:

(c) níɬ‿kɬ‿X̣'uʔ n-s-huẓ́ kʷzúsəm 'so (níɬ‿X̣'uʔ) I am going to work (kʷzúsəm) right now'

32.3.13. Combinations with ‿tuʔ and ‿X̣'uʔ
The enclitics ‿tuʔ and ‿X̣'uʔ were found in the combination ‿tuʔ‿X̣'uʔ as well as in ‿X̣'uʔ‿tuʔ. Examples with ‿tuʔ‿X̣'uʔ include:

(a) ka-qz'əx̌‿a‿tú?‿X̣'uʔ 'he just whizzed by'

(b) wéqʷ'‿tuʔ‿X̣'uʔ 'so he got carried away by the water'

(c) X̣'əX̣'aka-wít‿tuʔ‿X̣'uʔ 'they went right by'

Examples of ‿tuʔ‿X̣'uʔ in combination with other enclitics include:

(d) naqʷ'-xit-əm‿k'a‿hém'‿tuʔ‿X̣'uʔ kʷɬ‿kapúh 'his coats (kapúh) were apparently stolen (naqʷ') from (-xit) him'

(e) (ɬ‿)nas-an‿ká‿tuʔ‿X̣'uʔ ʔəkʷʔú pankʷúph‿a ʔi‿nátxʷ-as, xʷʔáẓ‿ka kʷ‿ən-s-húẓ' nas ɬkʷúnsa kʷu‿sq'ít 'if (ɬ‿) I would have gone (nas) to Vancouver (pankʷúpa) yesterday (ʔi‿nátxʷ-as), I would not (xʷʔaẓ) have had to go today' (ɬkʷúnsa kʷu‿sq'ít 'today')

(f) níɬ‿tuʔ‿tíʔ‿X̣'uʔ s-zuqʷ-s 'and so (níɬ‿X̣'uʔ) he died (zuqʷ)' (cf. [i] below)
For further examples of ‿tuʔ‿X̣'uʔ, see Section 32.5(af) and (ag).
Examples of ‿X̣'uʔ‿tuʔ include:

(g) níɬ‿X̣'uʔ‿tuʔ n-s-cixʷ ʔúx̌ʷal'-s ʔákʷuʔ 'and so (níɬ‿X̣'uʔ) I went (cixʷ) and brought it home' (ʔúx̌ʷal'-s 'to bring home')

(h) níɬ‿X̣'uʔ láti? s-ḷə́ṣ-c‿X̣'uʔ‿tuʔ ʔákʷuʔ ti‿s?ístkn‿a 'and then the underground house (s?ístkən) caved in (ḷəṣ) there'

(i) níɬ‿X̣'uʔ‿tú?‿ti? s-zuqʷ-s 'and then he died'; cf. (f)[7]

(j) xʷʔaz-as‿ká‿X̣'uʔ‿tuʔ ʔáti? kʷ‿s-x̌íɬ-c-an 'I wish I had not (xʷʔaz) done (x̌iɬ-c) that (?áti?)'

There are far more examples of ‿tuʔ‿X̣'uʔ than of ‿X̣'uʔ‿tuʔ in my material.[8]

32.4. Combinations of enclitics: special cases
Here we discuss double occurrences of ‿a (Section 32.4.1) and the status of demonstrative pronouns (Section 32.4.2).

32.4.1. Double occurrences of ‿a
When the enclitic ‿a is followed by ‿tuʔ, ‿X̣'uʔ, or ‿kʷuʔ, and the stress should fall on the last syllable before ‿a, there is often a second ‿a after ‿tuʔ, ‿X̣'uʔ, or kʷuʔ, and the stress (in accordance with the rules given in Section 2) falls on ‿tuʔ, ‿X̣'uʔ, or ‿kʷuʔ. Examples include:

(a) ka-xʷaz'‿a‿tú?‿a 'he disappeared for good, he died'

(b) húy'-ɬkan núkʷ'ʔan-cin, niɬ t‿s-nukʷ'ʔan-c-axʷ‿a‿tú?‿a 'I will (huy'-) help (núkʷʔan) you, because you helped me once (ni‿s-pála?-s‿a)'

(c) ka-qʷəzqʷaz‿a‿X̣'ú?‿a ti‿xá?‿a 'the sky is blue (qʷəzqʷáz)' (xa? 'high')

(d) ʔi‿nukʷ‿a‿X̣'ú?‿a ʔúxʷalmixʷ 'the other (nukʷ) people (ʔúxʷalmixʷ)'

(e) ka-xal‿a‿kʷú?‿a ʔákʷu? 'he got to the brow of the hill'

(f) ka-X̣'əp‿a‿kʷú?‿a ti‿s-ʔístkn‿a 'the underground house (sʔístkən) had gotten dark (ka-X̣'əp‿a)'

However, ‿a₂ does not always appear:

(g) ka-xím'‿a‿tu? ʔəkʷ?ú ni‿n-sqáx̣?‿a 'my dog (sqáx̣a?) disappeared'

(h) kʷʷúl'əm ti‿kʷíkʷs‿a‿X̣'u? sʔístkən 'she made (kʷʷúl'əm) a small (kʷikʷs) underground house'

(i) xʷʔáy‿X̣'u? kʷənswa‿ka-q'á?‿a, t‿ən-s-təx̣ʷ‿a‿X̣'u? ʔálṣəm 'I cannot eat (q'a?), because I am really (stəx̣ʷ) sick (ʔálṣəm)' (*t‿ən-s-təx̣ʷ‿a‿X̣'ú?‿a was rejected here)

(j) nít‿X̣'u? s-ka-ncqám'-s‿a‿kʷu? ʔət?ú ti‿sX̣'atálm‿a 'and then (nít‿X̣'u?) the grizzly (sX̣'atáləm) fell backwards (ka-ncqám'‿a)'

When there is more than one enclitic after ‿a, there generally is no second ‿a:

(k) ka-qz'əx̣‿a‿tú?‿X̣'u? káti? 'he just whizzed by'

I recorded one case each of ‿kət, ‿qa?, and ‿mat with double ‿a:

(l) ka-cət‿a‿két‿a 'he will sober up, come to his senses'

(m) xʷit‿a‿qá?‿a 'whistle!' (shouted by seeker in hide-and-seek game to find out where hidden players are: √xʷit 'to whistle')

(n) ka-X̣'ək'‿a‿mát‿a 'shut up, keep quiet!' (ka-X̣'ék'‿a 'to fall silent')

Note that the double occurrence of ‿a in ‿a‿xʷit‿a has nothing to do with the stress (see Section 32.1.10[g] to [k]).

32.4.2. Combinations of enclitics with demonstrative pronouns

As shown in Section 25.1, demonstrative pronouns of the shape C(V)V often occur as enclitics. When they are combined with adverbial enclitics in one stress unit, they usually appear at the end of the string:

(a) wa?-tkaxʷ‿há‿ti? zəwátən kʷu‿ʔúxʷalmixʷ 'do you know (zəwátən) that (‿ti?) person (ʔúxʷalmixʷ)?'

(b) sqʷəqʷəl'-s‿X̣'ú?‿ti? ni‿n-kʷ ə́kʷ?‿a 'that is a story (sqʷə́qʷəl') of my grandmother (kʷə́kʷa?)'

(c) qʷacac-s-as‿kʷú?‿?iz' 'he took those (‿?iz') with him' (qʷacác 'to leave')

(d) plan‿kʷu?‿tú?‿ti? ʔayt píx̣əm' ti‿skalúl?‿a 'that owl (skalúla?) had already left (qʷacác) to hunt (píx̣əm')' (ʔayt 'so, then')

(e) cukʷ‿wi?‿X̣'ú?‿ti? smútac-lap 'she is the only (cukʷ) sister of you folks' (smútac 'woman; man's sister or female cousin')

(f) nít‿kʷu?‿ti? sqʷə́qʷəl'-s Harry Carey ni‿səm?ám-s‿a 'that is a story (sqʷə́qʷəl') of Harry Carey's wife (səm?ám)'

(g) nít‿mat‿ti? sqʷəqʷʷl'ən-c-ás ni‿n-skíxəz?‿a 'that is what my mother (skíxza?) told (sqʷə́qʷʷl'ən) me'

(h) plán‿kʷuʔ‿tiʔ waʔ ʔan'w[as]-aszanuxʷ-ás‿k'a 'apparently, that one was two (ʔán'was) years (-aszánuxʷ) old'

(i) stam'-as‿k'á‿mat‿tiʔ 'whatever that was'

(j) xʷʔáz‿həm'‿tiʔ kʷas‿wənáxʷ 'that is not (xʷʔaz) true (wənáxʷ)'

Note that in (a) to (e) the presence of the enclitic demonstrative pronoun causes the stress to shift from the full word to the last enclitic before the pronoun.

In a number of cases, a demonstrative pronoun was recorded as the penultimate member in a string of enclitics. In most of these cases, the final enclitic is ‿ƛ'uʔ ([k] to [p]); in the remaining cases it is ‿tuʔ ([q] to [s]):

(k) cúkʷ‿tiʔ‿ƛ'uʔ 'well, that is finished (cukʷ)'

(l) cukʷ‿ha‿tíʔ‿ƛ'uʔ waʔ ka-száytən-sw‿a 'is that all (cukʷ) you can do?' (száytən 'what smb. does,' -sw 'your'; the combination of ka-..‿a with a nominal stem is highly unusual)

(m) c'ila‿tíʔ‿ƛ'uʔ kʷu‿wire 'that is just like a wire'

(n) n-cuwaʔ‿tíʔ‿ƛ'uʔ kah 'that is *my* car (kah)' (cúwaʔ 'own')

(o) wənáxʷ‿ʔizʔ‿ƛ'uʔ száytən-s ʔi‿ʔuxʷalmíxʷ‿a 'those are things that really (wənáxʷ) happen to people (ʔúxʷalmixʷ)'

(p) ʔayt-wit‿ʔízʔ‿ƛ'uʔ kʷán-twal' 'they had just (ʔayt) taken up (kʷan) with each other (-twal')'

(q) plan-as‿ká‿tiʔ‿tuʔ waʔ máysn-as 'he should (‿ka) have fixed (máysən) it already (plan)'

(r) plán‿niʔ‿tuʔ waʔ ptak 'that is already (plan) past (ptak)'

(s) q'ʷ'law'əm-wít‿nət‿tuʔ kʷu‿scáqʷəm 'those (‿nət) people went to pick (q'ʷ'láw'əm) saskatoon berries (scáqʷəm)'

Note also the following cases:

(t) q'ʷ'law'əm‿túʔ‿niʔ kʷu‿scáqʷəm = q'ʷ'law'əm‿níʔ‿tuʔ kʷu‿scáqʷəm 'that one (‿niʔ) went to pick saskatoon berries'

(u) kán‿ƛ'uʔ‿tiʔ ʔayt waʔ qəḷ-s = kán‿tiʔ‿ƛ'uʔ ʔayt waʔ qəḷ-s 'I dislike (qəḷ-s) him'

32.5. Enclitics after indicative and subjunctive forms

A number of enclitics and enclitic combinations were recorded both with words that have indicative subject suffixes and with words with subjunctive subject suffixes (see Sections 22.3.1 and 22.3.2 for indicative versus subjunctive forms). Where ‿ka occurs with subjunctive endings, it generally expresses a wish, whereas ‿ka with indicative suffixes expresses 'would, should.' Compare (a) and (b), (c) and (d), etc.:

(a) cukʷ-s-an‿ká‿tiʔ sénaʔ, nit s-natxʷ-s 'I hope I finish (cukʷ-s) that (‿tiʔ) by tomorrow (natxʷ)' (sénaʔ, Section 28.2.2; nit 'and then,' Section 29.1[6])

(b) cukʷ-s-kan‿ká‿ti? kə́la? ʔə́ɬ‿húy′-s-kan kʷu‿núkʷ 'I should finish that before (ʔə́ɬ‿) I start (huy′-s) another (nukʷ)′ (kə́la? 'first')

(c) plan-at‿ká‿tu? wa? cixʷ 'I wish we were there already (plan)′

(d) plan-ɬkaɬ‿ká‿tu? wa? cixʷ 'we should have been there already'

(e) plan-as‿ká‿ti?‿X̌′u? wa? máysn-as 'I wish he had fixed (máysən) that already'

(f) plan‿ka‿tí?‿X̌′u? wa? máysn-as 'he should have fixed that already'

(g) xʷʔáz-as‿ka ʔáti? kʷasu‿x̌íləm 'I wish you wouldn't do (x̌íləm) that'

(h) xʷʔáz‿ka ʔáti? kʷasu‿x̌íləm 'you should not do that'

(i) xʷʔaz-as‿ká‿X̌′u? kʷ‿s-nas-c 'I wish he wouldn't go'

(j) xʷʔáz‿ka‿X̌′u? kʷ‿s-nas-c 'he shouldn't go'

(k) xʷʔaz-as‿ká‿X̌′u? sə́na? kʷ‿s-nás-cu 'I wish you wouldn't go'

(l) xʷʔáz‿ka‿X̌′u? sə́na? kʷ‿s-nás-cu 'you shouldn't go'

(m) skán-as‿ka kʷ‿ən-s-cíxʷc ʔákʷu? band office‿a ɬ‿wə?áw-an 'I wonder if my voice would carry across to the band office if I shouted (wə?áw)′ (cixʷc 'voice/sound gets across'; skan question marker, Section 29.1[2])

(n) skán‿ka kʷ‿s-ka-nukʷa?-s-túmx-axʷ‿a 'would you help (nukʷa?-) me?' See also Section 24.1.2(d) to (i).

Combinations of ‿k′a with subjunctive forms seem to have only a very slight semantic difference from combinations of ‿k′a with indicative forms:

(o) kanm-án‿k′a 'I don't know what happened to me' (kánəm 'what happens?')

(p) kanəm-ɬkán‿k′a 'what happened to me?' (e.g., when a person has fainted, breaks out in blotches, has an allergy)

(q) kanm-ás‿k′a múta? ʔáti? nswa‿huy′‿cút 'I wonder why (kánəm) I said (cut) that' (comment by ML: 'when you are mad at yourself for saying it')

(r) kánəm‿k′a múta? ʔákʷu? nswa‿huy′‿cút 'I wonder why the heck I said that'

(s) skán-as‿k′a kʷ‿s-X̌′íq-i 'I don't know whether they have come (X̌′iq)′

(t) skán‿k′a kʷ‿s-X̌′íq-i 'I wonder whether they have come' (used when both the speaker and the addressee have stayed home; cf. [u])

(u) skan kʷ‿s-X̌′íq-i 'did they come?' (used, for example, when the addressee went to the railway station and back)

For combinations of ‿k′a with subjunctive 3S -as, see also Section 24.2(d) to (g), (k), and (m), and Section 26.1.4(d).

Combinations of subjunctive forms with X̌′u? generally express 'may (might) as well.' In combinations with indicative forms, X̌′u? has the elusive meaning discussed in Section 32.1.4. Compare (v) and (w), and note (x) and (y):

(v) wá?-an‿X̌′u? wa? kʷʷzúsəm 'I might as well stay (wa?) and work (kʷʷzúsəm)′

(w) wá?-ɬkan‿X̌′u? wa? kʷʷzúsəm 'I am just working'

(x) xʷʔaz-as‿máɬ‿X̣'uʔ kʷ‿s-nas-c 'he might as well not (xʷʔaz) go (nas)'

(y) xʷʔaz-as‿máɬ‿X̣'uʔ 'you may as well not go' (*xʷʔáz‿maɬ‿X̣'uʔ was rejected in [x] and [y])

For combinations of ‿X̣'uʔ with subjunctive 3S -as, see also Section 24.2(l) and 26.1.4(e).

Other enclitics were not recorded with subjunctive forms (except, of course, ‿an' [Section 32.1.3]) or they do not influence the basic 'optative' meaning of the subjunctive. Examples with ‿kəɬ include:

(z) ʔinwat-wít-as‿kɬ 'see what they will say' (ʔínwat 'to say what?')

(aa) ʔinwat-wít‿kɬ 'what will they say?'

(ab) kanm-áxʷ‿kɬ múta? 'I wonder what you are going to do again (múta?)' (kánəm 'to do what?')

(ac) kanəm-ɬkáxʷ‿kɬ múta? 'what are you going to do again?'

(ad) skan-as‿máɬ‿kɬ kʷ‿s-X̣'íq-i 'I wonder if they will come'

(ae) skan‿kɬ kʷ‿s-X̣'íq-i 'will they come?' (compare [ad] and [ae] with [s] to [u])

In one construction, the word waʔ 'to be (busy with, involved in)' enters into an enclitic combination with ‿tuʔ‿X̣'uʔ and follows a word with a subjunctive suffix. The connotation of this construction is 'I wish I had':

(af) nas-an‿wáʔ‿tuʔ‿X̣'uʔ ʔək̓ʷʔú pankʷúph‿a ʔi‿nátxʷ-as 'I wish I had gone (nas) to Vancouver (pankʷúpa) yesterday (ʔi‿nátxʷ-as)'

(ag) qʷusxit-an‿waʔ‿túʔ‿X̣'uʔ ni‿míx̣aɬ‿a 'I wish I had shot (qʷusxit) the bear (míx̣aɬ)'

32.5.1. Neutralization of subjunctive and indicative paradigms

The enclitic ‿an' (Section 31.1.3) always co-occurs with subjunctive forms. Second, the conjunctions ‿ɬ 'if, when' and ‿ʔi 'when' (Section 22.3.1) always require subjunctive forms. Third, there is no difference between subjunctive and indicative forms in cases with 3SP transitive subject (Section 22.3.2). It follows that in the first two cases we do not have a choice between various functions of enclitics depending on whether they follow a subjunctive or indicative form (because here they are limited to subjunctive forms). In the third case, the context must indicate an indicative or subjunctive reading. For enclitics after ‿an', see Section 32.3.1. With ɬ‿ and enclitics we have, for example:

(a) ɬ‿xʷʔáz-as‿kɬ kʷ‿s-X̣'íq-min'-as, níɬ‿kɬ‿X̣'uʔ [s-]snu-s kʷu‿kʷán-tali 'if he does not (xʷʔaz) come (X̣'iq) for (-xit) it, then (níɬ‿X̣'uʔ) you (snu) may take (kʷan) it'

(b) ɬ‿ʔac'x̣n-án‿kɬ kʷ‿s-John, sawən-ɬkán‿kɬ kʷ‿s-kʷuɬəns-túmx-as ni‿téx̣ʷʔac-s‿a 'if I see (ʔác'x̣ən) John, I will ask (sáwən) him to lend (kʷúɬəns) me his gun (téx̣ʷʔac)'

The enclitics ‿ka and ‿k̓a sometimes appear before a word that is preceded by ‿ɬ (i.e., they behave like proclitics here). Compare (c) with (d), and (e) with (f):

(c) ɬ‿xʷʔáz-as‿ka kʷ‿s-ʕʷúy't-su, lán‿ka‿tu? wa? x̌zum ʔi‿nkʷƛ̓'ústən'-sw‿a 'if (ɬ‿) you would not (xʷʔaz) have slept (ʕʷuy't), your eyes (nkʷƛ̓'ústən') would have been big (x̌zum) already (lan)'

(d) ka‿ɬ‿ʔác̓x̌n-an ʔi‿nátxʷ-as, sawɬən-xít-kan‿ka ni‿téx̌ʷʔac-s‿a 'if I would have seen him yesterday (ʔi‿nátxʷ-as), I would have asked (sáwɬən) him for (-xit) his gun (téx̌ʷʔac)' (in this sentence, ɬ‿ʔác̓x̌n-án‿ka was also allowed by the consultant)

(e) qʷən-qʷnúx̌ʷ-wit, ɬ‿stám'-as‿k̓a kʷu‿s-qʷnúx̌ʷ-i 'they were sick (qʷnux̌ʷ), whatever their (-i) sickness (sqʷnux̌ʷ) was'

(f) xʷʔaz kʷ‿s-zəwatn-ítas ɬ‿swát-as‿ʔiz' kʷu‿ʔús[-c]-tal'i, k̓a‿ɬ‿sámʔ-as, k̓a‿ɬ‿stám'-as 'they did not (xʷʔaz) know (zəwátən) who had thrown away (ʔus-c) these things (‿ʔiz'), whether it was a white man (sámaʔ), or whatever'

For ka‿ɬ‿ see also Section 28.2.7(f).

We may have ka‿ɬ‿ in a main (non-subordinate) clause, with the meaning 'I thought that,' as in:

(g) ka‿ɬ‿nas[-c]-tum'x-áxʷ‿tuʔ‿ƛ̓'uʔ ʔəkʷʔú pankʷúph‿a, xʷaz'wil'xs-káxʷ‿ha zam' 'I thought you were bringing (nas-c) me (-tum'x) to Vancouver (pankʷúpa), did you change your mind (xʷaz'wíl'xs) after all (zam')?'

Perhaps this expression (with ka‿ɬ‿ in the main clause) is considered to depend on an unexpressed main predicate (as a rule, expressions with ɬ‿ are subordinate [see Section 33]).

33
Proclitic Conjunctions

Lillooet has five proclitic conjunctions. Three of these link subordinate clauses to main clauses (see kʷ‿, ł‿, ʔi‿ in Section 22.3.1; for details, see Section 37). Of the remaining two, one (Section 33.1) links independent (non-subordinate) sentences, while the other (Section 33.2) links attributes to the heads of these attributes.

33.1. The conjunction ʔəł‿ 'before'
This conjunction parallels English 'before' exactly.[1] Examples include:
  (a) xín'‿X'u? ʔəł‿X'íq 'it took a long time (xin') before he came (X'iq)'
  (b) ʕap‿kł ʔəł‿X'íq‿kan 'it will be evening (ʕap) before I arrive'
  (c) cukʷ-al'c-káxʷ‿ha ʔəł‿X'ák-kaxʷ 'did you finish (cukʷ) eating (-al'c) before you went (X'ak)?'
In quick speech, ʔəł‿ is occasionally pronounced ł‿, phonetically not different from ł‿ 'if, when' (Section 22.3.1). However, ł‿ 'if, when' combines only with subjunctive forms, whereas ʔəł‿ was recorded only with indicative forms.

33.2. The conjunction kʷu‿ 'attribute-connector'
The conjunction kʷu‿ links attributes to their heads,[2] as in:
  (a) ʕálʕəl kʷu‿sqáyxʷ 'he is a strong (ʕálʕəl) man (sqayxʷ)'
  (b) ʕálʕəl-łkán kʷu‿sqáyxʷ 'I (-łkan) am a strong man'
  (c) x̌zum kʷu‿cítxʷ 'it is a big (x̌zum) house (citxʷ)'
  (d) cʔa kʷu‿sqáyxʷ 'it is this (cʔa) man'
The conjunction kʷu‿ is fairly often dropped without causing a change in meaning (e.g., ʕálʕəl sqayxʷ). We have mostly adjective-like intransitive verbs as attributes (see [a] to [d] above), but nouns may also occur as attributes, as in:
  (e) ʔúxʷalmixʷ kʷu‿sqʷə́qʷəl' 'it is an Indian (ʔúxʷalmixʷ) story (sqʷə́qʷəl')'
  (f) sqayxʷ skʷúza? 'son' (literally 'man [sqayxʷ] child [skʷúza?]')

(g) syáqcaʔ skʷúzaʔ M = smúɬac skʷúzaʔ F 'daughter' (syáqcaʔ, smúɬac 'woman')

With a non-adjective-like intransitive verb as attribute, we have, for example:

(h) ka-p'án'‿a xʷə́xʷk'tən' 'fold-in pocketknife (xʷə́xʷk'tən')' (ka-p'án'‿a 'to get folded')

Numerals usually do not take kʷu‿ when they function as attributes:

(i) pálaʔ sq'it 'one (pálaʔ) day (sq'it)'

We may also have an attribute linked to a head that is a verb. In this case the attribute-connector is kʷa‿ (a shortened form of kʷu‿waʔ‿), as in:

(j) ʕálʕəl kʷu‿sqáyxʷ, ʔáʔx̌aʔ kʷa‿píx̌əm' '(he was) a strong man, talented at hunting (píx̌əm')' (ʔáʔx̌aʔ 'talented, spiritually powerful')

34
Prepositions

Lillooet has a number of words that function as prepositions. These words fall into two groups: primary prepositions (Section 34.1), which are not derived from other words, and secondary prepositions (Section 34.2), which are derived from other words. Formally, these groups are different in that primary prepositions are proclitics whereas secondary prepositions are full words.

34.1. Primary prepositions
The primary prepositions are the following: l̩ 'in, on, at, with, among'; ʔə̰ (1) 'toward, along,' (2) 'by' (with agent in passive constructions); kən̰ 'around, via'; and ɬəl̰ (1) 'from, out of,' (2) 'than' (in comparisons). According to their functions, prepositions may be organized as shown in Figure 21.

Figure 21

Primary prepositions

	Static	Dynamic
Centripetal	l̩	ʔə̰
Centrifugal	kən̰	ɬəl̰

These prepositions combine with the complement forms of variable words (as described in Sections 22.6 and 22.7), and with proper nouns, demonstrative pronouns, and personal pronouns. Single proper nouns drop the article kʷ̰ (Section 31.5) after these prepositions (see [d] and [j] below). Demonstrative pronouns and articles starting in ʔ change ʔ to k after these prepositions (see Sections 25.3 and 31.3.1, respectively). Examples of primary prepositions include the following.

With l̩

(a) l̩‿ti‿cítxʷ‿a 'in the house (citxʷ)'

(b) l̩‿ti‿latám‿a 'on the table (latám)'

(c) l̩‿snúwa 'with you'

(d) l̩‿s-Peter 'with Peter'

(e) l̩‿kizá 'with these (ʔizá)'

(f) l̩‿ti‿xʷík'tn‿a 'with a knife (xʷík'tən)'

(g) l̩‿ki‿ʔuxʷalmíxʷ‿a 'with the Indians, with the people (ʔúxʷalmixʷ)'

With ʔə̩

(h) ʔə̩‿ti‿cítxʷ‿a 'towards the house'

(i) ʔə̩‿ti‿q'láx̌an‿a 'along the fence (q'láx̌an), towards the fence'

(j) níɬ‿X̌'uʔ s-cún-əm   ʔə̩‿s-máhyəqs 'and so (níɬ‿X̌'uʔ) he was told (cun) by Máhyeqs'

(k) pún-əm   ʔə̩‿ti‿kʷúkʷpy'‿a 'he was found (pun) by the chief (kʷúkʷpəy')'

The preposition ʔə̩ is easily dropped (so that, for instance, pún-əm ʔə̩‿ti‿kʷúkʷpy'‿a [k] becomes formally identical to pún-əm ti‿kʷúkʷpy'‿a 'we found the chief, the chief was found'). For the formal identity of 1P-3S and 3S passive forms, see Section 22.3.4.

With kən̩

(l) kən̩‿ti‿cítxʷ‿a 'around the house'

(m) kən̩‿ki‿tákm‿a 'about, around everything (tákəm)'

With ɬəl̩

(n) ɬəl̩‿ti‿cítxʷ‿a 'from, out of the house'

(o) ɬəl̩‿ti‿x̌éləmn‿a 'out of the wall (x̌élmən)'

(p) ɬəl̩‿kizá 'from these (ʔizá)'

(q) ʕəlʕəl-ɬkán   ɬəl̩‿snúwa 'I am stronger than you' (ʕélʕəl 'strong')

For the dropping of preposition-article combinations after local deictics, see Section 26.1.3.

We also have l̩, ɬəl̩, and kən̩ in l̩‿ənkáʔ 'where?' (pronounced [l̩ŋkéʔ, ʔl̩ŋkéʔ]), ɬəl̩‿ənkáʔ 'from where?,' and kə[n]‿nkáʔ [kɛ̩ŋkéʔ] 'around where, via which place?' (nkáʔ 'where? whither?' [Section 26.1.4]). It is possible that l̩‿ənkáʔ is a back-formation to specialize the meaning 'where?' as opposed to 'whither?' (The form nkáʔ in the meaning 'whither?' probably results from *ʔə-nkáʔ.) The form ɬəl̩‿ənkáʔ is also pronounced ɬənkáʔ.

Note that l̩, ɬəl̩, ʔə̩, and kən̩ are formally identical to the prefixes l-, ɬəl-, ʔə-, and kən- in the demonstrative adverbs (Section 26.1).[1]

34.2. Secondary prepositions

Secondary prepositions are derived from nouns with a locative reference, such as sqʷ'ʷut 'side,' nx̌ʔil'q 'a point across,' sʔuɬxʷ 'interior,' nƛ'pan'k 'area under,' x̌ʔiɬ 'other side,' szəháw's 'middle,' etc. These nouns combine with possessive affixes and (in principle) with primary prepositions into forms that correspond to English prepositions or prepositional phrases, such as 'on the side of' = 'beside.' The primary prepositions are often dropped from such forms, however, especially after local deictics, as in:

(a) húy'-ɬkan mícaʔq ʔáti? sqʷ'ʷút-sw‿a 'I am going to sit down (mícaʔq) beside you, at your (-sw) side (sqʷ'ʷut)': note the absence of ʔə‿ti‿ before sqʷ'ʷút-sw‿a

(b) nx̌ʔil'q-s‿a ti‿xʷəmanáɬxʷ‿a ɬən‿wáʔ 'I live across from the store (xʷəmanáɬxʷ)'

Part 3:
Syntax

35
Introduction to Syntax

Full sentences in Lillooet fall into two types: mono-clausal sentences and multi-clausal sentences.[1] As the name implies, mono-clausal sentences consist of one clause, i.e., one predicate (a predicate being a form with a subject suffix or a passive suffix or an imperative suffix),[2] with or without a subject complement and/or object complement,[3] and with or without enclitics and/or full-word adverb(s).[4] Mono-clausal sentences may be simply juxtaposed, as in:

(a) qʷacac-s-as‿kʷú?‿?iz̓, cíxʷ-s-as‿kʷu? ?ay‿ɬ ?ákʷu? ?ə‿ti‿skalúl?‿a 'he (-as) took off (qʷacác) with (-s) those (‿?iz̓), he brought (cixʷ-s) them to the owl (skalúla?)' (‿kʷu? 'allegedly' [Section 32.1.9], ?ay‿ɬ 'next, and then' [Section 28.2.8], ?ákʷu? 'that way' [Section 26.1.2], ?ə‿ 'towards' [Section 34.1])

On the other hand, they may be linked by a coordinating conjunction (see Sections 28.1 and 33.1 for such conjunctions).

Multi-clausal sentences consist of various clauses. One is the main clause, and the other(s) are subordinated to it or to other subordinate clauses. Only indicative and subjunctive (a) and (b) predicates may occur in, or by themselves constitute, a mono-clausal sentence or a main clause. Only subjunctive (c) and factual predicates may occur in, or constitute, a subordinate clause (see Section 22.3.1 for indicative, subjunctive, and factual predicates).[5]

In Part 3 of this book, we deal with mono-clausal sentences in Section 36, with multi-clausal sentences in Section 37, and with special questions in Section 38. Although this three-part discussion covers the main facts and a number of details about the syntax of Lillooet, a full description of the syntax remains a task for the future.

36
Mono-Clausal Sentences

Here we discuss first the word order in mono-clausal sentences (Section 36.1), and then the role of auxiliaries (Section 36.2).

36.1. Word order: general information
The basic structure of a mono-clausal sentence is discussed in Section 35. The order of the elements in a mono-clausal sentence is as follows. Note that the predicate is the only obligatory element.

conjunction   – <u>predicate</u>   – enclitic   – full-word adverb   – complement(s)
(coordinating)   (adverbial)

For the coordinating conjunctions, see Sections 28.1 and 33.1. The only element that may regularly precede the predicate (other than the coordinating conjunctions) is s-x̌ək 'maybe, perhaps' (cf? √x̌ək 'to count, figure out'), as in:

(a) s-x̌ək ʔac'x̌ən-ɬkán‿kɬ‿tu? kʷu‿c'íʔ 'perhaps I (-ɬkan) might (‿kɬ‿tu?) see (ʔác'x̌ən) a deer (c'íʔ)'

(b) s-x̌ək nas-wit‿kéɬ‿tu? 'they might go (nas), you never know'

It is possible that s-x̌ək has to be considered a mono-clausal sentence itself, paratactically linked to the sentence it modifies. We also have wáʔ‿ha s-x̌ək 'who knows?!' (waʔ 'to be [busy with, involved in]'; ‿ha question marker). This expression is best considered a separate mono-clausal sentence:

(c) wáʔ‿ha s-x̌ək, ʔac'x̌ən-ɬkán‿kɬ‿tu? kʷu‿c'íʔ 'who knows?! I might see a deer'[1]

(d) wáʔ‿ha s-x̌ək, ʔac'x̌n-ə́m‿kɬ‿tu? kʷu‿c'íʔ 'who knows?! we might see a deer'

36.1.1. Word order: subject and object complements
As we saw in Section 36.1 and earlier, a predicate may be followed by a

subject and/or an object complement (for the structure of complements based on variable words, see Sections 22.6 to 22.7). Where there is an intransitive predicate, we have two choices, depending on whether the stem used in the predicate is a 'with object' intransitive verb (see Section 18.1.1 for such verbs) or any other intransitive stem. Where there is a single complement after a 'with object' predicate, this complement usually refers to the object, as in:

(a) kʷʼúlʼəm ti‿n-ˁʷúyʼttn‿a 'he made (kʷʼúlʼəm) a bed (nˁʷúyʼttən)'

(b) húyʼ-ɬkan kʷʼúlʼəm kʷu‿X̣ʼlazʼ 'I am going to make a canoe (X̣ʼlazʼ)'

(c) waʔ k̓áxxal ki‿məxázʼ‿a 'she is drying (k̓áxxal) huckleberries (məxázʼ)'

(d) wáʔ-ɬkan ɬúɬxʷxal ki‿sk̓ək̓xús‿a 'I am stringing on (ɬúɬxʷxal) beads (sk̓ək̓xús)'

(e) waʔ nsʔáʔzʼəm ki‿smánʼx‿a 'he is trading (nsʔáʔzʼəm) tobacco (smanʼx)'

Where the predicate is not 'with object,' the complement refers to the subject, as in:

(f) X̣ʼak ti‿nkʼyáp‿a 'the coyote (nkʼyap) goes (X̣ʼak)'

(g) waʔ kʷʼzúsəm ti‿sqáyxʷ‿a 'the man (sqayxʷ) is working (kʷʼzúsəm)'

Although this situation is potentially confusing, we have in fact few problems here. For example, in (a) above the bed cannot make something, and the man in (g) cannot be worked.

In principle, the slot of subject and object complement may also be filled with a proper noun (Sections 27.2, 27.3, 31.5), a personal pronoun (Section 24.1), or a demonstrative pronoun (Section 25). Sentences with a subject complement are possible only when either the predicate refers to a third person or the complement is a personal pronoun (for the latter see Section 24.1.1[n] to [p], [r]; note that in [p] and [r] we have a third person predicate plus a personal pronoun complement).[2]

A 'with object' intransitive predicate (with a third person subject suffix) may also combine with both a subject and an object complement (usually in this order), as in:

(h) kʷʼúlʼəm ti‿kʷékʷaʔ-s‿a ti‿ˁiʔiʔ-icʼʔ‿a 'his (-s) grandmother (kʷékʷaʔ) made (kʷʼúlʼəm) a blanket (-icʼaʔ) out of magpie (s-ˁíʔiʔ) skins'

(i) kʷʼúlʼəm kʷ‿s-Mary ti‿kapúh‿a 'Mary made a coat (kapúh)'

(j) ʔazʼ kʷ‿s-Charlie ti‿káh‿a 'Charlie bought (ʔazʼ) a car (kạh)'

However, intransitive sentences with both a subject and an object complement are relatively rare: they do not occur often in texts, and most examples of such combinations had to be elicited.[3] (As we will see below, transitive sentences with both a subject and an object complement are also relatively rare.)

With transitive predicates, we have the following choices with regard to the function of complements.

First, a predicate with a third person object suffix. Here the complement refers to the object, as in:

(k) núk'ʷʔan-ɬkan ti‿sqáyxʷ‿a 'I (-ɬkan) helped (nuk'ʷʔan) the man (sqayxʷ)' (3S object suffix is zero [Section 22.3.2])

(l) núk'ʷʔan-as ti‿sqáyxʷ‿a 'he (-as) helped the man'

Second, a predicate with a non-third person object suffix. Here the complement refers to the subject, as in:

(m) núk'ʷʔan-c-as ti‿sqáyxʷ‿a 'the man helped me (-c)'[4]

In order to express 'the man helps him' (and other cases of a third person subject complement plus a third person pronominal object), we use a third person passive form (referring to the object), followed by a complement preceded by ʔə‿ 'by' (this complement then expresses the agent), as in:

(n) núk'ʷʔan-əm ʔə‿ti‿sqáyxʷ‿a 'he was helped by the man'

The preposition ʔə‿ is easily dropped, with possibly confusing results (see Section 34.1[k]). Only third person passive forms may be followed by agent-phrases; passive forms for other persons may not take such complements (hence, we may not use *nuk'ʷʔan-cál-əm ʔə‿ti‿sqáyxʷ‿a * 'I was helped by the man': the latter notion may be expressed only through [m] above).

Where we have a predicate with a third person object suffix and a third person subject suffix, we may have both a subject and an object complement, usually in this order, so we have PSO (predicate-subject-object) here, as in:

(o) pəl'ps-ás‿tuʔ ni‿n-skʷúzʔ‿a   ni‿kapúh-s‿a 'my son (skʷúza?) lost (pəl'ps) his (-s) coat (kapúh)'

(p) zuqʷs-twítas ʔi‿núkʷ‿a ʔi‿m'ə́ṣm'əṣ‿a 'some (nukʷ) would kill (zuqʷs) grouse (m'ə́ṣm'əṣ)'

(q) p'aman-ás‿tuʔ ti‿skixəzʔ-íh‿a   nəɬ‿qax̌ʔ-ic'ʔ-íh‿a 'their (-ih) mother (skíxza?) had thrown their dog (qax̌ʔ-) skins (-ic'a?) into the fire' (p'áman 'to throw into the fire')

(r) cíxʷs-as ni‿n-skíxəzʔ‿a ʔi‿stəm'tə́tm'‿a 'my mother (skíxza?) brought (cixʷs) the belongings (stəm'tə́təm')'

However, POS sequences are also used:

(s) cíxʷs-as ʔák'ʷuʔ ti‿swəlmín'k‿a ti‿kə́kəlʔamx‿a n-sqayxʷ 'my (n-) younger (kə́kəlʔamx) brother brought (cixʷs) a gun (swəlmín'k) over there (ʔák'ʷu?)'[5] (sqayxʷ 'man; woman's brother or male cousin')

Again, such constructions with two complements are relatively rare.

Where we have transitive predicates based on three-place verbs ('to give smb. smt.,' 'to point smt. out to smb.,' etc.), we may have one complement, which then refers to the direct object (i.e., the direct object from a Lillooet point of view, namely, that which is given, pointed out, etc.), as in:

(t) cúɬ-xi[t]-c-as ti‿cítxʷ-s‿a 'he (-as) pointed out (cuɬ-) his house (citxʷ) to (-xit) me (-c)'

(u) ʔum'ən-túmuɬ k'ʷu‿tíh 'give (ʔúm'ən) us (-tumuɬ) some tea (tih)'

(v) táwən-ɬkan ʔayɬ ni‿n-c'qáx̌ʔ‿a 'I sold (táwən) him my horse (c'qáx̌a?)'
(ʔayɬ 'and then, next')

Where a predicate with a three-place verb contains an object suffix for a non-third person and a third person subject suffix, as in (t), we may have two complements. The first refers to the subject and the second to the direct object, so the order is PSO, as in:

(w) ʔáz'-xi[ɬ]-c-as ti‿n-sqácəz?‿a   ti‿k̦áh‿a 'my (n-) father (sqácza?) bought (ʔaz') a car (k̦ah) for (-xit) me (-c)'

(x) ʔúm'ən-c-as kʷ‿s-Mom ti‿ɬkʷ'ál'us‿a 'Mom gave (ʔúm'ən) me a basket (ɬkʷ'ál'us)'

(y) kʷan-xi[ɬ]-c-ás‿tu? kʷ‿s-Johnny ni‿n-skʷazúz'‿a 'Johnny took (kʷan) my doll (skʷazúz') away from (-xit) me (-c)'

In a few cases I recorded the order POS, as in:

(z) ʔáz'-xi[ɬ]-c-as ti‿kapúh‿a ti‿n-skíxəz?‿a 'my mother (skíxza?) bought me a coat': note that in (w) to (z) there can be no confusion as to who does what, which accounts for the relatively free order.

Where a three-place predicate refers to a third person object, as in (v) above, we may also have two complements. The first expresses the indirect object, the second the direct object (PIO), as in:

(aa) táwən-ɬkan kʷ‿s-Bill ni‿n-cítxʷ‿a 'I sold my house (citxʷ) to Bill'

(ab) kʷán-xit-as ti‿skíxza?-s‿a ʔi‿q?ám-s‿a 'he grabbed (kʷan) his mother (skíxza?) by her breasts' (s-q?am 'breast,' here with dropping of the nominalizer s-)

(ac) ʔúm'n-as kʷ‿s-Sam ti‿c'qáx̌?‿a 'he gave Sam a horse (c'qáx̌a?)'

(ad) ʔáz'-xit-kan ni‿n-skíxəz?‿a ti‿n-kapúh‿a 'I bought my mother a coat'

(ae) n-X̌'ák'ʷ-xit-as ʔizú xʷ?i?t 'he poured (n-X̌'ak'ʷ-) those ones (ʔizú) a little bit more (xʷ?i?t)' (absence of article on xʷ?i?t is unexplained)[6]

Occasionally, we also have POI here:

(af) ʔáz'-xit-kan ti‿kapúh‿a ni‿n-skíxəz?‿a (id. as in [ad])

Sentences with three complements, as in 'the man pointed out the house to the woman' were not recorded.

Three-place predicates do not combine with only a subject complement (as in 'the man points it out to him') or only indirect object complements (as in 'he points it out to the man'). Where we have a single complement, it expresses the direct object (see [t] to [v]).[7] In order to express a third person pronominal indirect object (one to whom smt. is pointed out) with a subject complement and a direct object complement (as in 'the man points it/the house out to him'), we use a passive predicate that indicates the indirect object, followed by an agent phrase and a direct object complement, as in:

(ag) p'am-xi[ɬ]-tanəmwít‿kʷu?‿tu? zam' kʷu‿skíxəz?-i kʷɬ‿qax̌?íc'?-i 'after all (zam'), their mother (skíxza?) had thrown their dogskins (qax̌?íc'a?) into the fire for them' (p'ám-xit 'to throw smt. into the fire for smb.,' -tanəmwit 3P passive; for the absence of expected ʔə˳ before kʷu˳skíxəzʔ-i, see Section 34.1[k])

Without an agent phrase but with a direct object complement we have:

(ah) kʷan-xit-ə́m˳kʷuʔ ki˳x̌ʷʔucin-álqʷ˳a 'four (x̌ʷʔúcin) sticks (-alqʷ) were taken (kʷan) from him, I hear (˳kʷuʔ)'

(ai) nás-xit-əm ʔan'was-úlwił s-ʔúqʷaʔ 'two (ʔán'was) bottles (-ulwił) of booze (s-ʔúqʷaʔ) were brought to him' (nas 'to go')

36.1.2. Word order: adverbial elements

As the diagram in Section 36.1 indicates, predicates may be followed by adverbial elements (either enclitics or full words; for examples of the use of these elements, see Sections 32 and 28.2, respectively). The position of a full-word adverb may also be taken by a local deictic and/or a local non-deictic; see, for example, Sections 26.1.3(a) to (d) and 26.1.6(a). Where we have both a locative and a complement, the former may precede the latter (as in Section 26.1.3[d], where łtʔu x̌ʔíł˳a precedes ʔi˳waʔ˳záwəm), or vice versa (as in Section 26.1.3[c]).

36.1.3. Word order: auxiliaries

Where we have a predicate that contains an auxiliary, the enclitics and full-word adverbs regularly follow the auxiliary, as in:

(a) wáʔ˳X̌'uʔ kʷzúsəm 'he is (still) working' (˳X̌'uʔ 'well, but, still')

(b) húy'-łkan kaʔł cukʷ 'I am going to quit (cukʷ) for a while (kaʔł)'

Hence, in these cases we must adjust the formula in Section 36.1 as follows:

predicate (auxiliary) - enclitic - full-word adverb - predicate (base)

Where we have an enclitic demonstrative pronoun (see Section 25.1) as subject or object complement, this pronoun also follows the auxiliary, as in Section 32.4.2(p) to (r). These cases show the following structure:

predicate (auxiliary) - complement - predicate (base)

For the position of a demonstrative pronoun versus a variable-word complement, compare also (c) with (d):

(c) wáʔ˳tiʔ kʷzúsəm 'that one (˳tiʔ) is working (kʷzúsəm)'

(d) waʔ kʷzúsəm ti˳sqáyx̌ʷ˳a 'the man (sqayx̌ʷ) is working'

36.2. Auxiliaries: types and use

In Section 22.4.1 we saw that intransitive stems that are temporal/aspectual or modal in character may fill the slot of auxiliary. Verbs of motion may also function as auxiliaries. Stems most often used as auxiliaries include: plan 'bygone, past' (as auxiliary, 'already'), kə́la? 'first' (as auxiliary, 'very'), stəx̌ʷ 'true, real' (as auxiliary, 'truly, really, very'), huz̓ 'to be about to do smt.,' wa? 'to be (busy with, involved in),' x̌'ak 'to go along' (as auxiliary, 'to go in order to do smt.'; in combination with a base with final reduplication, 'to keep going at it, to get ___er'), nas 'to go,' x̌'iq 'to arrive (here),' cixʷ 'to arrive (there),' c̓as 'to come' (as auxiliary, see x̌'ak), papt 'always,' cáma 'to do smt. with effort' (usually cáma‿x̌'u?; for ‿x̌'u? see Section 32.1.4), ?álas 'really, very,' ?ílpa?ɬ 'barely, just about,' páwəl' 'finally,' tqiɬ 'almost' (usually tqíɬ‿x̌'u?). Two conjunctions also function as auxiliaries: zámas‿x̌'u? 'but,' mə́s‿x̌'u? 'but.'

Sometimes there are two or more auxiliaries (see also Section 22.4.1). In most cases, the last auxiliary is wa? 'to be.' The 3P intransitive subject suffixes may appear after the first auxiliary or after the base, but not after any of the intermediate (second, third) auxiliaries (we may therefore assign the intermediate auxiliaries to the base; see also [n] and [o] below). As we saw in Sections 22.4.1 and 22.4.2, transitive subject suffixes 3SP stay on the base, while the other subject suffixes attach to the (first) auxiliary, with the partial exception of 3P intransitive subject (see above). Examples of auxiliaries include:

(a) húz̓-ɬkan kʷzúsəm 'I am going to work' (also húy̓-ɬkan kʷzúsəm [see Section 1.7.1])

(b) cáma kəɬn-ás 'he did his best to take it off' (kə́ɬən 'to take it off')

(c) cama-ɬkán‿x̌'u? xʷíl'ən 'I did my best to find it (but I did not find it)' (xʷíl'ən 'to look for smt.')

(d) ?alas-káxʷ‿x̌'u? qíqc'min 'you chew (qíqc'-min) it really well!'

(e) páwəl'-wit ?ayɬ nkálim 'now they finally want to go' (nkálim 'to want to go, to want to come along')

(f) tqíɬ-kaxʷ‿x̌'u? ɬwəlawíɬ 'you almost missed the train' (ɬwəlawíɬ 'to miss the boat, train, taxi, etc.')

(g) tqíɬ-kan‿x̌'u? qam't-s-túmin 'I almost hit (qam't-s) you'

(h) x̌'ák‿x̌'u? x̌'ak 'just keep going!'

(i) x̌'ák‿x̌'u? ?állas 'he is getting worse (e.g., a sick person)' (?állas 'worse,' final reduplication of ?álas)

(j) plán-wit wa? x̌'iq 'they are here already' (x̌'iq 'to arrive here')

(k) plan wa? zuqʷ ti‿skíxza?-s‿a 'his mother (skíxza?) had died (zuqʷ) already'[8]

(l) stəx̌ʷ-kán‿x̌'u? wa? ?ál̦șəm 'I am really sick (?ál̦șəm)'

(m) ?ilpa?ɬ-kán‿x̌'u? wa? ka-tə́q-s‿a 'I can just about touch it' (ka-tə́q-s‿a 'to be able to touch it')

(n) plán-wit wa? kʷzúsəm 'they are working already' (cf. next item)

(o) plan wa? kʷzúsəm-wit (id. as in [n])

The conjunctions zámas‿ƛ'uʔ and mə́s‿ƛ'uʔ introduce information that was unexpected on the basis of earlier information (like Russian no), or information contrary to information on something else (like Russian a). Examples of zámas‿ƛ'uʔ include:

(p) ʔáma‿tiʔ kʷu‿sqáyxʷ, zámas‿ƛ'uʔ qəḷ ti‿skʷúzaʔ-s‿a 'he is a good (ʔáma) man (qayxʷ), but his son (skʷúzaʔ) is bad (qəḷ)'

(q) xə́ɫxəɫ ti‿skíxzaʔ-s‿a, zámas‿ƛ'uʔ kiʔkɬ'úɫ 'her mother (skíxzaʔ) is active (xə́ɫxəɫ), but she [the daughter] is really lazy (kiʔkɬ'úɫ)'

Examples of mə́s‿ƛ'uʔ include:

(r) plán-ɫkan waʔ xaʔs-áɬiw's, məs-kán‿ƛ'uʔ ƛ'ak kʷzúsəm 'I was already (plan) aching (xaʔs) all over (-aɬiw's 'body'), but I still went (ƛ'ak) to work'

(s) xʷʔuxʷ ʔi‿ləp'aɫkʷúnʔ‿a, məs-kán‿ƛ'uʔ waʔ ƛ'əx-s 'the cured salmon eggs (ləp'aɫkʷúnaʔ) stink (xʷʔuxʷ), but still I like (ƛ'əx-s) them'

(t) samaʔ‿kʷúʔ‿tiʔ, mə́s‿ƛ'uʔ waʔ ʔuxʷalmíxʷ-c 'that (‿tiʔ) is a white man (sámaʔ), but he speaks (-c) Indian (ʔúxʷalmixʷ)'

(u) waʔ ʔama-mín-cih-as, mə́s‿ƛ'uʔ xʷʔaz kʷasu‿xáƛ'-min' 'he is good (ʔáma) to (-min) you, but still you don't like (xáƛ'-min') him' (xʷʔaz 'not')

(v) ʔáma‿tiʔ kʷu‿sqáyxʷ, mə́s‿ƛ'uʔ qəḷ ti‿skʷúzaʔ-s‿a 'he is a good man, but his son is bad' (cf. [p])

With tákəm 'all' and plan 'already,' we have the following set of cases:

(w) takəm-ɫkáɫ‿ƛ'uʔ plan waʔ kʷzúsəm 'we (-ɫkaɫ) are all working already'

(x) plán-ɫkaɫ‿ƛ'uʔ tákəm waʔ kʷzúsəm (id. as in [w])

(y) takəm-wít‿ƛ'uʔ plan waʔ kʷzúsəm 'they (-wit) are all working already'

(z) plán-wit‿ƛ'uʔ tákəm waʔ kʷzúsəm (id. as in [y])

As (w) to (z) show, the auxiliaries tákəm and plan may change first and second places (waʔ is always third), while the subject suffixes select the first auxiliary.

37

Multi-Clausal Sentences

In this section we deal with the four types of constructions that form the predicates in subordinate clauses: kʷ-constructions (Section 37.1), s-constructions (Section 37.2), t-constructions (Section 37.3), and subjunctive (c) constructions (Section 37.4).

37.1. kʷ-constructions

kʷ-constructions are used in the following cases:

1 After sentence-equivalents in Section 29.1(1) to (4), (9): see there for examples.
2 After adjective-like intransitive stems and after numerals, which then function as adverbs to the kʷ-construction ('it is done in an X way, it is done X times'). Examples include:
   (a) x̌ʷəm kʷ‿s-cixʷ-s ʔúx̌ʷaľ 'she arrived (cixʷ) home (ʔúx̌ʷaľ) fast (x̌ʷəm)'
   (b) xʷʔít‿k'a kʷ‿s-ƛ'ak-s 'it seems (‿k'a) that she went (ƛ'ak) many (xʷʔit) times'
   For examples with numerals, see also Section 19.4.2. As mentioned in Section 29.2, the adjectives and numerals are variable words that appear here in an impersonal construction (in the form of a 3S subject main clause).
3 After *verba sentiendi et declarandi,* to indicate the content of what one knows, feels, declares, etc. Examples include:
   (a) wáʔ-ɬkan zəwátən kʷ‿s-ƛ'iq-s 'I know (zəwátən) that he came (ƛ'iq)'
   (b) waʔ ptínusəm kʷ‿s-huy'-s qʷacác 'he is thinking (ptínusəm) about leaving (qʷacác), he is planning to leave'
   (c) qan'ím-ɬkan kʷ‿s-núk'ʷʔan-axʷ ni‿n-sqácəzʔ‿a 'I heard (qan'ím) that you helped (núk'ʷʔan) my (n-) father (sqáczaʔ)'

(d) cún-łkan kʷ‿s-nas-c ʔálkʷ'ił 'I told (cun) her to go (nas) and babysit (ʔálkʷ'ił)'

(e) cun-tamaľap-ás‿ha kʷ‿s-nás-lap kʷ'zúsəm 'did he tell you folks to go (nas) and work (kʷ'zúsəm)?'[1]

37.2. s-**constructions**

s-constructions are used in the following cases:

1   After sentence-equivalents in Section 29.1(6) and (7): see there for examples.

2   After kánəm 'what happens? to do what?' which expresses 'why?' when used as an impersonal main clause. Examples include:

(a) kánəm su‿wəʔáw 'why are you hollering (wəʔáw)?'

(b) kánəm su‿qlíl 'why are you angry (qlil)?'

(c) kánəm səs‿qʷacác-wit 'why did they leave (qʷacác)?'

Instead of kánəm, we may also use waʔ kánəm:

(d) waʔ kánəm s-xʷʔay-s kʷasu‿nás núkʷ'ʔan 'why don't you go (nas) and help (núkʷ'ʔan) him?': note the use of a kʷ-construction subordinated to s-xʷʔay-s, which in its turn is subordinated to waʔ kánəm; for xʷʔaz 'not' > xʷʔay- see Section 1.8.1.

(e) waʔ kánəm s-xʷʔay-s kʷ‿s-núkʷ'ʔan-axʷ 'why didn't you help him?'

37.3. t-**constructions**

t-constructions are used in the following cases:

1   After the sentence-equivalent nił (Section 29.1[8]), or without nił, in order to express 'because': see Section 29.1(8) for examples.

2   After adjective-like intransitive stems and numerals, in order to express that the referent of the adjective stem or numeral is a fact actualized through the referent of the t-construction. For examples with numerals, see Section 19.4.3. With adjectives we have:

(a) ʔáma t‿s-X̓íq-sw‿a 'it is good (ʔáma) that you came (X̓iq)'

(b) ʔáma t‿s-ʔac'x̌ən-cín‿a 'it is good that I see (ʔác'x̌ən) you' ('glad to see you')

37.4. Subjunctive (c) constructions

Subjunctive (c) constructions fall into two types, depending on the proclitic conjunctions they employ: ł-constructions (Section 37.4.1), and ʔi-constructions (Section 37.4.2).

37.4.1. ł-constructions

ł-constructions are used in a number of cases that are summarized below.

The conjunction ɬ‿ easily merges with a preceding or following ɬ‿ in quick speech, but is usually restored in slower speech. Occasionally it is dropped when not adjacent to another ɬ‿. I write (ɬ‿) in cases where ɬ‿ was not used in the pertinent recording but where it is present in other recordings. We use ɬ-constructions in the following cases:

1 To express 'if' or 'when.' For examples see, among others, Sections 24.1.1(r), 24.3(a), 24.6(b), 32.1.6(a), and 32.5.1(a) to (d).
2 To connect subordinate clauses to demonstrative adverbs, e.g., Sections 26.1.1(a) to (d); 26.1.4(a), (b), (d), (e); and 26.2(c) to (f), (h).
3 To form relative adjuncts with the antecedent enclosed (as in 'I know who, what, where, whose, when ...'). ɬ‿ combines here with personal pronouns and related substitutes. Examples include:
   (a) xʷʔaz kʷənswa‿zəwátən ɬ‿swát-as‿ʔizʼ kʷu‿ʔús[-c]-taɬi 'I don't know (zəwátən) who (swat) threw those (‿ʔizʼ) away' (ʔus-c 'to throw away')
   (b) xʷʔaz kʷənswa‿zəwátən ɬ‿stámʼ-as kʷu‿waʔ‿skíʕʼʷ 'I don't know what (stamʼ) a skíʕʼʷ is'[2]
   (c) sawən-cál-itas ɬ‿swanʼuɬ-ás‿niʔ qmut 'they asked (sáwən) me whose (swánʼuɬ) hat (qmut) that (‿niʔ) was'
   (d) xʷʔaz kʷənswa‿zəwátən (ɬ‿)ɬənkaʔ-as‿kʼá‿tiʔ ɬ‿X̣ʼíq-as 'I don't know from where (ɬənkáʔ) that one (‿tiʔ) had come (X̣ʼiq)'
   (e) wáʔ-ɬkaxʷ‿ha zəwátən ɬ‿kánmas-as ɬ‿húzʼ-as cʔas 'do you know when (kánmas-as) he will come (cʔas)?'
   The phrase ɬ‿kánmas-as (see [e]) may also occur without subordinate clause in the meaning 'sometime':
   (f) húzʼ‿həmʼ‿X̣ʼuʔ X̣ʼiq ɬ‿kánmas-as 'he will (huzʼ) come (X̣ʼiq) sometime'
   (g) cʔás-kaxʷ mútaʔ ɬ‿kánmas-as 'come (cʔas) again (mútaʔ) some other day'
4 After the sentence-equivalent ʔuc, in only one recording (Section 29.1[9c]).

37.4.2. ʔi-constructions

The conjunction ʔi‿ expresses 'when' and refers exclusively to events in the past:
   (a) ʔi‿cíxʷ-wit-as, s-x̌áwʼ‿tiʔ‿X̣ʼuʔ 'when they got there (cixʷ), that was a surprise (s-x̌aw) for them'
   (b) níɬ‿maɬ‿tiʔ sqʷəqʷʼɬʼən-c-ás ni‿n-skíxəzʔ‿a ʔi‿wan‿wáʔ skʼʷúkʼʷmʼit 'my (n-) mother (skíxzaʔ) told (sqʷə́qʷʼɬʼən) me that when I was a child (skʼʷúkʼʷmʼit)'
   We also find ʔi‿ in expressions such as:
   (c) ʔi‿kánmas-as 'when' (used like ɬ‿kánmas-as in Section 37.4.1[e], but referring only to past happenings)[3]

(d) ʔi̯nátxʷ-as 'yesterday' (natxʷ 'tomorrow'; probably the underlying meaning of natxʷ is 'any day but today')

(e) ʔi̯sítst-as 'last night' (sitst '[late] night')

(f) ʔi̯xín'-as 'a long time ago' (xin' 'to last a long time')

Occasionally, ʔi̯ is used to link subordinate clauses to temporal adverbs (a task usually performed by ɬ̯), as in:

(g) láni? ʔi̯X̌'íq-as 'it is then (láni?) that he came'

However, ʔi̯ may be used in the latter function only when the main clause refers to a past event. ɬ̯ may be used both when the main clause refers to a past event and when it refers to a present or a future event:

(h) láni? ɬ̯X̌'íq-as 'it is then that he arrived'

(i) kanmas-ás̯k'a ɬ̯húz'-as X̌'iq 'I wonder when he will come'

38
Syntax: Special Questions

In this section we discuss the following syntactic questions: the use of the passive (Section 38.1), the structure of complex complements (Section 38.2), possessive complements (Section 38.3), single expression of the plural (Section 38.4), and the use of focusing elements (Section 38.5).

38.1. The use of the passive

Passive forms, i.e., predicates with a passive suffix (Sections 22.3.4 and 22.4.3) are used as a focusing device in running texts. One of the characters is in focus and when he or she is subjected to an action, this action is represented by a passive predicate, with the person in focus being the patient while the performer of the action is referred to by an agent phrase. (See Section 36.1.1[n] for a passive construction with an agent phrase). For example:

(a) wá?‿kʷu? láti? q'a? kʷ‿s-páhyəqs, wá?‿kʷu? ɬláti? s-xát-s-as ti‿pál?‿a skʷakst-s, ti‿pál?‿a x̌ʷuláka?-s, s-xát-s-as‿kʷu? ɬláti?. níɬ X̌'u? s-cún-əm ?ə‿s-máhyəqs: 'kánəm ti‿skʷákst-sw‿a?' 'Páohyeqs was (wa?) eating (q'a?) there (láti?), he was (wa?) holding up (s-xat-s) one (pála?) of his (-s) hands (skʷakst), one of his fingers (x̌ʷuláka?), he held it up from there. Then he was told (cun) by (?ə‿) Máhyeqs: "what is the matter (kánəm) with your hand?"' (-əm in s-cún-əm is the passive suffix)

The phrase s-cún-əm ?ə‿s-máhyəqs may not be replaced with s-cún-as kʷ‿s-máhyəqs, since the latter means 'he told Máhyeqs' (cf. Section 36.1.1[l]).

We also have passive forms, still serving to keep the main character(s) in focus, where an active form would not be ambiguous, as in:

(b) ka-q'sán'k‿a kʷ‿s-Thomas, ka-q'san'k-kán‿a múta?, [...] níɬ X̌'u? s-?uc'qa?-s-túmuɬ-əm 'Thomas burst out (ka-..‿a) laughing (q'san'k), I burst out laughing again (múta?), [...] Then (níɬ X̌'u?) we were made to go outside' (?úc'qa? 'to go outside,' -s causativizer, -tumuɬ 1P obj., -əm passive)

Here ?uc'qa?-s-túmuɬ-as 'he made us go outside' could conceivably be used, were it not for the fact that 'Thomas' and 'I' are already in focus, and not the grandfather who makes the two main characters go outside.

The focus may shift to another character, as when this character performs an intransitive action that does not involve the characters who were originally in focus. The character newly in focus may then perform a transitive action involving the characters who were originally in focus, as in:

(c) nq'san'k-m'íx-kał. kanm-ás‿k'a ʔáti? qlil ti‿n-c'éc'p'ʔ‿a, nił s-ʔuc'qaʔ-s-túmuł-as 'we (-kał) got carried away (-m'ix) laughing (nq'san'k). One way or another (kanm-ás‿k'a) my (n-) grandfather (c'éc'p'a?) got mad (qlil), so (nił) he (-as) made us go outside'

The shift in focus is possible only where there is a difference in grammatical persons, e.g., 'Thomas' and 'I' (together forming the first person plural) versus the grandfather (third person singular) in examples (b) and (c). Where there are two third persons, one will remain in focus, although the person not in focus may be mentioned as the subject of an intransitive action.

However, when the character not in focus performs an action on the character in focus, we must again use a passive construction (with the character in focus as patient and the other character in the agent phrase), as in the following fragment from a legend. One coyote (in focus) has been killed by Chickadee, and lies dead for an entire winter. He is then found by another coyote, who revives the first one by jumping over him four times (as part of a magic healing ritual):

(d) nít‿kʷu? láti?‿ti? s-kic-s, tákəm ti‿sútik‿a X'u sqapc. X'ák‿kʷu? káti? ti‿snúk'ʷa?-s‿a. 'tay, stám'-as‿k'a núkʷun' kʷu‿száytən-su [...].' q'əlxanʔan-ə́m‿kʷu?, q'əlxanʔan-ə́m‿kʷu?, x̌ʷ?úcin kʷ‿s-q'əlxánʔan-əm 'so (nił) that one (‿ti?) lay (s-kic), all (tákəm) winter (sútik) until (X'u) spring (sqapc). His (-s) friend (snúk'ʷa?) came by (X'ak). "Say (tay), you must have done something (stám'-as‿k'a) again (núk'ʷun')." [N.B.: This is said by the second coyote.] He [i.e., the first coyote] was jumped over (q'əlxánʔan), he was jumped over, he was jumped over four (x̌ʷ?úcin) times' (száytən 'business, what one does').

Note that in (d) we have in fact the same situation as in (a): interaction between two third persons.

38.2. The structure of complex complements

For the structure of complex complements, see Section 31.6.2. The last member (and nucleus) of a complex complement is a subject- or object-centred, or indirect object-centred, form (see Sections 22.6 and 22.7), while the preceding member is either an auxiliary or any of the words that may function as an attribute (for these, see Section 33.2). We may have more than one preceding member. Examples include:

(a) ti‿húz'‿a X'iq 'the one who will (huz') come (X'iq)'

(b) ti‿ʕélʕəl‿a sqayxʷ 'the strong (ʕélʕəl) man (sqayxʷ)'

(c) ti‿sqáyxʷ‿a núkʷˈʔan-c-as 'the man who helped (núkʷˈʔan) me (-c)'[1]

(d) ni‿plán‿a‿tuʔ waʔ ptak 'the past' (plan 'already,' waʔ 'to be,' ptak 'to pass, go by')

Where a complex complement is marked by a possessive affix, this affix is attached to the nucleus; see ti‿pálʔ‿a skʷakst-s, ti‿pálʔ‿a x̌ʷulákaʔ-s in Section 38.1(a), literally 'the one (pálaʔ) his (-s) hand (skʷakst), the one his finger (x̌ʷulákaʔ).' Note also:

(f) ti‿ʔuxʷalmíxʷ‿a skʷácic-s 'his Indian (ʔúxʷalmixʷ) name (skʷácic)'

(g) ti‿sqáyxʷ‿a n-skʷúzaʔ 'my (n-) son' (literally 'my man child')[2]

However, the possessive substitute cúwaʔ (Section 24.4) attracts the possessive affixes also even when it is not the nucleus of a complement:

(h) ti‿n-cúwʔ‿a citxʷ 'my (n-) own (cúwaʔ) house (citxʷ)'

(i) ti‿cúwaʔ-s‿a citxʷ 'his own house'

We may also have complex complements with a personal pronoun as the nucleus. This pronoun is then the first member of the complement, and the subordinated part of the complement is a subject- or object-centred form that follows the pronoun and takes no article:

(j) qʷaľut-sút-kan ʔayɬ sʔénc‿a waʔ kákzaʔ 'and so (ʔayɬ) I (sʔénc‿a) who had been telling lies (kákzaʔ) tried to cover it up by talking my head off (qʷaľut-sút)'

(k) pún-ci-m‿ha snúwa waʔ ləʕʷílx 'were you (snúwa) found (pun) while you were hiding (ləʕʷílx)?' (-ci-m 2S passive)

However, the personal pronoun is often dropped in these cases, as in:

(l) pún-cal-əm ʔayɬ waʔ ləʕʷílx 'I, who was hiding, was found' (-cal-əm 1S passive)

(m) X̌álləx-kan waʔ kʷˈzúsəm 'I quit (X̌álləx) working (kʷˈzúsəm)' ('I, who was working, quit')

When the attribute in a complement construction is a demonstrative pronoun (Section 25), it precedes the article, as in:

(n) ɬ‿X̌íq-as tiʔ cʔa ti‿sxʷápmǝx‿a 'when (ɬ‿) this (cʔa) Shuswap (sxʷápmǝx) came (X̌iq)'[3]

(o) nahn-ás tiʔ‿ti‿ľíľtm‿a smúɬac "Butcherknife" 'he called (náhǝn) that (tiʔ) old (ľíľtǝm) woman (smúɬac) "Butcherknife"'

38.3. Possessive complements

A complement following a form with a third person possessive suffix expresses the possessor of the thing in question, as in:

(a) ti‿cítxʷ-s‿a ti‿sqáyxʷ‿a 'the house (citxʷ) of the man (sqayxʷ)'

(b) ti‿káh-s‿a ti‿n-sqácǝzʔa 'the car (kạh) of my (n-) father (sqácza?)'

Proper nouns do not use the article kʷ‿ when they express the possessive subject:

(c) ti‿cítxʷ-s‿a s-John 'John's house'

Compare also the following cases:

(d) cixʷ haľa-xí[t]-c-as ti‿ḳáh-s‿a ti‿n-sqácəz?‿a 'he went (cixʷ) and showed (háľa-xit) me the car of my father'

(e) cixʷ haľa-xí[t]-c-as ti‿n-sqácəz?‿a ti‿ḳáh-s‿a 'my father went and showed me his car'

Note that the relatively free order between complements, as in Section 36.1.1(o) to (r) versus 36.1.1(s), or Section 36.1.1(w) to (y) versus 36.1.1(z), is absent in (d) and (e): we cannot change the order of the complements in (d) and (e) without completely altering the semantic structure of the sentence.

For the expression of plural possessive subjects, see Section 38.4(l) to (p).

38.4. Single expression of the plural

Where we have a plural complement based on a variable word (i.e., a subject- or [in]direct object-centred form with a plural article), or a plural demonstrative pronoun, the predicate may have a plural suffix referring to the complement, as in:

(a) c?ás-wit ?i‿xmán'‿a 'the enemies (xman') are coming (c?as)'

(b) xʷ?it-wit‿ḳá‿?iz' 'those (‿?iz') are many (xʷ?it), apparently (‿ḳ'a)'

However, in a large number of cases I recorded singular references in the predicate to a plural complement:

(c) X̌'iq ?i‿X̌'íq‿a 'some people came (X̌'iq)' (literally 'those who came, came')[4]

(d) qəḷ ?i‿sám?‿a 'the white people (sáma?) are bad (qəḷ)'

(e) húy'-ɬkaɬ x̌lítn-əm ?i‿?uxʷalmíxʷ‿a 'we are going to (huy'-) invite (x̌litən) the people (?úxʷalmixʷ)': cf. x̌litən-tánəmwit 'we invite them'

(f) n-snək'ʷnúk'ʷa?‿?iz' 'those (‿?iz') are my (n-) friends (snək'ʷnúk'ʷa?)'

Where the plural complement refers to inanimate objects, the use of plural suffixes in the predicate is excluded:

(g) x̌zum ?i‿cítxʷ‿a 'the houses (citxʷ) are big (x̌zum)' (x̌zúm-wit would be incorrect here)

Where the plural complement contains proper nouns or generic pet-names (Section 27.3), the predicate mostly has plural suffixes:

(h) wa? k'ʷzúsəm-wit wi‿s-John múta? s-Bill 'John and Bill are working'

(i) wá?-ɬkan lc?a ?alk'ʷən-tánih-an wi‿scəcəw'qín'kst 'I am babysitting (?álk'ʷən) the bear cubs (scəcəw'qín'kst) here (lc?a)'

Note, however, the following cases, which were all taken from a traditional song:

(j) xʷ?it wi‿s-kíka? 'lots (xʷ?it) of girls'

(k) xʷ?it wi‿s-?ápa? 'lots of boys'

Perhaps the absence of wi‿ in (j) and (k) is partially due to the need to fit these sentences into the rhythm and melody of the song.

Where we have a plural complement containing a personal pronoun, plural reference is preferred in the predicate (see Section 24.1.1[q]). Where we have a plural personal pronoun in the predicate, the complement may have a singular or a plural article; cf. Section 24.1.1(i) to (k) and 24.1.1(l).

Where we have a possessive complement (as discussed in Section 38.3) in the plural, and this complement is based on a variable word, the possessive marker is -i or -s:

(l) nít‿ti? qʷámqʷmət sztáytn-i ?i‿n?án'was‿a qəɬ-qəɬmə́mən' 'that (‿ti?) is a funny (qʷámqʷmət) thing (sztáytən) of the two (n?án'was) old (qəɬmə́mən') people'

(m) ti‿tmíxʷ-s‿a ?i‿?uxʷalmíxʷ‿a 'the land (tmixʷ) of the Indians (?úxʷalmixʷ)'

When the possessive complement is a combination of proper nouns, hence requiring wi‿ (Section 31.5), the possessive marker is always -i (3P). In contrast to kʷ‿, we do not drop wi‿ here:

(n) ti‿citxʷ-íh‿a wi‿s-John múta? s-Mary 'John and Mary's house (citxʷ)': cf. Section 38.3(c)

Where the possessive complement contains a personal pronoun and another term (together forming a plural complement), the possessive suffix is always plural, at least where the personal pronoun is that of a first or second person:

(o) nít‿ti? qʷámqʷmət sztáytən-ɬkaɬ s?ənc múta? s-Tom 'that (‿ti?) is a funny (qʷámqʷmət) thing that happened to me and Tom' (sztáytən 'business, what one does or what happens to smb.,' -ɬkaɬ 1P poss.)

(p) nít‿ti? sztáytən-ɬkaɬ ?ənc múta? ni‿n-kʷə́kʷ?‿a 'that is a thing that happened to me and my grandmother (kʷə́kʷa?)'

38.5. Focusing elements

Lillooet has three focusing elements: niɬ 'just, precisely' (see Section 24.5), ?í?wa? 'even' (a specialized use of ?í?wa? 'to go along'), and cúkʷ‿X̣'u? 'only' (a specialized use of cukʷ 'finished, to quit'). These elements form cleft constructions in which niɬ, ?í?wa?, and cúkʷ‿X̣'u? signal the focus.[5] Four types of words may be used as the focus of a cleft construction: subject- and object-centred forms (Sections 22.6 and 22.7), demonstrative pronouns (Section 25), personal pronouns (Section 24), and proper nouns, including generic pet-names (Section 27). With a demonstrative pronoun, we have, for example:

(a) nít‿ti? 'that's the one, it is precisely that one'

The focus may also be followed by an adjunct (corresponding to an English relative clause). The adjunct is always a subject- or object-centred form. Where the focus is a subject- or object-centred form or a demonstrative pronoun, the adjunct takes no article, but where the focus is a personal pronoun or a proper name, the adjunct does take an article:

(b) niɬ ti‿sqáyxʷ‿a núkʷ'ʷʔan-an 'it is the man whom I helped (núkʷ'ʷʔan)'

(c) niɬ cʔa núkʷ'ʷʔan-an 'it is this one whom I helped'[6]

(d) niɬ s-Bill ti‿nukʷ'ʷʔan-án‿a 'it is Bill whom I helped'

(e) niɬ snúwa ti‿nukʷ'ʷʔan-án‿a 'it is you whom I helped'

Note that when the focus is a subject- or object-centred form, as in (b), it takes an article, and that when the focus is a proper noun, as in (d), it does not take an article but rather the nominalizer s-.

Examples with ʔíʔwaʔ and cúkʷ‿x̌'uʔ include:

(f) ʔíʔwaʔ ti‿nskʷúzʔ‿a x̌'ák‿tuʔ ʔátaʔ Pemberton‿a 'even my son (skʷúzaʔ) went (x̌'ak) to Pemberton'

(g) ʔíʔwaʔ sʔənc ti‿cúkʷ‿a 'even I (sʔənc) quit (cukʷ)'

(h) ʔíʔwaʔ s-Bill ti‿cíxʷ‿a 'even Bill went (cixʷ)'

(i) ʔíʔwaʔ sniɬ ti‿waʔ‿kʷ'ʷzúsəm 'even he (sniɬ) is working (kʷ'ʷzúsəm)'

(j) cúkʷ‿x̌'uʔ ʔi‿sqʷ'ʷáx̌t-s‿a waʔ s-mul 'only his (-s) feet (sqʷ'ʷax̌t) were in the water' (s-mul 'dipped in')

(k) cúkʷ‿x̌'uʔ sʔənc ti‿cíxʷ‿a 'I am the only one who went, only I went'

(l) cúkʷ‿x̌'uʔ s-Bill ti‿cíxʷ‿a 'only Bill went'

For niɬ see also Section 38.4(l), (o) and (p).

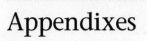

Appendixes

39
A Lillooet Text

The following text was tape-recorded in 1979 by Dr. Gordon Turner, who was at that time working as a curriculum writer for the Mount Currie Cultural/Educational Centre. The consultant from whom the text was collected is Mrs. Rosie Joseph of Mount Currie. The assistance of Mrs. Joseph and Dr. Turner is gratefully acknowledged.

The main character of the text is Mrs. Mathilda Jim, whose Lillooet name was máhyəqs, also affectionately known as máma. (máhyəqs consists of mah [cf. English 'Ma'] and the hypocoristic suffix -yəqs – Section 15.2[108.1]. máma is probably based on English 'Mama.') Mrs. Jim died in 1977, at the age of approximately 115 years.

The Lillooet text is given in Section 39.1, with interlinear morpheme-by-morpheme analysis and English translation. Section 39.2 provides comments on the morphemes in the text, with references to the sections of this book where they are discussed.

39.1. Text: 'Máhyeqs and the Mouse'
When shown in square brackets, the symbols [-] and [ ] represent an affix boundary or a clitic boundary that is not reflected in the English glosses in the morpheme-by-morpheme analysis of the text. See, for example, ʔám[-]ləx 'to get food' in sentence (2) and níɬ[ ]ƛ'uʔ 'so' in sentence (3). Such cases are analyzed in Section 39.2.

1 niɬ ʔayɬ   l[-]cʔa   s-máma   ti‿húz'‿a
   art. and now here, now nom.-Mama art.‿to be about to‿reinf.
   'This time it is Mama that I am going to talk about'

   qʷəl'[-]qʷal'əl't-mín-an
   talk-about-1S subj.

2 nás‿kʷuʔ   ʔám[-]ləx   ʔá[-]kʷuʔ   cípun-s‿a
  go‿quot.   to get food   that way   roothouse-3S poss.‿reinf.
  'As I was told, she went that way to get some food from her roothouse'

3 níɬ[‿]x̌ʼuʔ   s-x̌ʼák-s-as   ti‿x̌l[-]áka?-s‿a
  so   fact.-go-tr.-3S subj.   art.‿bucket-3S poss.‿reinf.
  'So she took along her bucket'

4 cixʷ   ʔá[-]kʷuʔ,   níɬ[‿]x̌ʼuʔ   səs‿wáʔ,   kʷán-as
  arrive there   that way,   so   3S subj.‿be busy,   take-3S subj.
  'She got over there, so she stayed around, taking potatoes'

  ʔə[-]ɬʔú   ʔi‿s-qáwc‿a
  that way   art.‿nom.-potato‿reinf.

5 wáʔ‿kʷuʔ‿x̌ʼuʔ?   ʔá[-]tiʔ   x̌íl[-]əm,   x̌ʼák‿kʷuʔ?   kná[-]tiʔ
  be busy‿quot.‿so   that   do like,   go‿quot.   around there
  'So, as I was told, she was busy doing that, and then a mouse came by'

  ti‿púʔyʼaxʷ‿a
  art.‿mouse‿reinf.

6 níɬ‿kʷuʔ‿x̌ʼuʔ?   s-kʷán-as,   lipʼ-inʼ-ás‿kʷuʔ?
  so‿quot.‿well   fact.-take-3S subj.   squeeze-tr.-3S subj.‿quot.
  'So she grabbed it, and she squeezed it'

7 níɬ‿kʷuʔ‿x̌ʼuʔ?   ʔayɬ   s-cut-s: 'wáʔ‿maɬ   ʔayɬ
  so‿quot.‿well   then   fact.-say-3S poss: 'be busy‿adh.   then
  'So she said: "get all squashed then!"'

  lá[-]tiʔ   ka-pə́ṭ‿aʼ
  there   res.-squashed‿reinf.'

8 níɬ‿kʷuʔ‿x̌ʼuʔ?   ʔayɬ   s-kɬ-aka?-mín-as‿kʷuʔ?   la[-]tiʔ
  so‿quot.‿well   then   fact.-take off-hand-from-3S subj.‿quot.   there
  'So, as I was told, she then released her grip on what turned out to be a

  ti‿s-qawc‿a‿xʷiɬ‿á‿k̓a,   naʔq̓   s-qawc
  art.‿nom.-potato‿reinf.‿after all‿reinf.‿apparently,   rotten   nom.‿potato
  potato it was, a rotten potato that she had caught'

ti‿kʷan-ən-s-ás‿a
art.‿take-final red.-tr.-3S subj.‿reinf.

9 n[-]ka?-as‿ƙá‿həm'‿tu?   ?ayɬ   ni‿pú?ýaxʷ‿a
   where-3S subj.‿apparently‿antithesis‿past event   then   art.‿mouse‿reinf.
   'The mouse must have run off somewhere'

10 níɬ‿ti?   qʷám[-]qʷm[-]ət   s-záytən-s   s-máma
    ant.‿that   funny   nom.-thing-3S poss. nom.-Mama
    'That is a funny thing that happened to Mama'

11 cúkʷ‿ti?
    finished‿that
    'That's all'

39.2. Comments

Here we refer each morpheme in the above text to the section in this book where it is discussed. Stress-shifts are not discussed here; for information about them, see Section 2. (For instance, in lip'-in'-ás‿kʷu? 'she squeezed it, allegedly' [sentence 6], there is a regular stress-shift from líp'-in'-as 'she squeezed it'; see Section 2.2[2]).

1 (a) niɬ: anticipatory pronoun. See 24.5 and 38.5.
   (b) ?ayɬ: '(and) then.' See 28.2.8. See also sentences 7 (twice), 8, and 9 in the text.
   (c) l-c?a: 'here' (in this sentence, with a temporal reference 'now,' perhaps because of its juxtaposition with ?ayɬ). For l-c?a and other local deictics, see 26.1 (with details on use and prefixation in 26.1.1 to 26.1.3).
   (d) s-máma: 'Mama.' For use of the nominalizer s- in combination with proper names, see 27.2. For proper nouns after niɬ, see 38.5.
   (e) ti‿..‿a: article 'known, present, individual-singular.' See 31.1.
   (f) huz': 'to be about (to do smt.).' For the use of huz' as auxiliary, see 22.4 and 22.4.1. For huz' in complements, see 31.6.2 and 38.2.
   (g) qʷəl'-qʷal'əl't-mín-an: 'the one I talk about.' The form qʷəl'-qʷal'əl't 'to talk, have a conversation' is a combined total reduplication and consonant reduplication of qʷal'-út 'to speak' (see type [5c] in 12.1 and references there). The form qʷal'-út contains the root qʷal'- 'to speak' and the formative -ut (15.4[7]). For all recorded derivations of qʷal'-, see 21.1. For the 'indirect' transitivizer -min, see 18.1.4. For -an 1S subject and its use in object-centred forms, see 22.6.

2 (a) nas: 'she went': combination of nas 'to go' and 3S indicative intransitive subject (which is zero). For 3S subject, see also 22.1(3) and 22.3.1.

   (b) ˌkʷuʔ: quotative enclitic indicating that the speaker has not personally witnessed the events in question. See 32.1.9. See also sentences 5 (twice), 6 (twice), 7, and 8 (twice).

   (c) ʔám-ləx: 'to get food (from roothouse or garden).' Contains the root ʔam- (cf. ʔám'-c-an' 'to feed smb., tr.,' with the suffix -c 'mouth,' which glottalizes a preceding resonant, and the transitivizer -an') and the suffix -ləx 'body' (15.2[77]), which is also used in reflexive formations. See 17.1.

   (d) ʔá-kʷuʔ: 'that way (invisible, non-pivoting).' See 26.1 and 26.1.2.

   (e) cípun-sˌa: 'her roothouse.' The word cípun means 'roothouse (cellar, larder).' The suffix -s expresses 3S possessive (see 22.1[1] and 22.2). The enclitic ˌa is required by certain articles (see 31.1), but articles are often dropped when preceded by local deictics (see 26.1.3).

3 (a) níɬ ƛ'uʔ: '(and) so, (and) then.' See 29.1(6).

   (b) s-ƛ'ák-s-as: 'she took it along.' The prefix s- is the nominalizer (Section 9), which is used here as a factualizer (see 8.1.3, 22 [introductory remarks], 22.3, and 22.4). For the use of so-called s-constructions after níɬ ƛ'uʔ, see 29.1(6) and 37.2. The word ƛ'ak means 'to go,' while the suffix -s is a transitivizer, here with a causative function; see 18.1.2 (type [Ia]) and 18.1.3. For -as 3S subject, see 22.1(3) and 22.3.2.

   (c) ti ˌx̌l-ákaʔ-sˌa: 'her bucket.' For ti ... ˌa see 31.1. The form x̌l-ákaʔ 'bucket' contains the root x̌l- (perhaps related to √x̌əl 'to build'), and -akaʔ 'hand,' 15.1(95a). For -s 3S possessive, see 22.1(1) and 22.2.

4 (a) cixʷ: 'to arrive there.' For the expression of 3S indicative intransitive subject, see (2a) above.

   (b) ʔá-kʷuʔ: 'that way.' See 26.1 and 16.1.2.

   (c) níɬ ƛ'uʔ: '(and) so, (and) then.' See 29.1(6).

   (d) səsˌwáʔ: 'she was busy.' For səsˌ proclitic factualized s-construction expressing 3S subject, see 22.4.1 and 22.4.2. For the use of s-constructions after níɬ ƛ'uʔ, see 37.2. The form waʔ means 'to be (busy with, involved in).'

   (e) kʷán-as: 'she took.' For kʷan 'to take, tr.' see 18.1.6. For -as 3S subject, see 22.1(3) and 22.3.2.

   (f) ʔə-tʔú: 'that way.' See 26.1 and 26.1.2.

   (g) ʔiˌs-qáwcˌa: 'potatoes.' For the article ʔiˌ ... ˌa 'known, present, individual-plural,' see 31.1. The form s-qawc contains the root qawc and the nominalizer s- (for s- see also Section 9).

5 (a) wáʔ ˌkʷuʔ ˌƛ'uʔ: 'as I was told, she was busy (with).' For quotative ˌkʷuʔ, see 32.1.9 and (2b) above. For ˌƛ'uʔ see 32.1.4. For the order of

enclitics, see 32.3. The form wa? 'to be (busy with)' is an auxiliary to x̌íl-əm, (5c) below. For auxiliaries, see 22.4 and 36.2.

(b) ʔá-ti?: 'that way.' See 26.1 and 16.1.2. In combination with x̌íl-əm (see [5c]), ʔá-ti? expresses '(like) that'; see 26.1.3(j) to (n).

(c) x̌íl-əm: 'to do smt. like smt.' See 20.2. Contains the root x̌il and the intransitivizer -əm (18.1.1[b]). For the expression x̌íl-əm ʔá-ti?, see (5b) above.

(d) X̣'ák̲k̲ʷu?: 'as I was told, it went by,' with X̣'ak 'to go.' For the expression of 3S subject (zero), see (2a) above. For ̲k̲ʷu? see 32.1.9 and (2b) above.

(e) kná-ti?: 'around there.' See 26.1 and 26.1.2.

(f) ti̲pú?y̓axʷ̲a: 'a mouse,' with pú?y̓axʷ 'mouse.' For ti̲...̲a see 31.1.

6 (a) nít̲k̲ʷu?̲X̣'u?: 'and then, as I was told.' For nít̲X̣'u? see 29.1(6). For quotative ̲k̲ʷu? see (2b). Note the order ̲k̲ʷu?̲X̣'u? (see also 32.3), breaking up the expression nít̲X̣'u?.

(b) s-kʷán-as: 'she grabbed it.' For s- factualizer see 8.1.3, 22.3.1, and 22.3.2. For the use of so-called s-constructions after nít̲X̣'u?, see 37.2. For kʷán-as see (4e).

(c) lip'-in'-ás̲k̲ʷu?: 'she squeezed it, I was told,' with líp'-in' 'to squeeze (líp'-), tr. (-in').' For -in' see 18.1.2. For -as 3S subject, see 22.1(3) and 22.3.2. For ̲k̲ʷu? see (2b) above. For the phonetics of l in this recording, see n. 20 of Section 1.

7 (a) nít̲k̲ʷu?̲X̣'u?: see (6a).

(b) ʔayɬ: see (1b).

(c) s-cut-s: 'she said,' with cut 'to say,' s- factualizer (8.1.3), and -s 3S possessive used in intransitive factual forms to express the subject (22.3.1). For the use of factualized forms after nít̲X̣'u?, see 37.2.

(d) wá?̲maɬ: 'be!,' with wa? 'to be (busy with, involved in),' ̲maɬ adhortative (32.1.1), used often in imperative forms (22.3.5 and 22.4.4).

(e) ʔayɬ: see (1b).

(f) lá-ti?: '(t)here.' See 26.1 and 16.1.2.

(g) ka-pə́t̲a: 'to get squashed.' Contains the root pət 'squashed' and the resultative combination ka-..̲a (10.1.3).

8 (a) nít̲k̲ʷu?̲X̣'u?: see (6a).

(b) ʔayɬ: see (1b).

(c) s-kɬ-akaʔ-mín-as̲k̲ʷu?: 'she released her grip on it.' For the factualizer s-, see 8.1.3, 22.3.1, and 22.3.2. For the 'indirect' transitivizer -min, see 18.1.4. For -as 3S subject, see 22.1(3). For ̲k̲ʷu? see (2b) above. The word kɬ-áka?-min contains the root kɬ- (reduced from kəɬ according to 3.2) 'to take off, apart,' and the suffix -aka? 'hand.'

(d) lá-ti?: '(t)here.' See 26.1.

(e) ti̲s-qawc̲a̲xʷiɬ̲á̲k̓a: 'what turned out to be a potato.' For the article ti‿..‿a, see 31.1. For s-qawc see (4g) above. The enclitic ‿xʷi⁴ expresses 'after all, as it turned out to be,' often preceded and followed by ‿a (see 32.1.10). For ‿k̓a 'apparently,' see 32.1.8; for the co-occurrence of ‿k̓a and ‿xʷi⁴, see 32.1.10(d) to (k).

(f) na?q̓: 'rotten.' Contains the root naq̓ (which does not occur as a free form) and the infix ? (see 13). The form na?q̓ is attribute to s-qawc (8g).

(g) s-qawc: see (4g).

(h) ti‿kʷan-ən-s-ás‿a: 'the one that she had caught.' For ti‿..‿a see 31.1. For -as 3S subject, see 22.1(3) and 22.3.2. The word kʷán-ən-s 'to catch' contains kʷán-ən 'to get caught' (final reduplication of kʷan 'to take, tr'; for final reduplication see 12.1[2a]; for the unusual intransitivizing effect of final reduplication in this case, see 18.1.6). The suffix -s is a transitivizer, functioning here as a causativizer; see 18.1.2 (type IIa) and 18.1.3. For the use of kʷán-ən-s-as 'she caught it' in the complement slot, see 22.6.

9 (a) n-ka?-as‿k̓á‿həm̓‿tu?: 'it must have gone somewhere.' For n-ka? 'where?' see 26.1.4. The form n-ka? contains the root ka? in combination with the locative prefix n- (see 10.1.5[1]). The 3S subjunctive subject suffix -as (22.1[3]), in combination with the enclitic ‿k̓a (32.1.8), expresses the indefinite pronoun (see 26.1.4). For ‿həm̓ see 32.1.13. For ‿tu? 'definite past' see 32.1.2. For the order of enclitics, see 32.3.

(b) ?ay⁴: see (1b) above.

(c) ni‿pú?y̓axʷ‿a: 'the mouse.' For ni‿..‿a see 31.1.

10 (a) ní⁴‿ti?: 'that's the one,' ni⁴ anticipatory pronoun. See 24.5 and 38.5. For ‿ti? 'that' see 25.

(b) qʷám-qʷm-ət: 'funny.' Total reduplication of the root qʷam (cf.? qʷan 'to desire') and the aspectual suffix -t (14.3). For combinations of total reduplication and aspectual suffixes, see also 12.5. For ə before -t see also 3.4 (under CREC). For adjunct phrases to a demonstrative pronoun (‿ti? in [10a]), see 38.5.

(c) s-záytən-s: 'what happened to her, her business,' with s-záytən (containing the nominalizer s-) 'affair, business, what happens to smb.,' and -s 3S poss.

(d) s-máma: 'Mama.' For proper nouns referring to a possessor (in this case the 'possessor' of s-záytən), see 38.3(c).

11 (a) cúkʷ‿ti?: 'that's all,' with cukʷ 'finished.' For ‿ti? 'that' see 25.

40
Comparison of Lillooet Orthographies

The list below shows the orthographic symbols used in this book and their corresponding symbols in the practical orthography that was developed by the author and that has been used since 1974 by the Mount Currie Community School, and more recently also by the Lillooet Tribal Council. Extensive examples of the use of the practical orthography are given in van Eijk 1978 and Lillooet Tribal Council 1993.

Another practical orthography is that developed by Bouchard, a key to which is given in van Eijk 1978. Bouchard's orthography is used mainly by the oldest generation of speakers, most members of which have now unfortunately passed away. Further comments on the orthographies are given following the table.

The vowels are shown first, followed by the consonants in the linear order of the chart of phonemes (Figure 1) found in Section 1: plain plosives, glottalized plosives, fricatives, plain nasals, glottalized nasals, plain liquids, glottalized liquids, plain glides, and glottalized glides.

This book	Practical orthography	This book	Practical orthography
a	a	c̣	t̲s̲
ạ	ao	k	k
ə	e	kʷ	kw
ə̣	v	q	q
i	i	qʷ	qw
ị	ii	p'	p'
u	u	ƛ'	t'
ụ	o	c'	ts'
p	p	k'	k'
t	t	k'ʷ	k'w
c	ts	q'	q'

This book	Practical orthography	This book	Practical orthography
qʼʷ	qʼw	l̥ʼ	l̲ʼ
ɬ	lh	z	z
s	s	y	y
ṣ	s̲	ɣ	r
x	c	ʕ	g
xʷ	cw	ʕʷ	gw
x̌	x	h	h
x̌ʷ	xw	w	w
m	m	zʼ	zʼ
n	n	yʼ	yʼ
mʼ	mʼ	ɣʼ	rʼ
nʼ	nʼ	ʕʼ	gʼ
l	l	ʕʼʷ	gʼw
l̲	l̲	ʔ	7
l̥ʼ	lʼ	wʼ	wʼ

In the practical orthography, the 7 (indicating ʔ) is not written word-initially, but it is written root-initially where a root is preceded by a prefix (as in áts'xen 'to see it' versus ka7ats'xsása 'he caught sight of it': ʔác'x̌-ən and ka-ʔac'x̌-s-ás̲a in the orthography of this book).

The underlined symbols t̲s s̲ l̲ l̲ʼ and the symbol ii are not given in van Eijk 1978. The underlinings are often omitted without causing ambiguity because of the rather low frequency of retracted consonants (see Section 1.7). The stress is indicated as in the orthography of this book, i.e., with an acute, but it is often omitted, again with little chance of confusion, because of the high degree of predictability of the stress (see Section 2).

The practical orthography indicates the schwa that arises in slow speech a bit more generously than this book does, as in k'wezusem versus kʷzúsəm. Before uvular consonants, the practical orthography indicates the underlying vowels (as in this book), but before 7 (ʔ) followed by uvulars it generally writes the retracted ones, as in nao7q' 'rotten' (naʔqʼ). However, because of my incomplete understanding of this issue when I developed the practical orthography, one does find the underlying vowels before 7 + uvular in a number of writings in the practical orthography.

Notes

Section 1

1 Occasionally, z̓ is pronounced [ɬˀ] in the position C—, or z is pronounced [ɬ] (after or before vowels). The phonemes ɬ ɬˀ do not allow the variants [z z̓], e.g., pəɬˀp 'lost': [pəɬˀp], never *[pəz̓p].

2 ʕ resembles the uvular trill in French 'rouge' or German 'rot,' but ʕ is pronounced further back. In its point of articulation it resembles Arabic pharyngeal ʕ, but it is more lax than Arabic ʕ, the latter being pronounced with 'very considerable force' (Heffner 1960:152, on Egyptian Arabic and Somali ʕ).

3 h allows a voiced variant [ɦ] between voiced sounds, e.g., náhən [nɛ́ɦən nɛ́ɦən] 'to name smb.,' nahnás [nɛhnɛ́š nɛɦnɛ́š] 'he names him.'

4 The absence of *γʷ *γ̓ʷ can be explained by the absence of *γʷ *γ̓ʷ (of which *γʷ *γ̓ʷ would be the velarized counterparts). We can also class w w̓ as the rounded counterparts of γ γ̓, thereby filling a gap in the chart (see also Thompson 1979b:715-716). Moreover, ə has the same phonetic variants when adjacent to w w̓ as when adjacent to rounded velar obstruents (see Sections 1.9.3 to 1.9.4). The troublesome etymological status of velar and uvular resonants (see Thompson 1979b:708) might indicate that they possibly result from filling a gap in the system (between the palatal and laryngeal resonants), instead of representing Proto-Salish phonemes (for gap-filling in phoneme systems, see also Heller and Macris 1967:13-18). For the status of ʔ, see also n. 8.

5 əz [z̩] is sometimes heard [əl], e.g., ʔúcəz [ʔócz̩ ʔócə]. Note that c in [ʔócə] has the same dental variant as in [ʔócz̩]. Where əz əz̓ are in close contact with a preceding consonant, z z̓ do not allow the variants [ɬ ɬˀ].

6 Cases of əR that normally have close contact occasionally have open contact (that is, are pronounced [əR]), e.g., xʷíɬ̓ən 'to look for, tr.': occasionally [xʷéɬ̓ən] instead of regular [xʷéɬ̓n̩]. On the other hand, sequences əR that regularly have open contact occasionally have close contact, e.g., kənčʔá 'around here': occasionally [kn̩čʔɛ́] instead of regular [kənčʔɛ́]. Cases of #RC are pronounced [R̩C], e.g., nkaʔ [n̩kɛʔ] 'where?' (see also Section 3.1).

7 Vowels do not occur initially in prefixes, in the roots of full words, or in proclitics. Vowels do occur initially in some enclitics and in a fairly large number of suffixes.

8 The fact that ʔ occurs frequently in the word-initial position (unlike other glottalized resonants), plus the fact that ʔ is frequent in general but h is relatively rare, casts some doubt on the status of ʔ as the glottalized counterpart of h (in other words, the relation between h and ʔ does not completely parallel that between the other plain versus glottalized resonants). However, in certain alternations ʔ clearly patterns as the glottalized counterpart of h (see Sections 3.5 and 4.1). Accordingly, we could accordingly posit two different phonemes, a resonant h̓ and an obstruent ʔ (although they would be phonetically identical). However, I reject this solution as being too abstract for the general framework of this book.

9   The only exception is -aluꞩʸʷ 'gall(?),' recorded only from MLaR, and only in kʷʼət-alúꞩʸʷ 'to spill (kʷʼət) one's gall.'

10 For details on the development of Proto-Salish *y *ý, see Thompson 1979b:705, 711, 719.

11 We also have y, rather than z, in a number of proper nouns, e.g., kíxya? (a woman's name, cf. s-kíxza? 'mother'), yáx-aɬqʼʷəlt (a man's name meaning 'long neck,' cf. √zax 'long,' -aɬqʼʷəlt 'throat'). In one legend, Owl casts a spell on his enemies' houses by saying yək-yík-almixʷ 'may they fall down!' (√zik 'log falls down,' -almixʷ 'land, earth'). The use of y in yək-yík-almixʷ is not entirely explained: it is possible that the use of y gives an archaic tinge to the curse (the use of archaic forms in magic formulae is a cross-cultural phenomenon). On the other hand, as Egesdal pointed out to me, Owl functions as a child-snatching bogey monster in Lillooet, Thompson, and elsewhere in the Plateau culture area (also in the legend in which yək-yík-almixʷ is used), and Owl and other bogey monsters often use or are associated with children's speech (Quileute, Nez Perce, Klallam, Thompson). According to Egesdal's Thompson consultants, the use of y instead of z by Owl in Thompson makes Owl 'more scary for children' (in the Thompson language, *y was also changed to z). For the use of special types of speech by certain animals in legends, see Boas 1918:xi, Egesdal 1992, Hess 1982, and Sapir 1915.

12 Some Salish languages (but not Lillooet) shifted Proto-Salish *l *ľ to y y', and Lillooet has borrowed a number of y y' forms, complicating the etymological picture, e.g., nk'yap 'coyote' (*s-n-k'l[ap] in Proto-Salish, cf. Kuipers 1982:84). Note also the hypocoristic suffix -ləqs/-yəqs, as in pípi-ləqs 'sweet little baby' versus máh-yəqs 'Mah' (a woman's name, from English 'Ma'): the use of y in máh-yəqs, and also the use of y' in ?ay'qs (a pet-name, cf. ?aľqs 'beloved person'), resembles the use of y in kíxya?, n. 11.

13 In the position —(?)Q, the vowels a i u prefer in slow speech the variants [æ ó ė] over [a ɔ ɛ] ([ȯ] is between [o] and [ɔ]), e.g., ɬa?qs [ɬæ?qš] 'to go ashore,' ?úqʷa? [?ȯˊqʷɛ?] 'to drink' beside [ɬa?qš], [?ȯqʷɛ?]. (Outside this note we write [a] for [a æ], and [ɔ] for [ɔ ȯ] in the position —[?]Q.) Uvular resonants (ꞩ, etc.) that are preceded by VˀV influence both vowels, with the first vowels having the [æ ó ė] variants, e.g., páˀəꞩ [pǽ?â?] 'faded' (for the pronunciation [â?] of əꞩ, see Section 1.9.4), ɬí?iꞩ [ɫė́ˊ?ėꞩʷ] 'to scatter (e.g., people leaving a meeting),' cí?iꞩʸʷ [čė́?ėꞩʷ] 'to bleed.' Uvulars normally require the variant [a] of preceding a(?) across a clitic boundary, but in slower speech one may hear [ɛ], e.g., sníɬ‿a‿qa? 'well (‿qa?), it's him (sniɬ)' (‿a reinforcing enclitic): normally [..aqɛ?], but in slower speech also [..ɛqɛ?]. Uvulars do not influence other vowels across a clitic boundary: nukʷ'ʷ?an-i‿qa? 'well, help him, you folks!': [..éqɛ?]. In the positions Q—Č and Q—T, the vowels a u allow [æ ȯ] beside [ɛ o], while i is generally diphthongized here: [eʸ] after unrounded uvulars, [oʸ] after rounded ones, e.g., qam't [qæm't] 'to get hit,' qʷul [qʷȯl] 'full,' kaɬqín [kɛɬqéʸn'] 'three-year-old buck,' qʷic [qʷoʸč] 'rich.' Outside this subsection we write [ɛ o e] for [æ ȯ eʸ/oʸ] in the positions Q—Č and Q—T.

14 In cases with epenthetic schwa and in certain suffixes, we do find irregular combinations of retracted and non-retracted phonemes, e.g., ?álsəm 'sick' M, with a final sequence ČəT. See also Section 5.2 for irregular sequences in suffixes.

15 The word qə̣l 'bad' yields the reduplicative form [qʌ́qʌɬʼ] 'good for nothing, useless (persons, horses, etc.).' Writing [ʌ́] (the first vowel) as ə would place the word orthographically in line with s-X̣'áX̣'əɬ-s (see main text), with which it belongs structurally. However, this would give us a unique case of VQ (otherwise excluded; see Section 1.8.1[1]), and therefore we write qəqə̣ɬ'. There are no other cases of QVC that are subjected to consonant reduplication, although we do have x̌ʷax̌ʷ s [x̌ʷax̌ʷs] 'forked,' which has no simplex.

16 The only exception is spukaní 'dun horse,' where we have unrounded k adjacent to u. We have no cases of y ý adjacent to u ụ.

17 Unrounded velars and uvulars that border on rounded ones within a morpheme are normally unrounded, but allow rounded variants in more rapid speech, e.g., qʷaqʷx̌ [qʷaqʷx̌ qʷaqʷx̌ʷ] 'nightmare,' x̌ʷéx̌ʷk'tən' [x̌ʷúx̌ʷk'tn̩ x̌ʷúx̌ʷk'ʷtn̩'] 'small knife, pocketknife.' We have the same situation where an unrounded velar or uvular is followed by a rounded one across a morpheme boundary, e.g., pəq-qʷ [pɔ̃qʷqʷ pʌqqʷ] 'white (pəq) animal (-qʷ)' (note also the difference in the vowels of the two variants; for an explanation of the phonetic symbols [ɔ̃ ụ], see Section 1.9.3). There is no rounding of a plain velar or uvular that follows a

rounded one across a morpheme boundary, e.g., X̌'əqʷ-qʷ-án' [X̌'ɔ́qʷqʷɛ́n'] 'to slap (√X̌'əqʷ) smb. on the head (-qʷ), tr. (-an')' versus n-X̌'əqʷ-q-án' [ṇX̌'ɔ́qʷqɛ́n'] 'to slap smb. on the buttocks (n-..-q).'

18 K'ʔ is often simplified to K' in more rapid speech, e.g., q'(ʔ)áɬmən 'hungry' M, núkʷ'(ʔ)ən 'to help.'

19 In slow speech we may have unassimilated variants in consonant combinations, e.g., s may be [š] before t or c', and sequences of identical consonants may have separate explosions.

20 Especially in relaxed speech, glottalized resonants tend to resemble non-glottalized ones. On the other hand, in emphatic speech plain resonants may sound like glottalized ones. For example, in one story RJ pronounces lip'in'ás‿kʷu? 'allegedly (‿kʷu?) she (-as) squeezed it (líp'in')' with tightened vocal cords, to suggest the force of the squeezing: the initial l here is almost [l']. In the positions C— and #—, plain and glottalized resonants are hard to distinguish anyhow.

21 In emphatic speech, the glottal stricture may be realized as a glottal stop, preceding or following the glottalized resonant (depending on whether the stricture normally falls near the onset or the outset; see main text). The resonant itself is still pronounced with 'creaky voice.' For example, in c'aw'án 'to wash it, tr.,' w' is normally [w'], but in emphatic speech it may be realized as [ʔw'], hardly distinguishable from ʔw in, for example, ha?w'áɬiw's [..?w'..] 'to sweat.'

22 BE pronounces a (when not in the position —[?]Q) as open [æ̀], hardly distinguishable from a [a], e.g., X̌'ak [X̌'æ̀k] 'to go along.'

23 For the pronunciation [ṇl..], see n. 6.

24 x̌ʷəys also allows the variant [x̌ʷéyɪš], with svarabhakti vowel [ɪ] (see also n. 1 of Section 3).

25 The words twiw't 'young man' and scwaw'xʷ 'creek' yield the reduplicated forms twə́ww'ət 'boy' and scwə́ww'əxʷ 'little creek,' phonetically [twó·w'ʊt   twó?w'ʊt] and [šč̓wów'uxʷ   šč̓wó?w'ʊxʷ] ([ow'] and [o?w'] varying with each recording and partially depending on idiolect). Other cases of wəww' (or wəw'w') were not recorded.

26 The word for 'to kick' is cúw'ən [č̓ów'un] in some idiolects, and cú?ən [č̓ó?ən] in other idiolects. (However, the fact that the root of both words is cuw', and not cu?, is shown by the reduplicative forms cúw'cw'ən   cú?cw'ən 'to kick repeatedly,' with a second syllable that is identical in both types of idiolects.) Speakers who use cúw'ən also have the derivation cw'úw'sa? 'to play soccer,' whereas those who say cú?ən have the derivation c?ú?sa? (both forms containing the suffix -usa? 'round object,' with reduplication of the consonant preceding -usa?). Before vowels, əy and iy are phonetically not opposed (the pronunciation being [ey]): we write iy except where əy is morphophonemically indicated, as in qʷéyən 'to use smt.' (regular variant of qʷézən id.; see also Section 1.7.1[1]). We have no cases of əy' or iy' before vowels. Before i əy', the resonant y' is occasionally pronounced [ʔ], e.g., sy'éy'qca? [šy'éy'qcɛ?   š?é?qčɛ?] 'girl' M.

Section 2

1 The pre-tonic vowels that serve as the counting bases in the assignment of the stress receive a secondary stress (`): ?ùxʷalmíxʷ-kan, cùɬun'-tùmuɬ-káɬap (aside from these examples, this secondary stress is not indicated in my transcriptions). All in all, Lillooet can be said to have what Marouzeau calls an 'accent binaire,' which is attested by, for example, Vulgar Latin (Marouzeau 1951:5), Seneca (Holmer 1954:15) and possibly other Iroquoian languages, and many Australian languages (Dixon 1980:128).

2 We do not have cases of several E's following a root (with the exception of the passive marker -əm after -ən, but here we have irregular assignment of the stress; see Section 2.1[8]). Neither do we have cases of several A?'s following a root, or of E and A? (in that order) following a root.

3 One could use the term 'syllable' or 'syllabifier' for vowels and for those clusters that play a part in the assignment of the stress. However, I hesitate to use the term 'syllable' here, since this would mean that I would have to assign a special meaning to this term. The term 'syllabifier' is not commonly used, and I refrain from using it for this reason.

4 One could synopsize the stress rules that pertain to roots, suffixes, and enclitics by stating that Lillooet has strong vowels (generally of the type A) and weak ones (E A? and any

vowel in an enclitic) to which the rules for placement and movement that are stated in Section 2.1(1) and (2) are applied. Such an analysis could be further formalized within the model of Metrical Phonology as discussed in, among others, Hogg and McCully 1987.

5 The fact that enclitics may attract the stress sets them apart from enclitics in most other languages. However, Hess has brought to my attention the fact that enclitics may occur stressed in Lushootseed, and possibly in other Salish languages. Enclitics are set apart from suffixes not only by the categorically 'weak' status of their vowels but also by certain syntactic factors (see Section 8.3).

Section 3

1 Sequences CRV are occasionally pronounced [CERV] besides regular [CRV], e.g., pľuk^w [pľok^w pəľók^w] 'to smoke' (same variants in pľuk^{w}sút 'to smoke away,' ʔúm'nas [ʔóm'nɛš ʔóm'ənɛš] 'he gives it to him,' qļáľq^{w}əm' [qɬá.. qʌɬá..] 'ugly.' In an unstressed syllable we have k'zuz-áłt [k'zu.. k'əzu..] 'to have twins' (s-k'zuz 'twins'). In x^{w}ənaʔm-ásk'aʔ 'power song' (s-x^{w}náʔəm 'Indian doctor'), the variant with epenthetic schwa was the only one recorded. We have [CR̩V] besides regular [CRV], where C and R are of the same place of articulation, e.g., ɬák^{w}uʔ [ɬɛ́.. ɬļɛ́..] 'from there.' Cases such as pľuk^w and others are opposed to cases CERV, which are always [CERV], e.g., pəľaɬcítx^w 'stranger, newcomer.' Sequences V́RK also allow [V́REK] besides [V́RK] (the latter being the usual pronunciation), e.g., ʕ^{w}əlp [..ļp ..ləp] 'to burn.' No schwa is pronounced in V́RK when K is -s (1) transitivizer, (2) 3S poss., -c 1S object (after transitivizers other than -s), or in the case of -tumx 1S object (after the transitivizer -s). See also n. 7.

2 Note that in [ʔļ ʔņ] we have [ļ ņ] in an unusual position (the sequences ʔəl ʔən are pronounced [ʔəl ʔən]; cf. also Section 1.4). The pronunciation [ļ ʔļ] is also used for ļ 'in, on, at.'

3 Sequences #REC allow in fast speech [R̩C] besides regular [REC], e.g., ləhác' [ləhéc' ļhéc'] 'otter.' Occasionally one has, instead of regular [REC], close transition from R to C, with a non-syllabic R, e.g., mļámən [mʌɬá.. mɬá..] 'medicine' F: [mɬá..] resembles the beginning of Serbo-Croatian *mlad* 'young.' Other examples are: zəmán [zəmén zmɛn] 'big bird's nest,' zəwátən [zəwé.. zwé..] 'to know.' Combinations of n- 'referent of root is situated in a larger setting' and stems beginning in C(V)V.. allow in slow speech [nEC] besides regular [ņC]: n-xʔ-ank [ņxʔ.. nəxʔ..] 'high, steep sidehill,' n-ʕəcúlm'əx^w [ņʕəč.. nəʕəč..] 'to stake a horse.' The prefix n- 1S poss. is never pronounced [nE].

4 There are a few irregular exceptions, where KEC retain E before a stressed suffix-vowel, e.g., sək-álk'-əm 'to phone, to telegraph' (√sək 'to whip,' -alk 'string'), also pronounced sk-álk'-əm. (In other derivations, √sək is regularly reduced to sk-, e.g., sk-ay'ɬ 'to whip a child [-ay'ɬ].') Note also √səx 'silly, crazy,' with regular reduction to sx-am 'crazy' but with retention of schwa in the retracted form sə̣x-ạm (a man's name, referring to his craziness, -am/-ạm formative).

5 Sequences ..səs allow both səs and ss when followed by a vowel, although the former variant seems to be more common, e.g., ka-lísəs̱ạ/ka-líss̱ạ 'dumbfounded,' lúsəs-əm/lúss-əm 'to work with a sluice-box.' Other cases of ..C$_p$əC$_p$ are regularly reduced to C$_p$C$_p$ before a vowel; see n-qáx^{w}x^{w}ək, etc. (Section 3.3.2).

6 Unstressed cases KEKC, where the first K is an obstruent and the second K is a fricative, are occasionally pronounced KKC, e.g., p(ə)ɬpúɬəɬ 'rapids,' or k'^{w}əsp 'to get singed' > k'^{w}əsp-ákaʔ 'hand gets singed': occasionally k'^{w}sp.. besides k'^{w}əsp... However, such cases are different from ksnán, which completely drops ə.

7 Occasionally one hears unstressed -alq^w, -alc, etc., instead of the forms with ə, but these forms seems to be limited to deliberate forms of speech where the consultant is aware of the fact that the forms with ə and those without it go back to the same base forms.

8 One exception is máʕəs 'maggot,' perhaps a borrowing from English.

9 Where a suffix -K is added to a word ending in an identical K, the result is usually ..KEK, e.g., n-ʕə́c-əc-tən 'bridle' (√ʕəc 'to tie,' n- 'in, on, at,' -c 'mouth,' -tən 'instrument'; however, ..KK was also recorded in some cases (e.g., n-ʕə́c-c-tən in the above case). I write ..KEK and ..KK in cases of suffixation as I recorded them, and I give all variants in the dictionary. Note also a case like n-wác-əc 'mid-winter bird' (√wac 'excrement, manure'; the bird's name might refer to the fact that these birds often pick kernels of grain out of manure):

the term n-wác-əc (never recorded *n-wác-c) either might contain the suffix -c 'mouth, food' or might have final reduplication.

10 The alternation -ílx/-ləx (see Section 2.1.[5]), might also be due to analogy to -ałp/-łəp (Section 3.3.1).

11 We also have CERC in the middle section of total reduplications of words RV́CER, e.g., lə́m'ən 'to break smt. (e.g., bread, dried salmon)' > *lə́m'ləm'ən > *lə́m'lm'ən > lə́m'əlm'ən 'to break it all up' (cf. *lə́m'ləm'ən > lə́m'əlm'ən with *sxʷápməxəc > sxʷápəmxəc). Note also cases of total reduplication such as *lip't > *líp'ləp't > *líp'ləp'ət (alleviation of final cluster) > líp'əlp'ət 'to be a nuisance' (√lip' 'to squeeze,' -t aspectual suffix [Section 14.3]). In contrast to líp'əlp'ət, the form wə́twətəx 'to itch (wətx) all over' was recorded without a change CREC > CERC in the unstressed part. Forms with unstressed CREC or CERC as a result of reduplication may undergo further changes when enclitics or suffixes are added. Besides cases like sqáyqyəxʷ > ʔi‿sqáyqəyxʷ‿a (CREC > CERC), we have cases like lə́m'əlm'ən > ləm'ləm'n-ás 'he (-as) breaks it all up' (CREC > CERC), with -as causing the reduction of -ən > n (cf. Section 3.2) and subsequent changes. Probably in analogy to such cases, we have cases with obstruents, e.g., tə́qtqən 'to touch all over' > təqtəqn-ás 'he touches it all over' (note that middle sequences with obstruents are allowed, but usually in words with a different structure; see Section 3.3.4).

12 The suffix -məx is the only productive suffix of the shape -REK (other than -ləx; see Section 2.1[5]). Occasionally one hears -məx where -əmx would be regular, or vice versa. For example, sáƛ'-məx was once recorded as sáƛ'-əmx.

13 The sequence ..REK in ʕʷə́lʕʷələp, záw'zəw'ət parallels ..REK in, for example, n-x̌ʷʔúʔcin'-əqʷ (Section 3.3.2). I also recorded ʕʷə́lʕʷəlp on one occasion, and záw'əzw'ət (which seems to be used about as often as záw'zəw'ət).

14 The fact that we have spzúzaʔ, rather than *spzúzəʔ, ties in with the fact that *EʔC does not occur in any word (see also Section 1.9.4).

15 Sequences uʔ/ʔu or iʔ/ʔi behave as though they were əw'/w'ə or əy'/y'ə. However, uʔ/ʔu are opposed to əw'/w'ə, and iʔ/ʔi to əy'/y'ə (see also Section 1.9.4).

16 For cases K'ʔ (like q'ʔ-ál'mən), see also n. 18 of Section 1.

17 Some speakers in M shift the stress to aʔ in words ending in Czaʔ when these are extended with suffixes or enclitics, e.g., ti‿n-skixzáʔ‿a. This is considered incorrect by more conservative speakers.

Section 4

1 Note that the stress moves first from ə to the final a of łə́nkaya, according to the rule in Section 2.1(2), and that then we have extension of á to áh (in other words, the assignment of the stress precedes other morphophonemic operations).

2 I have no cases of *CₚV́h > *CₚV́Cₚa (parallelling spzuʔ > spzúzaʔ). The only word with ..CₚV́h of which I do have a form with consonant reduplication is kapúh 'coat' > kapə́puh 'small coat,' with a totally irregular alternation V́h > ∴Vh.

3 ʔuqʷ?-ál'mən is also pronounced ʔəqʷʔ-ál'mən (cf. x̌ʷik'm-áłx̌ʷ/x̌ʷək'm-áłx̌ʷ [Section 4.2]).

4 The word ʔal'qs 'beloved person' yields the derivation ləqs-áy'ł 'favourite child' (-ay'ł 'child') with ʔa dropped and l' of ʔal'qs changed to lə (there is no #RC in roots; see Section 3.1). For the deglottalization of l' to l, see the general bar on word-initial glottalized resonants, in Section 1.7.

5 Other words ending in stressed as do not drop as, but shift or retain the stress according to the rules, e.g., nas 'to go' > nás-us-ən 'to look like one's parents, to inherit one's parents' looks' (-us 'face,' -ən transitivizer). From sƛ'uk'ʷəl'wás 'to be held around the waist,' I also recorded the derivation sƛ'uk'ʷəl'w-áx̌ʷac 'to have one's arms folded' (-ax̌ʷac 'chest'), with apparently a stress-shift *sƛ'úk'ʷəl'was > sƛ'uk'ʷəl'wás in the underlying form, and then deletion of as plus stress-shift to the suffix. However, the form sƛ'uk'ʷəl'w-áx̌ʷac is rejected by most consultants.

Section 5

1 For the irregular sequence i̧ł (V̧C) we have in this word, see also the last paragraph of Section 5.2.

2   The solution offered by Kuipers (1973, 1981) is that of a 'retracting feature' that operated on certain roots, changing V̄ C̄ to Ṿ C̣. Kuipers reconstructs this feature *in abstracto*, but comments on its phonetic nature (1973:11): 'one can think of a series of pharyngealized vowels, of an "emphatic" glottal stop, etc.' The retracting feature (if indeed it occurred) might have been a suffix that was dropped after leaving its mark on the root, comparable to, say, Old English *fōt-i > fēt; cf. Sapir 1921[1949]:172-180. (The suggestion of this mark-leaving suffix is mine, not Kuipers'.) Dr. M. Dale Kinkade informs me that the 'retracted feature' solution fails to explain certain developments in Columbian (a Southern Interior Salish language).

Section 6
1   There are no roots of the type CREC (or CKEC, for that matter), but roots CECC (CERC and CEKC) change to CCEC when embedded in ka ̣..̣a 'suddenly' (see Section 10.1.3[2]) for details.
2   In a few longer words we have a sequence ʔEC, e.g., s-ʔənc (1S personal pronoun), n-ʔə́x̌c-ək 'spine' (n-..-k 'back').

Section 7
1   Note that the initial clusters in pmi̬lx, X̌'laz̓, and ɬák̓ʷuʔ consist of an obstruent followed by a nasal or liquid of the same place of articulation (these are the only examples of such initial clusters). I cannot explain why we have aphaeresis in one case but syncope in the other cases.
2   The following terms might also have their origin in nursery talk: kíkaʔ (term of endearment for woman or girl; cf.? skíxzaʔ 'mother'), ʔáʔhan 'see?! didn't I tell you?!' (used when proving to smb. that he is wrong; cf.? ʔác'x̌ən 'to see'), lax̌ʷúx̌ʷzaʔ 'to play hide-and-seek' (ləˤʷilxúxzaʔ id.), ʔápaʔ (term of endearment for man or boy; cf.? s-pápzaʔ 'grandfather' F).
3   We have the alternative treatment of *cosho* in k̓ʷasú 'pig,' where the presence of a and u (both V̄) meshes with the presence of s [š] (C̄). Remarkably, in lapl̩áš [ɬapɬáš] 'board' (cf. French *la planche*) we have s [š] bordering on ạ.

Section 8
1   One could also use the term 'inflection' instead of 'personal affixation,' and 'derivation' instead of 'stem formation.' While I have no objection to using 'inflection' and 'derivation,' one must bear in mind that the functional and semantic range of these concepts is still under discussion (see Bybee 1985 and Jensen 1990:115-116), and it may be premature to suggest that this issue has been settled for Lillooet.
2   We could posit a zero-morpheme (written Ø) for 3S intr. subj. and 3S obj., and rewrite, for example, (j) and (k) as núk̓ʷʔ-an-Ø-as and X̌'ak-Ø ti ̣nk̓yáp-Ø ̣a, respectively. The advantage of positing Ø would be that we would have a visual marker, parallelling those cases that are represented by overt markers (e.g., -kan in [a-d] or -c in [i]). However, some linguists may not find this argument sufficient from a theoretical point of view of zero-morphemes. For discussions of zero-morphemes, see, for example, Martinet 1964:95-96, Matthews 1991:123-124 (with a bibliography on the topic on page 143), and Palmer 1973:118(e).
3   To bring out the parallellism between predicates based on nouns, e.g., ti ̣nk̓yáp ̣a, and those based on verbs, e.g., ti ̣X̌'ák ̣a, we could translate ti ̣nk̓yáp ̣a as 'the one who is a coyote' (and similarly, ti ̣sqáyx̌ʷ ̣a as 'the one who is a man'). However, I avoid such translations because they are too cumbersome, although they are grammatically more correct than 'the coyote' or 'the man'.
4   The issue of whether there is a viable distinction between noun and verb in Salish has been vigorously debated in recent years. For arguments against such a distinction, see Kinkade 1983 and Jelinek 1990; for the opposite view, see van Eijk and Hess 1986.

Section 9
1   The word k̓ʷúk̓ʷpəy̓ 'chief' may occur as such in sentences. However, when it attracts possessive affixes, it also attracts the nominalizer s-, as in ti ̣s-k̓ʷuk̓ʷpəy̓-ɬkáɬ ̣a 'our (-ɬkaɬ)

chief.' It is thus different from all other nouns, which either have s- or do not have it, regardless of whether or not they are combined with possessive affixes. For an irregular case of absence of s- (q?am instead of s-q?am), see Section 36.1.1(ab), obviously a case of aphaeresis (cf. Section 7.1). I also collected ti‿kʷúṣa?-s‿a 'his (-s) urine (s-kʷúṣa?),' again with aphaeresis.

Section 10

1 In emphatic speech, s- is quite often pronounced ?əs-. I do not know whether this represents an original pronunciation of s- or whether it results from influence by ?əs- 'to have, to own.'

2 M. Dale Kinkade (personal communication, 1984) makes the worthwhile observation that nəkʷ- may be a relic of Proto-Salish *nak-w 'one.'

3 In slow, deliberate speech one may also say s-ən-q'áyləx-s. With n- 1S poss. prefix, one may have a combination of the factualizer s- and n- (Section 10.1.5), as in nít‿X'u? n-s-ən-q'áyləx 'and then I swam' (literally 'and then the fact [s-] of my [n-] swimming [n-q'áyləx]').

4 The forms with -əltxʷ/-altxʷ were recorded from SM, who often pronounces CKK# where others pronounce CKEK# (see Section 3.3).

Section 11

1 Compare the retention of E in qə̣l-aɬ-tmíxʷ (and other compounds with #KEC) with the retention of E in roots KEC that are followed by a suffix that has the stress on the second vowel (see Section 3.2).

Section 12

1 Van Eijk 1990b and 1993b discuss Lillooet reduplication in terms of affixation, a position I would no longer support now. Instead I would now class initial and total reduplication as copying to the left of the targeted string, consonant reduplication as copying inside the string, and final reduplication as copying to the right. An argument against regarding partial reduplication as affixation comes from Lushootseed, which also has final reduplication (which in this language always copies the second consonant of the root with the preceding vowel, if available). Thus, from ?íbəš 'to walk' we get ?íb-ib-əš 'to pace back and forth,' and from ?úluɬ 'to travel by water' we derive ?úl-ul-uɬ 'to go boatriding.' If partial reduplication is affixation, then the above cases are infixation, but aside from cases like these, Lushootseed does not allow infixation (T. Hess, personal communication, 1995), and classing these reduplications as infixation would therefore complicate the morphological description of Lushootseed. Furthermore, Lushootseed final reduplication also gives sáqʷ-aqʷ 'to fly slowly in circles' (from saqʷ 'to fly') and ?úx̌ʷ-ux̌ʷ 'to go about in a dither accomplishing nothing' (from ?ux̌ʷ 'to go'). If the latter two cases are affixation, then they are suffixation, and the same reduplicative operation in Lushootseed must be described now as infixation, now as suffixation, which again is an unnecessary complication. (In the same way, Lillooet final reduplication copies at the end of the targeted string in púɬ-əɬ, but inside the string in pálla?.) One finds the kernel of this problem in Bloomfield's definition of partial reduplication, which reads: '*Reduplication* is an affix that consists of repeating part of the underlying form' (Bloomfield 1933:218); the reference to 'affix' is not essential for a good understanding of reduplication. (The Lushootseed examples here are taken from Hess 1966.)

2 When a word belongs to a productive reduplication type, it is considered to indeed have that type, even if no simplex can be found (as in the case of s-pəl'-púl' or qíqəl' 'weak,' Section 12.4). If a word formally shows an unproductive reduplication type but no simplex can be found, it is considered not to have that type but to be an unanalyzable root (see, for example, qʷ'əqʷ'ú? in Section 12.2 and n. 4).

3 It is possible that cə-cítxʷ results from *cət-cítxʷ, with the first t merging with c (cf. Section 4.4). If this is the case, cə-cítxʷ historically belongs with total reduplication.

4 qʷ'əqʷ'ú?ɬ, pəpíḷa? and other cases of 11(2)V̇.. without simplex are considered to be unanalyzable roots; cf. also n. 2.

5 Cases such as s-n'á-n'atxʷ, pá-pakʷ possibly represent not initial reduplication but a rare

type of consonant reduplication where the stressed vowel is repeated with the preceding consonant. The only proven case in this latter category is x̌əcp-qíqin'kst 'hundred' M (cf. x̌əcp-qíqən'kst in Section 12.3).

6 From one consultant I also recorded sá?x̌a? 'parent-in-law' > sá?a?x̌a? 'parents-in-law,' with a unique semantic function of the final reduplication. This formation (sá?a?x̌a?) is not used by other consultants.

7 A number of roots have the shape 12V2, e.g., pɬuɬ 'thick (of blanket or clothing),' qlil 'angry,' ṣṭut 'cricket' F. These forms might go back to a now totally unproductive reduplication type (1V2 > 12V2). However, I have no parallelling forms without reduplication here (although qlil might be derived from the same root as qíqəl' 'weak,' while besides pɬuɬ I recorded pɬ-ánis 'thick board [-anis]'). I do not find these cases convincing enough to postulate a reduplication type 12V2, and I treat pɬuɬ, etc. as roots of the type CVCC. Remarkably, in Shuswap there is a reduplication type 12V2 that is far more common than 1V22 (Kuipers 1974:38-40).

8 For other studies of final reduplication in Salish, I refer to the bibliography of my article. Some of the most important references given there are Carlson and Thompson 1982, Kinkade 1982, and Kroeber 1988.

9 The type of consonant reduplication that involves the consonant before the stressed vowel is limited to the Northern Interior Salish languages Lillooet, Shuswap, and Thompson. In Columbian, for example, consonant reduplication operates only on roots (M. Dale Kinkade, personal communication, 1990).

10 Note also laxʷúxʷza? 'to play hide-and-seek' (probably nursery talk for ləˤʷ-ilx-úxza?).

11 I also recorded pət-pátkʷa 'needles on bush or tree (i.e., collectively),' which is not used for individual (sewing) needles (pátkʷa 'needle'). Not all consultants use the reduplicated form.

12 I recorded kʷəp-kʷúkʷpəy' 'chiefs' (kʷúkʷpəy' 'chief') in a speech by an elder (in the form ?i‿s-kʷəp-kʷukʷpəy'-ɬkáɬ‿a 'our [-ɬkaɬ] chiefs'; for s- see n. 1 of Section 9). Not every speaker uses this reduplication.

13 An example is cəqʷ-cécqʷ sp'áq'əm 'little red flowers (sp'áq'əm).'

14 However, qʷən-qʷán-t 'poor, destitute' is of type (4a).

15 The meanings of s-kél-kla? and s-kəl-kékla? seem to overlap. I also recorded 'elders' for s-kél-kla? and 'ancestors' for s-kəl-kékla?.

16 A number of recent Salish studies (including Czaykowska-Higgins 1993, Galloway 1993, Montler 1986, and Thompson and Thompson 1992) make a semantic distinction between types (4a) and (4b) in that they ascribe a 'characteristic' function to type (4b) and limit the general pluralizing function to type (4a). I have strong reservations about this analysis, and I categorically reject it for Lillooet. For details, see van Eijk 1993a and 1993b and van Eijk, in press.

17 ƛ'ək-a-ƛ'ák-a seems to indicate a more thorough action than ƛ'ə-ƛ'ák-a (Section 12.2).

Section 13

1 There are also cases $C_1V?C_2$ that lack a simplex and do not fall in the same semantic category as cases with interior glottalization, e.g., x̌ʷu?ƛ' 'sturgeon.' These cases are considered roots of the type CVCC.

2 We have the opposite rule order in, for example, ká?əw' 'to go out further' > kék?aw' 'to go out a little bit further' (for ká?əw' see also Section 13.1; for á > é see Section 12.1[3b]).

3 Phonetically, i in n-zí?zəˤ' is like the first i in lí?əl?iˤ' and cí?c?iˤʷ (Section 13.1.2), varying from [é] to [e]. In other words, ˤ' keeps its influence on i even through the intervening consonants. We have no other cases of C_1?C_1Q where Q is a uvular resonant.

4 Note that -aɬ does not attract the stress, although it is preceded by a stem with A?.

5 An example of ?uc is: ?uc‿a‿xʷíɬ‿ti? kʷas‿cúwa?-s 'that (‿ti?) is not his' (‿a‿xʷíɬ 'after all,' kʷas‿ 'that it is,' cúwa? 'one's own,' -s 3S poss.).

Section 14

1 There are no cases of ləq' or cəx̌ʷ without -p. Hence, I do not know whether in these cases roots ləq' cəx̌ʷ attract -p or whether laq' cix̌ʷ irregularly attracts -p and then changes to ləq' cəx̌ʷ in order to fit the pattern CEC-p.

Section 15

1 The term 'ambifix' is from Kinkade 1963:348.

2 An interesting case is X̌'ak 'to go (along)' > s-X̌'ák-mən 'way of life' versus n-X̌'ák-mən 'track, trail,' as discussed in Section 15.2(9.1).

3 The difference between the abstract meanings of the suffixes and the concrete meanings of the roots is in a way parallelled (on an entirely different socio-linguistic parameter) by Guwal versus Jalnguy types of speech in Dyirbal (see Dixon 1980:61-62).

4 Nater (1984[20.4.1.1]) uses the term 'classifiers' for a comparable set of suffixes in Bella Coola. The use of these suffixes (in Lillooet, Bella Coola, and Salish in general) to a certain extent resembles the use of classifying prefixes in Bantu (cf. Welmers 1975:159-183), or the use of certain verbal stems describing the nature of the object handled, in Athabaskan (cf. Pinnow 1964:52-56, or Li 1946:405-409).

5 The order then is p p' m t c/ç c' s/ş n X̌' ł l/ḷ k k' kʷ k'ʷ x xʷ ɣ q q' qʷ q'ʷ x̌ x̌ʷ ʕ ʕʷ h w y z ʔ. The glottal stop is taken into account only where it begins a suffix; otherwise it is ignored. Glottalization in resonants is also ignored, except where the only difference between two suffixes is that between a plain and a glottalized variant of the same resonant, in which case the suffix with the glottalized resonant follows the one with the plain one (see 62, 63). Vowels are ignored, except in suffixes with an identical consonantal make-up, in which case the order is ə a i u (cf. 117, 119). The reason for largely ignoring the vowels is that we have only a few cases where a difference in vowel is the only difference between suffixes. Moreover, some suffixes have forms with different vowels but with an identical consonantal make-up, e.g., -us/-s (22), or -ílx/-ləx (77): it would be uneconomical to list the variants within 22 or 77 in different places because of the vowel differences between the variants. As we have seen in Section 1.7, velar and uvular resonants and h do not occur in suffixes, except for one case of ʕʷ. Retracted phonemes in suffixes are largely conditioned by retracted roots (see Section 5.2), and they are classed with the non-retracted phonemes.

6 As shown by n-ʔal-íməm (< [n-]n-ʔal-íməm), two consecutive occurrences of the locative prefix n- merge into one.

7 The retention of the nominalizer s- in s-psíʕ-tən and s-ʕáp-tən is remarkable: usually s- is dropped when a noun combines with a nominalizing suffix (e.g., s-xniź > xníź-aź [126]). On the other hand, in a few cases a nominalizing suffix requires s- (see s-X̌'ák-mən [9.1] or s-ləm-ála [51]).

8 One could very plausibly argue that -ílx/-ləx is not a lexical suffix but rather a special kind of reflexive suffix, or perhaps an intransitive marker with a reflexive tinge. For transitivizations of stems with -ílx/-ləx, see the last paragraph of Section 18.3.

9 There is some interplay in Salish between n and l (further complicating the situation outlined in Section 1.7.1 and n. 12 of Section 1). Cf. -alwas with ʔán'was 'two,' both items sharing the notion of 'in half, in two.'

10 The use of -qʷ to refer to 'animals' and to serve as a hypocoristic suffix resembles the use of consonant reduplication that forms diminutives but that refers to 'animals' in numerals (cf. Section 12.4).

11 Remarkably, X̌'aq' and q'áyləx do not combine with -əm unless they are followed by certain lexical suffixes (as in X̌'áq'-əm-kst [96], n-X̌'aq'-m-áw's, n-q'ayləx-m-áw's [118]). One could consider -əm to be a connective in these cases, but I have chosen not to do so. Note that the occurrence of -əm here is different from xʷik'-m-áłxʷ (48), where -əm is already in the stem to which -áłxʷ is added.

12 For the complex etymological relationships between l n y z, see n. 9 above and references there.

13 Phonetically, n- in n-wáł-ən is identical to the prefix n- [ṇ ʔṇ] (cf. Section 3.1).

Section 16

1 It is not impossible that -úł is (at least historically) the same suffix as -úł 'step-relative,' (Section 15.2[42]), through a common notion of 'exhibiting the quality of smt. (e.g., exhibiting the quality of a father, or of being unwilling to work).'

2 q'áylex/nq'áylex is often collapsed into q'əlx-/nq'əlx- in unstressed derivations: cf. nq'əlxmáw's (besides nq'aylexmáw's, Section 15.2[118]), nq'əlx-án?-an 'to jump over smb.,' with n-..-ana? 'surface' (Section 15.2[34b]).

Section 17

1 One of my consultants considers wəq'ʷ-ílx to be a 'baby-word' (i.e., a slightly substandard word). Other consultants consider both wəq'ʷ-ílx and wəq'ʷ-an-cút correct.

2 The transitivizer -Vn/-Vn' historically goes back to *-Vnt/-Vn't (with t probably having separate suffix status; see Thompson and Thompson 1992:62ff.). However, in Lillooet the t has been lost or it has been assigned to certain object suffixes. It is thus possible that -cút results from *-t-sút with a later 'condensing' of ts to c (synchronically, ts is different from c; see Section 1.9.1). One may not consider -cút as a variant of -sút (Section 16[4]) after n, since -sút occurs as such after n, in pun-sút-ən 'to find (pun) smt. by accident.' For historical information on the Salish reflexive, see also Kinkade 1981.

Section 18

1 Intransitive stems do take subject suffixes, e.g., ʔác'x̌-kan 'I am seen.'

2 The intransitivizer -xal is parallelled by formally similar intransitivizers in Colville (-xíx) and Columbian (-xíx and -xáx) (M. Dale Kinkade, personal communication, 1984). These intransitivizers (-xal, -xíx, and -xíx/-xáx) are less widely distributed than the m-intransitivizers, which are attested throughout Salish.

3 Summing up, we say that there are transitive verbs, which may take object (and reflexive and reciprocal) suffixes and object complements, versus intransitive verbs, which may not take object, etc., suffixes but some of which may take object complements whereas others may not, as follows:

	Object suffix	Object complement
intransitive: medial/reflexive, passive	–	–
intransitive: 'with object'	–	+
transitive	+	+

Besides intransitive verbs that are semantically passive (e.g., qam't 'to get hit'), there are transitive passive forms that are marked by an overt passive suffix (see Section 22.3.4).

4 I have no cases of consonant reduplication applied to stems with stressed -xal.

5 The stress patterns of núk'ʷʔ-an and páqʷʔ-an prove that in the former we have -ən in the underlying form, while in the latter we have -an: cf. núk'ʷʔ-an-as 'he (-as) helps him' and paqʷʔ-án-as 'he scares him': -an in the first form does not take the stress, hence it must go back to -ən (since -ən in suffixes generally does not take the stress; see Section 2.1[2]).

6 Referring to Shibatani 1976:31ff., we could say that causatives with total lack of control (e.g., qam't) or total control (of subject over object, in the form of relative ease of effort, e.g., k'áx-an') are 'manipulative,' while cases with shared control (e.g., x̌'iq-s, xáx̌'-xal-s) are 'directive.'

7 Many cases of -s seem to have an instantaneous aspectual tinge (e.g., qam't-s, x̌'iq-s, the latter referring to the actual delivery of smt. or smb., not to the being under way with smt. or smb.), while N often refers to a continuous action (e.g., k'áx-an'). However, we also have -s on verbs expressing continuous action (e.g., x̌'ak-s 'to take along (be underway with).' Also, it is precisely -s that is required by the stative prefix s- (see Section 18.8). The Lillooet information on -s and aspect is thus problematic, but in general in Salish the use of -s is partly a matter of aspect (see also Kinkade 1982).

8 S.C. Dik (personal communication, 1984) points out that ʔúm'-ən, sqʷéqʷʔ-ən, kʷútən-s, etc. may be called inherently three-place verbs, versus derived three-place verbs with -xit.

9 Note that usually the idea of 'talking (reporting, squealing) on or about smb.' is expressed by -min/-min' (e.g., pták'ʷt-min, sqʷáľ-min') rather than by N (as in máw-an).

10 The function of -xal in these cases is not different from that after plain stems.

11 We do not have -s on these nominal stems if they are not followed by -cút. Note also the difference in transitivizer between sama?-nún 'to think smb. is a white person (sáma?)' versus sama?-s-cút 'to pretend to be a white person.' The use of -nun versus -s here appears again to be a matter of objective versus subjective reasoning (see discussion on control in Section 18.1.3): in the case of sama?-nún one can test whether smb. is indeed a white person, while in the case of sama?-s-cút the matter is very subjective.

12 The choice of -an before -cút is not caused by the fact that -s-cút is already used in a specialized meaning (Section 18.6[1]). Since -s can have both function 1 and function 3 when -cút does not follow, there is no reason why -s should not have both functions before -cút (as the data show, however, the presence of -cút does not limit -s to function 3).

13 In van Eijk 1985 and van Eijk 1990a, the transitivizer -s is analyzed as indicating 'neutral control,' while forms with the stative prefix s- are analyzed as indicating control. As the discussion in Section 18 shows, I no longer support this analysis.

14 In descriptions of other Salish languages, it is the beneficiary/recipient that is called the direct object, and what is presented to the beneficiary/recipient is called the indirect object (in a number of languages, the complement expressing the latter is accompanied by an 'oblique' marker; for details see Thompson 1979b:741-743). Lillooet does not use an oblique marker on the object that is presented to the beneficiary/recipient, and the function of -xit can be adequately described by using 'indirect' and 'direct' object in their traditional sense.

Section 19

1 The fact that n- does not combine with pápla? suggests that it is associated more with plurality than with 'persons.'

2 From SM I also recorded ka?+ás instead of ka+ás on a number of occasions. The recordings of ka?+ás might be accidents, but they might also represent an archaic form of the numeral 3 (in CdA, 'three' is čí?+es, in Kal. it is če?+és). Besides n-x̌ʷə-x̌ʷ?úcin and n-kə-ka+ás, I also recorded n-x̌ʷa-x̌ʷ?úcin and n-ka-ka+ás in rather deliberate speech. Besides x̌ʷ?úcin, one also hears x̌?úcin, which represents an older pronunciation (cf. Squamish x̌a?úcin, Halkomelem x̌ə?áθəl).

3 For the absence of s- from kʷ̩ən-q'ə́m'q'm'əp-s (*kʷ̩s-ən-q'ə́m'q'm'əp-s expected), see Section 10.1.7.

4 pála? irregularly retains the stress with a number of suffixes. For example, in pál?-aləqʷ we would have expected the stress to fall on -aləqʷ since in the underlying form pála?-alqʷ the sequence lqʷ counts as a vowel (see Section 2.1[2] and [4]). Note also pál?-ulwi+ 'one container, conveyance,' pál?-usa? 'one piece of fruit, one potato, one dollar' (and cases with other suffixes).

5 nukʷ also means 'other.' The meaning 'some' appears in sentences such as ?i̠núkʷ̩a +əl̠kizá 'some of these (kizá)' (?i̠...̩a article 'plural, present, known,' +əl̠ 'of, from').

Section 20

1 The term 'relator-verb' is from Kuipers 1967:153. Morphologically and syntactically, relator-verbs are not different from other Lillooet verbs. They are treated as a separate group only because semantically (at least from an English point of view) they are rather special.

Section 21

1 The difference between qʷal and qʷaĺ is not conditioned by the formations in which these roots occur, i.e., ka-...̩a and total reduplication do not have a deglottalizing effect, and -ut and s- do not have a glottalizing effect.

2 A few examples with ka-qʷál̩a are: x̌ʷ?az̩ kʷas̠ka-qʷál̩a 'he couldn't say anything' (x̌ʷ?az̩ 'not'), ka-qʷál̩a̠ma+ lákʷu? 'say something! (don't just sit there!)' (̩ma+ adhortative; lákʷu? '[t]here' [see Section 26.1]).

3 An example with qʷəl-qʷál is x̌ʷ?az̩ kʷas̠qʷəl-qʷál 'he is kind of quiet' (literally, 'he doesn't speak').

4 Traditionally, one would ask for a woman's hand through a third party, hence one would 'ask about' a woman by asking her hand. See also Hill-Tout (in Maud 1978:105).

5 I do not know whether qʷaĺ-út-tən is a careless speech variant of n-qʷaĺ-út-tən (see Section 15.1.2), or whether we have in fact qʷaĺ-út-tən besides n-qʷaĺ-út-tən, each form selecting some of the meanings given for both. For a comparable problem, see also n. 2 of section 15, and Section 15.2(9.1).

6 The form s-qʷáqʷəĺ is both nominal and verbal. The nominal form may be considered to have the nominalizer s- merged with stative s-, thereby becoming indistinguishable from the verbal form.

7 For the interplay between tenses and aspects, see Comrie 1981:66-86.

8 In its broadest sense, Lillooet 'aspect' also includes the use of certain auxiliaries, such as waʔ 'to be (busy with, involved in)' (Section 22.4), and the use of certain enclitics, e.g., ˍtuʔ 'definite past' (Section 32.1.2).

9 For a discussion of the aspectual system of another Salish language (Songish), see Raffo 1971.

10 Control is also an important category in, for example, Austronesian languages. For instance, Ulu Muar Malay (as described in Hendon 1966) has a prefix to- (often in the shape t-) that indicates that 'an action is performed or that a condition comes about through no volition of the subject, or, if the subject is inanimate, through no volition of the person who is somehow involved in the situation,' as in tkono 'is victimized, is hoodwinked' (kono 'is caught, is hit, comes into contact with'). Similarly, Javanese has kegoreng 'fried by accident (together with other things)' (Uhlenbeck 1980:72), besides goreng 'fried.' (Because of font limitations, certain diacritics written in the sources of these examples are omitted.)

Section 22

1 The suffix -wit competes most strongly with -tan-i in the indicative (simple and complex) paradigms (some speakers even prefer -wit over -tan-i here after type I transitivizers). In the other paradigms, -tan-i is favoured.

2 On the basis of the fact that the Lillooet passive consists of an object suffix followed by an ending that takes the subject suffix slot, one could argue that here we do not have a passive at all but an indefinite subject paradigm. This is the position taken by Thompson and Thompson 1992 for the functionally (and partially etymologically) corresponding paradigm in Thompson. The situation is comparable to, for example, Cree (Algonquian), which has a paradigm that can be described as 'indefinite actor' (Ahenakew 1987:137-139) or as passive (Dahlstrom 1991:51-52).

3 We could argue that the intransitive subject suffixes (and, in the transitive paradigm, also the 1S and 2SP subject suffixes) are in fact enclitics, in that they select the first of two variable words (the auxiliary), whereas 3SP transitive subject markers are true suffixes in that they remain on the verb base. There is a difference between the intransitive subject suffixes and 1S/2SP transitive subject suffixes versus enclitics, however: suffixes by definition may not follow an invariable word, whereas enclitics may do so. There is also a stress difference between the suffixes and the enclitics (see Section 2.2). Note that the suffixes that follow the auxiliary (always an intransitive stem) are either exclusively intransitive or neutral as to (in)transitivity. The suffixes that stay on the verb base are precisely the ones that are exclusively transitive. Remarkable is the case of -as (3S subject), which moves to the auxiliary in an intransitive form (i.e., in the subjunctive [a] and [b] paradigm; see Section 22.4.1[a]), while it stays on the verb base when it is transitive (at least in the indicative paradigm; in the subjunctive [a] and [b] transitive complex paradigm, one has intransitive [subjunctive] -as on the auxiliary, and transitive -as on the verb base – see Section 32.5[e]).

4 There is some confusion as to which (in)transitive forms of 2P imperative (those with wáʔˍmaɫ X-wi/-i/-twi or with wáʔ-wiˍmaɫ X) are the more correct. The consultants select their favourite forms from the paradigm (one preferring wáʔˍmaɫ X-wi/-i/-twi, the other wáʔ-wiˍmaɫ X). The situation here is different from the declarative intransitive, where wáʔ-wit X and waʔ X-wit are used with equal frequency and are considered to be equally correct. I also recorded (with núkʷʔan 'to help, tr.') the pleonastic forms wáʔ-wiˍmaɫ nukʷʔan-c-ál-i (2P-1S), wáʔ-wiˍmaɫ nukʷʔan-túmul-i (2P-1P), and wáʔ-wiˍmaɫ núkʷʔan-i (2P-3S), and a special form for 2P-3P: wáʔ-wiˍmaɫ núkʷʔan-wit. I am at present unable to determine how correct these forms are.

5 As a rule, intransitive complement forms are based on the 3S indicative form. However, we do have a few cases based on the 3S subjunctive forms, all with stam' 'what?' or swat 'who?' (see also Section 24.2), e.g., tiˍstam'-asˍáˍk'a 'something, whatever it is' (ˍk'a indicates surmise).

6 S.C. Dik (personal communication, 1984) points out that instead of 'factualization' one could use the (perhaps better) term 'action nominalization.' Dik gives the following schema for English: (1) Agent nominalization: the catcher of the tiger, the one who caught

the tiger; (2) Patient nominalization: the thing caught by Peter; (3) Action nominalization: the catching of the tiger by Peter, Peter's catching of the tiger. For Lillooet, we could consider cases like s-cut 'what is said' as patient nominalizations (in this book they are simply called 'nominalizations'). The form t̠ən-s-cút̠a 'the fact that I said' would then be an action nominalization. Dik also remarks that 'it is a recurrent feature of Action Nominalizations that the central arguments (Agent and/or Patient) get possessive expression.' This holds for the intransitive factualizations (action nominalizations) in Lillooet.

Section 24

1 The Squamish counterparts to s-núwa and s-nulák are nəw and nə́wyap (Kuipers 1967:142). Instead of s-nulák I also heard in a hymn s-niw-lák (for i < ə see Section 7.2). Although u in s-núwa and s-nulák can thus be proven to go back to əw, it is no longer pronounced əw (for the opposition between u and əw, see Section 1.9.4).

2 For the use of -ɬk-an (rather than -k-an) in nk'yáp-ɬk-an, see Section 22.5.4.

3 This sentence was recorded in a hymn, where the word stəx̌ʷ was pronounced ʔəstíx̌ʷ (s > ʔəs in order to create an extra syllable needed by the melodical line; for ə > i see n. 1 above and Section 7.2).

4 The use of x̌ʷʔáz-as in combination with the complex form kʷaɬap̠ is somewhat unusual (see last paragraph of Section 22.4.4).

Section 25

1 The Lillooet system of demonstrative pronouns partially resembles Latin *hic ~ iste ~ ille*. However, 'that' and 'those' (ti?, ʔiz̓, ni?, nəɬ) may refer both to objects close to the addressee (like Latin *iste*) and to objects close to a third person (like Latin *ille*).

Section 26

1 Since lá-ti?, lá-kʷu? are often associated with the addressee, they are often best translated as 'there.' In the same way, other forms with -ti?, -kʷu? (see Section 26.1.2) are also often translated as 'from there,' 'that way,' rather than 'from here,' 'this way.'

2 Note the resemblance between lá-ni? and lá-kʷu?, and between ɬlá-ni? and ɬlá-kʷu?. The form *ʔá-ni? for 'up to that time' (parallelling ʔá-kʷu?) was rejected; kná-ni? was elicited, but is apparently used less often than piná-ni?.

3 The part kánmas in kánmas-as probably contains kánəm 'to do what?' (Section 20.1) and the 3S subjunctive subject suffix.

4 The suffix -s is probably the same as the possessive suffix 3S. It seems then that x̌ʷʔay-s forms a truncated s-construction, with loss of the factualizer s- parallelling the rather frequent loss of the nominalizer s- (see Section 9), and loss of the original function of the s-construction.

Section 29

1 The term 'sentence-equivalent' is chosen for lack of a better term. Note that from a Lillooet point of view, a term like x̌ʷʔaz 'not' is not different from a variable word like ƛ'ak 'to go' when both are used as predications, as in x̌ʷʔaz 'it is not the case' (Section 29.1[1a], [1b]), ƛ'ak 'he goes.'

Section 30

1 There is an accompanying gesture to this expression, in which one curves the index finger and middle finger (which are pressed together side by side) and thrusts one's hand down. For a description of the same gesture among the Flathead (where it is used only by women), see Turney-High 1937:45.

Section 31

1 The use of 'collective' ki̠ (i.e., not the variant of ʔi̠ after prepositions) is generally limited to 'natural' collectives, such as tobacco, meat, potatoes, berries, etc.; ki̠ was not recorded with terms for typically individual entities, such as 'man,' etc.

2 Sometimes kʷ̠ is dropped, e.g., wa? kʷ̠zúsəm s-John, or the whole combination kʷ̠s- is

dropped, e.g., wa? kʷˇzúsəm John. The dropping of kʷˇ or kʷˇs- is generally considered somewhat substandard.

3 Note that wiˍ combines with single pet-names, as in (d) to (f), but that we must have different proper nouns before wiˍ can be used; see (b). For 'the Mitchells' I recorded ?iˍMitchellˍa (with ?iˍ..ˍa instead of wiˍ), and for 'Bill and my wife' (proper noun plus regular noun) I recorded wiˍs-Bill múta? tiˍn-səm?ámˍa.

4 Note also the fixed combinations kʷuˍxá?ˍa kʷúkʷpəy' 'God, the Lord' (xa? 'high,' kʷúkʷpəy' 'chief'), kʷuˍxá?ˍa tmixʷ 'Heaven' (tmixʷ 'land'), kʷuˍƛ'épˍa ʕʷəlp 'Hell' (ƛ'əp 'deep,' ʕʷəlp 'fire'). These forms are often quoted xa?ˍaˍkʷúkʷpəy', xa?ˍaˍtmíxʷ, ƛ'əpˍaˍʕʷélp when cited as lexical entries.

Section 32

1 For double auxiliaries (such as kʷasˍhuy'ˍ), see also Section 22.4.1. I do not have enough examples of huz' as the second auxiliary to warrant a discussion of its behaviour there, but in Section 32.1.3(c) and in Section 32.5(q) and (r), it is proclitic (for huz' > huy' see Section 1.7.1).

2 I did not record any cases where ˍƛ'ɬ (Section 32.1.5) could attract the stress (so next to ˍkɬ we have ˍkéɬ, but next to ˍƛ'ɬ no * ˍƛ'éɬ).

3 In one case I recorded ˍxʷítˍa: nak'-alíc'?-am ?ayɬ niˍqéqcək-sˍa, səsq'ʷˈəz'-s-ásˍk'a, səsq'ʷˈəz'-sˍxʷítˍa 'so he changed (nak'-) his clothes (-alic'a?), her older brother (qéqcək), or was it her younger brother (sésq'ʷˈəz'), yes, it was her younger brother.' Perhaps the speaker's obvious confusion caused the use of ˍa in this uncommon position.

4 Note that ˍa as required by ka- appears after a later (not the first) word in a sentence in, for example, xʷˈ?əz kʷənswaˍka-c'uqʷaz'-ámˍa 'I am not (xʷˈ?əz) able to fish (c'úqʷaz'-am).'

5 The order subject-predicate in niˍn-sqácəz?ˍa kaˍɬˍzəwátn-as is highly unusual.

6 The form m?ám-min is the only form in my corpus that has initial RC [R̥C], rather than REC, in a root. It was recorded only in one story, where it may have resulted from dropping of initial s (cf. səm?ám 'wife') at high speed.

7 In fact, ML rejected (i) in a story by MLaR in favour of (f).

8 It seems that we may divide enclitics into four groups on the basis of their meanings and also with regard to the place they take in combinations: (1) 'validation of statement' enclitics (ˍan', ˍxʷiɬ, ˍqa?, ˍha, ˍkʷu?, ˍka, ˍk'a, ˍmaɬ, ˍwən, ˍwi?, ˍhəm'), which refer to the degree of certainty with which the speaker makes his statement; (2) temporal-aspectual enclitics (ˍƛ'ɬ, ˍkəɬ, ˍtu?), which refer to the time and mode in which an action is performed; (3) ˍƛ'u?, semantically almost all-embracing; and (4) ˍa, reinforcing, but mainly associated with type 1 enclitics ˍxʷiɬ and ˍqa?. Note that enclitics of types 1 and 4 are first in Figure 20, while enclitics of type 2 take the second position and type 3 is last (with ˍtu?, but it follows ˍtu? in most cases).

Section 33

1 Although ?əɬˍ translates as the English subordinating conjunction 'before,' from a Lillooet point of view it is coordinating (in that it does not require a kʷˍ, ɬˍ, or ?iˍ construction). In a number of cases, we can also translate ?əɬˍ as English coordinating '(and) then.'

2 Especially from an English point of view, kʷuˍ is a rather unusual conjunction. It is possible that kʷuˍ is somehow related to the article kʷuˍ (Section 31.1). However, the conjunction and the article should not be confused: the man in 33.2(a) is identified to the speaker, and semantically 33.2(a) is different from an identical construction with ʕélʕəl as predicate and kʷuˍsqáyxʷ (with the article kʷuˍ) as complement, which means 'an (absent, unknown) man is strong.' Certainly both the grammatical subject (and his manhood) of 33.2(b) are identified to the speaker: compare the latter sentence with 31.4(p), where what is communicated about the subject is still potential, and 31.4(q), where both the quality and the subject are identified. With its clear identification of both subject and ascribed quality, 33.2(b) is closer to 31.4(q) than to 31.4(p).

Section 34

1 It would be disadvantageous to consider lˍ, etc. in the local deictics as proclitics for two

reasons. First, they merge into new semantic units with the deictic roots (e.g., l-c?a 'in-this' > 'here'). The difference between l- and ḻ in a sense parallels that between English 'in' in 'in-law' (relative by marriage) and 'in' in 'in law and in life.' Second, if ḻ, etc. are considered proclitics, the elements la-, etc. in the 'non-pivoting' local deictics are also proclitics, which would be absurd – they are stressed but the conditions under which enclitics receive stress, i.e., extensive additions (see Section 2.2), do not apply here; or we must accept the idea that the pivoting local deictics take proclitics and the non-pivoting ones take prefixes.

Section 35

1 For a definition of 'full sentence,' see Bloomfield (1933:172): 'when a favorite sentence-form is used as a sentence, this is a full sentence.'
2 For subject, passive, imperative, and object suffixes, see Section 22.3.1 to 22.3.5.
3 For the structure of complements based on variable words, see Sections 22.6 and 22.7. For substitutes of such complements, see Section 36.1.1.
4 For enclitics and full-word adverbs, see Sections 32 and 28.2, respectively.
5 Simple subjunctive (c) predicates (as discussed in Sections 22.3.1 and 22.3.2) without the conjunctions ɬ, and ?iḻ (Section 22.3.1) yield optative subjunctive (a) forms, which may occur as full mono-clausal sentences. However, complex subjunctive (c) forms (see Sections 22.4.1 and 22.4.2) never occur without the conjunctions ɬ, and ?iḻ, and they contain auxiliaries (ḻwanḻ, ḻwaxʷḻ, etc.) that may never be used in a main clause or mono-clausal sentence.

Section 36

1 The form *s-x̌ə́kḻha, instead of wá?ḻha s-x̌ək, was rejected.
2 The fact that in Section 24.1.1(r) we have a third person predicate based on a first person pronoun is peculiar from the English point of view but not from the Lillooet point of view: Lillooet personal pronouns combine only with 3S intransitive subject suffixes (see Section 24.1.1).
3 The relative rarity of sentences with both a subject and an object complement is not surprising: in natural language one mostly uses a personal pronominal element to indicate the person that is already in focus (as in 'where is your father?' – 'he is fixing the car'). In Lillooet such pronominal elements are expressed through the subject and object suffixes.
4 Where the complement is a personal pronoun, rather than a complement based on a variable word, this complement may refer to the subject even though the predicate refers to a third person object (as in Section 24.1.1[m], which then contrasts with [k] and [l] in this section), or it may refer to the object even though the predicate refers to a non-third person object (as in Section 24.1.1[q], which then contrasts with [m] in this section).
5 In texts the ratio PSO:POS is roughly 4:1, so PSO is the normal construction here. Where we have POS, the object has usually been referred to already and is in the focus of attention (as in [s]: in the story, the gun has been requested in the sentence that precedes [s]). As is the case with intransitive PO versus PS sentences (see [a] to [e] versus [f] and [g], the role of complements in transitive PSO versus POS sentences is rarely confusing, since it is clear who undergoes the action and who performs it. (For example, the coat in [o] cannot lose the child.) Sentences where subject and object can switch function (as in 'my father helps the chief') were not recorded in texts. Where they were elicited, the results were contradictory, and confusing to the consultants (who, when I read the sentences back, switched the roles of the complements without changing their order). In general, sentences with both a subject and an object seem 'atypical of at least many Salish languages' (Thompson 1979b:740-741, to whom I refer the reader for further information).
   The above observations on the ratio PSO:POS hold for my own research. Remarkably, in a recent teaching manual of the Lillooet language (Lillooet Tribal Council 1993), the ratio is dramatically reversed: of the twelve sentences with both a subject and an object complement that are given in that book, eleven have POS, and only one has PSO. Details of these data, and my preliminary conclusions, are given in van Eijk 1995.
6 In the text from which (ae) has been taken, (ae) is immediately followed by nx̌'ák'ʷxit-as

ʔi‿sʔixʷɬúlmʼəxʷ‿a 'he poured it out to the strangers (sʔixʷɬúlʼməxʷ)': here we have a single complement referring to the indirect object, in contrast to the regular cases (t) to (v), where the single complement refers to the direct object. However, the fact that the situation has already been clarified by the preceding sentence, i.e., (ae), makes this deviant use of a complement possible.

7 See, however, n. 6.

8 The 'present' article is used here, because the mother is still present (her dead body is found by the child who is the protagonist in the story from which this sentence is taken); cf. Section 31.3(o).

Section 37

1 It is possible that kʷ‿ is related to (or derived from) the attribute-connector kʷu‿ (Section 33.2). There seems to be a parallellism between cases like (a) and (b):
   (a) ʕəlʕəl-ɬkán kʷu‿sqáyxʷ 'I am a strong man' ('I am strong with regard to [being] a man')
   (b) x̌ʷəm kʷ‿s-cixʷ-s ʔúx̌ʷalʼ 'she got home fast' ('it was fast with regard to the fact of her getting home')

2 Sometimes the main predicate is not expressed, in which case we have forms like ɬ‿swát-as or ɬ‿stámʼ-as by themselves, as in Section 32.5.1(e), where we would expect something like xʷʔaz kʷənswa‿zəwátən (such a form is present in Section 32.5.1[f]).

3 ML informs me that, instead of ʔi‿kánmas-as, some speakers use ni‿kánmas-as (the conjunction ni‿ is not used with other words). However, ML prefers ʔi‿kánmas-as.

Section 38

1 From an English point of view, (b) and (c) might seem to have a totally different internal structure, (b) containing an attribute (ʕélʕəl) and (c) an adjunct (núkʷʔan-c-as). However, from a Lillooet point of view they are of the same structure. We could also bring out this similarity by translating (b) and (c) as 'the strong male' and 'the male me-helper,' respectively. In (b) and (c) the order of the elements is the same as in English ('strong' precedes 'man,' and 'man' precedes 'who helped me'). However, we have a non-English type of ordering in ni‿s-ʔumʼən-c-áxʷ‿a mʼémʼsməs 'the calf (mʼémʼsməs) which you (-axʷ) gave (ʔúmʼən) to me (-c)' (ni‿s-ʔumʼən-c-áxʷ‿a is an indirect object-centred form). This type of ordering, on the other hand, seems to be less usual than the one where a noun follows a constituent that translates as an English adjective, but precedes one that translates as an English adjunct phrase, as in (b) and (c). I do not know whether this preference represents a traditional Lillooet grammatical pattern or whether it has arisen under English influence.

2 In the case of ti‿pálʔ‿a skʷakst-s or ti‿pálʔ‿a x̌ʷuláka?-s, we could not have possessive affixes on pálaʔ anyway, because pálaʔ is an intransitive verb and these do not take possessive affixes (see Section 8.1.1). However, the attributes in (f) and (g) are nouns, and therefore in principle able to take possessive affixes (which they indeed take when they are themselves the nucleus of the complement).

3 For the presence of two different demonstrative pronouns in this sentence, see Section 25.1.1(o) and comments about it.

4 For this type of construction, where we have the same word in predicate and complement, which then expresses 'some(body),' note also waʔ ʔílal ti‿waʔ‿ʔílal 'there was somebody crying (ʔílal).'

5 Lillooet constructions where we have a noun in the predicate and a verbal construction in the complement, such as Section 8.1.2(l) and (n), could be translated as English pseudo-cleft sentences ('a coyote is what is going along,' 'a man is the one who helped me'), but from a Lillooet point of view they are no different from their non-cleft counterparts in Section 8.1.2(k) and (m).

6 A number of speakers (mainly younger ones) use an article on the adjunct after a demonstrative pronoun that is in focus (e.g., niɬ cʔa ti‿n-qmút‿a 'this is my [n-] hat [qmut],' instead of regular niɬ cʔa n-qmut). For an adjunct with article, see also nəɬ‿ʔáyn‿a in Section 32.1.11(g). Most older speakers disapprove of the article on an adjunct after a demonstrative pronoun.

Bibliography

Ahenakew, F. 1987. Cree language structures: a Cree approach. Winnipeg: Pemmican Publications.

Bloomfield, L. 1933. Language. New York: Holt.

Boas, F. 1918. Kutenai tales. Washington: Bureau of American Ethnology Bulletin 59.

Bouchard, R., and D.I.D. Kennedy. 1977. Lillooet stories. Victoria: Sound Heritage, Vol. VI, No. 1.

Broselow, E. 1983. Salish double reduplications: subjacency in morphology. Natural Language and Linguistic Theory 1:317-346.

Bybee, J.L. 1985. Morphology: a study of the relation between meaning and form. Amsterdam/Philadelphia: John Benjamins.

Carlson, B. F., and L.C. Thompson. 1982. Out of control in two (maybe more) Salish languages. Anthropological Linguistics 24:51-65.

Comrie, B. 1981. Aspect: an introduction to the study of verbal aspect and related problems. Cambridge: Cambridge University Press.

Czaykowska-Higgins, E. 1993. CVC reduplication in Moses-Columbia Salish. Pp. 47-72 of Mattina, A., and T. Montler (eds.), American Indian linguistics and ethnography in honor of Laurence C. Thompson. Missoula: University of Montana Occasional Papers in Linguistics, No. 10.

Dahlstrom, A. 1991. Plains Cree morphosyntax. New York/London: Garland.

Dixon, R.M.W. 1980. The languages of Australia. Cambridge: Cambridge University Press.

Duff, W. 1964. The Indian history of British Columbia. Volume I, The impact of the white man. Victoria: Anthropology in British Columbia Memoir 5.

Egesdal, S.M. 1992. Stylized characters' speech in Thompson Salish narrative. Missoula: University of Montana Occasional Papers in Linguistics, No. 9.

Elliott, W. 1931. Lake Lillooet tales. Journal of American Folklore 44:166-181.

Galloway, B.D. 1993. A grammar of Upriver Halkomelem. Berkeley: University of California Publications in Linguistics, Vol. 96.

Heffner, R.-M.S. 1960. General phonetics. Wisconsin: University of Wisconsin Press.

Heller, L.G., and J. Macris. 1967. Parametric linguistics. The Hague: Mouton.

Hendon, R.S. 1966. The phonology and morphology of Ulu Muar Malay. New Haven: Yale University Publications in Anthropology, No. 70.

Hess, T.M. 1966. Snohomish chameleon morphology. International Journal of American Linguistics 32:350-356.

-. 1982. Traces of 'abnormal' speech in Lushootseed. Working Papers for the 17th International Conference on Salish and Neighbouring Languages. Pp. 89-97. (Mimeograph)

Hill-Tout, C. 1905. Report on the Ethnology of the StlatlumH of British Columbia. Journal of the Anthropological Institute of Great Britain and Ireland, Vol. 35. (Republished without the linguistics sections, which constitute pp. 156-176 and 206-218 of the original, in Maud 1978)

Hogg, R., and C.B. McCully. 1987. Metrical phonology: a coursebook. Cambridge: Cambridge University Press.

Holmer, N.M. 1954. The Seneca language: a study in Iroquoian. Upsala, Sweden: Upsala Canadian Studies III.

Jelinek, E. 1990. Quantification in Straits Salish. Working Papers for the 25th International Conference on Salish and Neighbouring Languages. Pp. 177-195. (Mimeograph)

Jensen, J.T. 1990. Morphology: word structure in generative grammar. Amsterdam/Philadelphia: John Benjamins.

Joseph, M., J. van Eijk, G. Turner, and L. Williams. 1979. Cuystwi malh ucwalmicwts: ucwalmicwts curriculum for beginners. Mount Currie, B.C.: Ts'zil Publishing House.

Kinkade, M.D. 1963-64. Phonology and morphology of Upper Chehalis, I-IV. International Journal of American Linguistics 29:181-195, 345-356 (1963); 30:32-161, 251-260 (1964).

-. 1981. The source of the Upper Chehalis reflexive. International Journal of American Linguistics 47:336-339.

-. 1982. Columbian (Salish) C_2-reduplication. Anthropological Linguistics 24:66-71.

-. 1983. Salish evidence against the universality of 'noun' and 'verb.' Lingua 60:25-40.

Kroeber, P.D. 1988. Inceptive reduplication in Comox and Interior Salish. International Journal of American Linguistics 54:141-167.

Kuipers, A.H. 1967-69. The Squamish language: grammar, texts, dictionary, I-II. The Hague: Mouton.

-. 1973. About evidence for Proto-Salish *r. Dutch Contributions to the 8th International Conference on Salish Languages. Pp. 1-19. (Mimeograph)

-. 1974. The Shuswap language: grammar, texts, dictionary. The Hague: Mouton.

-. 1981. On reconstructing the Proto-Salish sound system. International Journal of American Linguistics 47:323-335.

-. 1982. Towards a Salish etymological dictionary II. Lingua 57:72-92.

Levine, R.D., and F. Cooper. 1976. The suppression of B.C. languages: filling in the gaps in the documentary record. Pp. 43-75 of Levine, R.D. (ed.), Native languages and culture. Victoria: Sound Heritage, Vol. IV, Nos. 3-4.

Li, F.K. 1946. Chipewyan. Pp. 398-423 of Osgood, C. (ed.), Linguistic structures of native America. New York: Viking Fund Publications in Anthropology, No. 6.

Lillooet Tribal Council. 1993. Introducing St'at'imcets (Fraser River Dialect): a primer. Lillooet: Lillooet Tribal Council.

Marouzeau, J. 1951. Lexique de la terminologie linguistique (3rd ed.). Paris: Paul Geuthner.

Martinet, A. 1964. Elements of general linguistics. London: Faber and Faber. (Original title: Elements de linguistique generale. Translated into English by E. Palmer.)

Matthews, P.H. 1991. Morphology (2nd ed.). Cambridge: Cambridge University Press.

Maud, R. 1978. The Salish people: the local contribution of Charles Hill-Tout. Vol. II, The Squamish and the Lillooet. Vancouver: Talonbooks.

Montler, T. 1986. An outline of the morphology and phonology of Saanich, North Straits Salish. Missoula: University of Montana Occasional Papers in Linguistics, No. 4.

Nater, H.F. 1984. The Bella Coola language. Ottawa: Canadian Ethnology Service, Paper No. 92.

O'Connor, J.D. 1973. Phonetics. Harmondsworth, England: Pelican Books.

Palmer, F. R. 1973. Grammar. Harmondsworth, England: Pelican Books.

Pinnow, H.-J. 1964. Die nordamerikanischen Indianersprachen: ein ueberblick ueber ihren Bau und ihre Besonderheiten. Wiesbaden, Germany: Otto Harrassowitz.

Raffo, Y.A. 1971. Songish aspectual system. Pp. 117-122 of Hoard, J.F., and T.M. Hess (eds.), Studies in Northwest Indian languages. Sacramento, Calif.: Sacramento Anthropological Society, Paper No. 11.

Sapir, E. 1915. Abnormal types of speech in Nootka. Ottawa: Canada Department of Mines. Geological Survey, Memoir 62, No. 5, Anthropological Series.

-. 1921. Language: an introduction to speech. New York: Harcourt, Brace and World. Copyright renewed 1949.

Shibatani, M. 1976. The grammar of causative constructions: a conspectus. Pp. 1-40 of Shibatani, M. (ed.), The grammar of causative constructions. Syntax and Semantics, Vol. 6. Academic Press.

Teit, J.A. 1906. The Lillooet Indians. The Jesup North Pacific Expedition, Vol. 2, Part V. Reprinted by AMS Press (New York), 1975.

-. 1912. Traditions of the Lillooet Indians of British Columbia. Journal of American Folklore 25:287-371.

Thompson, L.C. 1979a. The control system: a major category in the grammar of Salishan languages. Pp. 154-176 of Efrat, B.S. (ed.), The Victoria conference on northwestern languages. Victoria: British Columbia Provincial Museum Heritage Record No. 4.

-. 1979b. Salishan and the northwest. Pp. 692-765 of Campbell, L., and M. Mithun (eds.), The languages of native America: historical and comparative assessment. Austin/London: University of Texas Press.

-. 1981. More on the control system of Thompson Salish. Pp. 126-131 of Mattina, A., and T. Montler (eds.), The working papers of the 16th International Conference on Salish languages. Missoula: University of Montana Occasional Papers in Linguistics, No. 2.

-. 1985. Control in Salish grammar. Pp. 391-428 of Planck, F. (ed.), Relational typology. The Hague: Mouton.

Thompson, L.C., and M.T. Thompson. 1992. The Thompson language. Missoula: University of Montana Occasional Papers in Linguistics, No. 8.

Turner, N.J. 1978. Food plants of British Columbia Indians. Part 2, Interior peoples. Victoria: British Columbia Provincial Museum Handbook 36.

-. 1979. Plants in British Columbia Indian technology. Victoria: British Columbia Provincial Museum Handbook 38.

Turney-High, H.H. 1937. The Flathead Indians of Montana. Menasha, Wisconsin: Memoirs of the American Anthropological Association, No. 48.

Uhlenbeck, E.M. 1980. Taalwetenschap: een eerste inleiding. The Hague: De Nederlandse Boek- en Steendrukkerij v/h H.L. Smits.

-. 1992. General linguistics and the study of morphological processes. Oceanic Linguistics 31:1-11.

van Eijk, J.P. 1978. Ucwalmicwts. Mount Currie, B.C.: Ts'zil Publishers.

-. 1981. Cuystwi malh ucwalmicwts: ucwalmicwts curriculum for advanced learners. Mount Currie, B.C.: Ts'zil Publishing House.

-. 1985. The Lillooet language: phonology, morphology, syntax. Ph.D. dissertation, University of Amsterdam.

-. 1988. Lillooet forms for 'pretending' and 'acting like.' International Journal of American Linguistics 54:106-110.

-. 1989. Coyote verdrinkt. Wampum 9:50-63.

-. 1990a. Intransitivity, transitivity and control in Lillooet Salish. Pp. 47-64 of Pinkster, H., and I. Genee (eds.), Unity in diversity: papers presented to Simon C. Dik on his 50th birthday. Dordrecht, Netherlands: Foris Publications.

-. 1990b. VC reduplication in Salish. Anthropological Linguistics 32:228-262.

-. 1993a. (Review of The Thompson language, by L.C. Thompson and M.T. Thompson.) American Culture and Research Journal 17:236-244.

-. 1993b. CVC reduplication and infixation in Lillooet. Pp. 317-326 of Mattina, A. and T. Montler (eds.), American Indian linguistics and ethnography in honor of Laurence C. Thompson. Missoula: University of Montana Occasional Papers in Linguistics, No. 10.

-. 1995. POS and PSO in Lillooet. Paper submitted to the 30th International Conference on Salish and Neighbouring Languages.

-. CVC reduplication in Salish. In Czaykowska-Higgins, E., and M.D. Kinkade (eds.), Salish languages and linguistics: current theoretical and descriptive perspectives. Berlin/New York: Mouton de Gruyter (in press).

van Eijk, J.P., and T.M. Hess. 1986. Noun and verb in Salish. Lingua 69:319-331.

van Eijk, J.P., and L. Williams (eds.). 1981. Cuystwi malh ucwalmicwts: Lillooet legends and stories. Mount Currie, B.C.: Ts'zil Publishing House.

Welmers, W.E. 1973. African language structures. Berkeley: University of California Press.

Williams, L. (ed.). 1981. Cuystwi malh ucwalmicwts: ucwalmicwts curriculum for intermediates. Mount Currie, B.C.: Ts'zil Publishing House.

Index

References are by section rather than page. However, in the case of a reference to an item that occurs on only one page of a section, the page number is given as well. The term *intro* in parentheses after a section number refers to the introductory remarks of a section.

Abstract suffixes, 8.1, 16; and (in)transitivizers, 18.5

Adhortative: adhortative enclitic ‿maⁱ, 32.1.1; use of adhortative ‿maⁱ in command forms, 22.3.5, 22.4.4

Adjective, 8.1.1

Adjunct, 37.4.1, 38.5, 38.5 n. 6

Adverbial elements. *See* Adverbs

Adverbs: demonstrative adverbs, 26; full-word conjunctions and adverbs (particles), 28; word order: adverbial elements, 36.1.2; enclitics as adverbs, 32 (intro); numerical adverbs, 19.4.2; numerical-distributive adverbs, 19.4.3

Affixation: status of affixation in morphology, 1.6, 8 (intro), 8.1; affixation in local deictics, 26.1.2. *See also* Infixation, Personal affixation, Prefixation, Suffixation

Affricates: glottalized uvular plosives as affricates, 1.9.1; articulation of the affricate c, 1.9.1

Ambifix, 15.1.2

Anticipatory pronoun, 24.5

Aphaeresis: and syncope, 7.1

Articles, 31; in combination with focusing elements, 38.5

Aspect: general information, 8.1 (p. 42); survey of aspectual operations, 21.2

Aspectual suffixes, 8.1, 14

Aspirated (plosives), 1.9.1

Attribute, 33.2, 38.2 (p. 239)

Attribute-connector, 33.2

Auxiliaries: word order, 36.1.3; types and use, 36.2

Bilabial: bilabial articulation of w w̓, 1.3

Borrowings: retention of y y̓ in, 1.7.1; treatment of, 7.5

Cardinals: and numerical substitutes, 19.1

Causative constructions, 18.1.4 (p. 116)

Causativization, 18.1.3

Centrifugal (prepositions), 34.1

Centripetal (prepositions), 34.1

Characteristic (reduplication), 12.5.1 n. 16

Cleft constructions, 38.5

Clitics: status of, in morphology, 1.6, 8 (intro); general information and difference with affixes, 8.3. *See also* Enclitics, Proclitics

Close contact, 1.4, 1.9.3

Closure: incomplete closure in glottalized resonants, 1.9.2

Clusters. *See* Consonant clusters

Collectivity (as expressed by initial or total reduplication), 12.2 (p. 57), 12.5

Complements: personal affixation: predicates and complements, 8.1.2; summary of complements, nominal forms and factual forms, 22.8; complex complements (in combination with articles), 31.6.2; word order: subject and object complements, 36.1.1; structure of complex complements, 38.2; possessive complements, 38.3

Compounding: status of, in morphology, 1.6, 8.1; functions and formal aspects of, 11

Conjunctions: full-word conjunctions and adverbs (particles), 28; proclitic, 33

Connectives, 15.3

Consonant clusters: occurrence and avoidance of, 1.7; cluster-avoidance in relation to the distribution of schwa, 3; stress rules and, 2.1 (p. 15)

Consonant reduplication, 12.4; interior glottalization and, 13.1.3; and (in)transitivizers, 18.1.1 (p. 109), 18.1.2 (p. 110). *See also* Reduplication

Consonants: general information on, 1 (intro); neutralization between un-rounded and rounded consonants, 1.8.3; morphophonemic changes of, 4.4. *See also* Consonant clusters, Obstruents, Resonants

Continued state, 14.2, 14.3

Control: general information on, 8.1 (p. 42); and transitivizers, 18.1.3; survey of control operations, 21.3

Coronal, 1.7.1

Creaky voice, 1.9.2

Deictics: deictic roots in demonstrative pronouns, 25; deictic roots in demon-strative adverbs, 26

Declarative: simple intransitive declara-tive paradigm, 22.3.1; simple transitive declarative paradigm, 22.3.2; complex declarative intransitive forms, 22.4.1; complex declarative transitive forms, 22.4.2

Deglottalization, 12.3 (p. 59), 12.4 (p. 61), 12.5 (p. 62)

Demonstrative adverbs, 26

Demonstrative pronouns, 25; combina-tions of enclitics with, 32.4.2; and focus-ing elements, 38.5

Dental: dental articulation of z z', 1.2; dental articulation of dental phonemes, 1.4; dental glides, 1.2. *See also* Dentals

Dental-alveolar (articulation of palatals), 1.9.1

Dentals (dental consonants): classification of, 1.4; phonetic influence of dentals on neighbouring vowels, 1.9.3. *See also* Den-tal

Derivation, 8.1 n. 1

Dialect: basic differences between Mount Currie and Fountain dialects, p. xxi; ar-ticulation of z z' in Fountain and Mount Currie dialects, 1.2; neutralization of vowels before z z' in Fountain and Mount Currie dialects, 1.8.1; total redu-plication of 'grandmother' in Fountain dialect, 12.5 (p. 62); use of auxiliaries in Mount Currie and Fountain dialects,

22.4.1 (p. 153); different articles in Mount Currie and Fountain dialects, 31.1; use of ˌwən versus ˌwiʔ in Mount Currie and Fountain dialects, 31.1.15

Diminutiveness, 12.4

Direct objects: and -xit, 18.1.4 (pp. 115-16); and word order, 36.1.1

Directive (transitivizers), 18.1.4 (pp. 115-16)

Distribution: of phonemes, 1.7; of schwa, 3; of intransitivizers and transitivizers, 18.1.5; of (in)transitivizers: special cases, 18.1.6

Dynamic (prepositions), 34.1

Ejectives: glottalized plosives as ejectives, 1.9.1; glottalized resonants not as ejec-tives, 1.9.2

Elision: of schwa (ə ə̣), 1.6, 3.2; elision of stem-final -as, 4.3

Enclitics: status of, in morphology, 1.6; general information and difference with suffixes, 8.3; functions and formal aspects of, 32; movement of the stress in combinations with, 1.5, 2.2

Epenthesis: of schwa (ə ə̣), 1.6; vowel-consonant alternations and h-epenthesis, 4.1; phonetics of vowels that result from, 1.9.3

Evasive pronouns, 24.3

Exclamations: greetings, exclamations, and interjections, 30

Factual. *See* Factualization

Factualization: status of, in stem forma-tion, 8.1; general information on, 8.1.3; and personal affixation, 22

Final reduplication, 12.3. *See also* Redupli-cation

Focus (and passive constructions), 38.1

Focusing elements, 38.5

Fountain dialect. *See* Dialect

Fricative off-glide (in glottalized uvular plosives), 1.9.1

Fricatives. *See* Glides

Glides: classification of dental, velar, and uvular glides, 1.2; dental, velar, and uvu-lar glides as voiced and lax fricatives, 1.2; pharyngeal glides, 1.2

Glottal release, 1.9.1

Glottal stop (ʔ): classification of ʔ as reso-nant, 1.3; frequent occurrence of ʔ word-initially, 1.7; alternation of ʔ with aʔ and ʔa, 3.5

Glottalized plosives: phonetics of, 1.9.1

Glottalized resonants: glottalized versus

plain resonants, 1.2; morphological status of, 1.6; non-occurrence of glottalized resonants word-initially, 1.7; phonetics of, 1.9.2. *See also* Resonant-glottalization

Greetings: greetings, exclamations, and interjections, 30

Hiatus (occasionally in geminated resonants), 1.9.2

High (quality of vowels), 1.9.3

Hypocoristic, 15.2 (pp. 94, 95, 100), 27.1

Idiolect: use of z and y as a factor of idiolect, 1.7.1; presence of schwa as a factor of idiolect, 3.3.1 (p. 21); total reduplication as a factor of idiolect, 12.5 (p. 62); distribution of n- as a factor of idiolect, 15.1.2

Immediate constituent (IC), 15.1.1, 15.1.2; consonant reduplication and interior glottalization, 13.1.3, 13.1.3 n. 2; total reduplication and consonant reduplication (12.5)

Imperative: simple imperative (intransitive and transitive) paradigm, 22.3.5; complex imperative forms, 22.4.4; imperatives 1P, 22.5.1; imperative stems, 22.5.2

Inchoative: inchoative suffix -wil'x and retraction, 1.1; inchoative function of interior glottalization, 13 (intro); inchoative function of -p, 14.1; semantic (inchoative) function of -wil'x, 16.1 (p. 104)

Incipient state, 14 (intro)

Indefinite local deictics, 26.1.4

Indefinite pronouns, 24.4

Indefinite quantifiers, 19.3

Indicative: subjunctive versus indicative paradigms, 8.1.2 (p. 45), 22; enclitics after indicative and subjunctive forms, 32.5; neutralization of subjunctive and indicative paradigms, 32.5.1

Indirect objects: and -xit, 18.1.4 (pp. 115-16); and word order, 36.1.1 (pp. 229-30)

Indirect object-centred forms (nominalized transitives), 22.7

Indirective (transitivizers), 18.1.4 (pp. 115-16)

Infixation: and reduplication, 12 n. 1; interior glottalization as infixation, 13 (intro)

Inflection, 8.1 n. 1

Ingressive, 13 (intro)

Initial reduplication, 12.2. *See also* Reduplication

Interdental (pronunciation), 1.2

Interior glottalization: status of, in morphology, 1.6, 8 (intro), 8.1; function and formal aspects of, 13

Interjections: greetings, exclamations, and interjections, 30

Internal sandhi, 4; unique case of, 12.2 (p. 58)

Interrogative: verbs, 20.1; pronouns, 24.2; local deictics, 26.1.4; enclitic ˌha, 32.1.12

Intransitive: simple intransitive declarative paradigm, 22.3.1; complex declarative intransitive forms, 22.4.1. *See also* Intransitivization, Intransitivizers

Intransitivization: transposition and (in)transitivization, 8.1.1, 21.4. *See also* Intransitive, Intransitivizers

Intransitivizers: and transitivizers, 8.1, 18; possible relationship between intransitivizer -əm and aspectual suffix -əm, 14.2; retraction of, 5.2. *See also* Intransitive, Intransitivization

Invariable words. *See* Word

Labials (labial consonants): and close contact, 1.4; phonetic influence of, on neighbouring vowels, 1.9.3

Laryngeal: resonants, 1.3. *See also* Laryngeal fricative

Laryngeal fricative (h): classification of h as resonant, 1.3; limited occurrence of h, 1.7; epenthesis of h, and vowel-alternation of h, 4.1

Lateral: release (release through lateral resonants), 1.4. *See also* Laterals

Laterals (lateral consonants): Classification of, 1.4; phonetic influence of non-velarized laterals on neighbouring vowels, 1.9.3. *See also* Lateral

Lax (articulation of glides), 1.2

Length (of vowels), 1.9.3. *See also* Rhetorical lengthening

Lexical suffixes: status of, in stem formation, 8.1; consonant clusters in (re stress rules), 2.1 (p. 15); and retraction, 5.2; functions and formal aspects of, 15; and proper nouns, 27.1

Long (pronunciation): obstruents pronounced long, 1.9.1; resonants pronounced long, 1.9.2

Main (clause), 35

Morphemes. *See* Morphology

Morphology, 8-34; introduction to, 8

Morphophonemic: general discussion of morphophonemic changes, 1.6;

morphophonemic changes of consonants, 4.4. *See also* Internal Sandhi, Resonant-glottalization

Mount Currie dialect. *See* Dialect

Neutral suffixes, 15.2

Neutralization: of phonemes, 1.8; between vowel-resonant sequences and vowels, 1.9.4; of subjunctive and indicative paradigms, 32.5.1

Nicknames, 27.1

Nominal stems: nominal versus verbal stems, 8.1.1; and (in)transitivizers, 18.5; summary of complements, nominal forms, and factual forms, 22.8

Nominalization. *See* Nominal stems, Nominalizer, Nominalizing suffixes

Nominalizer: nominalizer s-, 9; retraction of the nominalizer s-, 5.3

Nominalizing suffixes, 15.2

Non-retracted. *See* Retracted

Non-somatic suffixes: and (in)transitivizers, 18.3

Nouns: absence of noun-verb distinction on syntactic level, 8.1.2 (p. 45). *See also* Nominal stems, Proper nouns

Numerals: and numerical substitutes, 19

Numerical adverbs. *See* Adverbs

Numerical-distributive adverbs. *See* Adverbs

Numerical substitutes. *See* Substitutes

Nursery talk, 7.4

Object complements. *See* Complements

Object suffixes: general information on, 8.1; different object suffixes depending on transitivizers, 18 (intro, p.108); different functions of, 18.1.4 (p. 115); functions and formal aspects of, 22

Object-centred forms: object- and subject-centred forms, 22.6; object- and subject-centred forms with focusing elements, 38.5

Obstruents: general information on, 1 (intro); phonetic data, 1.9.1; schwa and obstruents, 3.3; -4k suffixes after obstruents, 22.5.4

Off-glide. *See* Fricative off-glide

Ongoing state, 14 (intro)

Onomatopoetic, 12.5.1 (p. 66)

Optative, 22.3.1 (p. 147)

Oral release (of glottalized plosives), 1.9.1

Ordinals, 19.4

Palatals (palatal consonants): classification of, 1.4; dental-alveolar articulation of palatals before t, 1.9.1; phonetic influence of palatals on neighbouring vowels, 1.9.3

Particles: full-word conjunctions and adverbs (particles), 28

Passive: passive forms from verbalized nominal stems, 18.4; simple passive paradigm, 22.3.4; complex passive paradigm, 22.4.3; use of the passive, 38.1; stress rules and the passive-former -əm, 2.1 (p. 16)

Personal affixation: general information, 8.1; predicates and complements, 8.1.2; functions and formal aspects of, 22

Personal pronouns: and related substitutes, 24; in complements, 38.4; and focusing elements, 38.5

Pet-names, 27.3; and focusing elements, 38.5

Pharyngeal (glides), 1.2

Pharyngealization, 1.9.4

Phonemes: general information and phonetic data, 1 (intro); retracted versus non-retracted (general information), 1.1; classification of sets of phonemes, 1.2, 1.3, 1.4; distribution of, 1.7; neutralization of, 1.8; retracted phonemes, 5

Phonetic data: phonemes, general information and phonetic data, 1(intro); phonetic effects of retraction, 1.1; phonetic aspects of dental, velar, and uvular glides, 1.2; phonetic aspects of laryngeal, velar, and uvular resonants, 1.3; phonetic aspects of dentals, laterals, and palatals, 1.4; phonetic data: details and special questions, 1.9; phonetics of obstruents, 1.9.1; phonetics of resonants, 1.9.2; phonetics of vowels, 1.9.3, 13.1.2; phonetics of vowel-resonant sequences, 1.9.4

Phonetics. *See* Phonetic data

Phonology, 1-7

Pivoting (deictics), 23, 26.1

Plain (non-glottalized) consonants, Figure 1 (p. 2)

Plain stems (and [in]transitivizers), 18.1

Plain (transitivizers), 18.1.4 (pp. 115-16)

Plosives: phonetics of, 1.9.1

Plural: and singular in personal affixation, 8.1 (p. 41), 22; and singular in personal pronouns, 24; and singular in demonstrative pronouns, 25; and singular in articles, 31; single expression of the plural, 38.4; plurality as expressed by initial or total reduplication, 12.2 (p. 57), 12.5

Plurality. *See* Plural

Polysyllabic, 1.5

Possessive: affixes, 22.1; paradigm, 22.2; personal pronouns and predicates with a possessive marker, 24.1.2; possessive substitutes, 24.4; syntactic aspects of possessive affixation, 38.3

Possessive prefix. *See* Possessive: affixes

Possessive suffixes. *See* Possessive: affixes

Predicates: personal affixation: predicates and complements, 8.1.2; predicates in word order, 36.1, 36.1.3. *See also* Predication

Predication, 8.1.2, 22 (intro), 22.3.1. *See also* Predicates

Prefixation: status of, in morphology, 1.6, 8.1; in cardinals, 19.1.2; in demonstrative adverbs, 26.1, 26.1.2. *See also* Prefixes

Prefixes: movement of the stress in combinations with prefixes, 2.3; lexical suffixes and the prefix n-, 15.1.2; nominalizer s-, 9; stem-forming prefixes, 10; possessive prefix n-, 8.1, 22.1, 22.2. *See also* Prefixation

Prepositions, 34; special forms of demonstrative pronouns after prepositions, 25.3

Pressure stops (ejectives), 1.9.1

Proclitic: status of proclitics in morphology, 1.6; general information and difference from prefixes, 8.3; auxiliaries as proclitics, 22.4.1; articles as proclitics, 31 (intro); enclitics as proclitics, 32.5.1; proclitic conjunctions, 33

Pronouns: personal pronouns and related substitutes, 24; interrogative and indefinite pronouns, 24.2; evasive pronouns, 24.3; anticipatory pronoun niɬ, 24.5; demonstrative pronouns, 25

Proper nouns, 27; and articles, 31; in complements, 38.4; and focusing elements, 38.5

Prosodic (structure), 13.1 (p. 68)

Pseudo-cleft sentences, 38.5 n. 5

Quantifiers. *See* Indefinite quantifiers

Quotative: enclitic ˍkʷuʔ 'quotative,' 32.1.9; use of quotative ˍkʷuʔ in a text, 39.2

Reciprocal suffixes: general information on, 17.2. *See also* Reciprocal and reciprocal suffixes

Relational (transitivizers), 18.1.4 (pp. 115-16)

Reduplication: status of, in morphology, 1.6, 8 (intro), 8.1, 12 n.1; functions and formal aspects of, 12; in cardinals, 19.1.2;

complex numerals and reduplication, 19.1.3. *See also* Consonant reduplication, Final reduplication, Initial reduplication, Total reduplication

Reflexive suffixes: general information on, 17.1; the reflexive suffix -cut (and transitivizers), 18.6. *See also* Reflexive and reciprocal suffixes

Reflexive and reciprocal suffixes: status of, in stem formation, 8.1; functions and formal aspects of, 17; detransitivization and retransitivization, 18.7; reflexive and reciprocal forms (and subject suffixes), 22.5.5

Relator-verbs, 20.2

Residual suffixes, 15.4

Resonant-glottalization: required by reduplication, 1.6, 12 (intro); required by suffixation, 1.6, 15.2 (p. 77); required by interior glottalization, 13 (intro); glottalization of the transitivizer -min, 18.1.4 (p. 114); glottalization of object suffixes after -s, 22.3.3

Resonants: general information on, 1 (intro); dental, velar, and uvular glides classed as resonants, 1.2; laryngeal, velar, and uvular resonants, 1.3; phonetics of, 1.9.2; phonetics of vowel-resonant sequences, 1.9.4; schwa and resonants, 3.1, 3.4; limited occurrence of velar and uvular resonants, 1.7. *See also* Glottalized resonants, Resonant-glottalization

Resultative: resultative combination ka-..ˍa, 10.1.3; stress rules involving resultative ka-..ˍa, 2.1 (p. 15); stative and resultative forms (and transitivizers), 18.8

Retracted phonemes, 5; versus non-retracted phonemes (general), 1.1; neutralization between retracted and non-retracted vowels before z z', 1.8.1; neutralization between retracted and non-retracted phonemes before uvulars, 1.8.2; rare occurrence of retracted phonemes, 1.7. *See also* Retraction

Retraction: of vowels: phonetic effects, 1.1; of suffixes, 5.2; of the nominalizer s-, 5.3; background of retraction, 5.4. *See also* Retracted phonemes

Rhetorical lengthening, 7.3

Root: status of, in morphology, 1.6, 8 (intro); movement of the stress in combinations of roots and suffixes, 1.5, 2.1; retracted roots, 1.1, 5.1; structure of, 1.6, 6; and interior glottalization versus -p, 13 (intro); total reduplication and aspectual suffixes, 14.2, 14.3

Rounded. *See* Consonants: neutralization between unrounded and rounded consonants

Sandhi. *See* Internal sandhi
Schwa (ə ə): elision and epenthesis of, 1.6, 1.7; stress rules and, 2.1; distribution of, 3; in root structure, 6.2; required by consonant reduplication, 12.1 (p. 56)
Segmental (phoneme), 1 (intro)
Sentence-equivalents, 29; and subordinate constructions, 37.1, 37.2, 37.3, 37.4.1
Sentence-word, 8.1.2
Sentences: mono-clausal, 36; multi-clausal, 37
Singular. *See* Plural
Slow song speech, 7.2
Somatic suffixes: and (in)transitivizers, 18.2
Speed of speech (in vowel-resonant sequences), 1.9.4
Static (prepositions), 34.1
Stative: stative prefix s-, 10.1.2; stative prefix s- involved in reduplication, 12.5 (p. 64); stative and resultative forms (and transitivizers), 18.8
Stem: definition of stem, 8.1 (p. 41); plain stems (and [in]transitivizers), 18.1; nominal stems and (in)transitivizers, 18.4. *See also* Stem formation, Prefixes: stem-forming prefixes
Stem formation: transposition and (in)transitivization, 8.1.1; summary of, 21. *See also* Stem
Stops. *See* Pressure stops
Stress: place within phoneme system, 1 (intro); general information, 1.5; movement of, 2; neutralization of oppositions outside the stress, 1.9.4; and distribution of schwa, 3; and internal sandhi, 4.1, 4.2, 4.3; and resonant-glottalization, 18.1.4, 22.3.3
Stridency (in uvular fricatives), 1.9.1
Strong suffixes (with regard to stress), 2.1 (p. 16)
Subordinate (clause), 22.3.1, 35
Subject complements, 8.1.2. *See also* Complements
Subject suffixes, 8.1, 8.1.2, 22
Subject-centred forms: Object- and subject-centred forms, 22.6; object- and subject-centred forms with focusing elements, 38.5
Subjunctive: versus indicative paradigms, 8.1.2 (p. 45), 22; subjunctive forms in indefinite pronouns and indefinite local deictics, 24.2, 26.1.4; enclitics after in-

dicative and subjunctive forms, 32.5; neutralization between subjunctive and indicative paradigms, 32.5.1; subjunctive (c) constructions, 37.4
Substitutes: numerals and numerical substitutes, 19; verbal substitutes, 20; personal pronouns and related substitutes, 24. *See also* Demonstrative adverbs, Demonstrative pronouns
Suffixation: status of, in morphology, 1.6, 8.1; in numerals, 19.2; with -wna/-na (in demonstrative pronouns), 25.2. *See also* Suffixes
Suffixes: retraction of, 1.1, 5.2; movement of the stress in roots and suffixes, 1.5, 2.1. *See also* Abstract suffixes, Aspectual suffixes, Intransitivizers, Lexical suffixes, Non-somatic suffixes, Object suffixes, Possessive suffixes, Reflexive and reciprocal suffixes, Residual suffixes, Somatic suffixes, Subject suffixes, Suffixation, Transitivizers
Suprasegmental (phoneme), 1
Syllabifier, 2.1(3)
Syllable, 2.1, 2.1(3)
Syncope: aphaeresis and syncope, 7.1
Syntax, 35-38

Tense: absence of tense distinctions, 8.1 (p. 42), 21.2
Tensing (and velarization, as part of retraction), 1.1
Total reduplication, 12.5-6. *See also* Reduplication
Transitive: simple transitive declarative paradigm, 22.3.2; complex declarative transitive forms, 22.4.2; expression of 1P transitive subject, 22.5.3; indirect object-centred forms (nominalized transitives), 22.7. *See also* Transitivization, Transitivizers
Transitivization: transposition and (in)transitivization, 8.1.1, 21.4; reflexive and reciprocal suffixes: detransitivization and retransitivization, 18.7. *See also* Transitive, Transitivizers
Transitivizers: Intransitivizers and transitivizers, 8.1, 18; type I (special cases of personal affixation), 22.3.2-5; retraction of, 5.2. *See also* Transitive, Transitivization
Transposition: and (in)transitivization, 8.1.1; survey of transpositional operations, 21.4

Unrounded. *See* Consonants: neutralization between unrounded and rounded consonants

Uvular: glides, 1.2; resonants, 1.3; neutralization of retracted and non-retracted vowels before uvulars, 1.8.2; rounding of uvular consonants adjacent to rounded vowels, 1.8.3; strident articulation of uvular fricatives, 1.9.1; uvular resonants and interior glottalization, 13.1.2. *See also* Uvulars

Uvularized counterparts of laryngeal resonants, 1.3

Uvulars (uvular consonants): articulation of uvulars (as being close to that of velars), 1.9.1; partial assimilation of velars to uvulars, 1.9.1; phonetic influence of uvulars on neighbouring vowels, 1.9.3. *See also* Uvular

Variable words. *See* Words

Velar: glides, 1.2; resonants, 1.3; rounding of velar consonants adjacent to rounded vowels, 1.8.3; velar pronunciation of n n' before velar obstruents, 1.9.2. *See also* Velars

Velarization: as part of retraction, 1.1; in vowel-resonant sequences, 1.9.4

Velarized: velar resonants as velarized counterparts of y y', 1.3

Velars (velar consonants): articulation of velars (as being close to that of uvulars), 1.9.1; partial assimilation of velars to uvulars, 1.9.1; phonetic influence of unrounded velars on neighbouring vowels, 1.9.3. *See also* Velar

Velic release, 1.4

Verba declarandi, 18.1.3, 22.3.1 (p. 146), 37.1

Verba sentiendi, 18.1.3, 22.3.1 (p. 146), 37.1

Verbal stems: nominal versus verbal stems, 8.1.1. *See also* Verbs

Verbs: absence of noun-verb distinction on syntactic level, 8.1.2 (p. 45); interrogative verbs, 20.1; relator-verbs, 20.2. *See also* Verbal stems

Vocal cords (tightened in glottalized resonants), 1.9.2

Voiced fricatives, 1.2

Voiceless articulation of h ?, 1.3

Vowels: general information on, 1(intro); phonetic data of, 1.9.3; phonetic data of vowel-resonant sequences, special cases,1.9.4; neutralizations involving vowels, 1.8; vowel-consonant alternations and h-epenthesis,4.1; reduction of full root vowels, 4.2

Word: questions of word phonology, 1.6; full words versus clitics, 1.6, 8 (intro); variable words, 8.1; variable words as sentence-equivalents, 29.2; variable words with articles, 31 (intro); invariable words: general remarks, 8.2, 23

Word order: general information, 36.1; subject and object complements, 36.1.1; adverbial elements, 36.1.2; auxiliaries, 36.2

Zero-morphemes, 8.1.2 n. 2

Books of Related Interest

The following titles are also available from UBC Press. Prices listed are in effect as of Spring 1997 and are subject to change.

Aboriginal and Treaty Rights in British Columbia:
Essays on Law, Equality, and Respect for Difference
Edited by Michael Asch
1996
0-7748-0580-3, hc, $65.00
0-7748-0581-1, pb, $24.95

Treaty Talks in British Columbia:
Negotiating a Mutually Beneficial Future
Christopher McKee
1995
0-7748-0586-2, hc, $65.00
0-7748-0587-0, pb, $19.95

Eagle Down Is Our Law:
Witsuwit'en Law, Feasts, and Land Claims
Antonia Mills
1994
0-7748-0513-7, pb, $24.95

Our Tellings:
Interior Salish Stories of the Nlha7kápmx People
Compiled and edited by Darwin Hanna and Mamie Henry
1995
0-7748-0523-4, pb, $25.95

Taking Control:
Power and Contradiction in First Nations Adult Education
Celia Haig-Brown
1995
0-7748-0493-9, pb, $24.95

First Nations Education in Canada:
The Circle Unfolds
Edited by Marie Battiste and Jean Barman
1995
0-7748-0517-X, hc, $24.95